The Book of Experience

Explorations in Philosophy and Theology

**Series Editors: Kevin Hart (University of Virginia, USA)
and Jeffrey Bloechl (Boston College, USA)**

This series promotes philosophical and theological works committed to drawing on both disciplines, without either holding them strictly apart or overlooking important differences between them. The series favours philosophical approaches covered under the umbrella of "continental European," by which is meant a general commitment to developments sharpened since the work of Kant, German idealism, and Nietzsche.

It provides a space for theological approaches historically informed and actively engaged via modern thought and culture. The series will focus on Christian theology in the first instance, but not to the exclusion of work in dialogue with multiple religions. Expanding the historical and cultural origins of both continental European philosophy and Christian theology, the series will embrace a global outlook. The series thus provides a platform for work from Africa, Asia, Australia, North and South America. Featuring edited collections, single-authored works, and translations managed by an active and global editorial board, the series is one of the main destinations for scholarship in the continental philosophy of religion today.

Editorial Board

Sarah Coakley, University of Cambridge, UK
Werner Jeanrond, University of Oslo, Norway
Jean-Yves Lacoste, Paris
Adriaan Peperzak, Loyola University of Chicago, USA
Pheme Perkins, Boston College, USA
David Tracy, University of Chicago, USA
Claudia Welz, Aarhus University, Denmark
Olivier Boulnois, École Pratique des Hautes Études, France
Nythamar de Oliveira, Pontifical Catholic University of Rio Grande do Sul, Brazil
James Heisig, Nanzan Institute for Religion and Culture, Japan
Robyn Horner, Australian Catholic University, Australia
Leonard Katchekpele, University of Strasbourg, France
Judith Wolfe, Durham University, UK

Available Titles

By Faith Alone, by Lev Shestov and translated by Stephen P. Van Trees

Forthcoming Titles

Anthropomorphism in Christian Theology, by William C. Hackett

The Poetics of the Sensible, by Stanislas Breton and translated by Sarah Horton

The Book of Experience

*From Anselm of Canterbury to
Bernard of Clairvaux*

Emmanuel Falque
Translated by George Hughes

BLOOMSBURY ACADEMIC
LONDON • NEW YORK • OXFORD • NEW DELHI • SYDNEY

BLOOMSBURY ACADEMIC
Bloomsbury Publishing Plc, 50 Bedford Square, London, WC1B 3DP, UK
Bloomsbury Publishing Inc, 1385 Broadway, New York, NY 10018, USA
Bloomsbury Publishing Ireland, 29 Earlsfort Terrace, Dublin 2, D02 AY28, Ireland

BLOOMSBURY, BLOOMSBURY ACADEMIC and the Diana logo
are trademarks of Bloomsbury Publishing Plc

First published in 2017 in France as *Le livre de l'Expérience*.
D'Anselme de Cantorbury à Bernard de Clairvaux by Les Éditions du Cerf
First published in Great Britain 2024
This paperback edition published 2025

Copyright © Les Éditions du Cerf, 2017
English language translation © George Hughes 2024

Emmanuel Falque has asserted his right under the Copyright, Designs and
Patents Act, 1988, to be identified as Author of this work.

George Hughes has asserted his right under the Copyright, Designs and
Patents Act, 1988, to be identified as Translator of this work.

Series design: Ben Anslow
Photography © Sashanna Hart

All rights reserved. No part of this publication may be: i) reproduced or
transmitted in any form, electronic or mechanical, including photocopying,
recording or by means of any information storage or retrieval system without
prior permission in writing from the publishers; or ii) used or reproduced in
any way for the training, development or operation of artificial intelligence (AI)
technologies, including generative AI technologies. The rights holders expressly
reserve this publication from the text and data mining exception as per
Article 4(3) of the Digital Single Market Directive (EU) 2019/790.

Bloomsbury Publishing Inc does not have any control over, or responsibility for,
any third-party websites referred to or in this book. All internet addresses given
in this book were correct at the time of going to press. The author and publisher
regret any inconvenience caused if addresses have changed or sites have
ceased to exist, but can accept no responsibility for any such changes.

A catalogue record for this book is available from the British Library.

A catalog record for this book is available from the Library of Congress.

ISBN: HB: 978-1-3503-8649-5
PB: 978-1-3503-8653-2
ePDF: 978-1-3503-8650-1
eBook: 978-1-3503-8651-8

Series: Explorations in Philosophy and Theology

Typeset by Integra Software Services Pvt. Ltd.

For product safety related questions contact productsafety@bloomsbury.com.

To find out more about our authors and books visit www.bloomsbury.com
and sign up for our newsletters.

Hodie legimus in libro experientiae
We shall read to-day in the book of experience.
(*Bernard of Clairvaux,* In Cantica Canticorum: Sermons on the Song of Songs [Song of Solomon])

Contents

Opening	x
Introduction: Talking about Experience	1
Part 1 The Theophanic Argument or Experience in Thought: Anselm of Canterbury	13
1 Of God Who Comes to Mind	17
2 The Theophanic Argument	29
3 The Debt for the Gift	49
Part 2 Hermeneutics and Phenomenology, or the Experience of the World: Hugh and Richard of Saint-Victor	69
4 God an "Open Book"	73
5 To Live One's Body	91
6 The Third Party of Love	113
Part 3 Affectivity and Spirituality or *Experience in Affects*: Aelred of Rievaulx and Bernard of Clairvaux	129
7 To Feel Oneself Fully Alive	133
8 Experience and Empathy	143
9 Openness [*apérité*] and Freedom	175
Epilogue: Hold Fast to Humankind	203
Notes	206
Name Index	256

Opening

We cannot read writers without having them in some way "pass through us" and being "transformed" by them. When we read in the "book of experience" along with them, like "dwarfs perched on the shoulders of giants,"¹ we enter into, and somehow participate in, *their* experience. Philosophy is experience: it is not above all conceptual. Or we might perhaps say that it is a matter of experience *because* it is conceptual. There has been too much separation of "writing" on the one hand and "life" on the other: treatises on theology have been separated from the source that gave rise to them. In the monastic world nobody thought without living or lived without thinking—for thought and life were connected in the liturgy as their ground and their most fruitful mode. To hide this is to abstract the medievals from a life-world into which they were once woven.

Whether or not one subscribes to their beliefs or indeed shares their faith is not what matters here. Because we can certainly read these pious authors without sharing *their* experience, and without denying that it is "theirs", and quite independent of "ours". This book has as its aim to read within the framework of the so-called monastic theology of the eleventh and twelfth centuries but first of all has a perspective that is unashamedly *philosophical*. What I have tried to do is not simply to clarify mysteries—whether it is a question of "the idea that comes to God" (Anselm of Canterbury) or actively "feeling oneself fully alive" (Aelred of Rievaulx or Bernard of Clairvaux). Rather I try to show how we can find at the heart of the medieval tradition what has probably been most sought after in contemporary philosophy, at least in the world of phenomenology, namely "experience as such."

This book *about* books, or *starting off from books*, opens, however, as a *book within books*. One can turn its pages as one might uncover a world, preferring landscapes to geography or opting to travel cautiously rather than staying at home. Nobody knows where they will be led as they tread on through the "book" (or the field) of experience, except perhaps the author who has made the journey through it and who leaves it open to others to accompany him at their own pace. Like the monks, but above all like their experience that proceeds from books without ever disrespecting them, we learn to read and decode a presence—perhaps that of God or perhaps of the Other. It happens in books certainly, and even more in our "thoughts" (Anselm), in "the world" (Hugh of Saint-Victor), and at the heart of our "affect" (Bernard). Just like the author of the Book of Revelations, we wait for the seals to be opened, without knowing *who* will come to open them:

> Then I saw in the right hand of the one seated on the throne a scroll written on the inside and on the back, sealed with seven seals; and I saw a mighty angel

proclaiming with a loud voice, "Who is worthy to open the scroll and break its seals?" And no one in heaven or on earth or under the earth was able to open the scroll or to look into it. And I began to weep bitterly because no one was found worthy to open the scroll or to look into it. (Rev. 5:1-4 NRSV)[ii]

Granges d'Ans, January 8, 2017
Feast of the Epiphany

Introduction: Talking about Experience

"However paradoxical it may seem, the concept of experience seems to me one of the most obscure we have."[1] Hans-Georg Gadamer's statement at the heart of his *Truth and Method* in 1960 came as a surprise because phenomenology had long been talking about experience, both in terms of experimental practice and quite simply in discussions of experience. Several years later, however, the phenomenologist Ludwig Landgrebe confirmed Gadamer's view at the start of a famous article on the phenomenological concept of experience: "Everybody believes he understands what the word 'experience' [*Erfahrung*] means. It is a fundamental word in the vocabulary of philosophy, and at the same time, it is a word used meaningfully in everyday discourse among people who know nothing about philosophy."[2]

There is no question in this book, it goes almost without saying, of repudiating all philosophizing on, or all statements about, experience. I simply wish to recognize a kind of understanding given to those who share an experience. Everyone "believes" they have more or less understood what the term "experience" signifies. Reservations do not arise so much from not knowing what it signifies but because we know the experience itself "always already beforehand"—and even know it extremely well. Those who live through an experience seem to grasp it immediately without having recourse to the slightest theoretical input. An understanding of (or a harmony with) experience is attributed spontaneously to those who know it by living through it, rather than knowing it from what they have been taught. The object of this present book is, however, to take a look at a certain *body of knowledge (or conceptualization) of experience*, born in the Middle Ages, in the context of the monastic theology of the eleventh and twelfth centuries, not just to agree with the practice of that period but to consider its theoretical formulation.

We speak in fact *of* experience both when there is wisdom that is authenticated in statements (as, for example, when foresters or masons hold forth upon their craft) and also when experience becomes the specific object of a statement (as in philosophy). Speaking *of* experience is thus speaking *on the basis of* experience (subjective genitive), as well as speaking *about* experience (objective genitive). And probably it is in the nature of phenomenology, which is fundamental here, never to separate discourse *about* experience (objective) from discourse *on the basis* of experience (subjective). Precisely in this respect phenomenology can be distinguished from the so-called empirical or analytic approach.[3] Phenomenology *also* "does its forestry" or "builds like a mason" in philosophy—not content with objectivizing (in a body of knowledge) or adjusting itself (having the know-how) but letting itself be transformed even by that which it works upon [*praxis*]. Experience "speaks" when we let it speak rather than when we make it speak. If there is, then, good practice in phenomenology that can be recovered today, it will have to go by way of a return to experience. Because, whatever the "turn" that has taken place in French phenomenology, it cannot simply be index-linked to the "theological turn" (Emmanuel Levinas, Paul Ricoeur, Michel Henry, Jean-Luc Marion): it must also be linked to a return to experience (Maurice Merleau-Ponty). Contemporary phenomenology, dissatisfied with both method and discourse, has tried to renew itself through relying upon other fields (for example, literature, theology, art, and psychiatry), though the risk remains of a certain sterility derived from too strong a self-sufficiency. Experience then becomes spoken of only in terms of "the experience of experience" and in daring to conceptualize experience. Probably the true task of phenomenology is to revise this, and it is monastic theology that can initiate such a revision.[4]

§1. Experience and Finitude

Tô pathei mathos: "Learning through suffering" or "knowledge by test or trial."[5] The famous formula comes from Aeschylus's drama and has often been cited and commented upon in contemporary philosophy. It is not a denial that there are things to be "learned," but it puts the case for a new form of apprenticeship. It suggests that we cannot be content simply with thought about things: we learn from life, from affect, and from the world—from the "chaos," from the "mass of sensations" from the "cinnabar,"[6] or from "the region of what can no longer be said."[7] Not everything can be spoken, and some things are better left unsaid. That is why we need to learn to say things *otherwise*. Denouncing any "ideal of transparency" or an "overhanging [*surplomb*] of transcendence," phenomenology belatedly teaches, following Merleau-Ponty, that there is a blessed obscurity in humankind. A *mixture* is sometimes more valuable than *purity*, and *chiasm* more valuable than *rupture*.[8] In short, as we shall see, "talking of experience" is not primarily talking about it but letting oneself be transformed and modified by it.

It is experience that establishes first of all for humankind the site of our own "limits" or "finitude." We talk, and talk frequently, about "events" or indeed "surprises," about a "coming into view" or *Ereignis*.[9] But we neglect all that limits such "learning through test or trial," when learning sends us back to our own thresholds. We have an experience, or some experiences, not first of all in that experiences "overflow" from us but in that they are what "contain" us. A sense of our "limits" precedes their "overflowing" from us, and it is only unpredictable insofar as we thought we knew what was coming. The transcendental is not so surprising: not even in the case of experience. It constitutes the primary sphere of what is human: nothing comes to us (including our sense of the other or God himself), if it does not *also* submit to our conditions for the reception of it (kenosis). Gadamer tells us in *Truth and Method*:

Aeschylus meant more than this ... What a man has to learn through suffering is not this or that particular thing, but insight into the limitations of humanity, into the absoluteness of the barrier that separates man from the divine. It is ultimately a religious insight—the kind of insight that gave birth to Greek tragedy. Thus, experience is *experience of human finitude*. The truly experienced person is one who has taken this to heart.[10]

It may seem surprising to connect "experience" and "finitude" in this way at the very start of a work concerning the status and sources of experience in monastic theology, a work where I am above all concerned with the relationship between humankind and God. Everything depends in what follows upon what we understand by "experience" in phenomenology, on whether it is "lived experience" (*Erlebnis*: Husserl) and/or "experience of an external event" (*Erfahrung*: Heidegger)—just as in theology so much depends upon "revelation" and/or "incarnation." Because paradoxically we could suggest that the "book of experience" signifies for the medievals, in particular in the Latin tradition, not so much a "saturated" phenomenon as a threshold or "limited" phenomenon.[11] Everything sends us back to our "limits," limits that even God will encounter. Thus, as we shall see, we go from (a) Anselm's God "than which nothing greater can be thought," where humankind is "little man" who accepts God (*Proslogion*), to (b) "the book of the world" of Hugh of Saint-Victor, where God's presence can be "deciphered" above all through nature and the artefacts of the world (*Didascalicon*), to (c) "affect" in the work of Bernard of Clairvaux, where God joins us so completely in our *pathos* that tears given to us overflow not in an excess but in sending us back to a pure and simple humanity (*Cantica Canticorum: Eighty-Six Sermons on the Song of Solomon*).

The "limited phenomenon" took root in the monastic experience of the eleventh and twelfth centuries when kenosis in humanity (Latin theology) plus deification (Greek theology) came to constitute the heart of the Christian experience. If one is tempted to forget this, one has only to look at a Gothic Christ of the twelfth century. From the "smiling Christ" of the abbey of Lérins, to the "compassionate Christ" of the altarpiece in the Sanctuary of Saint Michael of Aralar in Navarre, to "Christ in majesty seated within a mandorla" in the tympanum of the abbey of Vézelay, it is not a question of "suffering" but above all of "patience," or rather of "taking on board suffering" [*pâtir*]. Christ also learns through his suffering [*pathei mathos*] not simply in that he takes on himself our sins in a "dolorism" or exaltation of physical suffering that would be out of place but in rejoining the foundations of our humanity, indeed the foundations of our incarnate being.

Art, as I have often emphasized elsewhere, in particular in talking about various altarpieces, very often says more than straightforward language.[12] An image can supply us with words or suggest how we can find new ways of speaking. Because, if phenomenology helps us to see, we need *to have eyes* to see. Heidegger, talking of his predecessor, says, "*Husserl opened my eyes*."[13] And it is in looking, as well as in walking through, the abbeys of France that one comes to understand what the book of experience was *to them* in the past, plus how it is today *up to us* to decipher it.

I hope to show this without being reductive. I shall not discuss the "theophanic"[14] argument that we find in Anselm's *Proslogion* while ignoring the liturgy of the Benedictine abbey of Our Lady of Bec in Normandy. I shall not discuss the "deciphering of the world" in the *Didascalicon* of Hugh of Saint-Victor while neglecting the basis of the Victorine argument in contemporary disputes in Paris. I shall not be celebrating "affect" in the sermons on the Song of Songs by Bernard of Clairvaux in isolation from Cistercian spirituality rooted in the abbey of Cîteaux, associated with one of the founders of the order, Robert of Molesme. *What is lived in experience belongs to experience*, and it is forgetting this that leads too often to posing the monastic on the one hand and the scholastic on the other, or the contemplative against dialectic. The life of monks is "one"—as is, or ought to be, ours today. One did not go to the Scriptorium [the room where manuscripts were written and copied] in the Middle Ages without in practice also going to the abbey church and vice versa. We are not compelled to share their experience, but that does not prevent us from trying to enter into it or saying that what is in it can also be ours. We cannot truly build things anew without plunging to the roots of the past, without harvesting the fruits from an exploration of this kind for our own contemporaneity.[15]

§2. Ex-per-ience

What we say about "experience" and also how we read in the "book of experience" depends first of all upon the concept of experience we are using. One could certainly be accused of anachronism if one relied upon a *contemporary* concept of experience to speak of the meaning and standing of experience in the era of monastic theology. All the same, I would underline that there is no such thing as philosophical thought confined to its own pure historicity, nor is there a phenomenology that does not question tradition: "Each tree is known by its own fruit" (Lk. 6:44). I have frequently made the point elsewhere and incorporated it into my philosophical writings, but it may be useful to repeat it here, so that the reader does not suspect me of intentions for which I would not claim responsibility. In *God, the Flesh, and the Other* I wrote:

> Let me say it once and for all in order not to sink into gross anachronism: to *practice medieval philosophy phenomenologically* is not to require authors to respond to our questions—they already have enough to do with their own, and we ours. Rather it is to see *how* and *with what* they have responded to their own, in order to learn from them how to respond to ours. At this price (alone), philosophical anachronism reveals its prophetic vocation: not in being content to reread the old in the light of the new, but in interrogating the ancient itself so that it can teach us to work in the regions of the new.[16]

To "read the book of experience" during the monastic period was not just "relying on experience" (as in traditional empiricist philosophy), nor simply "knowing oneself" (as in the practical wisdom of Epicureanism, Stoicism, or skepticism), nor just relying on the experimental (as in modern science following the tradition of Galileo), but if so, it cannot either just be "living an experience" (as in Husserl) or "being passed through by the experience" (as in Heidegger and phenomenology).[17] Nonetheless the ex-per-ience in question has "something to say to us" that depends upon the language from which it was drawn. This is not simply a question of etymology (which as we know philosophers have performed with varying degrees of success—Martin Heidegger above all). We need to recognize, along with the philosopher Henri Maldiney, who will serve as our guide here, that "the power of a linguistic form is all the greater in that it expresses an even more fundamental attitude towards the whole of being."[18] Language speaks not simply because its roots are buried in the past (etymology) but also in that it unfolds a mode of being that remains open to our interrogation (ethology).[19]

Experiri[20]—"to experience," "to put to the test or trial." In fact, ex-*per*-ience, according to Henri Maldiney, is based on the root "*per*," which can signify at once: "The enemy (Sanskrit *pára-h*) and snow on a glacier (New High German *Firn*), the piercing of an arrow (Greek *péraô*—to pierce) and experience (Greek *emperia*, Latin *experientia*, German *Erfahrung*), the value of something (Latin *pretium*) and a ford or river crossing (Greek *póros*), proximity and transgression (the Greek prefix *pára*)."[21] Despite the diversity of these meanings, the Greek or Latin root *per* (*em-per-ia, ex-per-ientia*), like the German root *fahr* (*Er-fahr-ung*), does show a "crossing": an "attempt," a "try," a "test or trial" (*peïra*), the act of "experimenting" (*empeiros*), a "danger" (*periculum*), or a "passage" (*poros*), and indeed something "disquieting," or "no way through" (*aporos*).[22] In short, there is no experience in Greek (*em-per-ia*), or in German (*Er-fahr-ung*), or even in French (*ex-pér-ience*), without some change of the self, without the act of being transformed or metamorphosed or without recognition of "no longer being the *same*." Experience passes through us and changes us deeply. Maldiney affirms that "[t]o be put to test or trial by an illness, by mourning, by joy, to love, to travel, to write a book, to paint are 'experiences' in this primary phenomenological meaning, certainly very simple, but by no means trivial."[23]

It would have been better for our purposes (assuming that something was not quite right) if this primary meaning of experience in French [*ex-pér-ience*] as in German [*Er-fahr-ung*] had not been obscured or even obliterated by the widespread attention given, in particular by the father of phenomenology, Edmund Husserl, to a second German term: *Erlebnis*. Where German requires two words to talk of "experience," the original Greek and Latin languages only possess one. Thus, as far as *Erlebnis* (in contrast to *Erfahrung*) is concerned, Hans-Georg Gadamer, in *Truth and Method*, takes it from "to live" [*erleben*] rather than "to travel" [*fahren*]. And this means that it indicates above all a "lived experience," immediacy or the intimacy of the self to the self, rather than the fact of being transformed in and by something external. Gadamer says, "*Erleben* means primarily 'to be still alive when something happens.' Thus, the word suggests the immediacy with which something real is grasped … What is experienced is always what one has experienced oneself."[24]

This second lineage of *Erlebnis*, which is certainly taken up by Husserl and those who follow him (Max Scheler, Edith Stein, Hans Lipps, Eugen Fink),[25] until Heidegger takes a new turning toward *Erfahrung* (where he is followed in this respect by Henri Maldiney) and launches phenomenology in a kind of "swerve of the lived experience" (after the "swerve of the flesh"[26]), a direction that we shall be asking whether one can or should follow. Phenomenology has relied upon "a flesh without body" (Michel Henry[27]), and one might well ask whether it has not also recently produced a kind of *Erlebnis* without *Erfahrung* or a "lived experience that is immediate to and auto-affected from the self," but that lacks a "crossing" of the self or a "putting the self into danger." Have we not become satisfied with how it is just to "feel for oneself" or "to see (and think) that one has seen," instead of being concerned with seeing things *truly*, with seeing things—for better or worse—*certainly* something.[28] Isn't there *also* experience of being "transformed" by something exterior to ourselves that is not simply being "confirmed" in our own inwardness? Isn't it this time a question of the "*pathic*" and not simply the reflexive?[29]

Our questions are significant when we read the book of experience of the Middle Ages, in particular where the heart of monastic theology is concerned, as what is there in it *also for us*. Because if "lived experience" or "*pathic* experience" can be made out at the heart of the medieval epoch, to the extent that some readers have seen a source in the work of Meister Eckhart,[30] the eleventh and twelfth centuries are not really a period of their supreme preeminence. I hope to show that if one can interpret the so-called ontological argument as a theophanic argument, implying either the appearance of God in our own thought [see chap. 2: "The Theophanic Argument" (Anselm)], or, as it was first of all among the Cistercians, "feeling oneself fully alive" [see chap. 7: "To Feel Oneself Fully Alive" (Aelred of Rievaulx)]. There is nothing to guarantee that such a "putting oneself to test or trial" will not also be accompanied by a "modification of the self," in the sense of an "adventure." And this can be understood not solely as "a feeling of life in its totality" (Gadamer, Henry) but as "the transformation of an event by an occurrence" (Maldiney, Romano).[31]

If we go so far then we can also recognize that *experience as such is born in the Middle Ages, in the eleventh and twelfth centuries, in the context of monastic theology*. Not that it had been meaningless before (in empiricism or in practical wisdom), nor that it was to be without meaning afterward (in scientific experiment or in phenomenological definition), but in that *reflection upon experience* would suddenly come to belong *to* experience in such a way that "speaking of experience" would be done *on the basis of* the experience and at the same time as reasoning about it.

The point has been so often neglected that it really needs to be underlined. Certainly, there is no need to wait for monastic theology (for Anselm of Canterbury, for Hugh and Richard of Saint-Victor, or again for Aelred of Rievaulx and Bernard of Clairvaux), to "speak of experience" while living through it, to give an account of experience, or to give experience as an example. One could, it goes almost without saying, go much further back to St. Augustine to read "in the book of experience." But in St. Augustine, as also in the case of the "elders" of his time (Epicureans, Stoics, Sceptics) one "speaks" or "reads" less of experience than one just "has" or "lives through" experience.[32] One can recount one's experience, as St. Augustine importantly does (Book VII of *The Confessions*), and even give a theological reading of it, without establishing the experience as a *philosophical object* or at least without *conceptualizing it*. Certain medievalists writing today who belong to the modern monastic world understand this—recognizing from their status and their vocation an approach to *reflection on experience on the basis of their experience*. Philippe Nouzille says, "Monastic theology aims at a description of experience and the conditions of its possibility."³³ And Jean Leclercq tells us that the great difference between scholastic theology and that of the monasteries stems from the role played in the latter by the experience of union with God.³⁴

In what follows I aim to read the book of experience in the context of monastic theology of the eleventh and twelfth centuries, not simply as "having *an* experience" (accusative sense) but also as "having the experience *of* the theologians' experience" (subjective genitive). Experience and philosophy are linked together in an exemplary fashion in the Middle Ages that goes beyond a *philosophy of experience* and a way of thinking. In monastic theology there is no "experience" without an intellectual grasp of the experience, as there is not "life" without a hermeneutic or art of decoding that "life." Reflection upon experience, which is not at all the same as intellectualism, probably because it is a question of what is most intimate and of God himself, acts here as a line of defense against the evanescence of experience. It prevents us losing in the network of lived experience that ordeal of test and trial that can only be sustained because it has been thought through. The experience is "to be read" not because it is found in "books," as we shall see [chap. 6: "Reading the World"], but as it is *the mode of the book*—that is to say, reading—that sets itself up as type and model of all understanding of the world, as well as of oneself and of God. *Reflection on experience* depends upon a *possibility* and also depends upon *training*; it involves the potential of *recognition* and of being *invited* by it.

§3. The Book of Experience

Hodie legimus in libro experientiae—"We shall read to-day in the book of experience."³⁵ St. Bernard's formula, from his third sermon on the Song of Songs (3:1), taken up later by Aelred of Rievaulx,³⁶ lies behind the whole of this book, gives me my epigraph, and provides its leading thread. Although the "book of experience" [*liber experientiae*] takes such a leading place here, in fact there are numerous other "books" [*libri*] in the Middle Ages: there would be at least eight, perhaps ten, by the time of St. Bonaventure, a century later.³⁷ But all this would not have been so important and would not have led us *phenomenologically* toward the "book of experience" if statements by the Heideggerian, Otto Pöggeler, and Heidegger's personal assistant, Friedrich-Wilhelm von Hermann, had not been confirmed with the publication of Heidegger's notes on "The Philosophical Foundations of Medieval Mysticism."³⁸ Friedrich-Wilhelm von Hermann explains:

> In Heidegger's posthumous papers, a single sheet has been found that indicates a direct connection with Bernard of Clairvaux. It bears the title "on the *Sermones Bernardi in canticum canticorum*" and contains a manuscript copy by Heidegger (in minute handwriting) of sermon no. 3 [*sic*]. The materials gathered in this notebook were used in the preparation of a course planned [at Freiburg] for the winter semester 1919/1920—*the Philosophical Foundations of Medieval Mysticism*—that Heidegger did not, however, deliver. Probably it was never completed. In any event no [student] notes taken during this course have so far come to our attention.³⁹

The manuscript page, dated September 6, 1918, on which passages from Sermon 3 on The Song of Songs were copied, can now be read in its entirety in the volume translated as *The Phenomenology of Religious Life*.[40] The page quotes phrases from St. Bernard and grants them an appropriate interpretation. From Bernard of Clairvaux to Martin Heidegger there is certainly an immense distance, but Heidegger's interpretation has the great merit of "actualizing" the medieval philosophy, not simply in the sense of aligning it with today's tastes (actuality) but also in the deployment of its potentialities [*actualitas*].

St. Bernard begins Sermon 3: "We shall read to-day in the book of experience [*hodie legimus in libro experientiae*]. You must therefore turn your attention inward [*convertimini ad vos ipsos*]; each one must take note of his own particular awareness [*et attendat unusquisque conscientiam suam*] of the things I am about to discuss."[41] We see here how the book of experience [*liber experientiae*] marks a kind of return to the self [*convertere ad ipsos*] and an examination of one's own consciousness that is to be interpreted and deciphered "today" [*hodie*]. It can be put in the terms of the "hermeneutic of the subject" used by Michel Foucault: "Christian conversion, for which Christians use the word *metanoia*, is obviously very different from the Platonic *epistrophê*. You know that the word itself, *metanoia* is penitence and it is also radical change of thought and mind."[42]

In short, while experience in Greece is progressive in terms of wisdom or performance of the self (in the sense of *care of the self*), in the Christian book of experience, it becomes a sudden and unexpected way of "turning towards the self" or "into oneself." We can agree with Foucault when he says of the Greek "*gnôthi seauton*" [know thyself] that it "is, I think much less influential in our societies, in our culture, than it is supposed to be."[43]

Another interpretation, not hermeneutic this time (in Foucault's sense of the hermeneutics of the self), but phenomenological, can be offered of the same text, however, and it is this interpretation that will serve as a leading motif throughout this book. *Hodie legimus in libro experientiae* becomes in Heidegger's note: "Today we want to move apprehendingly (descriptively) in the field of personal experience. Turning back to one's own sphere of experience and paying attention to the manifestations of one's own consciousness. A strong, implicitly formulated consciousness of the exclusive principal value and right of one's own religious experience."[44]

Even the most devoted and resolute Heideggerian might deprecate the abstruseness of the language in this periphrastic paraphrase. Heidegger never goes in for straight translation, and moreover this note on the commentary on the Song of Songs does not offer itself as such, but it does lose the purity of St. Bernard's style in a proliferation of terms that seem very far from the Cistercian monk. At the same time, the philosophical "intention," that is in this case phenomenological, is clear, and not simply as regards what it performs: also as regards what it refuses to accept.

First of all, as far as what it performs: the book [*liber*] is no more a "text" here but becomes a "field," or in other words we belong to it, we live in it. We do not so much read the book of experience here as we step into the space of "ourselves" where we "make" experience. To read [*legere*] is not just to decipher but also to move ourselves, to gather into ourselves, indeed to be affected by our reading. Experience [*experientia*] is seen not as an act of reading but what sends us back to personal lived experience. And the today [*hodie*] is not the day of the analysis but of a comprehension understood simply as *description*. In other words, *we shall read to-day in is the book of experience* is saying philosophically, "Now we have to move into the field of our consciousness, or attend to what is going on there and which might change us." We enter not simply into the "book" but into the "world" of the monastic experience of the Middle Ages.

Next, as regards what it refuses to accept: what follows in Heidegger's text makes this plain to those who are able to take him at his word or at least decipher what he is saying. St. Bernard in fact goes on in the Third Sermon on the Song of Songs, also copied by the phenomenologist into this notebook: [*Est fons signatus, qui non communicat alienus*] "It is a sealed fountain to which no stranger has access."[45] One does not go toward, or at least one does not reach, the movement of an *other*, when an event arrives in the field of the other's consciousness. At most we can take note of it but never participate in it. We shall see this in detail later, assisted precisely by Bernard of Clairvaux [§26]. Nothing allows us truly to live what another lives, except God perhaps, though we must not confuse here what phenomenology will later carefully distinguish (in particular Edith Stein in her debate with Hans Lipps) as "empathy" on one side [*Einfühlung*] and intersubjective "affective fusion" [*Einsfühlung*] on the other. But it is the closing in of consciousness on the "lived-experience" as simply "auto-affection "[*Erlebnis*] that Heidegger refuses to accept here, and he does so from his earliest work of 1920–21. He maintains that such lived-experience is only "truly effective in a closed complex of experience (stream of experience)—not transferable, cannot be elicited, through description."[46]

Is this to say that such a lived experience of the book of experience can never be transmitted, in that I am myself the "field" where it is produced or realized? Certainly not. Because the "closed complex of experience" or the "stream of experience" changes or transforms me like things that come *to me* and are not *of me* (sickness, mourning, joy, love, travels, writing, painting[47]). "The constitution of the noetic religious experimental context is a 'historical' one (*qui bibit, ad hunc sitiat*) [he who drinks may be thirsty for this]."[48] The *Erlebnis* does not mean that one feels nothing, rather that the phenomenological constitution of the lived experience is not historical, or at least it is only so in its abstraction of the temporality of the world that can change me.

In short, the twists and turns of the book of experience as interpreted phenomenologically necessitate that we do not just see there simple lived experience (*Erlebnis*—Husserl), or the care of the self (*epistrophê*—Foucault), but the "passage of the self," the "putting to test or trial," or the "endangering" of the self (*ex-pér-ience* or *Er-fahr-ung*), through which one may be metamorphosed. Claude Romano, in *Event and World*, presents a version of what Heidegger had maintained in his *On the Way to Language* [1959]:

> To undergo an experience [*eine Erfahrung machen*] with something—be it a thing, a human being, or a god—means that this something befalls us [*es uns widerfährt*],

strikes us, comes over us [*über uns kommt*], overwhelms and transforms us. When we talk of "undergoing" an experience, we mean specifically that the experience is not of our own making; to undergo [*durchmachen*] here means that we endure it [*erleiden*], suffer it [*annehmen*], receive it (*accueillir*) it as it strikes us [*das uns Treffende vernehmend*] and submit to it.[49]

§4. Eating the Book

To read in this famous book of experience [*liber experientiae*], or to allow ourselves to be modified and transformed by what "happens" to us or "befalls" us in reading, it is still necessary to "eat the book"—the book of Holy Scripture [*liber scripturae*]. In monastic theology at least, one is not fed simply by the Eucharist (the "bread of heaven"); one is fed by the "page of the Holy Scripture" [*sacra pagina*] or the Bible listened to in a daily exercise of *lectio divina*. Philippe Nouzille says, "In this present world we have only one sole good, St. Jerome warns, in a teaching that will come to be adopted by the whole monastic community: we are nourished by his flesh and our thirst slaked by his blood, not simply in the sacrament (the eucharist), but also in reading the Holy Scripture."[50] To eat and read in the monastic period are thus "the one and the other an employment of the jaw"—what is sometimes called "rumination." The Scripture "is for chewing" just as it is to be understood. The good milk of its fermentation will be given to drink to those who have long experienced its fellowship.[51]

The Book of the Holy Scripture [*liber scripturae*] understood simply as "writing in a book" can gradually lead us to forget this, particularly as we meet its printed version, when infinite reproduction of repetition becomes possible. We have come to hide all that is really precious in a handwritten "manu-script" that is nonetheless "the word of God." The book of experience [*liber experientiae*] and the monastic theology that formalizes or conceptualizes it teach us newly to place ourselves at the table. Like Eugène Guillevic in his *Art of Poetry* we then become ruminants, who "graze" words. And, as Guillevic says, the words are then like grass, or like roads or houses, or like all those things that we see in the landscape and want to get hold of.[52]

I left out a *missing link*—in other words the book of experience—in both my studies of the Fathers of the Church (*God, the Flesh, and the Other*[53]) and my study of St. Bonaventure and the entry of God into theology.[54] That gap is filled here. It was not an absence that flaunted itself, but its "obviousness" is so apparent today that I could no longer work my way round the gap without being struck by it. My third volume of patristic and medieval philosophy, precisely in a place between the other two, has a role to link them, as well as standing in the structure of a larger edifice that now rests on three pillars: *Saint Bonaventure and the Entrance of God into Theology*; *God, the Flesh, and the Other*, and *The Book of Experience* (concerning patristic medieval philosophy); *Crossing the Rubicon*, *The Loving Combat*, and *Obstacles on the Route* (concerning the connection between philosophy and theology); *The Guide to Gethsemane*, *The Metamorphosis of Finitude*, and *The Wedding Feast of the Lamb* (concerning the philosophy of religious experience).

The book of experience is thus not solely a book that has to be read or deciphered; it offers itself in monastic theology of the eleventh and twelfth centuries as *the* source that we can still tap today. It provides insight into the experience of thought or the theophanic argument (Anselm: part 1), the experience of the world (Hugh and Richard of Saint-Victor: part 2), and experience as affect (Aelred of Rievaulx and Bernard of Clairvaux: part 3). We shall not find in it simply a philosophical version of experience, or the juxtaposition of authors or concepts that trace a genealogy of experience. We shall find life lived in a true "way of thought," where speaking of experience is above all a way of speaking *about* experience that *starts from* experience. It is not simply speaking of experience but also letting it speak. My hope is that the spiritual scansion of monastic theology analyzed here—all the more spiritual because also philosophical, and all the more philosophical because also spiritual—might nourish the reader as it has made the present author's life fruitful for many long years. "I am the food of the fully grown," St. Augustine hears a celestial voice saying to him at the time of his break with Manichaeism. "Grow and you will feed on me."[55]

Part 1

The Theophanic Argument or Experience in Thought: Anselm of Canterbury

"The only excuse one can make for adding a new interpretation of St. Anselm's argument to all those that we already have is that it is impossible to resist the temptation to do so."[1] Étienne Gilson's statement, in the journal of doctrinal and literary history of the Middle Ages, is not recent but dates from 1934 and should perhaps still serve us as a warning. One cannot add a new interpretation to an argument that has already received so many interpretations without obfuscating, even suppressing, the undertaking that seemed quite clear in Anselm's own preface to *Proslogion*: "I began to ask myself whether perhaps a single consideration could be found which would require nothing other than itself for proving itself and would suffice by itself."[2] Should we see in this "remembrance of forbidden fruit"[3] a kind of giving in once more to temptation, as though holding back from going down that route (that is to say, the route of a new personal interpretation of the so-called ontological argument), for a medievalist, would be like refusing one's own baptism? Not that it would be necessary to show one's credentials or knowingly be anointed in order to understand Anselm's argument (as Karl Barth or Michel Corbin sees it) but solely in that a *passage by argument* is also a "baptism of fire" for all medievalists. It represents a challenge that one day they will have to take, to measure themselves against the interpretative history of this most famous thesis of medieval philosophy. The great multiplicity of readings always remains possible, even if some today would plead for a unilaterally theological interpretation, preventing any other. But it is precisely because there are multiple interpretations that we can speak at the same time of the richness of the text and of different translations.[4]

Liturgy and Theophany

In light of such a diversity of interpretations, there are divergences in the exegesis to an extent that has rarely been reached in the history of philosophy. Certain commentators writing under the authority of their respective denominations prefer to see the *Proslogion* of Anselm, and the so-called "ontological argument," as a text whose content is mystical and theological (Karl Barth, Michel Corbin). In secular universities it is seen rather as a key work of philosophical logic and dialectic (René Roques, Paul Vignaux, Alain de Libera, Kurt Flasch). Henri Bouillard on the religious side, and Étienne Gilson on the secular side, can be seen as two special cases.[5] Should we limit the theological to the religious sphere and the philosophical to what is ultra-rational? That does not always work, or at least it is not self-evident. If the rediscovery of Anselm as the "last," or the "last but one," of the Fathers of the Church helps us to bring up to date the aspect of the argument that is properly speaking biblical, and if the perpetuation of his name as the "first of the scholastic thinkers" has authorized new developments in relation to logic and the dialectic in the Middle Ages, it is still doubtful that we need to be trapped between these insubstantial alternatives. Above all it is probably important to *let Anselm be Anselm*, within the quotidian that would have been his own lived experience of self-consciousness. Neither philosopher nor theologian, because such distinctions did not exist in the spiritual renaissance of the eleventh century, the abbot of Bec strikes us first of all as a *monk* or a Benedictine, and it is thus that we come to see the experiential emergence of the argument, understood as a vision of the world and at the same time as the translation of a certain manner of being in the world. As R. W. Southern points out in his book on St. Anselm, "[t]he old saw about his being the 'last of the Fathers and the first of the scholastic' has a certain fascination. It stimulates by vexing: he is neither one nor the other. He is a representative of that intermediate period between the Patristic and scholastic centuries, which may best be called the 'Benedictine centuries.'"[6]

Neither exegetic (scriptural) nor logical (dialectical), the argument is thus first of all *liturgical*. The thought that was shared, or was "in common," in the experience of reasoning with a Fool, or an *insipiens*,[7] that Anselm wrote out in his *Proslogion* in the monastic scriptorium, is invoked as lived experience, "in community," in the experience of faith among the brothers of the abbey. It is not a question here of proof, but of the confrontation with God, in the argument we refer to as "ontological." The true reality is not that of the existence of some kind or other of divine Being, but of the possible experience, in one's thoughts certainly (the "common understanding" of the concept that we share with the Fool), also in the reality of our experience (the "fulfilling of the concept"[8] by an experience of faith that corresponds to it). Whether God exists or not is not in question. But what is already an "experience in thought" in the realm of our intelligence (an asymptotic[9] perspective of the greatest) is also in the realm of revealed or manifest reality (to which the ultimate name of "God" corresponds). That is what the argument reaches out to, offering a kind of unity to Anselm the monk, who is at once praying *and* thinking.

Through what existential and cultural sources does God "come to mind"[10] constituting that which we interpret, like Anselm as "thought experience"? (chap. 1). What type of experience in common does the argument that is considered here as "theophanic" initiate? (chap. 2). And how does the so-called theology of "satisfaction" open a new formulation of the problem of *the debt and the gift* in Anselm's dialogue "On the Fall of the Devil"? (chap. 3). These are the three parts of a demonstration that I would no longer be bold enough to call ontological but rather "theophanic." "Praying through thinking" and "thinking through praying" are what produce unity within the framework of the emerging monastic theology of the eleventh century. Nothing could be falser than to oppose the manifestation of God in the incense at the altar (the liturgy) and his theophany in our spirit (theology). The one and the other participate in the same order—that of a God all the more "manifest" in that he also, and perhaps above all, searches to make himself seen in our thought, allowing nothing of us, and in particular our "reason," to escape him in his intimacy, where still "that very Spirit is joining with our spirit to bear witness" (Rom. 8:16 RNJB).[11]

1

Of God Who Comes to Mind

Where then does the first and most famous statement of the argument derive from? The statement is "[*Deus est*] *aliquid quo nihil majus cogitari possit*"—which can be translated as "[God is] something than which nothing greater can be thought."[1] There have been scriptural interpretations of the so-called ontological argument (as a prohibition of idolatry [Karl Barth], as the grandeur and beauty of divine glory [Michel Corbin], as kenotic manifestation of divine love [Balthasar]). Étienne Gilson, however, rightly points out that although the Scriptures give "many names of many different kinds," they "never give a name like this," nor did medieval theologians "add it to their list of names."[2]

To say with Anselm that we believe you are "something than which nothing greater can be thought" does imply that this belief, even if it is simply philosophical or theological, comes from somewhere. To adopt the striking title of a book by Emmanuel Levinas, the idea that we have or receive of God is *Of God Who Comes to Mind*, and this could be either "concept" or "life of God."[3] To put it another way, and going back to *Proslogion*, if we note along with Anselm that the Fool "hears" [*audit*] what is said to him and "he understands what he hears" [*intelligit quod audit*], and "what he understands is in his understanding" [*et quod intelligit in intellectu eius est*],[4] then this suggests that the author of the text himself has already heard, for himself; he has heard and understood, and understood where comprehension is taking place. This is not to say—far from it—that Anselm has invented anything. Simply (and this is what contributes to the richness of medieval studies), in the Middle Ages one did not ever think without recourse to "authorities" [*auctoritates*]. Such reasoning would not have been invented without first consulting, to some degree, the Fathers of the Church. The formula has a *source* in an experience but also its *sources* in a culture. And it is exactly in these two ways that God comes to mind in the *Proslogion* of Anselm of Canterbury.

§5. The Source of the Experience

We should then take into account the full narrative of the circumstances leading to the production of *Proslogion*, and indeed the circumstances of Anselm's life in general, in order to be in a position to evaluate the experimental, or rather the experiential, element that the argument had for the abbot of Bec, as well as for his biographer Eadmer in his

Vita sancti Anselmi.[5] An event, or rather a vision, something like St. Bernard's vision of the infant Jesus being born [§24], shows us that the predisposition of the young Anselm in the Aosta Valley in Italy was to rise to such heights:

> The child had heard his mother speak of God, who dwelt on high ruling all things. *Living in the mountains*, he thought that Heaven must be on their lofty summits. "And while he often revolved these matters in his mind, it chanced one night he saw in a vision that he must *go up to the summit* of the mountain and hasten to the court of God, the great King."[6]

The Aosta Valley

The mountains of the Piedmont region in northeast Italy seen from the Aosta Valley are certainly appropriate as examples of elevation toward the heights. But a mountaineer in his boots is not necessarily an alpinist in his thoughts, just as rising toward "something than which nothing greater [*majus*] can be thought" is not the same thing as reaching such heights. It is rather a case of recognizing, as we shall see later [§8], that such summits remain always inaccessible to us. In short, the vision of the child when "he must go up to the summit of the mountain" is more important than the realization of such a climb in practice. If the Infinite "comes to mind" when it comes as the "life of God,"[7] then to live for the young Anselm was already to raise himself toward the divinity, and to rise was to be called when necessary: "The child crossed the threshold; the Lord called him, and he obeyed; he approached and sat down at the Lord's feet; was asked with royal grace and condescension who he was, whence he had come, what he wanted; answered the questions, and was not afraid."[8]

Anselm's so-called ontological argument has its roots in an experience, a lived experience of the consciousness of the body, the heart, and the intelligence, and its search for the intellectual point of view takes off from there. Rather than seeing it as abstract, then, we should see the argument first of all as a translation—a transcription—of that world we all establish "as children." Our world "without speech" [*sans paroles*], or *infans*, forges our being more than all the philosophical or theological discourse that simply points to it: "'my' flesh, that which is most originally mine [*das ursprünglichst Meine*] ... The one that I am (as a *child*) is the first and most immediately appropriated."[9]

Se obtulit[10]

The circumstances of the argument's production in thought, of its being written out and of its preservation for posterity, as well as constituting its source, form part of the argument itself. It would be a mistake to reduce reading the Fathers of the Church in the Middle Ages simply to bibliographical details, to a number of available works which we would then have to show were also important for us. But the way in which we think for ourselves determines our understanding of the thought of others, as does the way in which we write. And it determines the way in which we read what others write, as well as the way in which we conserve by means of these texts an objective that we commemorate. Tradition is an accumulation: it is transmission. It is not scholastic learning but production: it is not a memory from the past but an opening toward the future. The actual discovery of the argument, at the time when he had just been made abbot of Bec (1078), was for Anselm the site of an experience, indeed of a challenge—not just in terms of his thought but also in the order of his daily life. The preface to *Proslogion* shows us this in exemplary fashion: "Despairing, I wanted to desist, as though from pursuit of a thing which was not possible to be found."[11] Eadmer's *Life of Anselm* dramatizes the circumstances: "An original and bold idea ... and one which, as he used to say, reduced him to great straits ...; for his tension of thought prevented him from taking either food, drink, or sleep, and, what was more distressing, distracted and worried him at matins and the other offices."[12]

The question then arises: how could an argument which was above all logical lead the monk to forgo his biological functions and spiritual duties? Is it going too far here to see it affecting his eating, drinking, and even his prayers? But the argument is not simply a question of logic: it is a spiritual matter before being dialectical. Or rather we find the integration of a *dialectical argument into the heart of the monastic life* that brings up questions and poses a problem. Far from suspecting any possible false reasoning, the abbot of Bec sees an obvious truth and asks himself who, either God or devil, can lie behind it. According to Eadmer, "[h]e at last made up his mind to banish an idea which he suspected must be a temptation from the enemy of souls."[13] In short, the process of integrating the dialectic into the heart of the monastic life (or the scholastic into the patristic if we decide to use those categories) became the site of the kind of spiritual combat which was distinctively a feature of the eleventh-century renaissance.

It was necessary to choose between the temptation of the devil and the illumination of God. Anselm wanted to use "unsophisticated argument and with uncomplicated disputation," obeying "rational necessity" and "nothing at all in the meditation would be argued on Scriptural authority."[14] Not that "rational necessity" would suppress appropriate argument but solely that integrating a logical necessity into the heart of the mystic life could not be done without undoing or shaking up some secular customs of the monastic world. With regard to God and the devil, however, as we shall see later (chap. 3, "The Debt for the Gift"), the young abbot was to find a true origin for his argument—inspiration and not temptation, *jubilation* and not mortification or ascesis, and spiritual exercise and not renunciation. According to Eadmer, "[o]ne night at matins ... suddenly the light broke upon him; the argument he had sought displayed itself clear and bright to his mental vision [*se obtulit*], 'and his inmost soul was deluged with unspeakable joy and gladness.'"[15]

Se obtulit—the thing displayed or offered itself to his mental vision. The key point is there, in something that becomes clear not from argumentation in reason but as displayed in his mental vision. God illuminates the intelligence as he conquers hearts, in an experience of thoughts that it would be wrong to set apart solely for theologians since it touches what is common to our humanity, which is precisely where the argument will lead. Three stages in a unique spiritual experience thus define the three moments or divisions into chapters of the *Proslogion* in the form of an *Itinerarium mentis in Deum* [journey of the mind into God].[16] First of all, there is grace of the heart (chap. 1), an "Arousal of the mind for contemplating God." This is followed by what the intellect makes clear (chaps 2–25), which is a development of the argument and all its consequences. Last there is jubilation (chap. 26), "Whether this is the full joy which the Lord promises."

The Name of the Rose

From a number of sources, or perhaps we should say, from the key source, we can then uncover an *experience* or even a double experience: experience of the child's vision, of a ride into the mountains toward an unattainable summit, and then, second, experience of conflict for the adult over the integration of scholasticism into the heart of the patristic. Moreover, there is a striking record of the many fantastic episodes that will lead to the conservation of the written record of this argument we call "ontological." Anselm had confidence in a fellow member of the monastic community and entrusted the "tablets"[17] on which he had recorded the argument to him, but the man could not find them. Anselm rewrote the work and, since this was the brother who had the charge of other tablets, gave the rewritten tablets to him. The brother hid them "in as safe a part as might be of his bed" but later found them "scattered about the floor of his dormitory." They were rescued and copied out, this time on parchment, on a "little scroll (*parvulum volumen*), modest in compass, but invaluable in its weight of thought and subtility of speculative effort."[18] And that was to be the volume entitled *Proslogion*.

The narrative sounds like something out of Umberto Eco's novel, *The Name of the Rose*[19] and helps us see something in the form of the argument that has been far too long neglected. The essential question concerning Anselm's reasoning was not whether it was philosophical or theological. The formulation and understanding of *aliquid quo nihil majus cogitari possit* (something than which nothing greater can be thought) is the site of an experience for the abbot of Bec himself, perhaps we might say of an apparition, and necessarily one of God himself, given directly to Anselm. It was an experience because he had to yield to the great weight or importance of the concept, to take it in charge and vouch for its custody: "One day when I was tired as a result of vigorously resisting its entreaties, what I had despaired of [finding] appeared [*se obtulit*] in my strife-torn mind in such a way that I eagerly embraced the [line-of-] thinking which I, as one who was anxious, had been warding off."[20] The force of the argument is neither simply theological (patristic reading) nor logical (scholastic reading) but phenomenological (a new type of reading): what appears to him and the way in which it appears [*se obtulit*] counts as much, or indeed more, than the internal coherence of the apparition itself. The experiential source of the argument demands then the deployment of its *cultural sources*: God who comes as idea reveals also a God who can be read in the texts so that the illumination of the concept can answer to the source in the manuscript which gives it rationality.

§6. The Source in the Manuscripts

Reading in the Middle Ages

Reading the pagan or Christian authors in the Middle Ages, or examining what their "philosophical re-appropriation" implies, invites material questions as well as philosophical questions about the tools Anselm had at his disposal, the tools that opened up a second millennium in Christian history for him. There is a significant danger of anachronism in believing, or seeing, the abbot of Bec as having a huge library, like Petrus Comestor (Peter the Eater), a century later—who is represented with a napkin tied round his neck and shelves empty because he "devoured" so many books.[21] In early Romanesque monasteries, the small size of the library, by the side of the abbey church, is striking. The monastery of the Abbaye Notre-Dame du Bec, in the village of Le Bec-Hellouin, is no exception to this rule. The Scriptorium is certainly large, but that cannot disguise what seems to us today to be the miniscule scale of the library. According to Michel Corbin, "[a]t the end of the eleventh century there were barely two hundred and fifty volumes in the library of Anselm's abbey. All had been copied by hand using the most rudimentary methods. A complete copy of the Bible was worth the equivalent of the price of a luxury car today."[22]

Rich in economic terms, the abbey appears then, as seen through our eyes, culturally poor: barely "two hundred and fifty volumes." That is not many—could indeed be called minimal—in comparison with the thousands of works that make up our university libraries or indeed some private personal collections. This indicates, as I would like to underline, that it is hardly necessary to overwhelm oneself with reading in order to display one's philosophical talents. What counts more is applying oneself to each point, figuring out where one needs to explore the cause in order to develop the soundness of a proposition.

If one has little, one had better settle for little. What counts is that the little one has provided enough to justify argumentation. It goes almost without saying that Anselm showed an exemplary originality in writing *Proslogion* (an originality that has perhaps never been equaled except in the *Cartesian Meditations* of Descartes): what makes Anselm's writing distinctive, however, derives precisely from a difference to his predecessors. It is not the absence, most often artless, of reference to what is woven into or "underlies" the text. He would have known the Bible, starting with the Psalms, by heart, but the little he was to settle for comes down in his case, as the Anselm scholar Michel Corbin suggests, to "the works of Saint Augustine, the *Consolation of Philosophy* and five *Opuscula Sacra* by Boethius, the *Sermons* of Pope St. Leo the Great, and the *Commentaries* and *Dialogues* of St. Gregory the Great."[23] The search for "manuscript" and "cultural" roots of *Proslogion* requires that we look for sources of his argument first of all in that list, not allowing ourselves to be deflected into the kind of philosophical ratiocination that the history of interpretation has shown to be nonsensical.

Christian Sources: Pseudo-Dionysius the Areopagite or St. Augustine?

(a) A first negative point needs to be made: Pseudo-Dionysius the Areopagite[24] does not appear in the list of works identified. There are, however, countless exegeses of Anselm's argument (including Michel Corbin's) that rely upon the apophatic overcoming of negation associated with Pseudo-Dionysius to give meaning to terms that can make up the different forms of the name of God, such as *"majus* [greater]," *"summum* [highest]," or indeed *"melius* [better]."[25] The medievalist Olivier Boulnois warns us, severely but appropriately, that "[i]t is Thomas and not Anselm who frequently cites Pseudo-Dionysius. We are confronted here with a novel intellectual synthesis, where it is not so much Anselm who practices negative theology as Corbin who submits Anselm to the rules of negative theology."[26]

And the criticism is extended this time by Boulnois to Jean-Luc Marion:

> "I shall not however follow Jean-Luc Marion in his note ['Anselm should be read as he understood himself—that is to say, in large part starting from Dionysius' corpus and the theology of divine names']; this seems to me *philologically untenable*. As one historian has agreeably pointed out, in Anselm's time Pseudo-Dionysius had more translations than readers: I have not found any quotations from Pseudo-Dionysius in Anselm's work."[27] It seems to me that this philological reason legitimates, as we shall see later (§8), another and new philosophical reading of Anselm's argument in terms of limit and finitude for the believer, rather than in terms of the unutterability of God. My reading stresses the manifestation of divine presence rather than its refuge in invisibility.[28]

(b) A second point, positive this time. Two important sources, or we might say, two great traditions are cited with regard to manuscripts that Anselm had at his disposal, and that could perhaps explain how, as he says, the idea comes to him (*se obtulit*): St. Augustine on the one hand and Boethius on the other. Commentators on Anselm at best make do with citing, very often at secondhand, possible references to scholastic and patristic reference to the argument (assuming that as in the past one has to start scholasticism and the Middle Ages with Boethius). I should like here to employ primary sources: one does not find sources in general without going back to "the" source.[29]

With regard to St. Augustine the reference is clear. Probably drawing upon Plotinus, Augustine seems to have fully—or *almost* fully—given the argument. That "*almost*," however, points to the originality of the abbot of Bec. The "One" is defined in Book V of the *Enneads* of Plotinus as "better" [*supérieur*], or utterly transcendent [*au-delà de tout*], "what could be better than The One or could exceed it in any sense?" [*ti gar an tou henos beltion kai epekeina holôs*].[30] The formulation of the argument in terms of "greater" [*majus*] by Anselm, or "exalted" [*sublimius*] by Augustine, has its origin in the "better" [*beltion*] of Plotinus. But St. Augustine's originality is seen in two respects: in his insistence not simply on the grandeur of God [*sublimius*] but also on his goodness or benevolence [*melius*]; and secondly in his including the movement of thought itself [*cogitari*] and not just positing The One [*henos*]:

> Now although he alone is thought of as the god of gods, he is also thought of by those who imagine, invoke, and worship other gods, whether in heaven or on earth, in so far as their thinking strives to reach a being [*ita cogitator ut aliquid*] than which there is nothing better or more exalted [*quo nihil sit melius atque sublimius*].[31]

The similarity with Anselm's argument, at least in its first formulation [*aliquid quo nihil majus cogitari possit*], is striking—proof, if we needed it, that God does not come to mind from nowhere. Experience allies itself to texts, and the personal world joins that cultural world from which it derives its contours.

Four characteristics thus unite the two authors:

1. Together Anselm and Augustine strive to reach God through the presentation of God or through an act of *cogitatio* (thought, reasoning, reflection).
2. In both cases this act is determined negatively such that "nothing is" [*nihil sit*] beyond what is declared and thought.
3. Both define this beyond as greater/exalted [*sublimius/majus*] or "better" [*melius*] in a way that combines the concepts as far as Augustine is concerned and that separates the two in Anselm's names of the divine (*Pros* chap. 2 *majus*; *Pros* chap. 14 *melius*).
4. Both describe in terms of "exertion" (*conetur attingere* [Augustine]) or an "act of faith" (*credimus te esse*—we believe that you are [Anselm]), an act that is a surpassing of the self, coming up against a God who is beyond all possible surpassing.

Cogitatio, negativity, exaltation and goodness, and an exertion of thought define then what is in common between the two protagonists. The movement here is not Pseudo-Dionysian but exclusively Augustinian. It is not a question of some kind of "ineffable beyond," which would be characteristic of the Eastern Fathers but rather of being this side of a limit or threshold concept for which St. Augustine is the principal source in the West, perhaps first of all through his doctrine of sin.

But there is more, and even better, in the work of St. Augustine. The Father of the Church, far from being simply satisfied with the superiority of the divine, also constructs an argument from that superiority which affirms the existence of God. This is found in his *De libero arbitrio* [*On the Free Choice of the Will*]. In his dialogue with Evodius in that book, Evodius insists: "I will plainly admit that this being, to which we agree none is superior [*quo nihil superius esse*] is God." Augustine replies:

> Very well. It will be sufficient for me to show [*ostendere*] that there is something of this sort that you will admit it is God—or, if there is something higher [*supra est*], you grant that *it* is God [*eum ipsum Deum esse concedes*]. Accordingly, whether there is something higher or not, it will be clear that God exists when with His help, I show as promised that He is higher than reason [*esse supra rationem*].[32]

The argument here is new and moreover comes close to Anselm's formula. Certainly, the superiority of the divine and the impossibility of thinking of what is beyond it make up its fundamental essence. But we can also take from it the conclusion that God is [*Deum esse*] because the thought of a being above that which I think of as superior cannot be other than God. The existence of a reality superior to reason, even if it is only a thinkable reality and not an effective one, proves that at the very least that such a being of reason exists, even though I myself, by my own means, would have no means to reach it.

Augustine's argument seems then to resemble Anselm's at every point, except that Evodius, far from objecting to Augustine with some form of the non-existence of God, even in thought, calls into question simply the possibility of reaching the superior [*superius*], and not that there actually is a superior. Evodius thus has nothing in common with the Fool in Anselm's work. The Fool directly puts the question of formulating the existence or nonexistence of God, and not just the superiority of God in relation to humankind. "Is there no such nature [as You]," Anselm asks himself, drawing here on Psalm 14 where "[t]he fool says in his heart, 'There is no God!'" (JB). While Anselm counters the Fool's question on the existence of God, even if only in conceptual terms, using the notion of superior [*majus*], or of better [*melius*], to resolve it, Augustine proposes along with Evodius the possibility of a superior [*superius*] as concept and draws from that concept the possibility of an argument for the existence of God that Evodius himself never puts forward.

The concepts used are thus the same—the superior [*superius*/*majus*] and the existent [*esse*], but they are developed in opposite directions: Augustine from the question of the existent to the possibility of a superior; Anselm from the question of the superior to the possibility of an existent. This is not a simple repetition but a transformation: or we could say it is the emergence of the problem of being and its significance—through the distinction Anselm makes between the presence of the thing "in the intellect" [*in intellectu*] and/or also "in reality" [*in re*], starting off with the case of the painter (see §7). As far as Augustine is concerned, he does not pose that problem in relation to the grandeur of God. In short, the basis of his argument is in the tradition of the Father of the Church, but its new form looks forward to the scholastic, that is to say a form of logic and dialectic capable of shaping by "'rational necessity' [*ratione necessitas*] and not by arguing 'on scriptural authority' [*auctoritate scripturae*]."[33]

Pagan Sources: From Cicero to Boethius

As far as *The Consolation of Philosophy* by Boethius is concerned, according to scholars of Anselm, a manuscript copy was also to be found on the shelves among the two hundred and fifty volumes in the library at Bec. It was this treatise that probably gave Anselm the possibility of taking one further step. While the fifth book of *The Enneads* of Plotinus was probably the source or first point of the formulation of the argument for St. Augustine (*supra*), Cicero's *Tusculan Disputations* served as a basis for Boethius and probably attracted Anselm with a more rigorously reasoned formulation. In Cicero's work, it is above all a question of philosophy, as it would be later for Boethius, so that there is a remarkable complicity with Anselm's formulation. Cicero, praising the feats of philosophy and above all the powers of memory and the mind's inventions, writes: "I am convinced entirely, that that which could effect so many and such great things must be a divine power. For what is the memory of words and circumstances? What, too, is invention? Surely they are things than which nothing greater can be conceived in a God [*ne in deo quidem quicquam maius intelligi potest*]."[34]

The closeness to Anselm's argument is evident, not to say striking, to the extent that one cannot help wondering if Cicero's *Tusculan Disputations* did not figure among the volumes in Bec Abbey, although there is no evidence to that effect. Several of the ingredients of Anselm's argument in the *Proslogion* are to be found there: the mention of the "greater" [*majus*] on the one hand, and the idea that "Nothing greater can be conceived in a God [*ne in deo quidem quicquam maius in intelligi potest*]." Cicero, however—and here we see the originality of Anselm, who can be placed with Augustine and Boethius—does not in any respect use the greatness of these faculties to prove the existence of God. The retrospective capacity of the memory [*memoria*] and the prospective faculty of invention [*inventio*] mean more to him than God, simply placed here as a term for all superior greatness or the eternity of God himself. Nothing can be conceived of "greater" [*majus*] than these faculties, according to Cicero, not even in God himself. But that says nothing of the existence of God as such.

We could add, concerning the pagan sources of the argument, that Seneca himself in his *Natural Questions* [*Naturales Quaestiones*] was the worthy successor of Cicero as far as the genealogy of the so-called ontological proof is concerned, although the French translation of Seneca's treatise unfortunately neglects to make this plain. According to the fifth Natural Question, which is often published as a kind of preface to the work, the soul "comes to learn what it has long sought, it begins to know God." But Seneca asks himself, "what is God?" His reply is that God is a "greatness" [*magnitudo*] that "exceeds the bounds of thought" [*qua nihil maius cogitari potest*].[35] There is a new and astonishing proximity to what will be Anselm's argument in *Proslogion*. This time it all seems more solid: not only do the faculties (the power of memory and the mind's "extension") have no greater extension than in God (Cicero), but God is the same as the one than whom nothing greater can be thought (Seneca). All that is missing here is reference in the development of the argument to "proving ... that God truly [i.e. really] exists,"[36] which will be characteristic of Anselm's reasoning as he refers back to both Augustine and Boethius.

In contrast to all the unilaterally theological interpretations and exegeses of the ontological proof, we need at least to recognize that a pagan, indeed two pagans, both Roman citizens and Stoics (Cicero and Seneca), were principal sources, while at the same time we come back to Anselm, who turned the philosophical formulation into its theological form. A certain purely metaphysical understanding of the argument would seem then to be not only possible but legitimate in terms of its origin—something that, within the Ciceronian tradition, is confirmed in every respect by the further steps in its formulation in *The Consolation of Philosophy* by Boethius.

It has often been suggested, but not fully considered, how the passage in Book III of *The Consolation* opens up a new perspective, which in turn wakes us up to how much Anselm depends upon the Father of the Church. Of course, Boethius is not one of the Fathers: or at least he is not simply classifiable as such. That is exactly what contributes to the originality of the Roman consul, not so much in terms of the content of his work, but as to what makes it a benchmark or reference. Throughout the Middle Ages, and above all through his master Lanfranc, Anselm would inherit Boethius's *logica vetus* (old logic), a logic that would move the philosophy of the patristic world into the scholastic world. The instrument has changed, as well as the perspective, and in that change we see an undeniable contribution of Boethius, giving the lie to all those who would reduce the Archbishop of Canterbury to a simple "Father of the Church," neglecting how he is a writer who opens a "new era."

(a) The instrument. The important passage in the *Consolation of Philosophy* (Book III) in a formulation that French translations never render literally adds a logical characteristic that Augustine's first argument does not contain:

> For nothing can be thought of better than God [*cum nihil deo melius excogitari queat*] ... [R]eason shews us [*demonstrat*] that God is so good [*bonum esse*], that we are convinced that in Him lies also the perfect good [*ut perfectum quoque in eo bonum esse convincat*]. For [*nam*] if it is not so, He cannot be the fountain-head [*rerum omnium princeps*]; for there must be something [*aliquid*] more excellent [*praestantius eo*], possessing that perfect good, which appears to be of older origin than God ... wherefore, unless we are to prolong the series to infinity [*ne in infinitum ratio prodeat*], we must allow that the highest Deity must be full of the highest, the perfect.[37]

First of all, the form differs, showing that a connection to the Fathers of the Middle Ages is not the same when it is a question of the patristic Augustine or the logician Boethius. The argument here distinctively takes on the pattern of a demonstration, with its rational observations ("reason shows"), its hypotheses ("were it not so"), its consequences ("there would be something"), the impossibility of a rebound from cause to cause ("lest we fall into infinite regression"), and its metaphysical terms ("the supreme God ... full of supreme perfect good."). We can say that the argument is more or less the same, at least with respect to St. Augustine. No more than Evodius and unlike the Fool in St. Anselm's work, Boethius does not question the existence of God, even in spirit. Moreover his target is uniquely the perfection of the sovereign God, and God's being, which suggests that, knowing better than anyone else the formulation of the argument that was to become metaphysical and Cartesian [Descartes, *Metaphysical Meditations* V.7: "The idea of a being supremely perfect"], Anselm had already rejected a use of terms that would be, to say the least, insufficiently biblical. As far as Boethius is concerned, Anselm did not adopt his language (metaphysical) but learned from his form of expression (logical). Thus the tools of the Roman consul could be used by the abbot of Bec (dialectic) though what he had in his sights was different (metaphysical in the case of Boethius).

(b) Thus, we find a radical difference in perspective. Boethius searches for the "consolation of philosophy," and in his work it is Philosophy that asks "whither I am attempting to lead you" (III, i) and considers "where lies this perfection of happiness" (III, x). Anselm expects nothing from philosophy valued as such, and philosophy in this respect is totally absent from *Proslogion*, as we can see even from the title of his work. Theology may serve as the entrance into the treatise, for example: "Arousal of the mind for contemplating God [*excitatio mentis ad contemplendum Deum*]" (chap. 1). While at the same time philosophical reasoning in a non-metaphysical language can easily take its place, for example, in chap. 2: "God truly exists."

Philosophy sets the tone for Boethius, while it is simply something that comes into play in the course of the argument for Anselm. The abbot of Bec knew what he was doing, or should have known, having at hand the works of St. Augustine (in particular *De doctrina Christiana* and *De libero arbitrio*) as well as Boethius's *The Consolation of Philosophy*. Anselm, as a Benedictine monk, did not choose one (Augustine) against the other (Boethius) and did not pit one against the other: patristic against scholastic, mystic against dialectic. As we shall see, out of the one and the other he constructed a new unity that reflected his own being (§5) as well as his own cultural roots (§6). The "experience in common" of Anselm along with his monks, as well as in his fictional dialogue with the Fool (§7), and in correlation of "The Threshold and the Manifest" at the heart of the *Proslogion* (§8), confirms his argument as a kind of "ode to limits," not in that it is to be confined by limits, but in that as far as Anselm is concerned, there is no theophany beyond anthrophony, no "saturated phenomenon" that is not a "threshold [or exceptional] phenomenon."[38]

2

The Theophanic Argument

As we have seen (chap. 1) the argument of *Proslogion* bears the mark of a double experience: that of the child's vision of going up "to the summit of the mountain" and the experience of the recovery of the "tablets" on which the argument was written. It also bears witness to multiple sources, taken on and nonetheless transformed. There are "patristic" sources certainly (Augustine, Boethius), but there is also a reliance on philosophy (Plotinus) and indeed on ancient "wisdom" (Seneca, Cicero). But just as Blaise Pascal's fragmentary "Mémorial," sewn into the lining of his coat, recorded the experience of an unforgettable night of 1654, so the *Proslogion* is a memorial of the year of grace 1076 for Anselm: "Behold, one night during Matins, the grace of God shone in his heart and the matter became clear to his understanding, filling his whole heart with an immense joy and jubilation."[1]

Is the experience here exclusively religious and of the order of an act of faith (immense joy and jubilation)? Or is it also and in a way that is distinctively original, philosophic, and phenomenal in terms of its thought ("clear to his understanding")? To put it another way, was there an "*experience in thought*" of God here, in a conceptual form new to the eleventh century, such that the understanding itself could be enlightened or illuminated by it, indeed inhabited by it? Was it an experience of the divine that seeks to make itself known? Was it that a "prophecy of the intelligence," in the sense of a light that one might carry rather than of something to be deciphered in the future, now allowed for different types of experience (conceptual and/or confessional), any one of which, shining into transcendence, could come to bear witness? All this applies certainly as far as the meaning of the hermeneutic and the conditions of interpretation of the lived experience are concerned, but there is a further possibility for us today, in the translation into textual form of an experience that can quite properly be universalized.

§7. Experience in Common

To Believe and to Understand

A first reading of the whole treatise certainly leads us to grasp it exclusively as the site of an experience of faith. It seems like an "Arousal of the mind for contemplating

God" [title of chap. 1] and not simply an argument showing that "God truly exists" [title of chap. 2]. Moreover, the often-cited ending of the first chapter provides ample excuse for such a perspective: "For I do not seek to understand in order to believe, but believe in order to understand [*neque enim quaero intelligere ut credam; sed credo ut intelligam*]. For I believe even this: that unless I believe, I shall not understand [*nisi credidero, non intelligam*]."[2]

The suggestion is then that one cannot understand the content of faith without adhering to faith. Thus the argument, at least at first, seems to be inaccessible to anyone who does not profess an attachment to the One by whom it is given to us to believe. In this hermeneutic circle of belief and knowledge, understanding is—as Paul Ricoeur sees it, when discussing Karl Barth and Rudolf Bultmann—"led by the object of faith."[3]

But there is more than this, and other than this, in Anselm's argument. While the hypothesis of the circle of faith and of our understanding of it demands that one remain entirely *within* the circle, Anselm, in the form of the ending of his chapter 5, and as it were to close the cycle of the argument (chaps. 2–5), outmaneuvers completely such argumentation. "What at first I believed through your giving [*te donante*], now by your enlightening [*te illuminante*] I understand to such an extent that (even) if *I did not want to believe that you exist* [*ut si te esse nolim credere*], I could not fail to understand [*non possim non intelligere*]."[4]

Certainly one could interpret this formula (as Karl Barth has done) as the persistent stubbornness of the speaker in his role of Fool, although everything in its formulation would seem to deny this. Barth suggests that even though we are submerged in the gift of God and illumined so that we might know him, "Man might not want faith. Man might remain always a fool."[5] But the sinful hypothesis of the Fool, as we shall see, is not enough to justify his argument and render the whole of the demonstration useless. This is evident even in the criticism of Anselm by Gaunilo of Marmoutiers. Gaunilo thinks that the figure of a Fool who is as logically erroneous as he is morally sinful is unsatisfactory: "For if [this thing] cannot [be thought to exist], why was your entire disputation enjoined against one who doubts or denies that there is any such nature [as this]? [*contra negantem aut dubitantem*]."[6]

We need to understand this following Anselm's own text. He affirms that one cannot not understand [*non possim non intelligere*] that God exists even if one wishes not to believe [*si nolim credere*], arguing on the basis of a certain shared understanding of the term "God," common ground between the Fool and the believer, independently of any position taken with regard to truth. As Henri Bouillard states, "[Anselm's] proof, discovered and included in faith and prayer, provides, *independently of them*, meaning and rigor." Paul Vignaux adds that "Saint Anselm and the Fool have accepted the *same concept of divinity*: one along with faith the other in refusing faith."[7] Seeking to resolve this paradox as we read the *Proslogion* today, we are not bound to a denial of the hermeneutic circle of belief and knowledge that would be entirely centered upon the stance of the act of faith. We need to recognize that a certain *knowledge without belief* can be both phenomenological and descriptive for humankind in general, independently of any confession of faith.

Believing in Order to Understand and Understanding in Order to Believe

"*Si non credideritis, non intellegetis*—if you do not believe, you will not understand" (Isa. 7:9). This formula, taken from the translation and version of the words of the prophet in the Septuagint, has its most explicit and fully developed statement in the works of St. Augustine, in this respect a precursor of St. Anselm: "believe in order to understand" or "understand in order to believe"?[8] One might think this had been decided authoritatively in the eyes of St. Augustine: "Someone says to me 'Let me understand, in order to believe, [*intellegam ut credam*].' I answer; 'Believe in order to understand [*crede ut intellegas*].'"[9] A third person or a judge [*iudex*] intervenes to settle the matter, the authority of St. Augustine submitting itself, legitimately, to the authority of the sacred Scripture: "You were saying 'Let me understand in order to believe'; I was saying 'In order to understand, believe.' ... Let the prophet make his reply: '*Unless you believe, you shall not understand*' [Isa. 7:9]."[10]

What follows then, from a reading of the prophet Isaiah, and a cursory reading of the *crede ut intellegas* of St. Augustine, is that the integration of knowledge into belief allows no room for any other possible interpretation. From *credere* to *intellegere* gives the desired result and not the opposite. A single-track leads only from belief to understanding and prohibits a return from understanding to belief, so that without faith nothing can be said and no formula can be found for what God is in himself.

St. Augustine, commenting very precisely in his sermon on the episode of the healing of a dumb and impure boy[11] (Mk 9:14-29), takes the boy's father as a link in an argument leading him to the prophet Isaiah as "referee" [*iudex*].[12] Like Anselm's Fool later on, the "boy's father" explicitly serves as adversary [*ille quem contra me constitui*] or objector in the "argument" [*controversia*] in order to illustrate this same question of the connection between belief and knowledge. Jesus himself, and the power of faith, is submitted to a prerequisite condition, or a kind of hypothetical imperative, of understanding—"If you can do anything [*si quid potes*], have mercy on us and help us" (Mk 9:23 RNJB). Jesus replies, conversely and *categorically*, to the father pleading for his child, "If you can believe [*si potes credere*], all things are possible to one who believes [*omnia possibilia sunt credenti*]."[13] Following in the footsteps of the prophet Isaiah ("unless you believe, you shall not understand"), Jesus himself seems to condemn once more in principle any question of explanation prior to the act of faith. Commitment to Christ is totally unconditional, or it is not commitment—and it certainly is not subject to rules of comprehension or to the possibility of healing ("if you can ..."). There is here, then, above all no hermeneutic circle. Any return to understanding in order to believe [*intellegam ut credam*] would be a de facto contradiction of the first imperative to "believe in order to understand" [*crede ut intellegas*].

That is not, however, the path chosen by St. Augustine himself, precursor in this respect of St. Anselm. Taking the interlocutor's questions seriously, and nuancing his own thesis that was such a single track (believe in order to understand), St. Augustine rules in favor, at least in part, of the hypothetical adversary whom he has set up: "And so, beloved, that other man too, whom I set up against myself, calling in the prophet as referee because of the argument that arose between us, he too isn't saying just nothing when he says 'Let me understand, in order to believe.'"[14]

The father "isn't saying just nothing" or is not entirely a stranger to the truth. But what is he saying when he makes a precondition (*if you can*) relative to the act of faith (*believe*)? As St. Augustine translates it, he says, "Let me understand, in order to believe" [*intellegam ut credam*]. The truth of the statement does not stem here from the minimal and common requirement of understanding which, as we shall see later, as far as Anselm is concerned, is based on an *argument communally acceptable* and precedes the hermeneutic circle. It is solely based, on the contrary, on the ambition to confirm those who already, even if unknown to themselves, move in the circle of faith:

> Do you imagine, beloved, that the one who says "Let me understand, in order to believe" [*intellegam ut credam*] is really saying nothing very much? After all, what are we on about now, but getting people to believe—not those who don't believe at all [*non qui non credent*], but those who do, though still not enough [*sed qui adhuc parum credunt*]. If *they didn't believe at all*, they wouldn't be here. It's *faith* that brought them here, to listen.[15]

Augustine's "understand, in order to believe" [*intellegam ut credem*] cannot be precisely understood independently of his "believe in order to understand" [*crede ut intellegas*]. Rather it is insofar as the "understand, in order to believe" is taken into "believe in order to understand" that he is truly intelligible. Someone who tries to understand is not in fact, in the eyes of St. Augustine, one of those who "don't believe" [*non credunt*], but one who believes "though still not enough"—and thus already believes. The premises of faith are part of the act of laying claim to an understanding of the faith, in such a way that the circle of believing and understanding is always already within the pre-understanding of the faith, whether or not it is confessed. The "understanding of the word of God," and not any conceptual argument, forms the boundary of a circle that is always *within the faith* as far as St. Augustine is concerned. "Belief in the word" is the condition of attaining understanding. The sermon concludes:

> What I am now saying, I am saying to help those people believe who do not yet believe [*loquor ut credant qui nondum credunt*]. And yet, unless they understand what I am saying, they cannot believe. So what this person says is partly true—"Let me understand, in order to believe" [*intellegam ut credam*]; and I on my side, when I say, just as the prophet says, "On the contrary, believe, in order to understand," am speaking the truth. Let's come to an agreement, then, [*concordemus*]. So: *understand, in order to believe; believe, in order to understand* [*intellege ut credas, crede ut intellegas*]. I'll put it in a nutshell, how we can accept both without argument: Understand, in order to believe, my word [*intellege, ut credas, verbum meum*]; believe, in order to understand, the word of God [*crede, ut intellegas, verbum Dei*].[16]

We have come full circle, or at least the circle has closed: faith is the condition of possibility of its comprehension, and comprehension confirms, indeed leads, those who still do not believe, if only in the act of searching how to understand.

Paul Ricoeur, without citing St. Augustine's sermon 43 (although it is the basis of what he is saying), sanctions this round trip under the title of the hermeneutic circle and makes this structure (which appears very early in his work [*The Symbolism of Evil*]) the center and heart of all his thought:

> What we have just called a knot—the knot where the symbol gives and criticism interprets—appears in hermeneutics as a circle. The circle can be stated bluntly: "We must understand in order to believe, but we must believe in order to understand." The circle is not a vicious circle, still less a mortal one; it is a living and stimulating circle.[17]

According to Ricoeur, we must "believe in order to understand" because it is only "from a prior understanding of the very thing," usually not subject to questioning, that all texts are "interpreted"; and on the other hand "we must understand in order to believe" because a "hermeneutics" of the text, in the form of a "second immediacy," always determines our relationship to the thing and to the world in general: "Such is the circle: hermeneutics proceeds from a prior understanding of the very thing that it tries to understand by interpreting it."[18]

We can see then how the philosopher of hermeneutics extends what was important in St. Augustine's thought to the whole of things in general. "Belief" in contemporary hermeneutics is not simply the act of faith inherited from Rudolf Bultmann's analysis in his *Jesus* but the act of prior understanding of existence in general that comes from Heidegger's existential analysis in *Being and Time*. One does not believe, or one does not exclusively believe, *in* God, or *in* the word of God, or *through* the word of God: one believes or rather one affirms an intimate filiation with existential presuppositions which orient our reading of these texts (believing in order to understand). And this reading then determines or modifies our being in the world in general (understanding in order to believe). The coming and going is that of faith and understanding but *not with* faith and *its* understanding; or rather it *starts off* from faith and its understanding even if it can philosophically get along without faith.

The payoff from this is huge: it means that we can transpose a structure of faith outside that faith, newly establishing if need be a possible philosophical secularization of theological schemata. The loss, however, or the danger is also great. It is a danger of forgetting what there is, in Christianity precisely, in the act of belief. It makes the simple philosophical clarification of our existential presuppositions (Heidegger) an act that will become separated from that of the theological confession of faith in Jesus Christ (Bultmann). And because the extension of the theological into the philosophical has to be paid for most often by the sacrifice of the theological, it will become necessary, as I see it, to find a communality between the believer and the non-believer, that is not just based upon the presupposition that a non-believer is on the road toward belief (Augustine) nor simply that the structure of belief can be extended to the whole of philosophy in general (Ricoeur). It seems to me that this is what we can derive from our reading or rereading of the structure of Anselm's argument, this time not within the *hermeneutic circle* inherited from St. Augustine's Sermon 43, but within our *common experience* simply as humankind—as believers or nonbelievers—who are confronted by, and come to grips with, thought that "comes to mind" about God.

To Not Believe and Understand

Anselm's Fool, who "has said in his heart that God does not exist,"[19] does not fall within any form of non-theism, or indeed atheism, in the modern sense of the terms. It would make no sense to suggest that he does. There are various reasons for saying this: first of all it is because this formula, cited twice in the Psalms (Ps. 14:1, 53:1) does not stem from a biblical hypothesis of the nonexistence of God but simply from his "absence of power on the earth."[20] Moreover, as Paul Vignaux says, "[t]he prior of Bec wrote for his Benedictines, who hardly resembled ... troubled believers who, by strengthening their certitude, relieve themselves of doubt."[21] Above all, that such a judgement could only be expressed in the inner self, that is to say in the heart [*in corde*], shows us that no public profession of atheism would have been acceptable: "the unbeliever is not directly addressed by St. Anselm, but he is nevertheless a person not to be overlooked."[22] In short, the Fool of *Proslogion* is not *somebody*: he is a kind of "methodological artifice" in the eyes of St. Anselm, like the famous and no less "malicious demon" [or "evil genius"] in the work of Descartes.[23] All the same, this Fool [*insipiens*] as he is interpreted by Anselm questions, or calls into question, the Augustinian radical rejection of any kind of "understanding without believing." Or rather, since Anselm had at his disposal a full set of the works of St. Augustine very likely containing the famous Sermon 43, the future Archbishop of Canterbury took quite literally what is most often forgotten, left out, or indeed not translated in editions that contain this passage. I would translate what St. Augustine says as: "Those who do not believe cannot come to believe if *they did not understand* what I am saying [*nisi intellegant quod loquor*]."[24]

Far from sticking simply within the hermeneutic circle, Anselm has a fresh interpretation of St. Augustine which he shifts to a central position: what counts is not to believe or to lead those who do not believe to the faith; it is first of all to understand what is in common between those who believe and those who do not believe; between what "I am saying" [*loquor*] and what it is that those who understand what I am saying have "understood" [*intellegant*]. Seeking rather for an overlap or a new tactical change of direction between philosophy and theology than for the simple back and forth of the hermeneutic circle, Anselm, does not wish to lose the ontological coherence either of those who believe (if we expand what they believe to all other forms of belief) or of those who do not believe (by dint of seeing them simply in the perspective of faith). From the Fool who is damned we pass on to the Fool who might be saved or rather from the senseless sense of the Fool we progress toward a certain meaningful face of the Fool, in that at least he shows how in all of us there is also our own distinct potential to exist quite simply as human beings. That is, we exist not independently of God but not relying upon an effigy of the divine that we are incapable of understanding, and we are capable of entering into a dialogue, at least of thinking the hypothesis of the nonexistence of God.[25]

In fact current interpretations of the argument often, if not always, conclude with a sweeping condemnation of the Fool. A number of theologians, citing the end of chapter 3 in *Proslogion*—"Why did the Fool say in his heart that God does not exist—why [indeed] except because [he is] foolish and a fool [*nisi quia stultus et insipiens*]!"²⁶—trace the figure of the *insipiens* back to that of the *nabal* in Hebrew, originally cited in the two psalms where the figure of the Fool appears (Ps. 14:1 and Ps. 53:1). Karl Barth emphasizes that the Fool is not stupid, but he behaves as though he were stupid; he is "quite clever, but he is following a principle that is from the outset perverse and pernicious, because he does not know the fear of the Lord, because he has fallen away from God."²⁷ I would like to emphasize, however, that there is a certain reasonable sense in what the Fool says. That is what makes Anselm seem modern, indeed the precursor of modern thought, less atheist and rather in search of a new style of community. The "reasonable sense of the Fool" is quite sensible, taken in a Cartesian way, that is to say as "reason" or "the power of judging correctly and of distinguishing the true from the false" that is "naturally equal in all men."²⁸ What does Anselm find out first of all in his indirect dialogue with the Fool? Not God. God never proffers himself independently of his words and concepts. Rather it is *humankind thinking of God* when God comes to our minds. The transcendental question of the conditions of our access to God is one that runs through all of Anselm's *Proslogion*, and the mystical enquiry will serve as the basis for philosophical and theological questions in the future (in particular for Kant and Karl Rahner).²⁹

We can cite, for example, the request that we meet at the start of chapter 2 of *Proslogion*, which does less to question God himself on his existence, than to examine the appropriateness *for us* of the way in which we describe God in our beliefs, and looks at how God truly appears in relation to the prior understanding we have of him. The abbot certainly speaks to his brother monks of Bec here and challenges them to confirm with their intellect what they have always held to in their faith: "Therefore, O Lord, You who give understanding to faith [*qui das fidei intellectum*], grant me to understand [*intelligam*]—to the degree You know to be advantageous—that You exist, as we believe [*sicut credimus*], and that You are what we believe [*quod credimus*]."³⁰

It is not a question here of showing what God *is* "quite simply," as though he could not be otherwise, but only that the formulation we have of God in our faith answers to a true understanding even of what we believe. The experience of the heights and lofty summits that, as we have seen, was physically and spiritually that of a native son of Aosta in his childhood [§5] was also the experience that the abbot of Bec wanted to share with his fellow monks, celebrating with them time and again, including during the offices of the night, the majesty of the divine. Interpretation of the argument must then be *liturgical* before it is ontological or gnoseological.³¹

We need to read closely what follows in the two psalms that both provided the inspiration for the figure of the Fool in *Proslogion* [Ps. 14 and Ps. 53]. Necessarily well known, sung, and recited by heart in slow repetition by the prior of Bec, these psalms formed part of a nourishment all the more spiritual in that it was at the same time intellectual [§4]. They established together the program of the whole of Anselm's treatise without it being necessary to quote them in full.

God looks down from heaven
on the human race [*prospexit super filios hominum*],

to see if any are wise [*ut videat si est intelligens*],
if any seek God [*aut requirens Deum*].

(Ps. 53 NJB)

The whole project of *Proslogion* is almost there, and it allows us to understand the project in its biblical dimensions: the appeal to the most high ("looks down from heaven"), the stipulation of intelligence in faith required in the name of the Lord himself ("God looks down"), and the unrelenting search of those who are bound to it ("if any are wise … any seek God"). But is there then a scriptural reading of *Proslogion*, where the treatise demonstrates its force and rootedness in the lived experience of a community praying and pleading in prayer? Certainly not, as we have already seen. On the one hand that is because the formulation of God to be believed in as something than which a greater cannot be thought [chap. 2] is not found in the Bible. It is rather to be found in Cicero, Seneca, Plotinus, Boethius, or St. Augustine. And on the other hand it is because the figure of the Fool goes substantially beyond the scriptural figure of the *nabal* in Hebrew, being as "intelligent" in his thought as he is "stupid" and "harmful" in his conduct [§7].

The Reasonable Sense of the Fool

We come back to our question: why the Fool? It is first of all a way of learning about Anselm in his indirect dialogue with the Fool. His dialogue is not then with God but certainly with man. And not just any man, but with one who could show his intelligence and understand that which Anselm himself understood. As we have seen, according to St. Augustine, dialogue and conversation are not possible with one "who does not understand what I say." But it is not enough to understand in order to believe; or rather one does not understand as long as *one does not understand that one understands*—and this is what underlies the outstanding originality of the abbot of Bec in comparison with all older formulations of the argument [§6]. The Fool and Anselm, thinking of God as "something than which nothing greater can be thought," agree at least on three points. No less importantly, they agree to say that they agree. They agree on the fact of "hearing" something [*audire*], and on "understanding" what they hear [*intelligere*], and on knowing where this has been comprehended [*ubi*], that is to say in the understanding or intelligence: "Surely when this very same Fool hears [*audit*] my words 'something than which nothing greater can be thought,' he understands [*intelligit*] what he hears [*quod audit*]. And what he understands is in his understanding [*et quod intelligit in intellectu ejus est*], even if he does not understand it [*etiam si non intelligat illud esse*]."[32] The result then is not tenuous, even though that has often been suggested. We could perhaps say that one is never as well "understood" as when in a discussion like this one between Anselm and the Fool, because if there is a point of conflict or something to be discussed between the two, it is skillfully placed on the basis of a common background. The commonality of their statements as well as of their experience in thought serves as a foundation for their potential difference. Together they try to understand/hear; together they try to understand/grasp; together they understand what they hear, and know the site where they can identify what they understand (in the intelligence). But they differ explicitly from one another as to the target or aim that they try to comprehend. It is in the understanding [*in intellectu*] for the Fool, and for Anselm it is in the "understanding" and "also in reality" [*in intellectu et in re*]³³ (*Proslogion*, chap. 2). It needs to be said that there are more points of agreement between Anselm and the Fool than disagreement, even though the one (Gaunilo of Marmoutiers, defender of the Fool) has difficulty in not drawing the same conclusions as the other. A consideration of the points of agreement is thus a basis that makes sense of the points of disagreement. It is not the disagreement that is new in St. Anselm's *Proslogion*, nor even the invention of a fictional objector to endorse the demonstration; what is new is the quasi-transcendental argumentation over the possible conditions of a common discourse about God when he comes philosophically into our ideas, whether one believes in God or not.

We can then make a further step forward. The definition—not biblical but strictly philosophical—of God as "something than which a greater cannot be thought" [*aliquid quo nihil majus cogitari possit*] is precisely philosophical in that it cannot, or should not, be first of all theological. We cannot simply attribute to chance the observation that the roots of the formulation of the argument are found just as much, or even more, among the pagans (Seneca, Cicero, Plotinus, Boethius) as among Christians (St. Augustine) [§6].

Probably this gives us evidence, if not proof, that Anselm is also looking for a kind of *commonality* between pagans and Christians. And in this he differs from St. Augustine. The act of direct and persuasive understanding for St. Augustine (Sermon 43) becomes in fact indirect and reflexive in St. Anselm (*Proslogion* chap. 2). While Augustine has no other end but to persuade those who do not believe, showing them that they do believe already even if only in seeking to believe, Anselm, confirming his brother monks in what they have always believed and justifiably have never doubted, tries instead to make them see that a true understating of faith requires them to enter into dialogue with that (or those) which in ourselves or outside ourselves does not believe as we do and even sets itself up in opposition to ourselves. We should not get this wrong. The challenge is not, or is no longer, just to make one believe— one cannot see quite honestly how the *Proslogion* could cater for such an exercise in apologetics in a purely monastic environment. It is to make those who believe already [*Deus est*] that their faith must also take them toward understanding what their faith is or understanding those who do not believe [*non Deus est*]. There is thus an overall coherence in the discourse on faith in St. Anselm's work, which distinguishes it from the persuasion of St. Augustine. It has a capacity to meet up with all human beings, including those who might refuse God in themselves, rather than a focus on God's power to choose certain people. "Infidels [*infidelium*] appeal to reason because they do not believe, but we, on the other hand, because we do believe; nevertheless, the thing sought is one and the same."³⁴

Unum idemque—"one and the same." Such is what is held in common and formed the basis of all attempts at encounter between those who believed and those who did not in the past just as it does today. The Fool of times past still has something sane to say to us now: the necessity and urgency of a joint understanding with those who say they do not believe but have, however, understood: we can at least understand one another on the minimal basis of *experience in common*. We share a common understanding of the word "God," a logical comprehension in terms of a shared formula, an agreement in relation to what is the site of its manifestation when it comes to mind (in the intellect).

Such a natural community was claimed, and was found in the past, in the *common experience of reason* of which Anselm lays down the first foundations. That community is claimed and found today, as I understand it, in the *common background of finitude*: as Foucault says, "modern man ... is possible only as a figuration of finitude."[35] A different era had a different natural community: where it was found through *reason* in the past, it is found through *finitude* today. But in one and the other we find the same ambition: that of not losing what it is that speaks, even if what is said "in one's heart" [*in corde*] is that "God is not" [*non est Deus*]. Not that a person who thinks like that would be lost if she or he did not follow us along what we think of as the "good route." But we lose one another if we do not know on what grounds or how we can come together.

It is not then to some kind of proof of the existence of God that we are invited by *Proslogion*. It welcomes us to a *common mode* of God's manifestation according to which, as we shall see later [§8], God is "so truly" [*sic vere*], that he must (or cannot not) appear to those who seek for him, even if only in terms of ideas and independently of any stance of existence. Unbelievers in this sense are not *without experience* of God, of whom they speak, since they hear his name, understand, and localize the site of their understanding. But their experience, shared with that of the believer, will not cease to be "different," relative to those other modes through which God himself gives access to believers through faith—although there is nothing that obliges one to follow one's faith other than the thrust of the Revelation itself in the act of "manifestation." Since it is limited simply to the purely conceptual mode of manifestation, the common understanding of that "than which a greater cannot be thought" perhaps awaits, legitimately, an experiential fulfilment. Divergence emerges then over the common basis of convergence: does the "that" [*aliquid*] than which nothing greater can be thought exist [*existit*] "only in the understanding" [*in intellectu*], or is it "both in the understanding and in reality"?[36]

We need to grasp what is going on here. The object is not to know if, purely and simply, God "is." It is rather to ask if, being established at least in the understanding, God could also be somewhere else rather than solely in the understanding. The questioning is not in relation to God *existing*, in an objective realism that as we shall see [§8] is no less than the complete opposite to Anselm's mysticism. It concerns rather the overflowing by God himself of the framework within which we have previously, and communally, fixed God: in the understanding [*in intellectu*] and not elsewhere, or otherwise. Foolishness is not then a matter of not understanding what this is all about. On the contrary, probably the believer is no wiser than the Fool in this matter, and Gaunilo is his worthy successor. What would be truly "foolish" [*insipiens*], even "stupid" [*stultus*] (*Proslogion* chap. 3), is not to say in one's heart that "God is not" [*Deus non est*]; it is to think that our common intellectual understanding of the being of God is the only thing that *is*—it is to think that there *is* only our common intellectual understanding of the being of God. That would prohibit, on the one hand, quite falsely, all individual experience of a God who comes to reveal himself to us. It would be a denial, on the other hand, of how we raise our communal logic of reflection into a mystical communion. As the psalm already cited recalls:

> Yahweh is looking down from heaven,
> > at the sons of men,
> To see if a single one is wise,
> > if a single one is seeking God.
>
> (Ps. 14:2)

§8. The Threshold and the Manifest

Quod vere sit Deus—"that God truly exists" (*Proslogion* chap. 2). The title of chapter 2 of *Proslogion* indicates, on its own, that there could be no question of some kind of "ontological proof" of the existence of God, at least as far as Anselm's project is concerned or indeed as opposed to the ambitions of the Fool and of Gaunilo his defender. In short, everything depends on the sense that we give to the Latin word *vere*. Either God *exists truly*, that is to say not simply in terms of thought or understanding [*in intellectu*] but also in reality [*in re*], and it is then the effectiveness of God that shows his beingness, as it is with all things in general. Or God is *truly God* [*vere sit Deus*], that is to say God is what is referred to in thought that is held in common between the Fool and the believer and is the One who responds to the appeal of faith—a unique case where the manifestation of the divine is also a criterion for the possibility of his appearance to those who are ready to accept or receive him. The supposed ontological argument thus gives way to the *theophanic*.

The Two Ways

What is often, not to say always, ascribed to Anselm's thought is a kind of objective realism which, as we have seen [§5], is very much opposed to his experience, as it is to the literal sense of the text of *Proslogion*. The first way out of this difficulty is then to suggest that God "exists truly" or "objectively" as a thing [*in re*], leading us to a form of reification of the divine: from Anselm's point of view one submits that there are no proofs of the existence of God because already "there is a God" (Étienne Gilson); and from the point of view of the Fool "someone who declares there is no God is not completely senseless. One has only to call him an empiricist" (Kurt Flasch).[37] In one or the other of these interpretations the real [*in re*] is considered in terms of its effectiveness, and the God found there (Anselm), or looked for (the Fool or Gaunilo), is no more than a shift into existence of a concept that is all the more empty in that it seems to be dying through not coming to fruition. All in all, if such is made the aim of the argument, the existence of God becomes thought of simply as "the positing of a thing or of certain determinations in themselves," a concept of "being" on which Kant relies in order to reject the ontological proof in *The Critique of Pure Reason* (see the example of a hundred actual dollars).[38]

The other way—according to which God "is truly God" [*vere sit Deus*] in that he shows himself through the mode of belief—is the sole one, as I see it, that makes sense of the general project of *Proslogion* as well as of the text.

(a) First of all, as I have already emphasized, we are talking about understanding that God is "as we believe him" [*sicut credimus*] and is "that which we believe" [*quod credimus*] (*Proslogion* chap. 2). Everything is then undertaken through an act of faith, even though the Fool does not share in it. We are not talking about showing or demonstrating that *God is*, but simply of showing that he is *such a one* and *what* we believe that he is when God comes into our thoughts.

(b) Secondly, definition in terms of "nothing greater" [*majus*] does not really work. Because if God is first of all defined in chapter 2 as "that" [*aliquid*] than which nothing greater can be thought, he then becomes a "that" or a "that which" [*id*] we cannot conceive anything greater, in chapter 4. The shift in terminology and the modification in meaning, so well understood and exploited by Karl Barth, leads us in fact to recognize in this formula a "designation" (of the name of God) and not a "definition" (of a doctrine concerning the existence of God).[39]

(c) Third, and we come here to the key point, it is precisely because the problem of the existence of God is "bracketed off" that God himself can and must reveal himself as manifest for us rather than just existing for himself. The case of the "painter" gives us an important example here. Certainly, one must agree that it is not the same when "the painter envisions what he is about to paint [*quae facturus est*]," having it "in his understanding [*in intellectu*]," and when "after he has painted [it] [*jam pinxit*]" he has it "in his understanding" at the same time as "he understands what he has done" [*et intelligit esse quod jam fecit*].[40] We must, however, be careful. The text does not say here that the painting exists: first and foremost because the word *existere* does not come before the end of the chapter, but also and principally in that the Fool can be said to "*understand that this is*" [*intelligit esse*] rather than to grasp some form of being beyond his comprehension. Paradoxically, although he does not fall into pure Cartesian idealism, the existence of God is a mode of understanding [Fr. *intelligence*] for Anselm, just as his comprehension of it was when it was a question of recognizing, and sharing along with the Fool, what they held "in common" about God. What differs between the protagonists (Anselm and the Fool), and is of no small importance here, is that in Anselm's view the *esse* does not speak of a quantifiable addition to "something" [*aliquid*], or to the understanding [*in intellectu*], or to reality [*in re*]. It speaks rather of a qualitative difference between a "that" [*id*] and a "someone" [*aliquid*], of which the believer can have experience. To move on from considering the Fool to considering a right-thinking person involved hard *work*. It was like when an artist strives so that a work of art that is "in the understanding" [*in intellectu*] comes to be realized [*in re*]—or perhaps we should say, becomes visible. The road taken counts far more than the result itself. The artist's picture is not solely the site of a reproduction exterior to what is going on in the interior, though certainly art would not have had any other office than pure representation in the Middle Ages—the work of art is the act of a "making" [*facturus est*], or of something "being made," but not yet made [*nondum fecit*]; and the "whole thing," as Bergson says, can mistakenly conceal what is in the process of being done.⁴¹ It is not important to consider whether God exists before or after this proof (Gilson), as that is not and has never been Anselm's question. What really counts is the *act of passing* into existence, which precisely makes the being of God as such, and is an action rather than a definition, giving us precisely "such as" [*sicut*] we believe, that is to say "greater" [*majus*] than the simple thought we have had of him. And this goes to make up the common nature that we share with the Fool.

From the Comparative to the Act of Signifying

The "something" [*aliquid*] or "that" [*id*] than which "nothing greater can be thought" [*majus cogitari non potest*] leads us to see a negative along with a comparative (*Proslogion* chap. 4). The text does not, as Karl Barth rightly stresses, say that "God is the highest that man has in fact conceived," nor even that God is the highest thing humankind "could conceive." As to whether this is really so, or could possibly be so, Anselm "leaves open the question of the givenness of them both."⁴² But this concession, almost what in phenomenological terms we could call an *epochê* (bracketing), opens up toward another signification—precisely that of the "greater" [*majus*]. Certainly this complement of the comparative [*quo majus*] remains without an object. And it is to the great merit of many commentators that they have shown this. There is an absence of limits in the comparison, and it moves thought on toward the limitless, but without ever reaching it. Jean-Luc Marion says, "Anselm's argument concludes that God exists starting from the very impossibility of producing any concept of God: God is known (as existing) as an unknown (through the concept of essence.)"⁴³

However, as I have briefly mentioned earlier [§6], the difference between Anselm and Pseudo-Dionysius the Areopagite lies in the movement of Neoplatonic anabasis [a going upward to the interior] to which Anselm would not have subscribed: "Anselm breaks with that Augustinian and Neoplatonic tradition in which he has often been placed."⁴⁴ The reason for this is simple: not only is it because, as we have already seen [§6], the abbot of Bec probably did not have the works of the Pseudo-Areopagite in his possession; in addition he would not have felt it right, nor would he have been able, to *climb philosophically* to the heights since it was more a question of God *descending theologically* downward. Or, we might say, the anabasis of common understanding undertaken by the Fool and Anselm goes far beyond conceptual sharing and meets up with what was already an experience—of the apparition of God when *he comes to mind* (as concept) and of an encounter of what constitutes *quite simply our humanity* (logic or reason in the Middle Ages). The ascent awaits then the descent, or the anabasis awaits a catabasis [a descent]. For, if God is that "than which a greater cannot be thought," *a fortiori* God is that which has *already* been thought—the thought itself or the reflexive understanding of that which has been understood beforehand along with the Fool: an understanding of the word "God," comprehension of its meaning and knowing the site of that comprehension (i.e., in the understanding) [§7].

The explicit absence of a complement to the comparative does not paradoxically prevent thought itself being overcome by thoughts. "That which is greater" [*quod majus est*] is just the thought that has been reached, and thus we move on from the understanding [*in intellectu*] to the thing [*in re*]. The "more" of Anselm, in the full meaning of the term, is paradoxically in the "less"—in the limit that it imposes on the power of thought since it wishes to achieve a "common reason" with the Fool and to arise from there toward God. That which was necessary—what is held in common by all humankind when God comes to mind—is now the very thing that we should, if not renounce, at least not be satisfied with. It is certainly a negative route, but one of "limitation" rather than of "surpassing," one of insisting on *difference* (Anselm) rather than on fusion through deification (Pseudo-Dionysius the Areopagite). Paul Gilbert points out: "The understanding of God imposes a negation on thought, a *negative* route *by limitation* ... the *aliquid* is not at all worldly; it differs thus totally from experience and we profess it solely in this difference."[45]

Experience and Manifestation

What then makes this difference, or this deferral of meaning ("*différance*" in Derrida's terminology), between Anselm and the Fool? It is precisely that movement of catabasis in which God descends and gives himself to those who, having done everything to climb toward him when he came to mind, await now for him to come to them so that he will give himself in and through experience. As I have noted earlier [§7], existence is a mode of knowing for Anselm and not something with ontic effectivity. It is not a question here of seeing two different things while looking toward God because the question of God's existence remains "limited" or "suspended," as does that of the possible thought of the unthinkable (Barth). But in seeing God, depending upon whether one is reasonable or foolish, one *sees the same thing differently*, just as there are variations in the attempts we make to see this same essence.[46] Certainly God is "one and the same" [*unum idemque*] for those who believe and those who do not [§7]. But the apprehension of the same is different this time according to whether one refers to the word [*vox*] or to the thing itself [*idipsum quod res*]: "For in one way a thing is thought when the word signifying it [*vox eam significans*] is thought, and in another way [*aliter*] when that which the thing is is understood [*idipsum quod res est intelligitur*]."[47]

It could not be clearer. There are various ways, not to say different modes, of intentionality focusing on God. And the experience of God that it is given to me to fulfil depends upon the mode. In the first way, that which focuses on the word [*vox*] rather than the thing, "God can be thought [*cogitari*] not to exist"—and such is the case with the Fool. In a second way, that which reaches the signification of the thing itself [*idipsum res*], it is necessary to "understand" [*intelligere*] what God is and to make of this a true *experience*. And what Anselm is saying boils down to this (*Proslogion* chap. 4). The meaning of *understanding* [*intellectio*] has changed here: understanding is not content simply with the "thought" of God when it comes to the idea [*cogitatio*] but identifies this time a specific mode of co-knowing "co-naissance" that, far from being satisfied with the pure abstraction of God, is enriched by an experience in which God himself comes to meet us. It is not in the words [*voces*], or in the utterance [*in prolatione*], but in the meaning [*sensus*] or in the signifying content [*quam in sententia*] that, according to Anselm in his *De Grammatico* (in this respect a precursor of Husserl) the terms of the syllogism are established grammatically.[48] Thus the Fool will continue at the level of words [*voces*] or simply at the level of utterance and conceptual comprehension of the name of God [*prolatio*]. The believer, on the other hand, passes through the sense [*sensus*], that is to say by what God signifies for him [*quam in sententia*], welcoming God at the heart of a lived experience or a challenge for himself in his relation to God.

The experience [*experientia*] which is at the core of what we seek here—not in the empirical sense of a recognition of the existence of God but in the phenomenological target of a shared conscious lived experience [§2]—gives us the key to a true understanding of St. Anselm's *Proslogion*, although the word is never explicitly pronounced, at least in this short treatise. *The Incarnation of the Word* [*Epistola de incarnatione Verbi*] (1092), written several years after *Proslogion* (1077), clarifies the meaning and helps us to see what hold together "understanding" and "belief" in the "experience." Belief certainly does not give understanding unless we follow the doctrine of pure fideism (that knowledge depends upon faith). And understanding cannot replace belief unless we go off into complete rationalism. Experience, according to Anselm, gives a lived quality [*un vécu*—lived experience] to belief and adjusts into conceptual form what was first of all given simply as faith. Thus is born a science of experience [*experientis scientia*] anticipating the "doctrine of experience" of Bernard of Clairvaux [§24] and going beyond the simple comprehension of the words that was shared with the Fool. It has real signification for the person who believes this time:

> Assuredly, what I am saying is this: He who does not believe will not understand [*qui non crediderit, non intelliget*]. For he who does not believe [*qui non crediderit*] will not experience [*non experietur*]; and he who has not experienced [*qui expertus non fuerit*] will not know [*non cognoscet*]. For the more experiencing-a-thing [*experientia*] is superior to merely hearing about it [*auditum rei*], the more knowledge from experience [*experientis scientia*] surpasses knowledge second hand [*audientis cognitionem*].[49]

A new form of knowledge said to be "from experience" or "on the basis of experience" [*experientis scientia*] emerges from Anselm's writings and will invigorate, as I hope to show, the whole of the monastic theology of the twelfth century (Hugh and Richard of Saint-Victor, Aelred of Rievaulx, Bernard of Clairvaux). This all happens as though it was already necessary for the abbot of Bec, like Spinoza later on, to distinguish "types of knowledge" where the believer and the Fool would differ. First, there was faith by "hearsay" of which everyone has heard today, as they had then. Second, there was understanding through "reason," which was shared by Anselm and the Fool in a conceptualization of God that they held in common. Third there was faith by "intuitive knowledge," reserved to theologians and the heritage of knowledge through experience, whose laws the theologians would sort out. Only this last type, which is characteristic of Anselm as it is of Spinoza, belongs to the true believer searching for knowledge. Having "the science of one who has the experience" (Anselm), the believer will always prevail over those who simply "have heard about it" (the Fool).[50]

The essential point, in fact, to return to the *Proslogion*, is not just to "understand" [*intelligere*] but rather to "rightly understand" [*bene intelligere*]. It is to harmonize the "God of knowledge" with the "God of belief" and to settle upon the second in order to nourish the first. "Anyone who rightly understands [*bene intelligit*] this, surely understands then that that [than which a great cannot be thought] exists in such a way [*idipsum sic esse*] that it cannot even conceivably not exist."[51]

The true understanding of God thus must be, in *rectitudo* [correctness], harmonizing the manner of being of humankind with the mode of being of God. Because, in Anselm's view, God is a "mode" [*modus*] rather than a "being." Anselm is not much concerned with defining God's beingness but attentive to the way in which God can manifest himself—in Anselm as well as his brother monks. God "*is not*," according to Anselm, as opposed to what we might think from a rapid reading of *Proslogion*. God is always in a way so real or "so true" [*sic ergo vere est*] that he is the being who has the manner of being "most truly and thus most greatly of all [*sime omnium et ideo maxime omnium habes esse*]."[52] The being of God is paradoxically a great asset or rather God's *habitus*. It would not matter so much what God is if he did not reveal himself at the same time in a *disposition* (or a *hexis*)[53] that allows humankind to know him. His "plus" is not a "plus" of being but a "maximum" in his manner of being—that of which the mode is "so real" [*sic vere*] that he surpasses all creatures. The *nihil majus cogitari possit* does not point simply to an ontic distinction between the Creator and his creatures; it points to what we find in the phenomenological differentiation between God the being, identifying himself when he appears, and human beings who could not reach such a fullness of phenomenality: "Whatever else exists does not exist as truly [*non sic est vere*] and thus exists less greatly [*idcirco minus habet esse*]."[54]

The ladder of beings is not then a ladder between beings but a hierarchy between modes of manifestation. The more the manner of being (*habitus*) proper to a being is manifest, the more it *is*—not ontically but phenomenologically. Here we find the true sense of the ontological proof, in reality a phenomenological argument: "Hence, something than which a greater cannot be thought exists so truly that it cannot even be thought not to exist [*sic ergo vere est aliquid quo majus cogitari non potest, ut nec cogitari possit non esse*]."[55] It is not the greatness [*majus*] of the being of God that makes his being, but that of his manner of being, or of his mode of manifestation. When God appears "in the understanding" [*et in intellectu*] and "in reality" [*et in re*] this apparition does not point to the exterior quality of the thing, as in a simple copy or a filling out of the concept, but the reality itself of God's *manifestation* or "theophany" in me, or my "experience in thought." Translated into phenomenological terms, God thought of "also in reality" [*et in re*] does not come to add something to his being but fulfills his initial mode of being as something that was made so that he could *manifest himself*.

The thing [*res*]—if we allow ourselves a shortcut here that at least helps to clarify matters—does not point simply to the empirical quality of God as being truly there but to the possibility of an *experience* of God as the "thing itself" [*Sache selbst*], that is to say as the lived experience of consciousness that makes him appear "in flesh and bone" or in a "presence in person" [*Selbstgegebenheit*—self-givenness].⁵⁶ To see God in the understanding [*in intellectu*] and/or in reality [*in re*] indicates then, as we have seen [§7], not two beings but two ways of seeing one and the same being—knowing that what differentiates one person from another, in particular in a monastic community, is not the empirical position of God as present in his presence (what is at least self-evident in a context such as this), but the capacity of each person to make of themselves the screen on which it is given to God to manifest himself. God is thus a "mode" in that he shows himself "so truly (or really) [*sic vere*] God" that he "cannot even be thought not to exist [*ut nec cogitari non esse*]"—that is to say as not giving all his power to his own capacity to manifest himself. "So much semblance, so much 'Being' [*Wieviel Schein, so viel 'Sein'*]."⁵⁷ The thing counts certainly for humankind, but even more for God, or especially for those who feel the obligation to let God be manifest in them, a task that a monk will discover on entering his cell, or the "inner chamber" of his mind, as Anselm recounts in the preface to *Proslogion*.

As we find the way of being of God so manifest that he would be unable *not* to manifest himself, so we find a kind of echo in the way of being of humankind that shows our particular aptitude to phenomenalize it. Fitting one way to the other is thus only an affair of *rectitudo* for Anselm, a capacity of joining along with God's manner of being rather than setting oneself up as the master when it comes to the question of existence and the understanding of God.⁵⁸ For it is not in fact thinking in the same way when "a thing is thought" as "word" [*cogitator res cum vox*] and when one thinks of "the thing" itself [*idipsum quod res*] because the "thing" itself points here to God as revealed, rather than God's being in his position of existence. In support of this we can cite the shift from a "so truly" [*sic vere*], formulated in philosophical terms ("this [being] exists so truly that it cannot even be thought not to exist"), to a "so truly" pronounced in the words of a confession of faith: "And You are this [being] O Lord our God [*et hoc es tu, Domine Deus noster*]. Therefore, O Lord my God, You exist so truly [*sic ergo vere es, Domine Deus meus*] that You cannot even be thought not to exist [*ut nec cogitari possis non esse*] and for good cause [*et merito*]."⁵⁹

The "cause" of God⁶⁰ is, taken literally here, God's merit. It is not simply that the merit and/or the glory of God is manifest to humankind, but that this is spoken in the terms of the believer or in a personal address to God—"you exist" [*hoc es*]—pronouncing that which was previously expressed in philosophical terms or with the anonymous sense of "one": "one cannot" [*non potest*]. If there is thus a filling in of the concept when the thing, like a picture being painted, passes from understanding [*in intellectu*] toward reality [*in re*], it is not in that it becomes truly existent or persistent. It is when humankind, also directed by faith, recognizes what we seek through reason, and faith alone gives full access to such a power of manifestation: "Grant me to understand [*ut intelligam*]—to the degree You know to be advantageous—that You exist, as we believe [*sicut credimus*] and that You are what we believe [*quod credimus*]."⁶¹

The Fool, in this perspective, is not without experience, but his experience is *other*—and it is precisely in this that we find what is held *in common* between the believer and the non-believer. The Fool has understood what God is [*intelligens id quod Deus est*], as we have noted along with Anselm [§7], but he has not, properly speaking, thought that "God does not exist" [*cogitari Deus non est*] in the form of simply negating the existence of God. The words he says in his heart—*Deus non est*—do not say anything from the simple point of view of the understanding because what they say means that one hears the word "God," that one understands it, that one understands one has understood it, and where one has understood it (in the understanding or *intelligence*). But what they say is "without any signification" [*aut cum aliqua extranea significatione*] relative to the full identity of the revealed God.⁶² Or we could say in another way, the Fool does not touch upon revelation, having access to it only through reason. But what he has access to is nothing, or almost nothing, in comparison with the power of the manifestation of God himself—which goes beyond one and thwarts all that we have anticipated (*prévu*) of him. God manifests himself already, including even to those who say "God does not exist," but this experience in thought ("even though he says these words") is not experience of "things" in a true "science of experience."

Hans Urs von Balthasar underlines that "the full realization of the true philosophical act is to be found in that theological experience of the *revelation* ... Herein lies nothing less than the overwhelming of the aesthetic reason of faith by the incomprehensibility of the divine love."⁶³

The Divine Exception

The stupidity [*stupidus*] or "non-sense" [*in-sipiens*] of the Fool, that is to say the impossibility of thinking that God does not exist, does not stem from a misunderstanding, far from it. He understands, and understands only too well. His error is not that that he does not understand God intellectually, but that he sees God, willfully and imperatively as "being":—or perhaps we should say, as waiting his true experience in thought [*in intellectu*] to become an objective reality of the thing and in the thing [*in re*], in the ontological sense of the term, independently of all subjective and personal experience of God himself. The so-called ontological proof suffers in fact for the Fool (and for those who defend him but not for Anselm himself) from ontology or beingness. Because, if [as in the attempted refutation of Anselm by Gaunilo of Marmoutiers] we imagine a "Lost Island" [*insula perdita*] as plentiful in its riches as it is inexistent in reality, it is not "lost" except in the eyes of Gaunilo, who relies here on the familiar model of the existent as "truly somewhere in so far as it is a thing."⁶⁴ What things most lack, according to Anselm, is phenomenality rather than their supposed reality. Thus he replies to Gaunilo, showing that he understands Gaunilo's objection perfectly well:

> If anyone can find me something [*mihi aliquid*] existing either in reality [*aut re ipsa*], or only in thought [*aut sola cognitione*] to which he can apply this inference in my argument, besides that than which a greater cannot be thought [*praeter quo majus cogitari non possit*], I shall find and give him that Lost Island never to be lost again.⁶⁵

To put it another way, Gaunilo like the Fool "makes the signification of Anselm's formula worldly,"⁶⁶ while Anselm himself phenomenalizes it. What Anselm's opponent does not see is the *divine exception* that goes right through the *Proslogion* and which precisely allows the phenomenality of God to emerge from his simple being: "You alone [*solus igitur*] exist most truly of all."[67] God exclusively and principally possesses the *unique privilege*, at least as far as his mode of manifesting himself to believers, of being fully that which he appears when he appears, prohibiting thus any falling away of his theophanic powers, "so true" for the whole assembly of other beings. The experience of the manifestation of God in thought through his word [*vox*], which is what is held in common through all humankind, waits then legitimately upon an intuitive fulfilling by "the thing itself" [*idipsum quod res*]—not in the existence of a supreme Being as the positing of a thing (ontological proof), but in the manifestation of his manner of being "most truly of all and thus most greatly of all" [*verissime omnium et maxime omnium habes esse*][68] (theophanic argument).

The Hypothesis of the "Third Man"

Paradoxically, it is not then, and moreover has perhaps never been, those who are explicitly mentioned in the *Proslogion* who are directly the target of the abbot of Bec. A *third man*—neither the Fool, nor Anselm, nor God himself—surreptitiously makes his appearance in chapter 3 of *Proslogion*, passing all the more unnoticed because he assumes the characteristics of the Fool [*insipiens*] as a mask for the figure of Pride [*superbus*] that he incarnates in reality: "If *any mind* [*si enim aliqua mens*] could think of something better than You [*aliquid melius te*] the creature would rise above the Creator [*super creatorem*] and would sit in judgement over the Creator [*judicaret de creatore*]— something which is utterly absurd [*quod valde est absurdam*]."[69] The insistence on a transition from *majus* (*Proslogion* chap. 2) to *melius* (*Proslogion* chap. 3), which is the guiding principle of an appropriate shift from ontology to agathology,[70] does not take full account, as I see it, of the transfer of the interlocutor on whom he relies. He goes from the Fool [*insipiens*], for a discussion of the "greater" [*majus*], to "any mind" [*aliqua mens*], for an argument over the "better" [*melius*]. The thought of this "any mind" would be "utterly absurd" [*absurdum*], which is more serious than the simple foolishness of the Fool [*stultus*], and it goes against the "logic of salvation" rather than challenging the "logic of proof or demonstration" or understanding God. It is not important if somebody, whether or not they are Fools [*insipiens*], does not understand the sense of the argument, or rather does not go so far as to live according to experience rather than just getting hold of the concept. That is a matter of apologetics rather than heresy, of a block in the road rather than a moral fault. But if someone, or "any mind" [*aliqua mens*]—whether or not that person identifies with the Fool—attempts to raise themself "above the Creator" [*super creatorem*], who is nonetheless seen as "better" [*melius*], then that is a most serious misstep against the economy of salvation. Believers, in their humility, especially the monk Anselm, since they want to make God known rather than humankind, or we might say to make God known in humankind, would not dispute with the divine over God's power to self-phenomenalize. "Any mind" then may raise itself up, rather than the "any body" [*aliquis*] that all of us might be—and not being foolish, or not more foolish than the Fool, who is always disposed to try to understand—may show *pride* (trying to rise above the limits of creaturehood) and thus may try to make a break with that disparity that permits the manifestation of the Creator.

The temptation of an elevation of the self by the self: such is what Anselm in the final analysis denounces in writing his *Proslogion*, separating off thus "any mind" or the prideful on the one side [*aliqua mens*] and Anselm or the humble believer on the other—the figure of the Fool or the logician serving here simply as a pretext for more serious matters: "I do not attempt to gain access to Your loftiness [*non tento Domine penetrare altitudinem tuam*] because I do not at all consider my intellect to be equal to this [task]. But I yearn to understand some measure of Your truth, which my heart believes and loves."[71]

The *Rule of St. Benedict* in its recommendation on humility reminds us that "*Omnis exaltatio genus esse superbiae*—all exalting is a kind of prayer."[72] In that respect the abbot of Bec was thoroughly in accord with his vocation. Following St. Benedict's rule throughout his life and commenting daily upon it during the chapter meetings, Anselm the monk could not hide or omit commenting upon it philosophically. Humility [*humilitas*] is what goes to make rectitude or right principle [*rectitudo*], and rectitude means a conformity of the manner of being of humankind (*Proslogion* chap. 3) with the manner of being of God (*Proslogion* chap. 2). Worse than the Fool [*insipiens*] in his obvious unreason is the proud [*superbus*] who aims to elevate himself to the same level as God. The ontological argument is *theophanic* insofar as it manifests an experience in thought (the Fool) and/or expression of faith (Anselm). We will thus find a remedy for the supposed aberrations of Anselm's interlocutors not by condemning the Fool, who, as I see it, cannot be confused simply with the sinful human,[73] but finding in Anselm's debate with the Fool the site of a legitimate *experience of reason* that is quite simply shared with humankind. It is found in between the faith of the believer obtained through revelation on the one hand (Anselm) and the inferences of "any mind" on the other (the proud). As Jacques Paliard points out, "[t]he essential signification of the argument does not at all consist in passing from logic to the real, but in seizing *at the very heart of a specifically intellectual experience* the *reality* that conditions it, and that it reflects: 'You cannot affirm your belief unless you already possess one.'"[74]

3

The Debt for the Gift

The sources of Anselm's argument (chap. 1), and what it makes clear (chap. 2), seem at this point to lead us to a threshold, and the question we are confronted with is the possibility of a gift received without a gift in return. There is no gift without a debt to the giver (chap. 3), at least as far as Anselm of Canterbury is concerned. The "threshold of the argument" [§8] means now that there is a greater "burden of the threshold" [§9], and far from condemning such a change, Anselm dedicates himself to acknowledging it. To reject of any form of reciprocity in gift-giving would seem to magic gifts into a pure abstraction that definitively reject fundamental and anthropological aspects of the given. "Giving the gift" would then lead to neglecting a crucial alliance in every donation. Paul Ricoeur notes decisively in his *Memory, History, Forgetting* that "it is important first to recover the reciprocal dimension of the gift in contrast to an initial characterization of it as unilateral." Ricoeur is taking stock here and opposing arguments about the "great swerve of the gift" [see Jacques Derrida, *Given Time* (1991) and Jean-Luc Marion, *Being Given: Towards a Phenomenology of Givenness* (1997)]. Ricoeur goes on:

> According to this commandment [the gospel commandment to love one's enemies] the only gift that is justified is the one given to the enemy, from whom, by hypothesis, one expects nothing in return. But precisely, the hypothesis is false: what one expects from love is that it will convert the enemy into a friend … Mauss does not oppose gift to exchange but to the market form of exchange, to calculation and self-interest. "A gift given always expects a gift in return," reads an old Scandinavian poem. The counterpart to the gift in fact, is not receiving but giving in return, giving back.[1]

A "ceremonial gift," something of which it could be that Anselm's argument, with its double form, both liturgical and theophanic, deploys the very highest example (chap. 2), comes down precisely to not forgetting the gift—or rather, to not making the highest degree of donation that of *forgetting the forgetting of the gift*. In reality all gifts contract a debt—not a "debt of influence" but a "debt of recognition" or indeed of "dependence." Marcel Henaff, commenting on "the price of truth" [*Le prix de la vérité*], suggests that "through this gesture which consists in presenting something to the other as *testimony of a pact*, it is *oneself* that one gives in the process of giving."[2] The threshold of the gift, or the gift as "threshold," in the theophanic argument, is not limitless donation (Pseudo-Dionysius the Areopagite). On the contrary the gift is thought of as a "kenosis within the threshold" in the form of a choice made by God himself (what will later be called "condescension" by Saint Bonaventure).³ The gift sends us back to our own limits or thresholds, while wrongdoing, or sin, wants us to be without limits. All limits are not limitations, even though limits may weigh heavily on our finitude or on our pure and simple humanity. But all true gifts cannot be given without some "burden of debt." In the same way that the infinite cannot constitute a point of departure here, where finitude marks the first steps in our existence, one does not *start off with a gift*, probably because the gift is not *heuristically* what belongs to our initial experience.⁴

We are thus above all "in debt"—whether it is a question of birth in some filiation, or of the economy of substances, or of politics that protect us, or of the juridical that defends us. The situation at the origin, at least for us, is not that of the donor but of the indebted. The turnaround that we need to operate in relation to our debt for the gift, or the "paying back of this debt" incurred through the merciful gift of God, is not simply a matter of course, at least for humankind. Friends rarely pay back debts, whether affective or financial. And the state or the financial establishment never (apart from a few exceptional cases) manages to "wipe the slate clean." We cannot pass easily, as we shall see, from a "debt without a gift" (the case of the devil) to the "gift without a debt" (mercy). That is the merit, as well as the originality of all the writings of Anselm, to have counterbalanced the absolute nature of the gift in *Proslogion* (the Theophanic Argument, chap. 2), with the burden of debt in his treatise *De casu diaboli* [*On the Fall of the Devil*] (The Debt of the Gift, chap. 3). We could also say that *De casu diaboli* provides a counterpart in theology to *Proslogion* as *Discourse* or *Address*, just as concretizing the gift in phenomenology cannot settle for abstracting the gift or separating it off.

What Anselm suggests in his so-called theology of "satisfaction," which has very often been misinterpreted, is that there is a "debt of the gift," or that it is characteristic of the debt to be inherent in the gift. "Satisfaction" in fact [§9] possesses at least the merit of not being "given" too cheaply. Because there is a donation, we often forget the extent or "measure" of its reception. Thomas Aquinas, in this respect the heir of Anselm, would later say, concerning just or limited proportion: "*nihil potest recipere ultra mensuram suam*—nothing can be perceived beyond its measure."⁵ It is only God who can be called the "true donor." But that is insofar as he is the "liberator" of a humankind that has been not so much humanized as it has been pardoned. The "limit of the gift" demands then that we connect it to the "gift of the limit" [§10]. That is why "God made man" or, according to Anselm, *Cur Deus Homo* [why God became man]. Anselm sees the grandeur of God not simply in his act of giving himself outside a context that is most often dismissed (the so-called anthropological reduction) but also in his act of complying with the limits of humankind in order to transform them and to inhabit them ("kenosis").

Donation and Satisfaction

To give is then first of all to make a claim for something that will be owed. But the "satisfaction" theory in theology, which stems from Anselm's work, has led into such territory that we probably quite rightly have neglected to consider the burden of the debt. Thus, we find Louis Bourdaloue, contemporary of Jacques-Bénigne de Bossuet (seventeenth century), saying in his sermon on the Passion that a vigorous "spirit of vengeance" definitively destroys any form of love in the Trinity as well as any commitment to mercy in Christianity:

> The Eternal Father, with a demeanor as adorable as it is rigorous, forgetting that he is his Son, and considering him as his enemy (forgive me those expressions) will declare himself as his *persecutor*, or rather the chief of the persecutors … Yes, Christians, it is God himself and not at all the council of the Jews who delivers up Jesus Christ … Strike now, Lord, *strike*: your only Son is ready to receive your blows; and without looking upon him as your Christ, do not look at him except to remember that in immolating him you will *satisfy* this hatred as you hate sin.[6]

Bourdaloue's words have sadly remained famous. The Father *satisfies* his own anger on the Son and makes him pay the *debt* of sin that humankind cannot pay. There has been no shortage in the history of theology, and even among the most important theologians, of attacks on Anselm and his *Cur Deus Homo* as the initiator of such aberrations. Louis Bouyer writes that "[t]he *Cur Deus Homo* is certainly the work that has had the *most pernicious influence* on all western thought … The whole problem of the incarnation was brought down to that of *divine honor* that has to be *satisfied*. The affront caused by human sin is beyond measure, because of the dignity of the affronted one."[7]

In short, humankind's unpayable debt and the surplus of the gift made by the Father lead, as it were, to the Son paying the debt in our stead—out of a kind of "feudal honor" and "juridical formalism" that comes from the developing society of the eleventh century, and that provides a context and a conceptuality too narrow for a true sense of divinity.

Hans Urs von Balthasar, however, warned that "Anselm's doctrine of redemption, his so-called doctrine of satisfaction, will have nothing about it of the 'juristic'"[8]—so that some of these condemnations of Anselm might merely raise a smile. Moreover, as I see it, there is in Anselm's thought about debt, and indeed about satisfaction, a *depth of existence* that contemporary overstatement in relation to the gift has probably wrongly neglected. Certainly, we can quite rightly underline, along with Balthasar, how the "objective figure of Revelation" goes beyond "subjective evidence." We can agree with Emmanuel Levinas that the "metaphysical desire for the absolutely other … deploys its en-ergy in the vision of the face [*vision du visage*], or in the idea of infinity." Michel Henry says that the extraordinary nature of the acts and deeds of the Messiah sent by God make him "a man who is not like others." And we might go along with Jean-Luc Marion, who says that the "saturated phenomenon" must serve as a "paradigm" for all "common-law phenomena" and through Christ of "poor phenomena."[9] But, all the same, we cannot think that through the *surplus of the gift* the *poverty of the debt* will disappear or, to put it another way, that the *extraordinary saturation of these phenomena* will somehow disguise the *ordinary experience of a human finitude that cannot be exceeded*. As Marco M. Olivetti says, "[i]t seems that the status of the debt as a *philosophical marvel* has been lowered by recent discussions of the gift ... Perhaps it has been found necessary to hide the link between the gift and the debt, as though it were something to be ashamed of, indeed the ultimate *metaphysical shame*."[10]

To rediscover the "marvel of the debt" today is not to indict the hypertrophy of the gift in a purely negative fashion. It is also and above all, this time in a positive way, to find in the work of the one who made the debt the heart of his enterprise (i.e., Anselm of Canterbury), a form of finitude that wrestles against excesses of over-Dionysian interpretations of *Cur Deus Homo*:

> Restoring freedom is not the same as making it all-powerful; it is allowing it the *power of its finitude*. Humankind was not supposed to have known the powerlessness that is sin ... But we could have known a *powerlessness that is not sin*. Satisfaction restores the *finitude of humankind*, rectifies it as an appropriate attitude, that is to say as a new desire and no longer as despairing.[11]

§9. Taking on the Debt

One thus "takes on a debt" as one might "take charge" [*prend la tête*], to the extent of never leaving off thinking about it, or referring to it, or weighing up the unbearable burden from which nobody can deliver us. Experience demonstrates this. A failure in this respect can sometimes be even worse than a setback in love, or at least it can lead to a drama where the elimination of the self (suicide) makes us see how, in some eyes, one could never raise oneself out of the debt. Obviously, beyond any economic or financial consideration, Anselm the monk, the newly promoted Archbishop of Canterbury [1093], found himself also "in debt" just when he starts drafting his *Cur Deus Homo* [1094]. No text can be read independently of the experience that it bears, even though we should not reduce it simply to that, but it has to be recognized how it is "in debt to himself," also "in debt to God," and "in debt to the Other," that the former abbot of Bec gets down to writing. Far from his abbey, and thrown into a situation that he had not coveted in the least (primate of Canterbury), the Archbishop underwent here the experience that Martin Heidegger was later to call *Schuldigsein*, "Being-guilty" [in French "*être-en-dette*"], introducing him to *Sorge*, "care," from which only God would come to relieve him.[12] Henri Declève suggests, commenting on *Cur Deus Homo*, that "what happens in these pages, what the reader is invited to, is the sharing and deepening of an experience of life."[13]

In Debt to Himself

Anselm confesses in the Preface at the opening of his treatise that he is in debt to himself: "With great tribulation of heart—God knows the source and the cause of my having suffered this—I began [this present work] in England."[14] What happened then, and where did this "tribulation" come from, when Anselm had just left the abbey of Bec? Assumptions explaining this abound: there was the absence of the king, William Rufus, who refused to respond to the call of Christianity, and there was the feeling of being forsaken when a soul like Anselm's was made for the monastic life rather than for a heavy pastoral burden.[15] But whatever the reasons, the Saint himself refuses to enumerate them, as though he feels that psychological knowledge of the causes would never be able to reduce the challenge of a hurt in his phenomenal *lived experience*: "God knows the source and the cause" [implied: I myself do not know and am not seeking to know]. The Archbishop suffers spiritually, and indeed bodily, while he prepares to establish the "necessary reasons" for the suffering of the Son. That is what makes him face the experience, "in debt to himself" in *Cur Deus Homo*. He is struck by his own "nullity" (to take up in another context the Heideggerian formula of "Being-guilty"), something that his secretary Eadmer describes in his *Life of Saint Anselm*: "[Anselm wrote a letter] complaining of the affliction in which he lived under a burden too heavy for him to bear, and regretting the tranquility of the solitude which he had lost."[16] Could he, and should he, then try to pay this debt for the life that God had given him, one in which through his sins he had become even more indebted, if the feeling of his own weakness and abandonment forced him to see his own radical incapacity to return the gift? At the very least the question is posed and serves as driving force for the justification of debt in *Cur Deus Homo*.

Debt toward the Other

The Archbishop is also in debt to others, and from several different points of view, not simply to himself.

(a) First of all, to Pope Urban II, to whom the dedicatory letter of recommendation, originally not part of the body of the work, is addressed. Certainly the discourse on method is exemplary here—as so many commentators on Anselm have been eager to indicate. But the discourse is more than a simple middle way for the intellect [*intellectum*] "between faith and sight [vision]."[17] The address makes us think of all the readers for whom *Cur Deus Homo* was written: *ad extra* for unbelievers "to confound [their] foolishness and to break through their hardheartedness," and *ad intra* for believers to "delight in the rational basis of our faith."[18] In short, the debt toward the papacy is one that has also been contracted toward all humanity: giving "the rational basis of our faith" [*de fidei nostrae ratione*] to those who do not have it (unbelievers), as well as those who have it (believers).

(b) But Anselm is not solely a "debtor to others" who bears responsibility for everything to everyone. He takes the monk Boso as his interlocutor in *Cur Deus Homo*, and writes: "In the following way Boso may ask [*Boso quaerat*] and Anselm answer [*et Anselmus respondeat*]." He explains elsewhere in *De conceptu virginali* [*On the Virgin Conception and Original Sin*] that he remained a debtor to Boso:

> I wish on all matters to accommodate your religious desire, brother and most beloved son Boso, I certainly count myself especially indebted [*maxime debitorum me iudico*] when I understand that this desire is aroused in you by

me ... in the *Cur Deus Homo* (which you more than the others urged me to write, and in which I have cast you in the role of my fellow-disputant).[19]

There is then a "debt within the debt" at the heart of the dialogue structure of *Cur Deus Homo* that not only deals with sin but also reveals that it is indebted to a young monk, Boso, from the Abbey of Bec, who would go on to become the fourth abbot [1124–36] after Anselm's death [1109]. Far from being used as a simple puppet figure to display the arguments of his master, Boso moves into the position of interlocutor, and promoter, of this abbot, who challenges himself "being in debt" and Boso's "debtor" [*debitorem*].[20]

(c) The debt toward others is most heavy and complete when it is extended to all readers in Anselm's dedication to Pope Urban II: "When I find some point which I did not previously see, I shall willingly disclose it to others, so that I may learn from another's judgment what I ought to safeguard."[21] This formula precedes the contents of the book but says everything, or almost everything, about the meaning of the debt. To philosophize is to see what one "did not previously see" [*prius non videbam*], to write or teach is to open what one has seen to others [*aliis libenter aperio*], and to be read or understood is to recognize oneself in the judgment of others [*alieno discam iudicio*]. From three points of view Anselm seems to bear the load of a debt: from the point of view of the Pope to the harshness of unbelievers and the joy of believers; from Boso as the clearest interlocutor whom he has enlightened; and from all readers as witnesses and guarantors of his philosophical vision. It is a debt toward the other where his feeling of indebtedness or his own nullity prevents him acquitting himself simply on his own.

In Debt to God

There remains then "God," who can bear the burden of the debt and indeed release us from it: "Come to me, all you that are weary and are carrying heavy burdens, and I will give you rest" (Mt. 11:28 NRSV). It is here we find, as I see it, all Anselm's originality, even beyond his existential situation and probably because of it. One is not easily relieved of the burden of a yoke unless one has it carried it oneself, indeed until one has proven it at full strength in one's own inwardness. The hypothesis of a "gift without debt," like a "God without being," is certainly audacious and no less seductive. But Anselm poses questions to himself, through the voice of Boso, who relays the objections of unbelievers:

> But since, indeed, He could have saved many by another means [*aliter*], [by pure spiritual love], why is it that in order to show His love He endured and performed these things which you are claiming [redemption, justice, power, will to punish etc.]? *Does He not show the good angels how much He loves them even though He does not endure such things for them?*[22]

The objections are significant and avoid a simple swerve away from the gift that would cancel the unbearable burden of debt—whether we refer to the debt of sin or simply to finitude. If the gift could be given wherever or whenever, based on the phenomenon as such, in a pure abstraction of "donor and receiver" [Derrida], or as the "gift itself" [Marion], independently of all conditions of transmission and reception, then what would happen to the *burden of the debt* and to our humanity per se? Through making too much of the gift, have we not come to misunderstand the debt? Or, to put it another way, and this time along the same lines as Anselm, if the salvation brought to the good angels out of "pure spiritual love" is enough for God to love them, why is it necessary for us to return always to the powerlessness of *our* "Being-there," as though we had to be shown that there is no hereafter for us except in and through this world?[23]

Anselm's reply does not precisely *release* us from the debt, suggesting a gift so diffused that we might neglect the price of discharging it. On the contrary, it traverses the depth of our *humanity* so as to find there the mercy (*misericordia*) of He who came to shoulder it. "He who sins ought not to be let-off unpunished," Anselm insists, in a formula that will serve as guiding principle and line of defense for the debt, as opposed to a hypertrophy of the gift, "unless mercy spares the sinner and frees him and restores him."[24] The hypothesis of a "gift without debt," or "pure love," or the complete "abstraction of the structure of givenness" in a triple *epokhé*[25] of donor, recipient, and the gift itself is not of something *gained directly from above* in Anselm's philosophy (recalling, as I see it, a certain valid questioning in contemporary phenomenology). The hypothesis has to deal with the depth and the burden of that which is first of all *given to us from below*: (a) the *debt without a gift* or the case of the devil; (b) the *gift of the debt* or honor; (c) the *debt for the gift* or satisfaction; (d) the *gift without debt* or mercy. Being in debt, according to Anselm, will gain an ontological value, in that the creature must make return to God independently of guilt. [Heidegger says, "*Being-guilty does not first result from an indebtedness (Verschuldung), but … on the contrary indebtedness becomes possible only 'on the basis' of a primordial Being-guilty.*"][26] But the moral coefficient should not be obscured here in suggesting that the ontological debt is just constitutive of our humanity. [Ricoeur says, "In this way, the rightful place of the notion of *debt* would be acknowledged, a notion that was too hastily ontologized by Heidegger at the expense of the ethical dimension of indebtedness."][27]

§10. Writing-Off Debt

Weighing up debt as "originary debt" (Heidegger), or in theology (Anselm), comes down then to calculating an eventual writing-off of debt. Having "taken on a debt" as one "takes the lead," as we have already seen [§9], one asks oneself *by whom* or *how* one will abstract oneself—not to be cleared of it (wiping the slate clean), but rather becoming recognized as not being a debtor in relation to a gift that one could never give back (mercy).

Things are not, however, simple. First of all, because in the "case" or in the "fall" of the devil, for example (*De casu diaboli*), the descent is so low that nothing guarantees he could rise again or somehow get out of it. And next, because in the collapse, or the vertigo, of being unable to render it up, forgiveness most often does not depend solely on the self but also depends on the Other accepting, at the very least, a moratorium in which one continues to exist or as a minimum does not perish. Finally, it is not simple because "satisfaction," that is to say the pure and simple "repaying of the debt," would not satisfy the contracting parties—neither the recipient nor the donor. The "writing-off" of the debt is not to be calculated simply in terms of the fulfilment of contract: it creates certainly a form of freedom or rather of liberation, but it is one in which the beneficiaries have unlearned what it is to be truly connected. Only a "heart full of wretchedness" or a "par-don," as we shall see later, will say what it is to be no longer indebted and will not deny being obliged and even "grateful" in an exchange that has been carried out. Far from becoming lost in a pure donation or an abstraction of the gift, the "gift without debt" of mercy is a kind of response to the "debt without gift" in the fall of the devil—not in that the first (mercy) comes to deny or forget the second (the fall of the devil), but on the contrary in that it comes to recognize the contract and prepares itself for the struggle that will necessarily accompany it.

The Debt without a Gift: The Fall of the Devil

The devil provides a "case," as we know by hearsay and as indeed we feel through experience. But what makes his "case" is also what makes his "fall"—*De casu diaboli*. The fall of the devil is not through the sin of mankind: far from it. To distinguish precisely the one (the devil) from the other (humankind), Anselm echoed and slightly modified the famous question of the "rights of devils" in the first book of *Cur Deus homo* ["The Devil had no just claim against man" 1:7]. Along with the "rights of the devil"—or rather the absence of such rights according to Anselm—goes the hypothesis of a debt that is contracted without a gift: that of "property rights" (Origen), or of a "power" of the devil (Augustine), which was to be avenged, even though the debt was not a *given*. With the collapse of the rights of the devil, Anselm definitively removes the debt from a mercantile system of exchange (but not of recognition), according to which there is at once "the obligation to give, the obligation to receive and reciprocate."[28] The rejection of Origen's ransom theory of atonement, or Augustine's theory of atonement as just punishment satisfying God's justice, leads Anselm toward seeing debt without a gift in the sense precisely that it comes back to the devil, and solely to the devil, who gives the illusion of a donation that he does not actually possess.

(a) Origen first of all or the hypothesis of the debt as *ransom for the gift*. This stems from a well-known passage by St. Paul that has been interpreted by theologians, including Anselm, in various different ways. St. Paul writes, "He has wiped out [*delens*] the record of our debt to the law [*chirographum decreti*], which stood against us, setting it aside [*et ipsum tulit de medio*] by nailing it to the cross [*affigens illud cruci*]" (Col. 2:14 RNJB).[29] For Origen the matter is straightforward.[30] The record of our debt, or the "leaf with the declaration of our sins" (*schedula*: leaf in Low Latin), contains not simply those that we ourselves have inherited but also those that the devil, in a contract with us would have put his stamp upon. Origen, in his *Homilies on Exodus*, asks himself, "But what sort of price did the devil, too, pay that he might purchase us? ... Murder is the money of the devil ... Adultery is the money of the devil ... Theft, false testimony, greediness, violence, all these are the devil's property and treasure ... With this money, therefore he buys those whom he buys."[31] What we have contracted with our debt, according to Origen, is sin as "the money of the devil" [*diaboli pecuniam*]. Thus, we are "debtors of the devil," while the Son of Man never himself contracted a debt: "And truly he did not *owe*, but each of us is a *debtor for sins*, and a debtor is one who has a bond" [*cheirographa*].[32] In short it seems that the devil has paid a duty on us because of our sins, and we have become the creditors. This debt is the ransom of the gift such that the Son, through the cross, redeems us, almost in the financial sense of the term: "But perhaps Christ, who gave his own blood as the price for us, is rightly said to have bought us back."[33] Did Anselm have direct access to Origen's sermons? It is hardly likely. The problem of how the debt can be redeemed was nonetheless one that passed down through tradition. We find Ambrose of Milan saying: "[Christ] redeemed with His own blood those that had been sold by their sins."[34]

(b) In the lineage of a "good practice" where debt remains in the logic of an exchange of gifts, even poisoned gifts, Augustine cannot be left out. His emphasis is, however, different. Not content with the juridical model of debt (debt as the ransom or the price of the gift), he substitutes a political model (debt as just retribution or punishment). What counts, according to St. Augustine, is less the price that has to be paid (the amount of the bills) than the obligation to pay it (the contractual nature of what is due). Certainly the devil has a *right*. But this right is also exercised, according to Augustine, through the exercise of a *power*—in which the model is rather political than judicial. "By the justice of God in some sense, the human race was delivered into the power of the devil [*in potestatem diaboli*] the sin of first man passing over originally into all of both sexes in their birth, and the debt of our first parents [*et parentum primorum debito*] binding their whole posterity."[35] The "record of our debt" (Col. 2:14 RNJB) is paid for in an *empire of sin* that the devil holds over humankind. And certainly, in terms of the Augustinian political model, there is not injustice here, insofar as the adversary, who has won the fight, or provoked the fall, is able to exercise his sovereignty. The problem is not when he plays on his power and burdens us with debts, but when he extends his power to that which does not belong, and never has belonged, to him: the Son of God who is himself exempt from all debt. St. Augustine asks himself how it is that the devil can be conquered: "Because, when he found in Him nothing worthy of death, yet he slew Him" [*cum in eo nihil morte dignum inveniret*].[36] It is in the devil's nature that he sins—or rather it is what he has become by choice against nature (the fallen angel), but what goes beyond the limits of his empire is that he abuses his power and makes him who has never contracted the debt (sin) pay this debt (through his death on the cross). The devil does not simply receive payment or ransom for the debt [Origen: payment of ransom]: it is a just punishment for his sins [Augustine: overstepping his powers]: "But the devil was to be overcome, not by the power [*potentia*] of God, but by his righteousness" [*justitia*].[37] According to St. Augustine, in his treatise *On the Free Choice of the Will*, humans die a temporary death "to repay what they owed" [*debitum exsolvant*], but they feed on the hope of eternal life that will be lived in "Him who repaid on their behalf what he did not owe" [*qui pro eis quod debeat exsolvit*].[38] In short, the Son pays the debt of sin that he has never signed up to, not simply to discharge the ransom of humankind but to strike down the abuse of power by the devil in relation to God (inflicting death on the Son as a punishment for sin to Him who was liable to sin but not a sinner).

(c) Anselm of Canterbury, emblematic figure for those who attribute all the evils of the debt to the "theology of satisfaction," is then paradoxically the writer through whom the debt *presses with all its weight* and at the same time loses its rights, at least as far as the case of the devil is concerned. Origen and Augustine both "sin" in a sense through excess—either of jurisdiction or deliberation—the first (Origen) because he believes the devil himself established a *contract* with humankind, albeit against God. The second (Augustine) because he thinks the adversary still deserves punishment as he had taken steps against God, who is the only judge. Anselm thinks entirely differently—the debt is in neither *ransom for the gift* (Origen) nor *just punishment* (Augustine); it is quite simply *without a gift*, precisely in the case of the devil. We regularly make the claim, according to *Cur Deus Homo*, that "in order to free man, God has required to deal with the Devil in terms of justice [Augustine] before dealing with him in terms of power [Origen]—so that … the Devil … justly lost the power which he had over sinners." Anselm goes on to say, "I do not see what cogency this claim has."[39] The strength of the devil is in a way without force in Anselm's eyes because to attribute force [*vix*] to him is to make too much of it and to retard in some way his fall. "Evil truly is nothing" [*vere nihil est*], Anselm emphasizes with very striking precision in *De casu diaboli*, and for that reason "is not something" [*et idcirco non est aliquid*]. But because it is necessary to speak of evil and nothing, we "speak about them *as if* they were something," and Anselm, with real originality, suggests evil is "only as-if-something" [*quasi aliquid*].[40] With regard to this "as-if-something" which is not "nothing," at least for us who speak of it, the devil "was not entitled to punish man" [*meritum nullum erat ut puniret*][41] quite simply because punishment was not something that belonged to him and had never belonged to him. Punishment was only possible, within the scope of the contraction of the debt [Origen], or in the exercise of power [Augustine], by one who precisely recognized himself as a debtor. And that is exactly what the devil does not recognize. His devilishness could very well consist on the other hand in making us believe that he possesses these rights, or these powers, that are solely the responsibility of God. Anselm says, "Neither the Devil nor man does belong to anyone except to God [*non sit nisi dei*], and … neither of them exists outside God's power" [*et neuter extra potestatem dei consistat*].[42] In short, there is no true debt. For the devil that is because there is no gift, or at least no recognition of the gift. If the authentic gift is "the gift of a gift," as many contemporary phenomenologists have insisted, true debt is perhaps also above all *the debt of a debt*. Certainly the gift appears as a gift even when the giving or donation is unknown. But debt, on the contrary, is evident as debt when the indebtedness is fully known—albeit by the sinner. *Consciousness of debt* is the opposite of a *learned ignorance of the gift* and defies the burden of the first (the debt), emptying the second (the gift) of the true liberation that it performs.[43]

Admittedly we have *first of all* the experience of debt because we are at once "sinners" and "created (but not fallen) with certain limits." But in order for there to be debt, there must be a gift, and thus we come back to the donation— the hypothesis underlined by Anselm that "evil is just a privation of good," even though it seems to be something [*videatur esse aliquid*].[44] And when this something that is nothing or "not-being" "seems to be something," in making us contract debts or believe it is exercising its power, we must then, *on our part*, continue to hold it to be "nothing" [*nihil*] or "not anything" [*non aliquid*]. That is the sole method of focusing on a "debt without a gift" and thus overthrowing the rights of the devil. St. Paul says, "[Christ] has wiped out the record of our debt to the Law" (Col. 2:14 RNJB). Anselm concludes tersely, "And suppose someone thinks that the apostle's reference ... signifies ... the Devil, as if by an agreement in writing, justly required man to continue sinning ... I do not think the matter is at all to be understood in that way [*nequaquam ita intelligendum puto*] ... [That] decree was not the Devil's decree but God's" [*sed dei*].[45]

The Gift of the Debt: Honor

Debt, definitively extracted from devilry or the simulation of a gift (as if the gift of God could be the counter-gift to a gift of the devil) is then only contracted in the orbit of the gift, that is to say in God himself. The *debt without a gift* in the case of the devil leads to a *gift of the debt* for humankind, in that it depends first of all on the donor from whom the donation is received. Anselm, justifying (it is said) the fall, releases paradoxically the *ontological meaning* of the debt that has been frequently misunderstood even among Anselm scholars, in a way that does, however, echo what Heidegger scholars have been looking for—to the point where one might wonder who is the reader of whom (except that Heidegger never cited Anselm) Heidegger wrote, "The idea of guilt [i.e. debt] must not only be raised above the domain of that concern in which we reckon things up. But it must also be detached from relationship to any law or 'ought' such that by failing to comply with it one loads himself with guilt [debt]."[46]

The debate here is difficult and can be disturbing to the participants, as Anselm and Boso were well aware. Boso says in *Cur Deus Homo*, "It is up to you to explain [*tuum est ostendere*] and me to pay attention [*et meum intendere*]."[47] Anselm, replying, says that sin is not debt itself, it is the act of not repaying what is owed to God: "to sin is nothing other than not to render to God what is due" [*non est itaque aliud peccare quam non reddere deo debitum*].[48] If sin is not the debt itself but the act of not rendering to God what is due, then humans are in a way already-in-debt, even before sinning. Without sin there would be positively nothing to render up to God, sin consisting negatively in not rendering up to God. To put it another way, one can only render up what one has (a debt) and what one is (an indebted being)—apart from, as we shall see, the case of the Son of God, where what he gives back to the Father represents neither what he has (sin) nor what he is (a sinning being).[49] Reason imposes this acknowledgement: human beings have already contracted a debt independently of sin, such that precisely our debt is a *gift of the debt* (as creatures turned toward God) before it turns into a *debt for the gift* (through the fall that is to be satisfied). But it must nevertheless slip into becoming a *debt without a gift* (the case of the devil).

What then does the "being-in-debt of humankind," pre-sinful or in a pre-lapsarian state, actually mean? Above all it is a *mode of being of our being*, or an "attribute of Being," to take up the term used by Heidegger in *Being and Time*,[50] and it is not a *quantity of "what is due*," which would be as unbearable in its load as it would be unassailable in any conflict. Anselm insists that, whatever may be the case with the fall or satisfaction, "the will of every rational creature ought to be subordinate to the will of God [*subiecta debet esse voluntati dei*]," and "this is the debt which angels and man owe to God [*hoc est debitum*]."[51] The first "due" or the first debt [*debitum*] is not then of sin or within its purview. The phenomenological bracketing off of the debt is such here that the extent to which humankind is indebted does not really matter—even as far as the most "capital" sins are concerned. What counts is *the way* in which this debt is felt, with regard to the possibility of its being settled, if that is by another, or if it is always ingrained in oneself, where *Sorge* or "care" has the final word. The definition of justice in Anselm's *De veritate* as "uprightness-of-will kept for its own sake [*rectitudo voluntatis propter se servata*],"[52] and not as some kind of superfluous balancing between punishment and merit is what shows us this. What is just is not simply someone paying or discharging a debt, it is the One who makes the *manner of being of the debt* positive or negative for his creatures as gift:

> No one who pays this debt [of being, I would like to add] [*quod solvendo*] sins [*nullus peccat*], and everyone who does not pay it does sin. This is the justice [*justitia*] ... which makes men just, or upright, in heart (i.e. in will) [*id est voluntate*]. This is the sole and complete honor [*solus et totus honor*] which we owe to God [*quem debemus Deo*] and which God demands from us [*et a nobis exigit deus*].[53]

The *honor of the debt* or its *justice* in the context of the "upright in heart" helps us then to understand the "due of the due," which sounds strange when we speak it aloud—as almost like a "gift of the debt." Not in the sense that we would be in debt to sin, which only leaves us overextended in debt, but in the sense that *to be created* is already to recognize that we depend upon another being to whom we are "obliged," in the sense that Levinas describes, that is, open to the dimension of the Infinite that "puts a stop to the irresistible imperialism of the Same and the I."[54] Anselm writes: "You ought to consider that you are required to give [by virtue of a debt] [*ex debito*]—even as you recognize that what you give, you have not from yourself [*quod das non a te habes*] but from Him whose servant both you and the one to whom you give are."[55] What we have already seen as the philological "wonder of the debt" appears strikingly here. To be in debt is not to yield under the hypertrophy of the gift (as in the phenomenology of the extraordinary), nor is it to bow under the burden of sin (as in many wrong-headed interpretations of Anselm): it is to recognize our "dependence upon an other" [*ab illo*] through which we acknowledge our being in its finitude and our non-sinful vulnerability. Claude Bruaire, in his attempt at an ontodology as a *being-in-debt even to oneself*, says,

> It is in exactly the same manner of being that the spirit is a gift to itself and in debt in all its being. To pay the debt is *to give the other*, honor the other's alterity, give what one is not … a blind task that indicates in an indelible fashion, the finitude given to the being exactly *because* it is a gift.[56]

The Debt for the Gift: Satisfaction

But humankind does not unfortunately remain in debt for his created being—as we know. Even in the case where the debt is not settled by submission to the will of God, when neither angel nor man "sins" [*nullus peccat*], it is not discharged. Sin precisely comes back. *Et quod omnis qui non solvit peccat*—"And anyone who does not pay it does sin."[57] Sinning is not then paying the debt, as a certain caricature of the theology of satisfaction maintains; it is on the contrary *not paying* it—the debt here understood as our created being and our radical dependence on the Creator. There is then no debt without a gift (the case of the devil). It is on the contrary, and solely, in the context of the *gift of the debt* (humans as created beings) that the *debt of the gift* arises (sin to be satisfied by the Son). And it is because the honor owed has not been rendered up (the gift of the debt) that it comes down to the Son to satisfy the unforeseen offence (the debt of the gift).

In the so-called theology of satisfaction, certainly there is no primacy of the gift over the debt; it is only seen *as far as we are concerned* "afterwards." The Father's choice that the payment of the debt (sin) is performed through his Son, by that which is its consequence (death), is not made *a priori* but *a posteriori*. In other words, the gift is not given by God in redemption of the debt—as if it were only offered to get back the gift—it is the recognition *a posteriori* of the debt that imposes such a modality on the gift. Anselm underlines, for those who are prepared to listen:

> Suppose that I can cross a certain river either by horse or by boat. And suppose that I decided to cross only by boat. If I do cross [*si transeo*] the river after a boat has become available [*cum iam praesto est navis*], then it is right to say of me: "A ship was ready, there [*propterea*] he crossed over" … [We] speak in this manner not only when we determine to do something else *by means of* [*per*] a thing which we will to occur beforehand but also when we determine to do something else only *subsequent* to the preceding thing [*post illud*] and not by means of it.[58]

Obviously, then, it is only *after*, or after the fact, that the gift (the cross) appears to be befitting for the debt. Anselm, as we find in all good theology, does not maintain that there is a necessity of debt (sin) in order to accept the gift (of the cross). For Anselm, simply, factually and necessarily, the Father "*willed* the Son's death because He did *not will* for the world to be saved otherwise [*non aliter voluit mundum salvari*]," in the same way that we say of someone "he *wills* to extinguish the lamp [*lucernam extinguere*]" because he "*does not will* to close a window through which a draft enters and extinguishes a lamp."[59] As the wind has burst into the house of God through sin, God intervenes to put out the lamp or at least to close the window because of which the light was extinguished. In short, there is in God neither love for the debt (sin) nor enjoyment in the satisfaction of the debt (suffering). Bourdaloue's interpretation cited earlier in this chapter and the interpretations that are common among scholars of Anselm (see Louis Bouyer, note 7) go against the letter of the text. Anselm underlines, as it were to counteract in advance all these interpretations, that "the Father is rightly said to have willed that the Son undergo death so graciously and beneficially—even though the Father did not delight in the Son's torment" [*quamvis poenam eius non amaret*].[60]

Why then is there "satisfaction for sin"[61] if the Father himself "did not delight" in the suffering of the Son? It is here that the "notion of *debt*," according to the work by Paul Ricoeur already cited, does not become, as it does with Heidegger, "too hastily ontologized ... at the expense of the ethical dimension of indebtedness."[62] Anselm's insistence on the burden of the debt, so often decried by his detractors, has at least the merit of sticking within the limits of our "finitude"—a finitude that is both consubstantial with humankind (the dependence of the creature on the Creator) and sinful (enclosure within the self in sin). What *Cur Deus Homo* has principally in its sights is that the debt *weighs* and that it is difficult, indeed impossible, to liberate oneself from the debt: such is the principal aim of *Cur Deus Homo*, according to which "in the absence of satisfaction [*sine* satisfaction] it is not fitting for God to elevate sinful man."[63] As opposed to the Heideggerian claim of a "summons to Being-guilty," as a "calling-forth to the potentiality-for-Being which in each case I as Dasein am already" (Authentic Dasein),[64] Anselm, according to Charles Bruaire, shows that it is *inauthenticity* that produces the authenticity of our Being-there and of Being indebted: "[Our] ordeal is not the anxious existential recognition of being thrown into the world, of being placed there, deposited like an abandoned child."[65] Boso again shows his alarm here, since a descent into the heart of our fragility threatens to wipe us out. He says to Anselm: "You have already placed before us so many things required for us to do that whatever you add to them cannot more greatly frighten me" [*non me magis terrere possit*]. Anselm tells him to "[l]isten anyhow [*audi tamen*]," and Boso replies, "I am listening [*audio*]."[66]

The disciple listens to the voice of his master since he is resigned to complying with the enumeration of reasons why "it is no less difficult [*non minus difficile*] for man to be reconciled with God."[67] They are:

(a) An irreparable injury not done to something but to someone (God Himself). [To do something that is "contrary to the will of God" is "extremely grave" and "comparable" to no other injury.[68]]
(b) An offence against a third party that a person could not satisfy (the devil). ["Man ... freely permitted himself ... to be conquered according to the Devil's will."[69]]
(c) An incapacity to render up to God what humankind had lost in sinning (a part of our nature). ["Sinful man cannot at all accomplish this justification, because a sinner cannot justify a sinner."[70]]

(d) Injustice with regard to oneself that is unpardonable, in that humankind "cast [themselves] into a pit … from which [they] would not at all be able to get out." ["(Humankind) voluntarily became obligated to that debt which (they are) unable to pay."]⁷¹

The *burden of the debt* is such that we keep coming back to Boso's contributions to the dialogue in relation to the paradoxical necessity of a liberation from it that is, however, impossible to realize: "I see both that reason requires this [*rationem video sic exigere*] and that it is altogether impossible [*et omnino esse impossibile*]."⁷²

The impossibility of man "making satisfaction by himself" [*pro te ipso redimendo*] because of the burden, or measure, of sin, does not impede satisfaction [*satisfactio*] but on the contrary reinforces it: "Everyone who sins is obliged to repay to God the honor which he has stolen [*honorem deo quem rapuit solvere*]. This constitutes the satisfaction [*haec est satisfactio*] which every sinner is obliged to make to God."⁷³ But the inability to repay, in a negative that this time becomes positive, summons up anew the figure of the Other [the Son] in order to satisfy the satisfaction—no longer solely depending on the created being (the *gift of the debt* in honor) but in the salvation of sinful humankind (the *debt of the gift* in satisfaction): "The Son says that the Father wills his death, which He, the Son, prefers to undergo rather than to see the human race not be saved."⁷⁴ The gift (of the Son) is then at least in proportion to the debt (of sin), since according to Anselm "satisfaction ought to be proportional to the measure [*secundum mensuram*] of the sin."⁷⁵ But there is more here because, since the *Proslogion*, as we have already seen, Anselm has held that the greater [*maior*] in the lesser [*minor*] is what gives us the very name of God: "Something than which nothing greater can be thought" [*aliquid quo nihil cogitari possit*]: "You do not make satisfaction unless you pay something greater [*aliquid maius*] … [If] nothing is greater [*nihil maius*] or better [*aut melius*] than God, then Supreme Justice (which is identical with God Himself) keeps nothing more justly than God's honor in regard to the governance of things."⁷⁶

The specific character of the gift is thus that it is disproportionate to the debt and that is precisely what makes for satisfaction in the etymological sense of the term. Bernard Seboüé, commenting on Anselm, clarifies that the term "satisfaction" comes from Roman law: "The first thing to state is that it does not *express the total discharge of debt*, or the *strict compensation* of a wrong perpetrated. *Satis-facere* translates as *doing enough*."⁷⁷

Humankind then *does enough* in trying to replace the ontological debt (honor) within an ethical debt that would fall short of being delivered if it were not for the Son (satisfaction)—because God Himself does *everything* and *more than everything* (mercy) in order to take the debt in charge and change its meaning.

The Gift without Debt: Mercy

Let us return then to our point of departure, as it were to the guiding principle and bulwark of the debt with regard to the hypocrisy of the gift: "Now, he who sins ought not be let-off unpunished—unless mercy spares the sinner and frees him and restores him [to God]."⁷⁸ Could there then be a *gift without debt* (mercy), the reverse of the *debt without a gift* (the case of the devil), that was capable of liberating us? Just to suggest this seems to indicate at once that we have not completely thought it through. Because, according to Anselm, the excess of the gift does not efface the debt, and in this context, as we have already seen, *Cur Deus Homo* is a useful corrective to the "great swerve of the gift" described in contemporary philosophy. It is on the contrary, in that he travels through it—whether the ontological debt of the created being (honor) or the ethical debt of sinful humankind (satisfaction)—that the Son shoulders the debt through and through. Anselm replies to the question as to "whether it is fitting for God to forgive sin out of mercy alone" [*sola misericordia*]: "It is not fitting that God should forgive sin that goes unpunished."[79] Further, if we take on board what the Lord's Prayer says, "forgive us our debts, as we have forgiven our debtors" (Mt. 6:9 RNJB) [*et dimitte nobis debita nostra, sicut et nos dimittus debitoribus nostris*], then it is in that negative ["it is not fitting"] that we experience mercy: God alone has the capacity to *judge* the measure of sin and *by choice* to forgive our debts, a forgiveness that we ourselves only offer through obligation. Anselm says, "There is no inconsistency here, because God gives us this command so that we should not arrogate to ourselves His prerogative [to judge, redeem, punish]."[80] Mercy does not supplant justice, nor does the surplus in the gift supplant the payment of the debt. It passes through the first (the debt) to show us the second (the gift).

And so that *the gift* appears as gift, not forgetting the *gift of the debt* (honor) or the *debt of the gift* (satisfaction), and without falling into the trap of the *debt without a gift* (the case of the devil), it must seem in some way that it is a *gift without a debt* or a *pardon*, where the gift navigates and shoulders through and through the debt by means of its par-don ("par"—through: "don"—gift):

> Now regarding forgiveness [pardon] I will say briefly that vengeance does not at all belong to you [*nec tuus es*] (as I stated earlier), since you are not on your own. And he who has wronged you is neither yours nor his own [*nec ille tuus aut suus qui tibi fecit iniuriam*], rather you are both servants of one Lord and have both been created by him out of nothing.[81]

According to Paul Ricoeur, "the experience of fault adheres so strongly to imputability that it becomes its organ and its means of revelation." In his chapter on "Difficult Forgiveness" Ricoeur says, "There is forgiveness ... But the proclamation summed up in the simple phrase ... resonates like an opposing challenge."[82]

To par-don, and thus to show mercy, is not simply a giving back [*redonner*], nor even giving an additional gift in order to efface, or indeed to wipe out, the debt. It is on the contrary to give in such a way that one could never give back [*re-donner*]. And thus we find the necessity not of a reduction of the gift [see Jean-Luc Marion] but of a third party who alone can liberate us from the debt. The Son, as we have seen, according to Anselm has nothing to give back: "Nor did he ever owe anything which could be forgiven him." All that belonged to the Father belonged to him: "All mine are yours, and yours are mine; and I have been glorified in them" (Jn 17:10 NRSV). How then can "a reward be bestowed on one who needs nothing [*nullius rei egenti*], and to whom no gift or release can be made?"[83] Only one response is possible because it breaks open the circle of the debt and the gift: "It is necessary for the Father to reward the Son ... on the other hand it appears impossible ... The reward then must be bestowed upon someone else [*ut alicui alii reddatur*], for it cannot be upon him."[84] Once again the figure of the Other emerges here not in the obligatory asymmetry of an ontological debt (honor), nor in unlooked for liberation from an ethical debt (satisfaction), but as the ultimate recipient of a gift without debt (mercy)—himself of humankind. Anselm writes, "[If] the Son wished to give some one else what was due to him, could the Father rightly prevent it? ... Upon whom [*quibus*] would he more properly bestow the reward accruing from his death, than upon those for whose salvation, as right reason teaches, he became man [*hominem se fecit*]?"[85]

It is for humankind that the Son renders or satisfies the debt because he himself has nothing to repay. Or rather, the Son "satisfies" the Father not for what he has done (sin), nor for what he is (a sinner), so that the Father "through mercy" restores everything to mankind (salvation).

The "Third party of this love" as we shall see later (chap. 6), with the help of Richard of Saint-Victor, is probably what is most importantly lacking in the abstractions of certain phenomenological accounts of donation [e.g., Derrida and Marion]. They confirm their abstractions through a neglect of the *positive* meaning of the debt. What is shown by the relation of filiation, which is generated mutually between Father and Son, and includes humankind with respect to God, is then a *new possibility* of donation—without abstraction of the gift, that is to say, without suggesting at once "the indifference of a father with respect to his gift" or "the absence of debt and understanding on the part of his son." Emmanuel Gabellieri, in the course of a severe diatribe against apologists for the abstraction of the gift, maintains that,

> The son not being able to render up to his father the life that he has received, can on the contrary respond to the gift of life *in giving life in his turn*. He thus gives back, but *indirectly* the gift he has received ... The son does not give back to the father what he has received from him, but *he gives life* to other sons, setting up a chain of recipients where the gift is always open to a *third party* with respect to the point of origin of the donation.[86]

If there is a mercy in God (*misericordia*), according to Anselm, it is not a kind of watered-down mercy, such that it would be enough for humankind in our powerlessness to plead to God in his all-powerfulness and thus obtain "satisfaction." Anselm says, "This kind of divine mercy is utterly contrary to God's justice. It is impossible for him to be merciful in this way [*ita hoc modo illum esse misericordiam impossibile est*]."[87] Like Anselm, we have to look for, and plead for, a different divine mercy. It is one that cannot be reduced to the poverty of debt (sin), nor heightened into the pure abstraction of the gift (spiritual love), but is found in a *gift without debt* that demonstrates the taking on board of debt through the gift and the par-don of humankind—a humankind that also "gives" and "pardons." This "mercy" [*miséri-corde*], like a heartfelt con-cord, is not just found in God himself, who is not only "greater" [*maior*], more "just" [*justior*], or "better" [*melior*] but, especially, "more merciful" [*misericordium*]. It is just at the heart of God's secret Trinitarian conversation, addressed to and above all made for humankind:

What compassion can [be more merciful (*misericordius*) than] ... these words of the Father, addressed to the sinner doomed to eternal torments and having no way of escape: "Take my only begotten Son and make him an offering for yourself [*accipe unigenitum meum et da pro te*]"; or these words of the Son: "Take me, and ransom your souls [*tolle me et redime te*]." For these are the voices they utter, when inviting and leading us [to Christian faith]. Or can anything be more just [*iustius*] than for him to remit all debt [*dimittat omne debitum*] since he has earned a reward greater than all debt, if given with the love which he deserves.[88]

The "limit of the gift" paradoxically establishes here the "gift of a limit." Humankind looks for an "other mercy" [*aliam misericoridam*] and God responds. It is not enough to receive or to wait to receive, or indeed to be one of the elect in the Lutheranism of the *sola gratia* [by grace alone] that is not so far from phenomenology with its pure abstraction of the gift.[89] It is necessary to participate, or at least to give oneself, not in order to win through by good works alone (a Pelagianism), but at least in committing oneself in the movement of the gift (*cooperation of good works and grace*). Anselm, in receiving "God who comes to mind" (chap. 1), does not lean solely on the side of the pure gift of the "theophanic argument (chap. 2), but also weighs up the finitude of humankind in the case of the 'debt of the gift' (chap. 3). The well-known formula of Thomas Aquinas in *Contra Gentiles* ("*Deus est causa operandi omnibus operantibus*—God is the cause of operation for all things that operate"[90]), which identifies humankind as capable of "cooperating" with the actions of God, has its first source in the works of St. Anselm. This cooperation does not "limit" the power of the divine but recognizes for God himself, in his kenosis, his unique power of stooping as far as humankind—establishing also for humankind a capacity to give themselves, at least in order to gain par-don. The *Cur Deus homo* (the burden of the debt) and the *De casu diaboli* (the debt of the gift) take over here from *Proslogion* (the theophanic argument). The unity of these works shows us the equilibrium of Anselm's thought—a flow of ideas that moves without dragging too far into the abstraction of the gift (gift without return) or to a humankind always indebted (satisfaction).

An "experience in thought" is thus characteristic in an exemplary fashion of the monastic Being-there. The "liturgical" is fundamental to it, and consequently the theophanic that speaks in the heart of the life of the abbey is *the same* as what emerges in thought in the scriptorium. God can thus *appear* and give himself also to the understanding—theologians and philosophers know this. It is something that can make the experience of "thinking through praying" every day become "praying through thinking," and that establishes thought as an "act of prayer," elevating prayer to a "modality of thought." A "summa of revealed theology" thus becomes possible, starting from Anselm, abbot of Bec. Saint Bonaventure will later conceptualize it in his *Breviloquium*.[91] Because this has later been forgotten, experience has been placed on the side of *praxis* and thought on the side of *theoria*. But the *contemplatio* [or fourth stage of the Benedictine *Lectio Divina*], in the abbey of Bec of the eleventh century, maintained and already put together theory and practice, the "thought about experience," and the "experience of thought." In the abbey of Saint-Victor, thinkers like Hugh and Richard of Saint-Victor would also remember this in the twelfth century, turning the "book of experience" [*liber experientiae*] from the interior to the exterior, from the "book of consciousness" [*liber conscientiae*] to the "book of the world" [*liber mundi*]. Hermeneutics and phenomenology follow on from the theophanic, in that for them it is no longer solely a question of letting God "show himself" (in our thought), but rather of "interpreting" (the world), indeed also "living it" (through one's body). The "book of experience" makes *ex-per-ire* a challenge to the self (an *Erlebnis* experience) but also, as we have seen [§2], a "travelling through the world" [*Erfahrung*].

Part 2

Hermeneutics and Phenomenology, or the Experience of the World: Hugh and Richard of Saint-Victor

From "experience in thought" we move now then to "experience of the world" (Hugh of Saint-Victor) and to "experience of God" (Richard of Saint-Victor). We are still reading the same book—the book of experience [*liber experientiae*], but in moving from one century to another, from the eleventh to the twelfth century, monastic theology gains a new status, and not simply thinking [*cogitari*], or rather learns to speak and to live what "reading" [*legere*] wants to say, and not simply "thinking" [*cogitari*]. Books undoubtedly multiplied with the flourishing of the monasteries. There was an urbanization that led to the foundation of more monasteries and the installation of Victorine monks in Paris "*hors-les-murs*" (outside the city walls), in what is now *Jussieu—5th arrondissement—* site of the main campus of the Science Faculty of the Sorbonne. They were thus close to the Sorbonne or the *École cathédrale de Paris*. Typical of the area was the distribution of copies, the spread of reading, the designing of disciplines, and the formalization of a society that would gradually define reading as an "art"—the "art of reading" [*ars legendi*]. Not that everyone there could read, far from it, but in that everyone might have a "book in the hand." Even the lay brothers who could not read sang the Psalms with the aid of a book (a psalter), signifying in this way how the "symbols" always want to say something, even if we do not know how to decipher them. The illuminations of the psalter were not only the work of talented artists, most often anonymous, they served also as page-markers, for those who did not know how to read the books, even for those who would never learn to read. What was significant in monastic theology of the twelfth century was not just "knowing" how to read but recognition that everywhere one could *read* and *decipher* the presence of God. That presence might not be limited to books; it was to be found in the fields, with the animals, in the art or the "works" of the woodcutter, blacksmith, or baker. God "who is everywhere" would appear above all to *those* who know how *to see him* or *to find him* there. The *Didascalicon* (or *The Art of Reading*) of Hugh of Saint-Victor marks a key turning point relative to St. Anselm's *Proslogion* or *Cur Deus Homo*, in that it moves in another direction "toward the world." The *Liber Mundi*, or "book of the world," as I have tried to show elsewhere,[1] and as we further shall explore here, represents the first words of a hermeneutic that we can call "Catholic" of the "body and voice," since in the prelapsarian state there is no need for "the book of scripture" [*liber scripturae*] because Adam and Eve can be satisfied with seeing God in "nature" [*liber mundi*].[2]

Reading to Love

"Read, therefore, and love [*legite ergo atque diligite*]; and what you read on account of love, read it so that you might love [*et quod propter dilectionem legitis, ad hoc legite ut diligatis*]."[3] This is the formula that deserves to figure as the frontispiece for all philosophical writings and indeed, as we shall see later, for hermeneutics and contemporary phenomenology, as long as they put interpretations and descriptions that go along with a certain "experience" at the heart of their procedures [§2]. The "art of reading" deployed by Hugh of Saint-Victor along the lines of the new disciplines or philosophical styles defines itself at the same time as an "art of living," indeed an "art of loving." There are in fact no other criteria for reading than its fecundity, and there is little point in deciphering the marks on the page if they do not at the same time clarify the enigma of our lives.

"To read" [*legere*] is also to choose [*e-ligere*] according to a wordplay that remains famous in Latin. There is a kind of "re-ligion" [*re-ligere*] in reading that holds us, and keeps us, together.[4] But we find more and better among the School of Sait-Victor, or "Victorines," of the twelfth century, whether it is a question of Hugh of Saint-Victor, who was a philosopher, or his brother Richard, who was more of a theologian.[5] What was at the time simply a rhetorical formula becomes the starting point for the deployment of a mystical theology, indeed for the writings of the Victorines themselves. The act of reading [*legere*] in the *Didascalicon* [Chapter 4] and the manner of living [*vivere*] in Hugh of Saint-Victor's *Training of Novices* initiate a new way of "loving" [*diligere*], along with the "Third Party in divine love" or "condilection" in Richard of Saint-Victor's *On the Trinity*.

It is surprising that contemporary philosophy has not made more of this shift from the "art of reading" to the "art of living" and even to the "art of loving," particularly as far as questions in hermeneutics are concerned. Simply with regard to the *Didascalicon*, otherwise entitled by Hugh of Saint-Victor, "The Art of Reading" [*De studio legendi*], we may wonder why and how it has been so little studied, or even mentioned, in the corpus of the hermeneutic tradition in general—from Hans-Georg Gadamer's *Truth and Method* to Paul Ricoeur's *The Conflict of Interpretations*. The medieval tradition, and in particular the monastic theological renaissance of the twelfth century, contains still buried treasures that would certainly merit being brought to light. We find that the "book of experience" [*liber experientiae*] is characteristically not simply a matter of experience as such but is truly speaking concerned with building up the conceptuality of experience [§3]. And in the same way "to read" is certainly not new in the monastic period, but one discovers or, more precisely, one reads what it is that this "to read" attempts to say. The "reading of experience," as we shall see later, goes along with a certain "experience of reading."

Like the network of the World Wide Web today, the "page" of parchment of the past served as a principle for deciphering of the whole of creation. In going from the "page" to the "web" we now pass from the line to the network. And although the processes are different (perhaps the least one can say), the model nonetheless encompasses them both. It is the manner of learning, but also of living, that was to be profoundly shaken by both.[6] One no longer simply reads "books" with Hugh of Saint-Victor; one interprets the *mode of reading*, the totality of the "world," indeed one's own "life." The hermeneutic of the text is also a hermeneutic of contingency in the twelfth century before writing freezes into reproduction in print in the sixteenth century or multiplies into infinity in the web and the virtual of the twenty-first century. The "Art of Reading" [*De studio legendi*]—*Didascalicon*—comes down to "linking" the text to life, as hermeneutics are bound to phenomenology. A "grafting" [*greffe*] takes place here, as in the well-known hermeneutic wager of Paul Ricoeur, where the hermeneutic is not simply "attached" to phenomenology but *is* phenomenology.[7]

4

God an "Open Book"

The Roots of the Hermeneutic

The "book of experience" takes us back to the "experience of the book," and that is probably what constitutes the great originality of Hugh of Saint-Victor's *Didascalicon*. That is why one could not consider the "book of experience" [*liber experientiae*] of the eleventh century without both looking at the act of reading and experiencing. There is no book of *experience* without an experience of *reading*. If we take it too much for granted we miss what we are searching for—not just experience but the hermeneutic that underlies it. The act of "interpreting" is a kind of experimenting, and interpretation itself is a form of experiment. What one might have thought was an absolute novelty (Dilthey, Schleiermacher, Ricoeur, Gadamer, etc.) has in reality its neglected roots in the work of Hugh of Saint-Victor. We cannot really separate off contemporary investigations of the status of the "hermeneutic of the text" from what happened among the Victorines. After reflection on the meaning of scripture in the tradition of Origen, closely tied in to exegesis, what springs into existence, most probably following Hugh of Saint-Victor, is the first secular hermeneutic of the text and of the world in general.

As far as Hugh of Saint-Victor is concerned, and precisely in the renaissance of the Middle Ages, "reading" itself changes in meaning, or perhaps we should say that it had not yet been given the significance that we accord it today. Far from passing silently from a visual graphic, where the pages resonate in our heads, as in the empty space of a cash register, reading, for the medieval, comes down always to speaking or pronouncing in the form of a real physical and acoustic exercise on that which, depending on the parchment, was either for murmuring in a low voice [*silentia lectio*] or proclaiming as one read aloud [*clara lectio*]: "In the Middle Ages, as in antiquity, one read normally, not as we read today, principally with the eyes, but with the lips, in pronouncing what one saw in speaking it aloud; and with one's ears, in listening to the utterance that one pronounced; in understanding, as was said, the voices of the page."[1]

The "art of reading" is thus an "art of seeing" as well as "understanding" so that we work back from the *ars legendi*, or God as an "open book" in the *Didascalicon* (chap. 4), to an *ars vivendi* or a way of "living one's body" in Hugh of Saint-Victor's book *On the Training of Novices* [*De Institutione novitiorum*] (chap. 5). As I have tried to show elsewhere, one cannot take the "long route" (the hermeneutic of the text) without also bringing up the "short route" (hermeneutics of the contingent).² To read is to "live," and to "learn to read" is to "learn to live." That is what the Victorines teach us, and it is a tradition that Meister Eckhart would strongly continue in demanding of the "reading master" [*Lesemeister*] that he should be at the same time a "master of life" [*Lebemeister*]: "A *master of life* is worth a thousand *masters of reading*, but to read and live in God is something that nobody can achieve."³ Far from remaining a simple conflict between hermeneutics (master of reading) and phenomenology (master of life), it is "experience of the world" that resolves the confrontation [Part 2: Hermeneutics and Phenomenology, or *the Experience of the World*]. Hermeneutics *and* phenomenology—not hermeneutics *or* phenomenology. That suggests how much the route through interpretation is both an experience of the self and an experience of the world and how on that route there is neither experience of the self nor experience of the world aside from the act of interpreting. Hugh of Saint-Victor does not simply root hermeneutics in the "text" (in establishing the first great theory of interpretation or of "reading"); he also enriches it and expands it to the "world" and to "life" in general. The "book of the world" [*liber mundi*] does not supplant the "book of scripture" [*liber scripturae*]; on the contrary, it recalls the hermeneutic to the contingent and obliges us to attend to what it is to "read," sending us always to what it is to "see," as well as what it is to "live."

§11. From the Book to Reading

Learning to Read

To come back to the Victorines, and to underline paradoxically the thesis, rather than the reflective taking into consideration of the "book" by Hugh of Saint-Victor [The Art of Reading—*De studio legendi*], is to focus less on the "book" and more on the "manner in which it is read." That is to say, it is to accept that reading appears in the renaissance of the Middle Ages, not as a "form of text" but as a "feature of life"; not as a considering of the "parchment of writing" but as an appreciation of the "deciphering of creatures." Hugh of Saint-Victor writes impressively in a statement that was later to be fully taken up by St. Bonaventure:

> This sensible world [*mundus iste sensibilis*]⁴ is like a book written by the finger of God [*quasi quidam liber est scriptus digito Dei*]. All the creatures taken in themselves are like figures [*quasi figurae*] which have not been discovered according to the whims of humankind, but instituted according to divine judgment in order to manifest the invisible things of the wisdom of God [*ad manifestandum invisibilium Dei sapientiam*].⁵

Thus, God writes. Such is the thesis and as it were the rediscovery of Hugh of Saint-Victor. But if God writes, he does not write texts, and that is what makes for the originality of Christianity, as of Judaism, with respect to Islam, for example, and the writing of the Koran. Rather than "texts," God writes through an "action." By means of His "creative finger" He makes the "sensible world" a "book" where the creatures are like "signs" or "figures" which manifest his splendor. That is to say, we are the letters or the graphic designs of this parchment of the world—letters which it is also up to humankind to make themselves able to decipher. Medieval culture was certainly a "culture importantly based on reading," as Jos Decorte stresses in his book on medieval manuscripts, but this was not "in that the books were present everywhere in great numbers or read assiduously (books were rare and expensive and the majority of people were illiterate) ... It was just that people did not read the books: but they read *reality* itself."[6] One might learn to read certainly but not, as we have seen, solely manuscripts; one also read the world and one's own life.

It would be possible then to "read without knowing how to read." That is the whole paradox and the originality of the Victorine form of reading—something we really ought to learn again today. Reading, far from being reduced simply to following the trace of writing, is extended to the whole of reality, to "the world itself," insofar as everyone, including the lay monks who do not "know how to read," has to recognize that creation is also made up of "signs" [*signa*] and of "traces" [*vestigia*] that are to be interpreted. Finding the sense or meaning [*sensus*] beneath letters [*littera*] or the meaning [*significatio*] under the text [*textus*] was not solely the task of the monastic theologians or copyists. What became clear and was newly practiced in the scriptorium (the art of reading or interpretation), under the fatherly eye, as we have already seen with Anselm (chap. 2: the theophanic argument), of God the "greatest," was to be extended not simply to the abbey church (to God the greatest celebrated in the singing of the psalms) but to all the activities of the monks (in the fields, the kitchen, the hostelry, or the stable). The Fool is not someone who does not *know* how to read but someone who does not *want* to read. "Just as when an illiterate sees an open book," says Hugh, making reference here implicitly to the lay-brothers who would carry the Psalter around with them but were not able to read or decipher it, "and [when he] notices the shapes [*figuras ascipit*] but does not recognize the letters [*litteras non cognoscit*], so stupid ... people [*stultus*] ... see on the outside the beauty in these visible creatures [*foris speciem*] but they do not understand its meaning [*sed intus non intellegit rationem*]."[7]

We need to grasp this important point. In such a statement, and in the view of Hugh of Saint-Victor in particular, it is not a question of deploring the almost general illiteracy of an era when they had neither a program nor the means to teach everyone to read; on the contrary, it is precisely to honor the lay-brothers and raise them to the rank of "readers" even though they cannot read. Thus the Victorines made less of reading a form of text than of reading as a condition of life, a considering of the deciphering of creatures rather of the parchment of the Scriptures. Not knowing how to read, dunces or illiterates must also and paradoxically *learn to read*, whatever their status or faculties. To read here, as we have seen, is to "decipher," indeed to "interpret," whether one is in the library studying, in the scriptorium copying manuscripts, in the abbey church praying, or in the fields cultivating. As Ivan Illich rightly says in his *In the Vineyard of the Text*: "The individual monk might be a *rudis*—an unlettered servant or uncouth dullard. Even so, he attends the seven daily assemblies in the choir and, in front of the book, sings the Psalms. They have become part of his being, and like the most learned brother, he can mouth them while he watches goats."[8] An anonymous

Marian devotee of the twelfth century, cited by Dom Jean Leclercq puts it in another way: "A monk in his monastery is like the Samaritan's beast in the stable. Hay is given to one in his stall, the other assiduously chews, nourishing himself on the memory of Jesus Christ."[9]

To read in the Middle Ages is then not first of all a way of relating to some writing or to Scripture [*liber scripturae*], but to creatures [*liber creaturarum*], to the world [*liber mundi*], to Christ [*liber Christi*], or to one's own life in general [*liber vitae*]. Exactly what one reads is not important, or even whether one can read or not, if we fully understand the Victorines. What counts is the "way of reading" [*modus legendi*], which must not in any way be neglected, that is to say, the function or operation particular to humankind by which we decipher the meaning [*sensus*] behind the "figures" [*figurae*], as well as the "inner understanding" [*intus intellegere*] behind the "external appearance" [*foris speciem*]: "While the Fool [*insipiens*] only views the appearance of things," Hugh of Saint-Victor insists, "the wise man [*sapiens*] is committed, through his slant, towards what he sees of the outside, to the way of unfathomable thought in divine wisdom."[10] Saint-Victor's innovation thus comes down neither to relying on the book of nature (a theme developed at length by St. Augustine) nor to relying upon the visible world as a way of moving toward the invisible (a movement initiated by John Scotus Eriugena and finally completed by Thomas Aquinas) but to "making nature like a *second language* that contributes to the shaping of humankind" (Gilbert Dahan). As in the song by Alain de Lille, "*Omnis mundi creatura*":

> On earth dwelling every creature,
> Like a [book] or a picture,
> Mirrors forth our mortal sphere:
> Of our being, of our ending,
>
> Of our [condition] of our tending,
> Is a signet true and clear [i.e., it is a faithful symbol].[11]

In short, I hope to show in what follows that for Hugh of Saint-Victor the scriptural text and indeed writing itself are not a "medium" which the reader turns to in order to be transformed, but the direct site of "self-exposure as it were of one's own life," in which what matters is not what is passed on by language, but above all the way, always mute and silent, of being and living in the world. At the end of *De diebus tribus*, Hugh of Saint-Victor explains, "The fool and the wise man may well have the same book before their eyes [*una eademque Scriptura*]," but while some "enjoy the color and the execution of the figures [*alter colorem seu formationem figurarum commendet*] ... others appreciate the meaning and signification [*alter laudet sensum et significationem*]."[12]

The Art of Reading and the Art of Living

According to the Victorines, the "art of reading" [*ordo legendi*] will become, and in a sense always remains, an "art of living" [*ordo vivendi*]—and vice versa. The formula, indeed the matching up of reading and life, does not just imply, as we frequently assume today when we talk about an avid reader, that opening books and turning the pages suffice in order to understand one's own life, or even that life could above all principally be found among books. Returning to the act of reading rather than just to books (and here the Victorine approach can also serve to clarify things in our contemporary culture, where we rely so much on screens rather than on written material), the call to read [*ordo legendi*] and the call to live [*ordo vivendi*] are the *same* for Hugh of Saint-Victor, in that the "mode of reading" is something that must pervade all our lives. It becomes such a clear and obvious way of deciphering the world and living through our customs that letters or text are almost unnecessary—they are what teaches us to decrypt or decipher our own lives or, it might be better to say, they teach us what decrypting and deciphering really mean. Hermeneutics is wholeheartedly a "hermeneutics of life," even of the "contingent," since to live is to interpret, but interpretation goes beyond the sphere of language. Hugh of Saint-Victor underlines strongly in his chapter "On Discipline" in *Didascalicon* that the "wise person" adds "principles of living [*praecepta quoque vivendi*]" to principles of reading. Through the principles of living the reader [*lector*] comes to recognize "the way of life he should undertake [*modum vitae suae*]" as well as "the manner of studying [*et studii rationem*] he should pursue."[13]

In this sense, and following this time the preface to *The Art of Reading*, which addresses those who read (understood as those who have learned to decipher through study or otherwise), it "outlines [for readers] the discipline of one's life that is necessary [*vitae suae disciplinam praescribit*]." The call to read is a call to life in the *Didascalicon* not only because the work teaches us what we "should read [*quid legere debeat*]," "in what order [*quo ordine leger debeat*]," and finally "how one should read [*quomodo legere debeat*]."[14] Whatever there is of a Discourse on Method, and that is something we shall return to, the *Didascalicon* is not first of all a "method," nor even a mapping out, or an encyclopedia of knowledge.[15] The book, written in his own hand by Brother Hugh, is an "art of reading"—a *studio legendi*, as the subtitle maintains—and thus also an art of, or an apprenticeship to, life: *de studio vivendi*. To convince oneself of this one has only to see and read in *Didascalicon* that books are not the end of life and that what one learns from books is simply the meaning of living—in the sense of a hermeneutic of life or a "deciphering" accessible to all mankind that is independent of the simple act of reading: "After a while," Hugh confesses to his readers, "I want you to stop. There is only suffering in those books [*labor est in chartis*]! Go run outside [*curre per area*]!"[16]

The Meaning of Reading

It should be evident that in the Middle Ages one did not read in order to understand life, just as one did not live in order to read. But one *read in living* and one *lived in reading*, and this reading was the manner of living itself [*ordo legendi (et) ordo vivendi*]. What was presupposed, and what progressively unfolds in the form of a thesis in *Didascalicon*, relied upon a certain conception of "reading" we no longer share today, and from which we probably have much to learn. "Reading [*lectio*]," the *Didascalicon* states, in a landmark definition, "is when we are formed by principles and precepts [*cum regulis et praeceptis informamur*] from various writings [*ex his quae scripta sunt*]."[17] Certainly the text forms the basic support for reading, as it does in the monastic tradition of the *lectio divina*, or daily rumination over the scriptures, a tradition respected in the life of the cloisters of Saint-Victor. But Hugh of Saint-Victor, expanding it to what would later become *lectio scolastica*, draws from it an in-formation of the self and for oneself (*informamur*) according to rules and precepts. In other words, when the master read at Saint-Victor, he was not content with what he read, nor even with understanding or contemplating what he read: he strove to read in such a way that reading was his raison d'être as well as a reason for living, insofar as precepts for living (*ordo vivendi*) could be identified in the same way as prescriptions of how to read (*ordo legendi*). We can see this in the extension of *lectio* that has been reduced in our day to a simple relationship with the text but was expanded in those days to the whole relation with the Other: the way in which one read being the determining factor in the act of reading, rather than the books themselves:

> There are three kinds of reading: that of the teacher [*docentis*], that of the learner [*discentis*], and that of the person examining the book on his own [*per se incipientes*]. For we say, "I am reading the book *to* him [*lego librum illi*—the teacher]," "I am reading the book *under* him [*lego librum ab illo*—the learner]," and "I am reading the book [*lego librum*—the beginner]." In reading, the order and method must especially be considered.[18]

What is it then that makes a book, as the Middle Ages understand it, and in particular in the twelfth-century renaissance, something on the borderline between the *lectio monastica* and the *lectio scolastica*? Not simply the mumbling or murmuring of the text in private (*lectio monastica* or *lectio divina*) but a type of relationship to the text (*ordo legendi*) which is also, and always, a relationship with the Other (*ordo vivendi*). One should not just read anything, according to Hugh of Saint-Victor; everything depends upon the "order" [*ordo*] and the method or manner [*modus*] in which one reads. Reading is "an addressing (to)" not just a simple "prowess" or achievement, even for an era when there were so few readers. One reads simply "a book" [*lego librum*] when one is starting off, but when one becomes a learner or student one reads the books "of someone" [*ab illo*], and one reads the book "to somebody" when one is nominated teacher or master. According to Michel Lemoine, in his edition of *Didascalicon*, "[w]e should note that reading ['lecture' in French] is to be taken in the sense of the Latin word *lectio*." The word signifies at once "deciphering a text," "study," and "meaning."[19] As we shall find in relation to gesture and speech (chap. 5), according to Hugh of Saint-Victor, it is the *modality of the relation that* moves always toward *action* and not the other way around. The Anglo-Saxon languages moreover retain this sense when it is a question of reading, a "lecture" identifying not that one has gone through a text but an act such as studying a passage in the context of a course and indeed of giving a talk during a conference.

To come back to Hugh of Saint-Victor, what counts for the reader reading is not simply understanding what one reads—something to which we nowadays most often reduce reading: it is the appropriateness of the connection with the person "to whom" and "with whom" one reads. No reading takes its place in the canonical life of the Victorines independently of the community that sustains it. Abbot Gilduin confirms this, word for word, in the "rule of life" of the order of Saint-Victor: according to his *Liber ordinis*, "nobody should be seen without a book in his hand"—including those who could not read.[20] Living in the Middle Ages is thus also a way of reading or deciphering the world so that one does not go simply from "the book to reading" [§11] but rather from "utterance (*parole*) to books" [§12].[21]

§12. From Utterance to Books

What is most surprising when one reads Hugh of Saint-Victor at length is how much he is concerned about "books" and how little about "texts"—making the hermeneutic not simply the crucible of the act of "interpretation" but also the site of "sacramentality" or of "efficacious speech." We could say that where the Bible speaks it is first of all entirely understood as the "Word of God" [*De verbo Dei*] and not as "book" (or text) of Scripture [*liber scripturae*]. Thus we find Hugh's treatise *On the Word of God* which, far from consecrating a "text" in the spoken word, sees rather an "act," joining the "speech of humankind" and the "speech of God" into the one and only "great sacrament" [*magnum sacramentum*]: "God speaks through men [*per hominem*]; he speaks himself [*per se*]; through men, many spoken words [*multos sermones*], himself only one [*unum*] … Let us examine then this great sacrament [*videamus ergo magnum sacramentum*]."[22]

The Great Sacrament

It might seem surprising that the "utterance of God" [*sermo Dei*] could be called a "sacrament," and even "this great sacrament," since it would not be, or would no longer be, included in what were subsequently to be seen as the seven sacraments (baptism, eucharist, confirmation, penance, anointing the sick, marriage, and holy orders). But it is not so surprising if we recall that in the renaissance of the twelfth century sacramentality was not yet definitely fixed. Thus we find, for example, Lanfranc giving a non-comprehensive list of four *sacramenta*, Abelard five, Bernard of Clairvaux ten, and Pierre Damien twelve.[23] But with Hugh of Saint-Victor something new is taking place which makes him somehow "turn over a new page," where what will arise is strictly speaking a kind of "thematization" of the book insofar as it is a "book of life."

The double development of *sacramentum* by St. Augustine on the one hand, and St. Isidore of Seville on the other, had in fact led to a hesitation of the part of theologians between the sacrament as "outward and visible sign" (*sacrum signum* [Augustine]) and the "secret and hidden power" on the other [Isidor of Seville]. Moreover in almost the same period we find the argument over the eucharist between Berengar of Tours and Lanfranc of Pavia which keeps sparking off two extremes: the symbolic presence or in the form of the sacrament as sign (Augustine, Ratramnus, Lanfranc) and the presence later called "real presence" or the reality of the sacrament as thing (Isidore, Paschasius Radbertus, Lanfranc).[24] As for Hugh of Saint-Victor, he stands in a watershed period when the notion of the sacrament as efficacious cause (Peter Lombard and then Thomas Aquinas) had not yet been brought up and when a solution was sought between "sign" and "thing," where later "cause" would be found. To make the word of God itself into a "great sacrament" [*magnum sacramentum*] is then to see at once a sign and a thing until a cause is found there. Many features can thus be read into and deciphered in *De verbo Dei* of the Victorine master.

The formula from the Letter to the Hebrews serves as a guide and justification for the deployment of the *verbum* as sacrament: "The speech of God is something alive and active [*vivus et efficax*]: it cuts more incisively [*penetrabilior*] than any two-edged sword" (Heb. 4:12 RNJB).

The word of God is *life* in that it "is unchanging in its promise" and "is fulfilled in truth"; it is *active* in that it "operates with force" so that it achieves "hope" for us; it is *sharp* in that it "does not deceive in its judgement" and leads us to love or "charity."[25] It becomes apparent, at least in a retrospective reading of *De verbo Dei*, that the sacramentality of the spoken word of God implies that what is said is not simply the "sign" of He who says it (the spoken word proffered by the Word) but also the "thing" that He is himself (the Word as spoken Word)—until the one and the other will be identified as "cause" or "efficacity" (the word proffered as uncreated Word, incarnate and resurrected.)

But in order that such speech can achieve its "performativity," it is necessary that humankind participate in the act of "proffering." According to Hugh of Saint-Victor there is no grace without a cooperation with grace. And thus there is no book unless the reader takes part in the story being read, as well as what is being recounted. In the same way all sacramentality demands a joining of humanity and divinity, at least in the sensible signs that it lays claim to (the water for baptism, the oil for confirmation, etc.). Hugh talks of the "great sacrament of the word of God" demanding that we are "spokespersons" or the "mouthpiece" of He who, in being the spoken Word, gives the Word to us so that we can speak it for ourselves and with Him:

> We must understand that God speaks in one way through the mouths of men [*aliter per hominum ora*], in another way by himself [*aliter per semetipsum*] … But in all these words that he has pronounced through the mouths of men a unique word is present [*iste unus in omnibus fuit*], and in its uniqueness all becomes only one [*et omnes in isto uno unum sunt*].[26]

It is no longer necessary to show that God speaks: that is clear in Christianity as it is in Judaism or Islam. But that he speaks "through the mouths of men" [*per hominum ora*] is a belief that Christianity shares only with Judaism: "Almost all the Scripture of the Old and the New Testament shows that God in fact speaks among men [*in hominibus*], and through man [*per homines*]."[27] The fact remains that, entering here into what is specifically Christian, the word of man (that is, of humankind) can never be separated from, or divested of, He who is the Word. The unique speech of the Word contains in itself all our speech [*omnes in isto uno unum sunt*], in that the *Ark of Speech* (the Word himself) measures us up with regard to our own capacity to welcome other beings in the act of speaking (by our own words). *De verbo Dei* celebrates not simply the word that God intends for us (subjective genitive) but also how we ourselves confide in God in speaking of him and for him (objective genitive): "There is first of all the word of God addressed to us [*sermo Dei ad nos*]," Hugh specifies, "and then there is our word addressed to God [*postea sermo noster ad Deum*]."²⁸

But with the act of speaking, or rather with the words spoken, albeit the multiplicity of words that humankind uses to speak the oneness of the word of God, Hugh of Saint-Victor still does not believe, quite correctly, that he has reached the essence of the "great sacrament" that is the speech of God. Even though the spoken word (*parole*) may be living, efficacious, and sharp, it awaits being embodied in the flesh of humankind (integration of human speech with divine speech), as well as, and above all, becoming embodied through the flesh of God (the incarnation of the Word to the point of consecrating *flesh itself* as unique and principal utterance). Thus, where Christianity finds itself, and where the book definitively leaves the text to become body, is when the Word becomes "flesh" and when its mode for us today can be called "voice." Reading is so little the text and so much life in the work of Hugh of Saint-Victor that we can still recognize today the Word through his "voice" [*vox*], just as the apostles once recognized the Word through his flesh [*caro*]: "The voice of the Word *is to be understood* in the present day *as* the flesh of God *was* then understood"—[*hic intelligenda est vox Verbi quod ibi caro Dei*].²⁹ In this masterly analogy between the flesh and the voice in *De verbo Dei* we find the strongest and most original element of the corpus of Hugh's work. It is what I have described elsewhere as fundamental for my own work—a hermeneutic that can be called "Catholic" of the body and voice.³⁰

The Flesh and the Voice

If God "spoke once only" [*semel locutus est*] in engendering his Word, this was spoken many times [*multi*] but otherwise [*aliter*] when the mouths of humankind took over from the mouth of God.³¹ What was produced by utterance, by the spoken word—the oneness of the *Verbum* and the multiplicity of the *verba*—acted in the same way when it was a question of the flesh and the incarnation: "The Word of God clothed in human flesh [*humana carne vestitum*] appeared only once in visible form [*semel visibile apparuit*] and now, every day [*quotidie*], this same Word comes himself to us under the guise of the human voice [*humana voce conditum*]."³² Here, despite the soundness of the analysis, the originality is such that it is not easy for us to grasp what is being said.

Certainly it is no surprise to read that God is given in his Word or indeed in our spoken words that carry on from his own Word. That is the usual way of rendering justice to God "speaking," where what he says is not reduced to a single text. But since the closing of the canon of Scripture, or rather since the end of the apostolic era, it is also common to call an end to all forms of the sensible presence of God. His flesh that was previously "visible" (Jn 1:1) is no longer accessible today, and talk of his utterance, previously heard, describes nothing other than the abstraction of a message disconnected from the body as from the "voice." This way of thinking is what Hugh of Saint-Victor rightly denounces—in a tradition that Hans Urs von Balthasar will later recover for us under his own title "The Spiritual Senses."³³

Even if we can no longer see the "flesh" (*caro*) today, that does not mean that we have lost the "voice" (*vox*)—and for several reasons:

(a) First of all, and Hugh of Saint-Victor seems to remember it in this passage, the "human voice" (*vocem humanam*) of Christ certainly needs a body, but there is no necessity for the body to be visible in order to be heard. It is not that the voice indicates the absence of the body, but it specifically allows the phonemes of a body that is sometimes absent to be heard. I can hear without seeing. Moreover, I sometimes hear better when the prism of seeing stops intruding upon me, and I am enabled to be completely present to the voice. If the Word resurrected *is not "seen"—not seen in the flesh—he is still heard or understood in the voice* since we recognize him not through an absence of body but just as a body that is "absent" or "hidden" but is always nonetheless a bearer of a "voice."

(b) Further, and this is again something that the Victorine Master could not forget, since every day he celebrated and meditated upon the Scriptures, it is by the "voice" (*vox*) that God is recognized by us in the Bible—from the shepherd who cries out with a "loud voice" (Mk 15:34), indeed to Mary Magdalene recognizing him probably by the voicing of her name "Mary" (Jn 20:16). In every case, as Jacques Derrida has shown, the voice understood as "phenomenon" represents the strongest "thisness" (*haeccity*) of the one who speaks, independently, or at least less, than what is being said: "No consciousness is possible without the voice … the voice *is* consciousness."[34]

(c) Finally, and Hugh of Saint-Victor formulates this explicitly, the voice resounds with such interiority that hearing comes down first of all to recognizing that what is being shown is internal (*intus*) and is not that which in an exterior way (*foris*) would seem simply to have been given:

> The wicked and the unbelievers were also able to see the humanity of Christ, and even to kill it, and still every day they hear the Word of God from the outside [*foris audiunt*] and have contempt for it. In the same way that those of long ago would not have dared to kill the man if they had been able to recognize God, those today would by no means despise the divine words if they had understood, if they had been able to taste the excellence and the inner savor [*si virtutem eorum interno sapore gustare valerent*].[35]

This is then what is at stake with the voice (*vox*) and with the gate (*porta*) in the parable of the good shepherd, which explicitly talks of them or at least makes a connection between them: "I am the gate [*porta*]. Whoever enters by me will be saved … I am the good shepherd. I know my own and my own know me … they will listen to my voice" (Jn 10:9-16 NRSV). The "voice" like the "gate" is essentially a "passage" [*transitus*], understood here as a transit from within to outside for the one who speaks and a movement from without to within for those who listen or understand:

> Thus the Word of God is "living" because there is life in it. It is in that which is outside [*foris*] which stimulates the hearing, in that which is inside [*intus*] which invigorates the heart; it is in that which affects the ears [*auribus illabitur*], and in that which inspires the heart [*cordi inspiratur*]. That which is outside passes on [*foris est*

transit]: that which is inside does not suffer any change [*intus est mutabilitem non recipit*]. That which develops discourse outside [*foris decursus verborum explicat*], tells the immutable truth within [*intus veritas incommutabilis dictat*].[36]

The "voice" [*vox*], in (a) the trace of an absent body but not of the absence of the body; in (b) the singling out, or thisness, of he who speaks rather than in attention to what is said; in (c) a reciprocal passage of the internal and the external through which it essentially passes, takes on the role for us today, as it did originally for Hugh of Saint-Victor, that the "flesh" [*caro*] held in the past for the disciples. The Word incarnate, no longer visible in its flesh, remains nonetheless audible to us in terms of voice. What is to be understood in its utterance is not solely what is said but also the way in which it is said. The sign of the voice feeds back to the sign of the flesh in that a particular "style" identifies them, something we also have to decipher today. The "voice here is made flesh" not simply in that it is incarnate in a body but also because of what it takes over. No voice without flesh, and perhaps in the absence of flesh or in a "hidden flesh," what remains always for us is the voice: "Different [*aliter*] certainly, is the way in which God is made known to mankind, according to whether it is through the flesh [*per carnem*] or through the human voice [*per vocem humanam*]. However, in a certain way [*quodammodo*] the *voice of the Word is to be understood today as the flesh of God was understood then*."[37]

Through the "voice" we recognize the footstep of he who comes, and here the Master of Saint-Victor remembers perhaps the Augustinian attribution of "voice" to the figure of John crying in the desert and of the Word to He who comes to be baptized in the Jordan: "John is the voice [*vox*], but the Lord at the start was the Word [*verbum*] … It is difficult, you see, to distinguish word from voice and that is why John himself was thought to be the Christ. The voice was thought to be the Word; but the voice identified himself, in order not to offend the Word."[38]

The *readable* is thus also the *audible* before it leads us, as we shall see later, toward the visible. We should learn to read or rather open "the books of our lives" to measure them up "to the book" of the wisdom of God, the example of how all books are to be read, as are all voices to be heard.

The Book and the Books

To read "God as an open book" (chap. 4) is thus above all to commit oneself to opening books. But, since books are so often closed and sealed, or not present for those many readers to whom they remain impenetrable, we might ask, which books are in question here? This has already come up in my introduction [§4], and the *Book of Revelation* is unambiguous on this point: the sacred book in Christianity is not the first that is read (the book of the text) but that which is "eaten" (Rev. 10:9), or that which is the "book of life" (Rev. 20:12). Hugh of Saint-Victor will remember this lesson which, throughout *De verbo Dei*, and opening "the books," asks what standing should be given "to the book"—that of "life," not simply the Scriptures. He cites the book of Revelations: "The books lay open. And another book was opened, which is the book of life [*liber qui est vitae*], and the dead were judged from what was written in the books [*in libris*]" (Rev. 20: 12 RNJB). The "book of life" (singular) thus refers explicitly to "*the* books" (plural) in the Book of Revelations. Nothing, in the singular or plural, indicates here that it is still a question of the written text, in that the hermeneutic seems able neatly to leave behind the traps of the text, to rejoin the lived experience of life that remains originary. Hugh magnificently states that "books are the heart of humankind [*libri sunt corda hominum*] and the book of life is the wisdom of God [*liber vitae est sapientia Dei*]."[39] As with the utterance (*parole*) of God and *the* words (plural) of humankind or, as with the comprehension of the Word *once* only in the flesh and *many times* in the voice, the plurality of the these books of our lives seems to be in agreement with unity of the book (singular) of God: "The dead are judged according to the content 'of the books' [*in libri*] and not 'of the book' [*in libro*], because sinners shall be judged according to their works [*ex sui operibus*]."[40]

This is the Christian tradition, and the Catholic tradition in particular will further emphasize not simply what we "think" (intentions) but also what we "do" (acts). The books of our lives are written in the world, as a seal makes its mark on wax and fixes it in a definitive way. Our books are then "our hearts," but what reveals their particular character is how their intentions are translated into "works." As for the book of God— the Wisdom rather than the text—it is still exemplary, or rather it is the Life on the basis of which our own lives were written or copied: "Our books were written according to the book of God [*ad librum Dei scripti sunt*], because our hearts were formed in the likeness of the wisdom of God [*ad similitudinem sapientiae Dei condita sunt*]."[41]

Here, even more than elsewhere, the metaphor of writing and reading is in full play and points to something other than a simple gesture of the text or the course followed by the lines of the text. Once again it does not matter whether or not the monk can read a text, as long as he has the keys necessary to decrypt his own life. In the "cabinet of books" of the library of the abbey he will learn things which seem to controvert his own example. And whatever his standing in the society of the monastery he will learn to order or "collate" the book of his own life in the Book that is God Himself in his Wisdom in a heart to heart rather than in a text to text. If he is a copyist in the scriptorium he will learn from this art to "correct" or "underline" his own errors in his sinful existence, to match up his own example against the divine example, and to resemble the divine example always more. Not knowing how to read the letters does not exempt him from the interpretation of life; it is a puzzle to be put together with the divine life that the relationship of parchment to text can show him, even though it may not necessarily instill the divine life in him. "Even after they have been written, our books must at least be corrected [*corrigendi sunt*]. Let us therefore collate our book with that book, to correct the discrepancies that can be encountered there, fearing that during the final collation [*in ultima collatione*], if some discrepancy is found, they will be discarded."[42]

It will be plain then that the "voice of God" is heard and recognized when the "books of our lives" are in accord with the "book of God" and in that coincidence a "style" can be read that allows us to set about decrypting them. The text is no longer simply *readable*, nor even *audible*, but *visible*, since it is given to us to read in our lives [*liber vitae*] as in the world [*liber mundi*]. In this "surge of the visible" we find the movement that is particular to Hugh of Saint-Victor and that the Franciscan lineage, in particular as it follows on from St. Bonaventure, will take care never to forget.[43]

§13. From the Readable to the Visible

Going from the "readable" to the "visible" has important consequences. If we insist too strongly on the "readable" we tend to forget the "visible."[44] Certainly we must *interpret*, but even more we need to *show*. As I have pointed out at the start of part 2, a hermeneutic is either phenomenological or it is nothing. Concentrating too much on "meaning" we lose the symbolic. The depth of the created world is not fully deployed unless *deciphering* is at the same time *looking at*, or letting oneself be transformed by, that which is there *to behold*. The *Commentary on the Celestial Hierarchy* by Hugh of Saint-Victor takes over from the *Didascalicon* or *De verbo Dei*, in that it moves from "reading" to "seeing" and also indicates a different direction from that of Pseudo-Dionysius the Areopagite. Far from taking refuge in the ineffable (negative or apophatic theology), reading the book of experience in the twelfth century brings us into the realm of the figurable (positive or cataphatic theology). From the "world of the book," passing to the "book of the world," according to a distinction that was already popular at the time, was another way of saying that God is not simply "above us" [*supra nos*] (mystical theology), but "in us" [*in nos*] (illuminative theology), and also "outside us" [*extra nos*] (symbolic theology).[45]

The Way of the Visible

In a passage of the *Commentary on the Celestial Hierarchy* that was to become celebrated, at least as far as medieval posterity was concerned, Hugh of Saint-Victor distinguishes clearly between two theologies: the theology of this world [*theologia hujus mundi*] and the theology that is called divine [*theologia quae divina nominator*]. It has not been sufficiently noted that, far from opposing the upward movement of "human theology" and the descending movement of "divine theology," as we find later, for example in the work of Thomas Aquinas, Hugh of Saint-Victor actually identifies the same act in both (the one and the other taking place for us in the same world), while he places them in opposition in their form (human and divine). A single maxim in fact guides all Hugh's thought and demands "passing through the visible," albeit in order to get to the invisible. "It is in fact impossible to make the invisible known other than through the visible [*impossibile enim est invisibilium, nisi per visibilia demonstrari*]," Hugh writes, as if to join together the natural movement and the movement as revealed in thought. "As a consequence, all theology [*omnis theologia*] must necessarily be based on visible signs [*visibilibus demonstrationibus uti*] in order to express the invisible [*uti in invisiblium declaratione*]."[46]

Whether one follows the secular wisdom of the Greeks, or the divine theology that comes to us through revealed religion, "both are based on the visible world and endeavor to reach the invisible," as Dominique Poirel says, "but the humility of the second can be opposed to the over confidence of the first."[47]

What counts most in the distinction between these two theologies (worldly and divine) is less their separation than their unity. Certainly, and it is much to the credit of Hugh to have shown this, one cannot so easily identify the secular wisdom and Christian Wisdom when the first becomes integrated and transformed in the second (*Didascalicon*). But what brings them together—that is to say their ascending movement—is also what demonstrates the originality they have in common:

> But the theology of the world [*mundana theologia*], as we have seen, took for its object the *works of creation* and the *elements of the world* with their created beauty, and based its statements on them. Divine theology [*theologia divina*] applied itself to the work of restoration with regard to the humanity of Jesus and his sacraments, and based its teaching on it.[48]

In other words, the specific route taken in Christianity is neither that of opposing the descending way of Revelation to the ascending way of philosophy nor even of partially uniting them (Thomas Aquinas). Characteristically, and in common with the secular world in form if not in content, it never goes from the invisible to the visible but only from the visible to the invisible. Because God was made human, we have no other way to go to God but that of passing by way of the human, according to a leitmotif that I have developed elsewhere.[49] The route of the incarnation determines, at least for us, that we above all consider "the humanity of Jesus and his sacraments [*secundum humanitatem Jesu et sacramenta ejus*]" because it is on that above all that we live.

As for the Trinity, the hypostases, the generation of the Son by the Father etc.—all that does not remain always inaccessible. But we shall reach it only through passing by way of the "flesh" of the visible Son or by his audible "voice." Certainly, as Kant says, "The light dove in free flight cutting through the air, the resistance of which it feels, could get the idea that it could do even better in airless space."[50] However, such is not the case. We are made of "flesh and bones," and Christ *with us* and Christ *for us*. The "world" itself *speaks to us*, telling us to read it, but also to see it, in the way that it shows God because God also (and here we find the Victorines anticipating the Franciscans with even more "naturalism") speaks through it and through its creatures. The two theologies—"theology of the world" (*mundana theologia*) and "divine theology" (*theologia divina*)—open thus above all the *way of the visible* rather than divide into two movements of thought. The pretensions of philosophy or of a supposedly unmixed theology are capable of separating paganism from Christianity but that does not happen in the justified quest for a way to pass through humankind toward God, albeit by way of a Man-God. Inculturation [i.e., adapting Christian theology to a non-Christian background] is important for revealed religion, and it is only through forgetting this that we have come to magnify the separation of the orders.[51]

Stripped Bare

If there are then "three orders" for Hugh of Saint-Victor, as there were later for Blaise Pascal,[52] we need to interpret them in another way—less in a leap to *revealed religion* and more in a taking on board of *incarnation*. Thus it is only the Victorine who distinguishes in a very original fashion, this time in *De verbo Dei*, "the eye of the flesh [*oculus carnis*] exterior and not interior [*foris est et non intus*]"; "the eye of the heart [*oculus cordis*] interior from one point of view and exterior from another [*intus est ad aliquid et ad aliquid foris*]"; and the "eye of God [*oculus Dei*], exclusively interior and not exterior [*intus est tantum et non foris*]."⁵³ We could certainly go further into analysis of texts by Bonaventure and Blaise Pascal that, as we have seen, take up this whole movement: the "eye of the flesh" [*oculus carnis*] seeing what is exterior to the body but not what is interior in the heart; the "eye of the heart" [*oculus cordis*] seeing what is interior to the heart but not what is interior to the body; and the "eye of God" [*oculus Dei*] seeing the exterior and the interior as well as the heart of the body. But all that is not the subject of this present book.⁵⁴

There remains an essential difference in Pascal's aim and Hugh's ambition: the "order of charity" for one (Pascal) and the "order of visibility" for the other (Hugh of Saint-Victor). Hugh goes on to say, "There is no invisible creature before him" [*non est ulla creatura invisibilis coram ipso*], taking up the Letter to the Hebrews: "And before him no creature is hidden, but all are naked [*nuda*] and laid bare [*aperta*] to the eyes [*in conspectu eius*]" (Heb. 4:13 JB). As we have already seen, the "book of our lives" shall be opened at the last days (Book of Revelations) and God shall read what we have done on the exterior [*foris*] as well as what we have thought internally [*intus*]. The stripping "bare" [*nuda*] on the day of the coming of the Kingdom will then be that of the total manifestation of God in the world [*liber mundi*] and of his theophany in our hearts [*liber cordis*]. The *intent of visibility* for the divine is not to spy on us but rather to make us see for ourselves what we have still wished to hide. All will be laid "bare" for us even if that is above all for Him and through Him. In that new way we shall see ourselves without coat or veil, and in this nakedness we shall also be revealed to ourselves:

> In the eyes of God then, all is exposed [*omnia sunt nuda*] because he sees all the actions of mankind, where they are done, because there is neither darkness, nor shadow of death where those who do evil can hide; no coat that covers our eyes [*nec operimentum tegit*], no veil that protects us [*nec velamen protegit*], no wall that screens us off [*nec paries intercludit*], no cloud that hides us [*nec caligo abscondit nos ab oculis eius*]. All is bare [*nuda*] because then he sees what has been done; all is *uncovered* [*aperta*] because then he sees the intent with which we have done it.⁵⁵

Rather than fearing the "eye of God," humankind will profit first of all by submitting. Seeing the exterior through "the eye of the body," and the interior by "the eye of the heart," we can learn to see the accord [*conformitas*] of the exterior [*foris*] and the interior [*intus*] that is so dear to the Victorine, through a coincidence of acts and intentions, even if we are seeking for a unity that we cannot find in ourselves, we can receive it above all from Him who made that unity.

The Wonder of the Visible

Aesthetic experience of beauty, or wonder at the visible, does not come then in this sense from that which we see but rather from the *way* and the *unity* with which we see it. Visible reality, or the works of God, "speak[s] to us" [*nobis loquitur*], as do all God's words. And we are given eyes to see them and to recognize them, as long as we dare at last to turn our gaze toward the world to find it and decipher it. Far from fleeing terrestrial reality, Victorine spirituality, like so much in the twelfth-century renaissance, leads us back toward it. Yet it was necessary for the faithful to be converted sufficiently to believe this and for them also to have that unique experience of how in the most striking visibility what speaks in secret is the invisibility of Him who remains hidden there:

> Nobody should think that viewing visible reality [*visibilium rerum aspectum*] is harmful to the chaste soul, since if looking at the works of God was something culpable, he would by no means have created the faculty of looking at them. The works of God are in effect like his word [*opus enim Dei quasi verbum illius est*] and the eyes are like instruments by means of which the words of God are perceived through contemplation.[56]

The "word" and the "works" are not then to be separated any more than the "word" and the "flesh" are separate in the figure of the incarnate Son. The world, or the works, "speak to us" [*nobis loquitur*] because it is itself also word and speaks in the same way that Mount Saint-Victor spoke to the painter Cezanne because he waited for it to "emerge." We can cite Merleau-Ponty as a *philosophical* pioneer of such Expressionism as when he wrote in "Eye and Mind": "The painter's vision is not a view upon the *outside* ... it is the painter to whom the things of the world give birth by a sort of concentration or coming-to-itself of the visible ... For henceforth, as Klee said, the line no longer imitates the visible; it 'renders visible,' it is the blueprint of a genesis of things."[57] Nothing in the sphere of visibility will then be irrelevant for the believer since God is also given there to be seen. Specialists in the works of the Victorines have grasped this and pointed out that it can be seen in the several graphics and drawings in the pamphlet on the making of *Noah's Ark* [*De archa Noe*] or the *Description of the World in the Form of Maps* [*Descriptio mappe mundi*]. Some architects, geographers, and abstract painters have also on their own account come across this when they have taken the time to look at these works by Hugh of Saint-Victor.[58] Like the "phenomenon" that hides nothing of what it is but is "at the same time an 'appearance' as an emanation of something which *hides* itself in that appearance,"[59] "appearance" is defined almost phenomenologically in *De tribus diebus*, as containing shapes and colors: "Species is the visible form which contains two things: the shapes and colors" [*species est forma visibilis, quae continet duo, figuras et colores*].[60] What is original here is that the appearance, or "species," does not deceive or at least no longer deceives. Moreover figure [*figura*] and color [*color*] make it emerge and make it iridescent in such a way that one cannot be separated from the other unless they disappear into invisibility. For Husserl the essence of the phenomenon will no longer appear independently of the appearance of its figure and color, or rather of its color that goes along with its figure (as in the example of red slips of paper), and similarly appearance in reality is not denied by Hugh of Saint-Victor; it is confirmed as the pre-eminent site of the manifestation of visibility.[61]

But things in their "figures" and "appearances" would not really be so wonderful in Hugh of Saint-Victor's eyes if they did not show themselves to be "wonderful in a thousand ways" [*multis modis mirabiles*]. What arouses wonder is, once again, less what they are and more the *way* we have of seeing them and knowing how to read in them the code of the presence of God. Probably once more Hugh is a precursor for the thought of Pascal here, this time in describing the site of *wonder* rather than an abyss of *terror*; neither the infinitely great nor the infinitely small escapes the excitement of the believer deciphering God in the world and recognizing God as in a "book of pictures." Thus Hugh of Saint-Victor refigures, but with a different significance, what will become notorious in Pascal's philosophy (the "two infinities"):

> One pays attention to the figure according to its magnitude when the thing exceeds the size of its kind in quantity, it is thus that we marvel at a giant among men ... Ask yourself therefore which one you marvel at more [*vide ergo quid magis mimeris*]. Is it the teeth of a boar or a mite, the wings of a gryphon or a mosquito, the head of a horse or a grasshopper, the thigh of an elephant or a midge, the snout of a pig or a louse, an eagle or an ant, a lion or a flea, a tiger or a tortoise? Here you marvel at the great size [*hic miraris magnitudinem*]: Here you marvel at the smallness [*hic miraris parvitatem*]. You marvel at a tiny thing created with great wisdom. And great is this wisdom in which there is not a trace of negligence. It has given eyes to these beings that our eyes can hardly see, and in their tiny bodies are so well distributed, in a complete fullness, the lineaments appropriate for their nature, that you can see how for the smallest of them there is nothing lacking of all that nature has provided for the greatest [*nihil deesse in minimis eorum ominium quae natura formavit in magnis*].[62]

Apart from recognizing the naturalism, indeed the formulation of humankind as microcosm that we find also and concurrently in the School of Chartres, the description here—of the teeth of the boar or of the mite (?), the wings of the gryphon and the mosquito, the thighs of the elephant or the midge—is sufficient to make us see how *nothing of what is visible* is forgotten by Hugh of Saint-Victor in order precisely to grasp the presence of a God hidden, but never far away. God is read by Hugh of Saint-Victor definitively "as an open book" (chap. 6). He proceeds forcefully, whether it is a question of the book of life [*liber vitae*], the book of the heart [*liber cordis*], or the book of the world [*liber mundi*]. And this is done without the book of Scripture [*liber scripturae*] coming into view—at least as the *first* book.

I have been trying to emphasize the originality of Hugh of Saint-Victor. It is not necessary *to know how to read* in order to read or to learn to read in the twelfth-century renaissance, as long as reading points less to the act of going through a text than to that of "deciphering" the presence of an other in the events of one's existence (book of life), in the depths of one's inner being (book of the heart), or in the visibility of appearances (book of the world). Not being satisfied simply with texts or with the Scripture [*liber scripturae*], one thus passes on to the world [*liber mundi*]. The "body" itself also speaks, as Hugh of Saint-Victor saw and showed. From "gesture as utterance (*parole*)" we then pass on to "utterance (*parole*) as gesture." Hugh will not be satisfied this time with decrypting the presence of God in the world as though it were a text. He tries to see and to show the extent to which the attitudes and manner of being of the body, indeed of its kinesthesis, speak what there is in the gesturality and interiority of us all.

Hugh of Saint-Victor's treatise on *The Training of Novices* [*De institutione novitiorum*] takes over from the *Art of Reading* [*Didascalicon*], moving us from a kind of hermeneutics to phenomenology—as it were from Paul Ricoeur to Maurice Merleau-Ponty. "Discipline" for novices in Latin [*disciplina*], as in French [*discipline*], speaks to us of both a method and a faculty of "learning to read" (hermeneutics), as well as of a certain stringency or style of inhabiting or "living one's body" (phenomenology). Thus is born, in Hugh of Saint-Victor's *De institutione novitiorum*, the first great definition of "gesture." One can only be surprised that Merleau-Ponty was able to overlook this Victorine source just as Paul Ricoeur seemed unaware of the "art of reading" of *Didascalicon* in his hermeneutics of the text. But what is important is not whether they knew or did not know. It does not matter, after all, if certain texts have not been read or cited, just as long as the work of translation and exegesis by historians of medieval philosophy has truly brought to light what was previously passed over and is still neglected. It is left for us now to draw fully upon the source of these texts, and also upon experience, to allow them to teach and even transform us. The possibility of replenishing ourselves and making fruitful our own thought depends upon what took place and was said yesterday.

5

To Live One's Body

Toward a Phenomenology of Gesture

God is given as an "open book" (chap. 4) in the monastic theology of the twelfth century. It is necessary to "learn to read" [*ars legendi*] before "learning to live" [*ars vivendi*]—or rather it is necessary to recognize that "to read" is "to live" since reading is not just a matter of texts but extends also to the world and indeed to the deciphering of our hearts. *Reading in the book of experience* in the works of Hugh of Saint-Victor is not simply "to interpret" but also "to experience," indeed to be "incarnate" in, or to "live one's body" (chap. 5).

> At the time [in fact] when the young master of the Parisian abbey gave his students their program of study and of his teaching, and advised them on how to engage with it (in 1125), he was drafting *De institutione novitiorum* [*The Training of Novices*], alongside *Didascalicon*. If the one is an 'art of reading' [*Didascalicon*] ... the other is an 'art of living' [*De institutione novitiorum*].[1]

The "art of living" in *De institutione novitiorum* is thus contemporary with the "art of reading" in *Didascalicon*. A hermeneutic of the text is not possible without a hermeneutic of facticity, even in the Middle Ages.

In moving from the "art of reading" [*Didascalicon*] to the "art of living" [*The Training of Novices*] and thus from the individuality of the reader to the community of reading monks, we enter what Heidegger rightly refers to as "everydayness" [*Alltäglichkeit*]—an act of "Being-with" Others [*Mitsein*] in an "environment" [*Umwelt*] and under the mode of solicitude [*Fürsorge*]: "By 'Others' we do not mean everyone else but me—those over against whom the 'I' stands out. They are those from whom, in the most part, one does *not* distinguish oneself—those among whom one is too."[2] And thus we encounter the astounding paradox of the "ears," which in Hugh of Saint-Victor's work aim precisely at "Being-with" (*The Training of Novices*), while the "eyes" search only for "Being-there" (*Didascalicon*): "In the human body the eyes are places appropriately *in front* to contemplate the works of God in the world. But the *ears* are also placed appropriately: situated *at the side*, so that we understand that our purposes should only be directed toward our neighbors secondarily, and toward God primarily."[3]

The art of reading God in the world or in Scripture (*ars legendi*) teaches the art of living with others by spoken word or gesture (*ars vivendi*). Corresponding to the verticality of seeing in *Didascalicon* (relationship to the book of the world) is a horizontality of understanding in *The Training of Novices* (relationship to brother monks or rather to colleagues living under monastic rule).

Given the relevance of this approach, one has to wonder if the "phenomenology of gesture" (Merleau-Ponty) does not have unsuspected roots in *The Training of Novices*, just as hermeneutics (Ricoeur, Gadamer) could or should have found their sources and renewed them in light of *Didascalicon*.

The world to be read by what one "sees" (or the hermeneutic duty of "deciphering") demands that one live by one's "understanding" (or the phenomenological challenge of our "being in common"). The symbolic, or the "Good use of the Sensible" (Bonaventure), is not what *I* discover alone or what *God* works in me.[4] It is shared *with others* since in a monastic community, or a community living under canonical rule, the individual goes also and above into the world along with his brothers, in that God makes the community before wishing for each one to individualize himself. *The Training of Novices* is neither "scholastic work" like the *Didascalicon* nor a compendium of theology like Hugh's *De sacramentis christianae fidei* [*On the Sacraments of the Christian Faith*], nor even "spiritual writing" like his *Soliloquium de arrha anime* [*Soliloquy on the Earnest Money of the Soul*]. It is a kind of "manual on how to live directed at novices," not simply as a supplement to the universal project of the Victorine author but as a true psychology of "daily life" at Saint-Victor (Dominique Poirel).[5] What is at stake in gesture and spoken word in *The Training of Novices* is preserving "the discipline inside" [*interior custodia disciplinae*] and "connecting the members of the body with the outside [*foris*], so that inside [*intresecus*] they will be consolidated upon a firm spiritual basis."[6] "Wearing the habit" [§14], the "position of the limbs" [§15], and the "delivery of speech" [§16] are seen as a way of being for the self and toward God and above all a way of being toward others and the world.

Far from any division of being and appearing, in a theology of invisibility, or in a philosophy of the thing in itself, both of which should be ruled out (chap. 4), the "discipline" [*disciplina*] newly interrogated here by Hugh of Saint-Victor helps us in truth and in true-seeing to understand what and who we are—in the face of the world and others, where we show the nature of our relationship with God. In a definition that will become famous, Hugh emphasizes that "discipline [*disciplina*] is *a way of living* [*conversatio*] ... that is committed to appearing irreproachable in everything."[7] We humans do not lie, it would seem, about our relationship with the Other, as long as it is spoken in terms of the sensible. The tongue is always ready to lie and probably never as persuasive as when it is being deceitful but the body does not deceive: it expresses the truth of its being when it neither can nor should conceal itself in appearance: "Whoever loses their spiritual basis slides outwards [*foras*] towards an unsteady agitation [*inconstantiam motionis*]," Hugh warns, "and through their exterior mobility [*exteriori mobilitate*] forestalls sustaining roots in their interior [*indicat quod nulla interius radice subsistat*]."[8] The Victorine makes us see, in a way that is justly famous, the good consequences of going from "interior" to "exterior" [*intus et foris*]. "Making seen" is what helps us understand—precisely that it is our bodies that see, and the symbol, as "the good use of the sensible," will move us above all through a "good usage of ourselves" and indeed of "the other," if we are able, and certain, in "using" it.[9]

§14. The Habit Makes the Monk

Examining the Self and Examining the Other

It was in the canonical period, more precisely in the twelfth century, that the art of the "examination of the conscience" was born or reborn. After having reached its zenith among Stoics and Epicureans, it had been absent, or almost absent, from the ancient monastic rules of the East but regained respectability among the Victorines in an increased emphasis on interiority born of penitential practices as the "rule of life": "By a daily consideration [*quotidiana discussione*] the novice examines before him [*apud semetipsum examinet*] his thoughts, his words as well as his acts … Because experience [*per experientiam*] of what men do makes them more attentive as to what they will have to do subsequently."[10] Coming back to enrich the "book of experience" Hugh adds on self-examination that makes a "re-reading" the site of his interpretation.[11] The quotidian is faced every day and thus becomes the object of examination—as does "quotidian-ness" as such.

But there is more than simple self-examination in the renaissance of the Middle Ages: there is also and above all the examination of the Other. Hugh of Saint-Victor anticipates, or almost anticipates, what will become "style" in Merleau-Ponty's "Synthesis of One's Own Body," and what leads him to say, "everyone recognizes his own silhouette or a filmed version of his own gait," but "we do not recognize our own hand in a photograph."[12] Hugh sees in the "style" described in Ecclesiasticus and applied in *The Training of Novices* the source of one's own relationship with oneself as well as one's relationship with others:

> You can tell [*cognoscitur*] a man by his appearance [*ex visu*],
>> you can tell a thinking man [*cognoscitur sensatus*] by the look on his face [*ab occursu faciei*].
> A man's dress tells you what he does,
>> and a man's walk tells you what he is [*enutiant de illo*].
>
> (JB Si 19:26-27)[13]

In order to be it is sufficient to become visible, and that is the truth of one's relationship with oneself as it is of one's relationship with others. The *symbol* or "good use of the sensible" according to Saint Bonaventure (heir in this respect of Hugh of Saint-Victor)[14] establishes first of all that the sensible is seen. And what is seen of me, as what I see of others, ensures first of all what I am for myself, and what others are for themselves, as they are for me. "What is done outside [*foris*], for good or evil in the eyes of those who witness it, makes obvious the interior quality of the spirit [*interior animi qualitas*]. That is why it is necessary, to calm this confusion, to place against it the discipline that keeps each member to his duty."[15]

There is a risk of falling into crude anachronism in order to make sense of this, but it is nonetheless clear. What makes the "structure of conduct" for the novices of Saint-Victor is not simple "exterior compliance" (behaviorism), nor even their "global form" (Gestalt theory). The significance of gesture, as Maurice Merleau-Ponty shows, is as "signification for a consciousness," mine or that of another. The external [*foris*] certainly speaks of what is internal [*intus*]—something that can easily be understood from simple observation or from globalizing the situation—but this exteriority is directly addressed to an otherness, insofar as the novice monk says *something* to his brother monks and to the master of the novices by disturbing conduct (his laughter, his gait, or his attire). The "discipline" of the life of a canon is a "way of living," or "being in conversation" with the other [*disciplina est conversatio*], as it is defined very precisely by Hugh, in that it "makes appear" [*apperere*] that which the monk is intrinsically for himself and for others, sometimes unbeknownst to himself (in uncontrolled laughter, a red or blushing face, or indeed a staggering gait).[16] Far from sticking to the "teaching material" or "educational and pedagogic process" as we find, for example, concerning the art of reading in the *Didascalicon*, *disciplina* is transformed here into "norms" or "rules of conduct" through which the novice can see something of himself: an art of living described in *The Training of Novices*. There is nothing here of the boarding school—which perhaps goes without saying for the true novitiate. We find simply the mode of being from within [*intus*] which, according to the "symbolic" or the "good use of the sensible," also allows the outside [*foris*] to be seen and shows the abbot what the latest arrival is really like.[17]

The Manner and the Mode

The habit *makes the monk* at Saint-Victor in an unusual sense, in that all that is perceptible exhibits at the same time the mode of being of the consciousness. We need to focus on this, and experience makes it seem glaringly obvious. The "interior control" [*interior custodia*] that keeps "order in the members of the body outside" by virtue of a "bedrock of the spirit within" is not always found in humans and in particular was not always found among the young Victorine monks.[18] Hugh reminds us, as the Wisdom of Solomon also underlines, "[a] scoundrel and a villain goes around with crooked speech, winking the eyes, shuffling the feet, pointing the fingers, with perverted mind devising evil, continually sowing discord" (Prov. 6:12-14 NRSV). Inhabiting our bodies badly leads to wrong-doing or doing evil. And it is not just a question of doing things wrongly: disordered action is most often a sign of intention wrongly oriented.

It is significant in this context to note the *manner* in which the monk is clothed. Life is certainly "more than food" and the body "more than clothing" (Mt. 6:25 NRSV), but the kind, the "genre" of clothing ("more or less valuable"), its quality ("neither too delicate not too soft"), its color ("not too bright or beyond what the rule specifies"), and its form ("decent and in conformity with the religious condition"), all say something about the person who wears it. The habit makes the monk, not in that it is enough to wear chasuble and tonsure to believe one is totally consecrated to God, rather because the choice of exterior [*foris*] clothing always says something about the interior [*intus*], whether or not one has a religious calling. It is the manner [*le mode*] that makes the mode [*la mode*]—reflecting the double sense of the Latin word *modus*—at least in canonical life. But we can all understand this because we have all experienced it. The *quomodo* [in what manner] garments are worn produces its own harmony, more than the *quid* [what they are] or the garments themselves. The Victorine Master appropriately insists that "harmony is related to the way of wearing them" [*coaptation ad modum portandi pertinet*].¹⁹ If there was not strictly speaking a "fashion" in the monastic world, some brothers would nonetheless distinguish themselves by "their fashion" or "their way of wearing" [*modus portandi*], that which should not be a fashionable object. Hugh adds, not without a touch of humor:

> Certain fools who foolishly want to please use little tricks in wearing their clothes. Others with a still greater buffoonery distort their clothes in a ridiculous way; others, to make themselves the subject of conversation, unfold the clothes and spread them out as widely as they can. Others gather them up with little wrinkles: others mess them up in twists and folds. Others wrap them round as tightly as they can, splitting them, exposing the contours of their bodies with shameful indecency, so that spectators can see them in detail. Others, waving their fripperies in the wind, show the superficiality of their minds in restless inconsistency. Others, in walking, sweep the floor with the twists and turns of their long robes, wiping out the trace of their steps by trailing the fringe, or rather, like foxes, with tails that follow behind them.²⁰

We cannot help smiling at this, but in Hugh's eyes it is very serious: because undoubtedly all this is a way of hiding oneself from others. Canonical life, like that of monks, and probably like life in general, is always "Being-with" [*Mitsein*], in order to show oneself, and at the same time "Being-there" [*Dasein*]. The buffoonery is not that of the professional Fool [*le bouffon*] but of a dolt who is unaware of what he is doing [*le sot*]. Knowing what one is doing one can mimic foolishness (the Fool), but if one is unaware one can only show oneself up (the dolt). Self-respect is thus linked to respect for others. Or better, we might say that respect for others says something about oneself: "There are a thousand other ways by which the vainest and the most fatuous of men want to make a spectacle of themselves in the eyes of the other [*spectaculus de se intuentibus prebere*]. But the servant of God will, with great consistency, scorn all that."²¹ Does this mean that the other has nothing to teach me? And in particular nothing to teach me about myself? Or is it that we have to flee the sensible (symbolic theology) in order to take refuge in the nets of the intelligible (speculative theology) or the distance of the ineffable (mystical theology)? Not at all. Or at least not for Hugh of Saint-Victor. The canonical rules are concerned with the exposure of the self to others not with withdrawal. Brother Robert, Canon of Saint-Victor, whose statement of these rules has recently been rediscovered, says precisely, that "in all settings, in all your acts and in what you say, behave with humility, measure and maturity, so that you do nothing that will be offensive in the sight of anyone else [*nihil a te fiat quod cuisquam offendat aspectum*]."²²

The Virtue of Example

In fact one wonders, and quite rightly, why so many precautions, indeed precisions, were included by Brother Hugh in his instructions for novices or beginners in the canonical life. A few general recommendations would surely have been enough to give the gist, as in the Augustinian or Benedictine rules, and not an array of precepts so coordinated that it seems nothing has passed unnoticed But this is because it was not enough, or was no longer enough, just to initiate oneself into the mystical life, in this twelfth-century renaissance. It was up to the monks to imitate the saints—to imitate as when the shape of a stamp or seal is impressed upon some wax. Hugh specifies that "What is embossed, or in relief, in them [*quod in illis eminet*] must be embedded into us [*in nobis introsum recondi debet*]; and what is hollowed out in them [*quod in illis depressum est*], must be made in relief in us [*in nobis est erigiendum*]."[23] We are, then, in a way hollowed out where the saints have their fullness and vice versa. We must learn from them to become what they were, not simply in order to imitate them, but so that in imitating them "the form of resemblance to God that is expressed in them" will also be expressed in us [*similtudinis Dei forma expressa est*].[24] Resembling the saints we can also come to resemble God, insofar as, through imitation, we shall be "configured in the image of that resemblance" [*ad eiusdem similtudinis imaginem nos quoque figuramur*].[25]

It should be apparent that the "art of living" in *De Institutione novitiorum* makes a step further relative to the art of reading in *Didascalicon*. It is not enough, or no longer enough, just to read. Reading must be extended to all those who cannot read so that they can at least decrypt the presence of God in the book of the world (chap. 4). The question is no longer that of reading but of living (chap. 5). Or rather, we might say that if there is already life in a reading or in the hermeneutic of a text, or of the world, what is found in the descriptive or phenomenological experience of the surrounding world as an intersubjective structuring world is an expression that is not just a speaking, but also a seeing. *Disciplinam doce me*—"Teach me your statutes." This verse, taken from Ps. 119:68 [Vg 118:68], which structures the whole of *De Institutione novitiorum*, along with "good sense" and "knowledge," shows that for Hugh neither "knowledge" [*scientiam*] nor good sense [*bonitatem*] on their own is quite enough. The "discipline" teaches through the spoken word [*verbum*], but it teaches also by example [*exemplum*]. *Docere verbo et exemplo*—"teach by spoken word and example": that is probably the origin and the originality of the canonical mode of being in the twelfth century, and it is through this teaching that one's relationship with oneself is at once mediated into a relationship with the other and a relationship with God:

> In every case the novice must consider how much he should show himself full of reverence ... in the service of God [*in Dei servitio*]; how much he should appear spontaneous, joyful, ready to succor the needs of his neighbor [*necessitatibus proximorum*]; how much he must show himself small, modest and not importuning anyone else when he tries to find and accomplish what he needs himself [*in his que ad se pertinet*]. Thus he will always be frugal for himself [*parcus sibi*], available for his neighbor [*proximo promptus*] and devout toward God [*et Deo deotus*].[26]

In the tripartition in *De Institutione novitiorum* of "science" (chaps i–ix), "discipline" (chaps x–xxi), and "good sense" (end of chap. xxi), *example* plays a central role (chap. vii), and constitutes specifically the "book of experience." Thus arises the role and the image of the saints, alone capable of leading us to, and making us into, the image of

God. The *virtue of example* is so significant that the play between the internal and external unity for each of us (the discipline as a visible unity of body and spirit) sends us back at once to the confrontation of two externals (oneself and the other, or the saint). Novices must call upon these models in order to interrogate their own unity between their heart of hearts and their external selves. "Saint Paul says to the Corinthians, 'I appeal to you, then, to be imitators of me [*imitatores mei estote*]' (1 Cor. 4: 16 NRSV), as I am imitator of Christ [*sicut et ego Christi*]." If I imitate Paul, I also imitate Christ. Paul, in the form of prototype, represents and makes Christ (who is to be imitated) if not possible, at least visible. In this *chain of imitations* we find the so-called lost likeness (Gen. 1: 26) and the unity of the internal and external is restored.[27]

The symbol becomes mystical here in that the "use of the sensible" does not simply bring us back to the intelligible; it works in such a way that the manner of being for humankind and for human beings among themselves is through the "style" of God that is to be imitated, according to prototypes that the saints unceasingly give us. The novice or the future monk in his habit will no longer be satisfied, or will not solely be satisfied, with appearance [*apparere*] or the making of the monk by his habit. The monk's gestures and words will also be important indicators of his way of being in the community, in a world that he will make through his body and his speech—so he will not see himself as having suddenly arrived in a monastic world for which he had not been prepared. *Gesture is utterance* [*parole*] for the novice, as for all the brothers in the community, in that his gestures are addressed to others, creating time and space through his own bodiliness. *Utterance is also gesture* for the monk, and even more for the canons (priests), in that the way of speaking in the canonical sphere (in certain circumstances in the cloister, for example) was to give sense, indeed to give a "sound" and a "tone" to the spoken word that was addressed with a precision that has probably never been equaled. According to Brother Hugh it was, then, necessary to recommend to the novice, to the listener, and to the reader that they should here and now have "the mouth closed and the ears open[*os clausum et aures apertas*]" because "the more you hold back in speaking [*quantum estis ad loquendum modestiores*] the more insightful will you be in your understanding [*tantum estote ad intelligendum sagaciores*]."[28]

§15. Gesture as Utterance [*parole*]

From the "way" and the "mode" [§14] we move on then to "gesture" [§15]. What the monk's habit says is what the body expresses—and it makes the "art of living" the site of its visibility. A structure of engagement, or what has been called "metaphysics," was to shape philosophy for a long time: it was based upon consciousness in the body and the body in the world, much as though we were talking of some content held in great containers. But, according to Heidegger's *Being and Time*, "[b]eing-in-the-world" we do not yet know "the world."[29] And as we seek the other through our consciousness it is discovered as originally woven from our own bodies (See Husserl, *Cartesian Meditations*: "Reduction of transcendental experience to the sphere of ownness").[30] It was, however, Hugh of Saint-Victor who, at least in part, discovered this, if not in theory at any rate in practice. *Gesture makes the world* rather than being executed in the world, and *utterance speaks to the body*, rather than conversing between consciousnesses. The gestures of the novice, constitutive of spatiality and temporality, are what make the community: they are not just made in the community. A monk's spoken utterance ensures that he becomes a Brother, not simply a colleague or fellow member. With extraordinary modernity, the body of the canonical community is then seen to make the world worldly, rather than the body being made worldly by the community. The monks' talk engenders fraternity rather than being based upon it. And with this back and forth another way of being in the world speaks to us, where the form (style) of the body betokens a manner of being in the world, and through the way of speaking it is built up in another manner. *Gesture is utterance* in that it speaks through the body what there is in the community: *utterance is gesture* in that it shows by its style or tone what intersubjectivity is. In both cases, and in every case, the symbolic, or the "good use of the sensible," depends precisely upon the way in which one uses the "gestural," as well as the way in which one "speaks" it, telling by this what there is in our common bodiliness and our community.

Definition of the Gesture

There are of course sins of the tongue, as we shall see (§16). But "vices of gesticulation" [*vitia gesticulationum*] are also given to us to see, perhaps even more so, and faced by them it is necessary to impose a "disciplinary measure" [*modus discipline*].[31] It is not new to suggest that the Middle Ages can and should be seen as a "civilization based on gesture."[32] In Jean-Claude Schmitt's work we have a brilliant demonstration that there is a "rationale in gesture" that can be explained in historical terms.[33] But what the philosopher can bring to this discussion today, being guided by what Hugh of Saint-Victor achieves, is the sense that this rationale—of gestures—could metaphysically and almost transcendentally set up the world that it innervates. Merleau-Ponty underlines how "the body is not in space like things: it inhabits space" so that the child holds out her or his hand to grasp an object without looking at the hand.[34] Hugh of Saint-Victor in *The Training of Novices* says, with astonishing modernity, that "gesture is a measure and a positioning of the members of the body for all manner of acting and behaving."[35] In both cases, as always where an objectivizing attitude to the world is suspended, either by phenomenology (Merleau-Ponty) or by mystical theology (Hugh of Saint-Victor), we *set up the world through our bodies* rather being set up by the world. That is, we make space through our fleshly mode of being. Our bodiliness does not just follow a natural attitude that phenomenology and mystical theology have both learned to correct.

"Gesture is a measure and a posing of the members of the body for all ways of acting and behaving [*gestus est modus et figuratio membrorum corporis ad omnem agendi et habendi modum*]."[36] This definition of gesture that we find in Hugh's work is, according to the authority on the rationale of gesture, Jean-Claude Schmitt, "the most complex of all those that we encounter in all western history of the ancient Middle Ages." Moreover, "hardly is it stated than it becomes the canonical definition, reproduced by ecclesiastical authority of the twelfth and thirteenth centuries."[37] It remains for us to interpret what has for the moment simply been formulated.

(a) The mode [*modus*], (b) the figuration [*figuratio*], and (c) the manner of being and acting [*agendi et habendi modum*] constitute thus the three measures of a gesturality that configures the world to the extent that it makes bodiliness the site of a new beingness.

(a) It would be appropriate to agree at least that gesture [*gestus*] is a "measure," since gesture marks out (in a musical sense) our relation to space in travelling through time. All the same *modus* implies more than simply "measure." It refers at the very least to a qualitative manner of being of the gesturing subject. Like "the way to love without measure" (rather than "the measure of life without measure") of Bernard of Clairvaux, that we shall return to later [§26], the *mode of gesture* marks a qualitative difference independently of all quantitative considerations.[38] Gesture is "a mode" in that it identifies "my mode" (of being or acting) in a way that nothing else does in the same way. As further demonstration we can point to the repetition of *modus* in Hugh's definition of gesture which finally takes our gestures as modes, talks of our individual mode of acting [*modus agendi*], and of being in our relation with the world [*habendi*].

(b) As for the "figuration" of gesture [*figuratio*], its setting in motion or kinesthesia is more than simple "posture" (Poirel).[39] It is not a question here of a summary of the "structure of behavior '*comportement*,'" but strictly speaking of an *ethical mode of being* that is at the same time *phenomenological*, this time like a "phenomenology of perception." *Figuratio* is "figuration" not solely in that the gesture "takes on a figure" *in* the world, but in that it "con-figures" *a* world. Thus Husserl emphasizes, as he is relayed to us by Edith Stein, how humankind "figures the world (is figurator)" through our world view [*Weltanschauung*]. We make the world in making worldly the world, precisely by our bodies.[40]

(c) We are not speaking solely here of ways of "acting" and of "behaving" (Poirel), in a kind of behaviorism that would be reductive with regard to Hugh's *De Institutione novitiorum*. The way of being (or *habitus*) and way of acting form in reality two modes of gesture. I stipulate *mode* rather than measure, gestures themselves being divided into "modes" those of the manner of being through their "style" (as in Merleau-Ponty's view, for example), and those of the manner of acting through "praxis" (as we find in Aristotle).[41]

> Humankind moves in the world through gesture, through so many configurating transcendental categories of the world rather than just being immersed in the world. As I see it the definition of gesture might also be translated as follows: "Gesture is a mode [*modus*] and a figuration [*figuration*] of the members of the body in respect to all ways of acting [*agendi*] and of being disposed [*habendi*]." "Mode" rather than "measure" (Poirel) or "movement" (Schmitt): "figuration" rather than "posing" (Poirel), "manner of acting" and of "being disposed" and not "behaving" (Schmitt). Hugh of Saint-Victor in saying what gesture is precisely indicates what it is not and could not be. It is not "some thing" in the world (*quid*); it is the *how* or the *mode* of a being in the world as such (*quo-modo*).

Categories of Gesture

Hugh of Saint-Victor's categories of gesture in *The Training of Novices*, which break new ground and are astonishingly modern as far as kinesthesia is concerned, convincingly verify a transcendental structure of the body that probably only gesturality can perform. If there is an "anthropology of gesture" (Marcel Jousse) whose initiation is flagged in the canonical life in the form of definition and reflection, it exists above all in the *transcendental function of gesture*, through which active bodiliness is able to synthesize a world that is not just a given.[42] The typology takes on a genetic function and cannot be reduced simply to its pedagogical role: "Through his reason man must consider diligently and must discern on his own, as far as he can, what is permissible and what is not, what is appropriate and what is not: in all *acts* [*in omni actu*], in all places [*in omni loco*], at all times [*in omni tempore*], and with regard to all persons [*erga omnem personem*]."[43]

The "categories of gesture" (act, place, time, person) take us on after the definition of gesture (mode, figuration, manner of being, and acting). On the basis of what we do (act), of the location where we move (place), of the "moment" when we do it (time), and of "the one" to whom we address it (person), Hugh of Saint-Victor revisits and transforms the Ciceronian categories of *loquacity* (utterance), to see them differently in terms of *gesturality* (the body). Thus, we newly set up the world, where all the members of the body, or of the community, have as their task and also their vocation, setting up space in the way in which it will be lived.[44]

(a) In every "act" (*in omni actu*), as we have already seen in relation to the monk's "habit" or the "chasuble" (§14), the gesture is a question of taking into consideration the triple relation of the novice "to the service of God" [*in Dei servitio*], to the "needs of his neighbor" [*in necessitatibus proximorum*], and "to himself" [*ad se*]. The novelty here is not simply in the relationship itself but in the *manner* of generating it through bodiliness. The novice *is not* in a relation with God, his neighbor or himself such as would be with two independent poles that are to be connected, but his gesturality as act *makes* the alterity of God and his neighbor, as well as his identity for himself. It is in order that divine mysteries can "be fulfilled" [*impleri*], Hugh insists, that the beginner becomes practiced in prayer or liturgy in his relationship with God. Thus righteousness "is practiced" [*exercere*] in that the novice fulfills his human duties to others, and his use of his body is organized [*ad usum corporis*] so that he gets in touch with himself through his own flesh. God, the other, and the flesh (identical in every way with the trilogy of "*God, the flesh, and the other*") is not just a given but is constituted through the self. "In every act" [*in omni actu*], to "do some thing" [*agendum*] is above all the way of making oneself—as it is in phenomenology for Bergson, and in mystical theology for Péguy, who never sees humankind or the world *ready-made*, but only *becoming*.[45]

(b) Performing a gesture in every "place" [*in omni loco*]—and the transcendental function of the body is only the more clear here—comes back precisely to the *setting up of place*. It is as though the *modus of the gesture* always corresponded with the *topos of the world*. We do not come into the world with our bodies just to make gestures here: we mobilize the body through gestures to make the world here. Thus we find it stated authoritatively in the work of Hugh of Saint-Victor that there is a topology of gestures to which a topology of places closely and immediately corresponds. "Otherwise is the way [*alius est modus*] of standing in a place where one adores God; otherwise [*alius*] is a place where one replenishes the body; otherwise [*alius*] is a place designated for conversation; otherwise [*alius*] is a place where one keeps silent; otherwise [*alius*] after all inside, otherwise [*alius*] outside; otherwise [*alius*] in private, otherwise [*alius*] in public."[46]

What is interesting here, but what we should note in order to understand Hugh's intentions, is that the places in question are not named, or perhaps we could say that they are not named in their alterity (*alius, alius, alius*); they are gesturally different. The church is "to stand where one adores God"; the refectory where "one nourishes the body"; the parlor, being-with others, is "designated for conversation"; the dormitory is where one "keeps silent"; the enclosure is "inside" and the world "outside"; the monk's cell is "in private," and the chapter hall "in public." These are not places [*topoï*] as such, but places are made in that they are acted out. Moreover, if there is a "hall" of "events" or acts (well known because it has been the subject of a long and rather different reflection by Jean-Luc Marion[47]) it is such in that there is "acting out"—of the spoken word naturally— and not simply because it is for the festive gathering together of a community that needs to assemble.

Here symbolic theology is not then, or not only, "the good use of sensible things." It becomes more radical in *making* or *setting up* the sensible. Even more, it makes the world into the sensible, so that there are no things or places beyond what we are dealing with and making into what they are. To demonstrate this, we can point to the kind of confusion of gestures (typology) that is often found in a confusion of places (topology). Hugh warns in *The Training of Novices*: "Nevertheless even what is necessary in public [in the chapter hall] needs to be first of all given a kind of test in private [in the cell or *studium* of the novice master], because if we are careless about it in private, we shall not be able to make use of it in public when necessary."[48] Like the habit that makes the monk [§14] the place thus makes the community [§15], not simply in that the monastery brings the monks together, but in that the brothers in their *way of fraternizing with one another* make a community, defining spaces that start from their own bodiliness. The canonical community represents the body of Christ (1 Cor. 12), consequently its members are made capable of gesturing it, indeed of choreographing it.

(c) After the space or topos of gesture follows then its "temporality" or its chronos: "*quid in omni tempore agendum*—what to do at all times."[49] Hugh could not doubt, given his epoch, that there was a time to work and a time to take a rest since the division of the days made the day of rest on the Sabbath the sign and significance of our sometimes-dramatic busyness. We read in *De Institutione novitiorum* that "the feast days require also another kind of diligence [*aliud studium*] and another type of life [*aliud conversationis*], different from the days when it is permitted to work." The rotation of day and night, or indeed of the working days and the Sunday rest, tells us more than a simple division of days. If we set up a space through our gestures (the church in praying there, the refectory in eating there, the parlor in conversation, the dormitory in sleeping there etc.), we also set up, and just as effectually, a time. Gesturality generates temporality, just as it gave birth to spatiality. Hugh recommends to novices that "at night [*in nocte*] the men must be by themselves [*secum*] and must rebuild their tired limbs through sleep ... In the day on the other hand [*in die*] emerging from their privacy [*de secreto suo*], they assemble and show themselves so as to be seen [*coeunt et ad invicem videndos se*] and to be like one another [*et imitandos ostendunt*]."[50] All this is clear and speaks for itself. The temporality of the gesture is what constitutes alterity, and the changeover from day to night sets up relationships in the community. The Victorines, as we have seen, started as a canonical order, living in the cloister but not closed off. It was, then, appropriate at Saint-Victor to "show oneself" [*ostendunt*], precisely "to be seen" [*se vivendos*], or to "be like" one another [*imitandos*]. In giving and receiving from one another [*dare et accipere alterutrum*], obviously in instances of good works, phenomenality was what guided the opening of the day.[51] The time of day, constituted through gestures of imitation, made meaning of their expression which was also a showing forth. Withdrawal on the other hand would inhabit and nourish the nocturnal rhythm. The night took place removed and holding one withdrawn from the community. One did not seek then to imitate or be like the others, but just to sleep to rest oneself. The body that rests is also a body that is exposed and was definitely not to perform a gesturality that would have been inappropriate in terms of its temporality. "It is necessary to respect the time [*discretio temporum*] as far as good works are concerned. Because, in the same way that evil work is never laudable at any moment, good works are, in a certain way, judged as reprehensible if they are not done at the right time [*si tempore opportuno factum non est*]."[52]

(d) We come then, to conclude this account, to the fourth modality of the constitutive gesture, to alterity. "*Quid erga omnem personam agendum*—what to do toward every person."[53] What is at stake here is not thought but "affection" for "those who are for loving" [*ad dilectionem*] because love above all offers signs rather than dry concepts. Necessary tokens of respect in fact make us see love. Without them there is no proof of love, as it remains hidden. "Respect without love is somewhat servile [*reverentia sine amore magis servilis est*], and love without respect should be judged trifling [*et amor sine reverentia puerilis iudicari debet*]."[54] But it is above all in the modality of the gesture that love appears such as it really is, that is to say as something directed. There is no need to speak to express oneself. We all know this, not just through having made ourselves understood through gesture when in foreign countries, but also in that a "look that kills" can say more than many "wounding words." Bodiliness or the phenomenological descriptivity of our ways of being through our bodies (chap. 5) overrides here the linguistic sphere or the hermeneutic analysis of the way we speak (chap. 4). Moreover, and we shall return to this later, the spoken itself is a "gesture" [*gestus*] as far as Hugh is concerned, in that it comes through integrating "sense," "sound," and "tone." The "ways of moving" [gestures *ad extra*] are also so many ways of "making seen" [what is lived *ad intra*]: softness in lasciviousness, brazenness in pride; slackness in negligence and indolence in laziness; restlessness in impatience and precipitation in inconstancy.[55] The body speaks, and it speaks to us. It sends to the other a message of alterity that always has to be deciphered: Jean-Claude Schmitt, commenting on Hugh of Saint-Victor, underlines that "gesture is always perceived by someone. It is 'the gaze of the other' (whoever he is) that so to speak makes it exist."[56]

We may then well ask, if gesture creates spatiality as well as temporality, and indeed also otherness, what about the "members of the body" [*membrorum corporis*] through which these aspects are figured or configured [*figuratio*]? Here it is the face and its distortions that show us what a well ordered, or badly ordered, corporality is.

From the Face to the Republic of the Body

It is important, according to Hugh of Saint-Victor, to teach the novice that he possesses in himself a "mirror of discipline" because in seeing he is seen, or rather, he sees that we can see that which he himself, on his own, does not see. The definition of the "face" [*facies*] as the "mirror of discipline [*discipline speculum*] toward which one must be all the more attentive because the smallest fault cannot be hidden there" serves exactly as a guide to a life that would be shown without veil or lies.[57] Before and after taking our nourishment, Hugh insists, by way of example, "the face [*facies*] should not be the same: Before it is rather 'happy' about the idea of eating, and afterwards rather 'reserved' so as not to become overheated."[58] As Levinas will say later on, the face here "is not seen." Or rather it is "meaning" and "meaning without context."[59] What is seen of the face is not its figure as such, and is very unlike the figuration that, as we have already seen, sets up the world. The face is the unseen, as it were a back view rather than the figure since it very often signifies precisely what the novice does not wish to show and allows that to be seen in an uncontrolled gesturality:

> Some close one eye and open the other when they look at something, aping I know not what model; others, even more ridiculous, speak with one half of their mouths; furthermore there are thousands of grimaces, thousands of affectations and quivering of the nostrils, thousands of pouts and distortions of the lips that distort the beauty of the face [*quae pulchritudinem faciei deformant*] and the decorum of the discipline [*et decorum discipline*].[60]

We can understand then that because the face "shows" that which the novice does not always want to show, and shows it unbeknownst to the one showing it, it sometimes approaches "monstrousness"—showing [*monstrare*], exactly what monstrousness tries not to show [Fr. *montrer*].

The "vices of gesticulation" [*vitia gesticulationis*] stated above then define a veritable teratology [study of malformations] of the gesture, such that "all exterior and dishonest movements of our bodies [*omnis exterioris hominis inhonesta figuratio*] lead always to the corruption of the inner spirit [*ab interiori mentis corruptione manaret*]."[61] In this "lived unity" of the soul and body, in which the mystic intimacy of the *intus* and *foris* can rival that of the metaphysical scheme of hylomorphism,[62] rests the true sense of the human body, in its justice and harmony. Hugh says, following Plato and many others, that "the human body is like a republic [*quasi quaedam respublica corpus humanum*]." But he makes the "public thing," or the *respublica* the body of God, indeed our own bodies, rather than the city. In a way Hugh "incorporates" the city, so far as to make the canonical community, and individual bodiliness itself, a site of great openness. The justice of this is evident, and he manages to take up the Platonic *dikê* (*Republic* Book 4, 432b-449a) just as much as Pauline harmony (1 Cor. 12:12-31). His point is that "every member [of the body] has its own office [or functions] [*in quo singulis membris sua officia distributa sunt*]." The foot no longer says, "Because I am not a hand, I do not belong to the body." The eye cannot say to the hand, "I have no need of you"; nor again the head to the feet, "I have no need of you" (I Cor. 12:15-21 NRSV). It is the totality of the body, not in terms of behavior (behaviorism) nor in a global manner (Gestalt theory), but simply in a signifying intention of the flesh, as we have seen already in the definition of gesture, that makes meaning so that it can be directed at both the other and the world.

The message is then clear because it is figured; that is, it gives figure in taking on figure. The office of the body of the novice, as also the bodies of sages in the past, according to Hugh, is that of representing (figuring) the order wished by God in the use of individual members that will also come to represent the community [*respublica*]: "Let the eyes see [*oculi videant*], let the ears hear [*aures audiant*], let the nose smell [*nares olfaciant*], let the mouth speak [*os loquator*] etc."[63] Here, where it might seem that thought is taken up with trivial matters, it shows in reality its most extensive exemplarity. Because, whatever one might say, the body of the novice, like that of all of us, can quite often make every effort to be dysfunctional without his being aware of what is taking place. While it would be appropriate in the eyes of the Victorine to "laugh without showing the teeth, to see without staring, to speak without brandishing the hands or pointing the fingers, without twisting the lip, without nodding the head, without raising the eyebrows, to walk without swaying the hips, without waving the arms, without rolling the shoulders etc.,"[64] what we frequently see is:

> Certain people who do not know how to listen without their mouths open, and opening their buccal cavities to the speaker ...; others who, when they listen, stick out their tongues like thirsty dogs, and at each action, twist their lips as though they were grinding a mill; others who, when they speak point their finger and raise their eyebrows ...; others who nod their heads ...; others who, as if both ears were not made to listen, just offer the one.[65]

The "republic of the body" [*respublica corpus humanum*] can thus lose the sense of its publicness once it forgets that it is being looked at. The look, or gaze, at the other, which is at the heart of the canonical community, does not protect the subject from shame (Sartre). On the contrary, it shows the subject's distinctive identity (Levinas).[66]

In doing that, however, it points up the subject's alterity in an almost disembodied face, but it takes total charge of the subject's own bodiliness. Interchange between the Saying and the Said, in a language act that lacks bodiliness, is not sufficient to reveal the subject to himself.[67] Only gesturality, as Hugh sees it, marks and individualizes a subject's style. The other, through his look, shows me what I am through my body, and teaches it to me, sometimes despite myself.[68]

A connection with the sensible in the symbolic cannot be avoided and must also be regarded as mediated: by God certainly but also by humankind and the world. The "monstrous body" [*monstrum corporis*], in that it is not satisfied with its own "republic," shows precisely that it is making shown to us what should never have been shown. And at the same time it allows a "teratology" (or study of abnormal physiological development) to be made through noticing its uncontrolled gestures:

> Some in walking throw their arms like flippers, and like some double monster [*duplici quodam monstro*], at the same time use their feet. They walk down here on the earth, and with their arms fly up above in the air. Tell me, I pray you, what is this monster [*quod est, queso, monstrum hoc*] that in himself imitates at once the gait of a man, the oars of a boat and the flight of a bird?[69]

Without identifying a listener here, or indeed a reader or an author who could feel targeted, it is the *body* in its "ways of being" or in its "gestures" that takes over from the "appearance" of the monk's habit, which, as we have already seen [§14], is sometimes sufficient to make the monk. Merleau-Ponty suggests at the heart of *Phenomenology of Perception*, coming strangely close to Hugh of Saint-Victor, that "just as speech [*parole*] does not merely signify through words, but also through accent, tone, gestures, and facial expressions … supplemental sense reveals not so much the thoughts of the speaker, but rather the source of his thoughts and his fundamental manner of being."[70] All the same, one does not cease to speak in the works of Hugh of Saint-Victor or in phenomenology as written by Merleau-Ponty. The "pure, and so to speak, still dumb—psychological experience"[71] merits passing on, not only in language acts (the hermeneutic of the text) but also through life or voice, where it is incarnate (hermeneutic of imitation). Gesture as utterance (see definition and categories of gesture: §15) operates upon utterance itself as gesture (see definition and categories of utterance: §16) and makes of the spoken itself a mode of bodiliness.

§16. Utterance [*parole*] as Gesture

Along with the definitions of "gesture" in *De Institutione novitiorum* (chap. 12) we find that of the utterance or the spoken [*loquere*]: *de disciplina in locutione servanda et primo quid loquendum*: "concerning the discipline to keep in utterance, and what should one say?" (chap. 13). Along with the categories of gesturality that set up spatiality as well as temporality or indeed alterity (chaps 1–5), we find as it were an echo, authoritatively analyzed, of the categories of utterance that go to make up our own truth (chaps 13–18). The extraordinary construction of this treatise must be apparent to anyone who wishes to analyze it from a metaphysical standpoint. Pedagogy is not in question here, and even less a discourse or method for the use of instructors in need of concepts. What is at stake is *phenomenology* and also *theology*. The "republic of the body" awaits its manner of speaking, as flesh without words would never be capable of full signification. The symbolic as a "good use of the sensible" [§14] must then *also* work by verbalization, not against bodiliness but exactly on the basis of bodiliness, and certainly in its most exemplary mode.

Definition of Utterance

As far as definition of utterance, or the spoken, is concerned, there is no short statement that can sum it up. The reason behind gesture (as in Jean-Claude Schmitt's *La raison des gestes*), echoes to a certain extent the sins of the tongue (as in Carla Casagrande and Silvana Vecchio's *Les Péchés de la langue*[72]), where the circumstances of utterance [*circumstantiae loquendi*] are finely analyzed. But there is a wide gap between the two. Where the Ciceronian "circumstances" remained rhetorical, they become metaphysical in the works of Hugh. Utterance is elevated to a "discipline" [*disciplina*], not simply to be controlled, but also becoming matter that can be questioned conceptually—giving a double sense to *disciplina*: "Concerning the discipline to be kept in utterance [*de disciplina in locutione servanda*]." According to Carla Casagrande and Silvana Vecchio there is a decisive turning point here: "Up to this time, the schema of the circumstance had been used in the formal and empty structure of the list ... For Hugh of Saint-Victor the schema becomes discipline, the *disciplina in locutione*, a distinct collection of rules to follow, an integral part of the general discipline with regard to behavior."[73] What makes it, as I see it, the turning point of "the discipline to be kept in utterance" is not simply the way it is laid out or even its orientation toward discipline in a collection of practical rules for life. At stake in reality is the metaphysical and is the possibility of expanding upon a mode of "utterance" which is not disconnected this time from "bodiliness." In asking "what to say" [*quid loquendum*] (chap. 13), "who to speak to" [*cui loquendum*] (chap. 14), "where to speak" [*ubi loquendum*] (chap. 15), "when to be silent and when to speak" [*quando tacendum et quando loquendum*] (chap. 16), and "how to speak" [*quomodo loquendum*], Hugh of Saint-Victor fails to mention the first and most obvious question: "who speaks" [*quis loquendum*]? But what is omitted leads us in reality to a precise definition of utterance. "Who speaks?" is not asked because the "speaker," whether he is a novice or simply a Victorine monk, is always *already-there* in the community in the mode of being of his speech (in a certain part of the cloister or sometimes in the refectory according to the Victorine rule), and he should never retreat into a self-sufficiency that turns aside from utterance that has been addressed to him.

The speaking subject is not discharged from the act of utterance; he is convoked to it. But this subject, who should present himself first of all in the nominative case [*quis*]—which precisely explains the absence of his being named—finds himself first of all responding, before speaking, to the accusative case [*quid*], to the dative [*cui*], and to the ablative [*ubi, quando, quomodo*], rather than to the nominative. The heroism of the subject would be shown if a novice who was a "good speaker" started to declaim or boast, when it would have been more appropriate for him to stick to being spoken to rather than speaking, to listening rather than being heard. Here we can pick up well-known linguistic categories (Saussure) and say that the mode of "enunciation" of the "utterance" [*parole*] takes precedence over the statement or what is enunciated. Or again, we could say that the mode of being of the person to whom [*cui*] one says something takes precedence over what [*quid*] one says. Hugh of Saint-Victor notes that "in everything we wish to say [*omnino quicquid dicere*] we derive above all the quality of what we say from the one to whom we say it. [*volumus cui dicendum ex ipsa prius nostri sermonis qualitate colligamus*]."[74] If there is then a definition of "speaking" in Hugh's work, it holds above all that the speaking subject, even more than the gesturing subject, always directly envisages the addressee in addressing him. And the modalities of the spoken which are appropriate (where, when, how) demand precisely the hyperpresence of the other, rather than the other's absence.

But there is more, and as I see it even better, in this implied definition of the spoken by Hugh, in that it fully rejoins gesture and the symbolic world as good uses of the sensible. Hugh insists: "The quality of a discourse, that is to say, the manner of speaking [*qualitas, id est modus loquendi*] derives from three points, namely: gesture [*gestu*], tone [*sono*] and meaning [*significatione*]."[75] True utterance is not simply saying the truth (matching the *quis* with the *quid*) but saying it in a "true manner" (matching the *quis* with the *quomodo*)—as with God, who is, according to Anselm "so truly true" that he "is manifest" (Chap. 2: "The Theophanic Argument"). Gesture, tone, and meaning of the utterance go to make up its import, as we recall all the more because that was what Merleau-Ponty repeatedly stated. Moreover, it is not simply because we think that we speak: it is because we speak that we think. The utterance does not precede gesture in a false sequence going from thought to speech and then from speech to action. Utterance itself is a gesture so that in speaking we paradoxically learn to think and thus also to act. Merleau-Ponty writes, in a passage that shows how we can find traces of the Victorine in phenomenology: "The orator does not think prior to speaking, nor even while speaking: his speech *is* his thought."[76]

We learn from the Letter of James, astutely cited by Hugh of Saint-Victor, that the tongue is like "bits in the mouths of horses to make them obey us" or like "a very small rudder" that can steer ships no matter how large they are. It is "a small member, yet it boasts of great exploits" (Jas 3:3-5 NRSV). But if one should control the tongue, that does not mean clamping down upon it or indeed suppressing it. Certainly, Hugh emphasizes, speaking at a time when one should not, or must not, speak is just gossiping [*per licentiam*]. At the same time, it is possible through carelessness [*per negligentiam*] that one might "not speak at a time when one could or should speak." It is appropriate certainly to know when to keep quiet, as it is to learn when to dare to speak, and this is especially important for novices, to whom the recommendation is addressed. Hugh then adds to the categories of gesture (what, where, when, to whom [chaps 1–4]), those of speaking (what, to whom, when, where, how [chaps 13–16]) so that what corresponds to the transcendental setting up of space and time by the body (the *corpus* as *exemplum*) is the establishment of the other and the world through utterance (the *verbum* as *actum*).

Categories of Utterance

(a) To resolve problems concerning speaking it was necessary first of all to ask "what to say?" [*quid loquendum*]. Paradoxically what is useful and harmful in what one speaks—because "For me everything is permissible but not everything is helpful" (1 Cor. 6:12 RNJB)—depends less on what is stated (the enunciated) than on the way it is spoken (enunciation). But the Spoken and the modes complement, or complexify, one another. The Spoken speaks not simply of the person "who" speaks [*per quas*], or "to whom" one speaks [*ad quas*], but also and above all "of which" [*de quibus*] one speaks. The third party in the Spoken makes the meaning of what is said. One knows this from experience, maybe without admitting it to oneself, and that is what Hugh wants to communicate to the beginner. One should be careful not to "speak ill" or "denigrate" those who are not present, in that it is only their physical absence that allows us to use a language mode about their presence abusively. "These three kinds of speech, that is to say the harmful, the dishonest and the useless, respond to ... the quality of the people who speak [*qualitatem personarum per quas*], to whom they speak [*vel ad ques*] and *of whom* [*de quibus*] they speak."[77]

(b) The addressee "to whom one speaks" [*cui loquendum*] is thus designated as having a regular role in every act of speech. One did not speak first of all to oneself, or to God, in a canonical order which allowed one to speak in certain places (in the scriptorium, or in some part of the cloister with the master of the novices, for example[78]), but one spoke to the other whom it was necessary to address purposefully. Hugh notes that "after having chosen what to say [*quid dicat*], one should check carefully the person to whom one speaks [*cui dicat*]," because Ecclesiasticus tells us that "anyone who addresses speech to someone who does not listen is like someone who wakes a man plunged into a deep sleep" (see Sir. 22:14).[79] The criterion for speaking does include "vain curiosity"—of which Hugh is always suspicious. In this respect, as we shall see [§25], he looks forward to the attentiveness of his contemporary, the Cistercian abbot, Bernard of Clairvaux. It is only the prospect of "edifying" that makes speech fecund: "When we speak for our own edification [*cum propter nostram edificationem loquimur*] we are speaking with those whose teaching can carry us toward righteousness. But when we speak in order to edify our neighbor [*cum autem propter edificationem proximi loquimur*], we are speaking with those who we hope can be corrected of their vices through our exhortation."[80]

(c) The place, or the places, "where to speak" [*ubi loquendum*] (chap. 15) reflect then and add to the places "where [and through which] to act" [*quid in omni loco agendum*] (chap. 3). The setting up of the place by speech corresponds to the setting up of place by gesture: "The 'silence' of the dormitory or of the abbey Church; the 'disputing' in the school in the cloister; the 'conviviality' of the canonical cloister." Casagrande and Vecchio point out that to the "hierarchy of words there corresponds here a hierarchy of places."[81] This is not to say that the places where they should remain silent were more highly valued than the places where they could speak, but that "through the spoken" the conviviality of the community was formed, just as "through gesture" its spatiality and temporality were constituted.

(d) There is a question about "When to keep silent and when to speak?" [*quando tacendum et quando loquendum*]. What is original here is probably the *loquere*. Because if one did not speak just "anywhere" [*ubi*] among the Victorines, nor did one speak at "any time" [*quando*]. The times are distinguished, as in Ecclesiastes: "A time to keep silence, a time for speaking" (Eccl. 3:7 NRSV). It was important that both beginners and all the brothers should be careful. The time for speaking was not one for an unceasing flow of utterance, coming from a novice who might be frustrated because he had so few occasions to express himself. "It is never the time to say everything" [*quando omnia numquam*], Hugh warns with authority, because it is important to learn that whole of Speaking could not take place in the necessarily limited time of the Spoken. Rather than a muteness that silences utterance when it wants expression, and finds itself restrained, true speaking is born in reality from a basis of silence, which the novice must learn. Hugh places this at the heart of certain formulations, the contemporaneity of which could put our best linguists to shame: "It is through silence while keeping quiet that one learns what one will then express through utterance at the moment of speaking ... It is first of all in silence [*prius in silentio*] that the utterance takes shape [*forma loquendi sumitur*]."[82] The "hospitality of silence" is the basis of speaking, and we might recall here the very appropriate formula of Jean-Louis Chrétien in *The Ark of Speech* that is strangely close to the most profound of the Victorine secrets, when he says that far from denying utterance, silence is its source.[83]

(e) How then to speak [*quomodo loquendum sit*]? Because it is no longer enough just to speak. It is necessary to act, or rather to "gesture" that which "speaking" wishes to say, and our most profound unity stems from that. No longer is there gesture on the one hand with its own categories (chaps 1–4) and utterance on the other with its own paradigms (chaps 13–16). There is now the "gesture of utterance" which itself marks out a "style," its particular fleshly way of being, and a most certain way of being listened to (chap. 17): "The discipline demands that, as far as the one who speaks is concerned [*ut loquentis*], gestures should be humble and measured [*gestus modestus et humilis*], the tone moderate and melodious [*sonus demissus et suavis*], the meaning of the speech true and gentle [*significatio verax et dulcis*]."[84] Such are the characteristics that define the modalities of the spoken, in the strictest sense, in the eyes of Hugh of Saint-Victor, since the spoken is embodied.

We should recall that the "gesture" was defined as a mode "and a figuration, or posing, of the members of the body for all ways of acting [*agendi*] and behaving [*habendi*]," and "discipline" was seen "connecting the members of the body with the outside [*liganda sunt foris membra corporis*], so that inside [*intresecus*] they will be consolidated upon a firm spiritual basis [*ut intresecus solidetur status mentis*]."[85] When the spoken becomes gesture it has recourse to the bodily: when it is connected with the discipline it speaks also of the unity of the bodily and the spiritual. The novice speaking with a "measured gesture" should then avoid, according to the Victorine Master, "haphazard movements of the arms, brazen and violent, so that he does not disrupt the calm of his discourse by blinking his eyes or with an inappropriate facial look."[86] With his "moderated tone" he will strive also "not to frighten or to offend for no reason his listeners in storming or throwing tantrums with an intemperate voice."[87] And, finally, in taking care about "meaning," that is to say "what the discourse signifies" [*id est sententia sermonis*], "he must be true, because false speech, even when spoken with art and eloquence, is nonetheless judged to be either harmful or idle by the listener who has understood it."[88] We need to be careful here: it is not a question of making simple recommendations, as if there were method and training (pedagogy), so that the spoken could deceive or indeed mislead (rhetoric). Utterance is not sufficient on its own, to be able to plead a cause. It needs the body to embody it, even simply to express it. Accompanied by "gestures" it is also in its own right "gesturality," and Hugh underlines this, borrowing what is almost a "walking" metaphor from the Book of Proverbs: "Unreliable as a lame man's legs: so is a proverb in the mouth of fools" (Prov. 26:7 JB).

The Voice

It is important, according to a wordplay in French, to speak for the flesh (*chair*) when one speaks from the pulpit (*chaire*). As we have seen already (§12) utterance (*parole*) without voice remains always mute, and that is why it needs to be embodied:

> The Word of God clothed in human flesh [*humana carne vestitum*] appeared only once in visible form [*semel visibile apparuit*], and now, every day [*quotidie*] this same Word comes to us under the cover of a human voice [*humana voce conditum*] … In a certain way the voice of the Word [*vox Verbi*] is to be understood at the present time [*hic*] as the flesh of God [*caro Dei*] was then [*ibi*].[89]

This is so original in Hugh of Saint-Victor's work that it deserves much further development. Paradoxically we recognize the Word today through its "voice" [*vox*], as the Apostles in their day recognized it through its "flesh" [*caro*]. That is not to say that we can see it. The apostolic era is definitively closed and completed, but we can and must try to understand it, and utterance on its own cannot satisfy us. Because the "book of Scripture" [*liber scripturae*] becomes the "book of the world" [*liber mundi*] when the hermeneutic of the text catches up with the hermeneutic of contingency and utterance becomes body in gesture to the point of recognizing the "style" of He who is incarnate there. The parable reminds us:

> He who enters through the gate is the shepherd of the flock; to him the gatekeeper opens the gate, the sheep hear his voice, he calls his own sheep by name and leads them out. When he has brought out all his sheep, he goes ahead of them, and the sheep follow because they know his voice. They will never follow a stranger, but will run away from him because they do not recognize the voice of strangers. (Jn 10:3-5 RNJB)

Voice [*vox*] must be identified and listened to; it expresses "discipline" in the relation between master and his disciple or novice, more than just utterance (*parole*) because the spoken is made bodily through it and recognized through it. The voice is the phenomenon of the "actually present now" for those who hear it, and we could add to this, as Derrida points out, that "the phenomenon of the voice, the phenomenological voice, is *given*."[90] It speaks the Being-there of one whom I hear without necessarily seeing him—whether he is hidden or linked with it in some other way. Hearing it then in the kind of understanding that makes our community, we find together in voice the very heart of symbolism, precisely where utterance and gesture come together to be unified—providing, as Paul Claudel suggests, a *book of images* where "what is seen" is also "what is heard," where "*the eye listens*."[91] Alain of Lille, a generation after Hugh, in his "*Omnis mundi creatura*," tells us that all the creatures of the world are like a book, or an *image*, and serve us as a *mirror*. They are *faithful* symbols of our lives, our death, our condition, and our destiny.[92]

Everything about the "body" is thus given in *De Institutione novitiorum* clarified "phenomenologically" in light of the modes of being or the kinesthesia of the body (chap. 5: To Live One's Body). A comparison can be made with how all the "world" is deciphered in the *Didascalicon*, where the "hermeneutic" could achieve so much, given what it can draw upon (chap 4: God as an "Open Book"). After St. Anselm and "experience in thought" in the theophanic argument (Part 1), Hugh of Saint-Victor in "experience of the world" (Part 2) does not simply mark out a further stage in *The Book of Experience*. He is strictly speaking at the heart, or at the center of the book, even if experience "as such" is not fully conceptualized until Bernard of Clairvaux brings in "experience in affect" (Part 3).

But we cannot pass as smoothly as all that from the Victorines to the Cistercians. *En route* to the experience of the world we meet the "other." Not simply the other of humankind (Origen), or the angelic other (Thomas Aquinas), or the singular other (Duns Scotus), as I have discussed them in *God, the Flesh, and the Other*,[93] but the other of God—in the Trinity. If we learn that the world is a text "to be read," and that the body, like utterance, is "to be expressed," it is still necessary to establish what is the key to our reading as well as to exposition and expression "*in*" *God himself*. Because if the act of "loving," as I have tried to show and explain (part 2: Reading to Love), brings together the act of "reading" and that of "experience" ("Read, therefore, and love; and what you read on account of love, read it so that you might love"[94]), it is still necessary to show how this so-called love is special and original in Christianity. Richard of Saint-Victor, more of a theologian than his brother Hugh the philosopher, takes up the baton here, rooting all love in a "Third Party" who forbids a shutting up in the reciprocity of the act of giving—a reciprocity that, as we have already seen (Chapter 3), is nonetheless necessary. And this we find in exemplary fashion represented by the perichoresis—that is, the relationship—between the three persons of the Trinity.

6

The Third Party of Love

The Necessary Third Party

As far as the *relation to the world* is concerned I have been opening a "horizon" that helps us to "read" or indeed decipher—leading from the *Didascalicon* of Hugh of Saint-Victor to *The Conflict of Interpretations* of Paul Ricoeur (chap. 4). As far as *relation to the body* is concerned, where we link up with an other in our "mode of expression," we have been moving from the *De institutione novitiorum* [*The Training of Novices*] of Hugh of Saint-Victor to *The Phenomenology of Perception* of Maurice Merleau-Ponty (chap. 5). But—"in the relationship with another I am always in relation with the third party"[1]—and we move from the *Treatise on the Trinity* of Richard of Saint-Victor to *Totality and Infinity* by Emmanuel Levinas (chap. 6). This last formula from the phenomenologist, enigmatic to say the least, puts forward the "three" as a condition for the "two." If donation, as we have seen, could not, according to Anselm, be so simply abstracted from exchange in the context of satisfaction, it is precisely because (and we follow Levinas here), "to make possible a dis-interested responsibility for another [that] excludes reciprocity ... a third party is necessary."[2] The necessity of a third party, in the form of an investigation (analysis and query), becomes the driving force because, as I have previously suggested (chap. 3), neither the "non-reciprocity" of the gift nor its "pure abstraction" is sufficient. The "debt for the gift" for Anselm (chap. 3) is found thus as the "third, loved person" in Richard of Saint-Victor's work (chap. 6). If that is not an answer to the problem of debt, it is at least a full liberation—understood here as an insertion and a transformation *in God himself*.

The *condilectio*, or shared "love for the third" in Richard of Saint-Victor's *De Trinitate* [*On the Trinity*], exhibits precisely this possibility, unique in its genre, of inscribing *in the Trinity* a form of remedy for sin, as it were an "anti-jealousy" in God. The Son, in fact, to follow the Hymn to Christ in the Letter to the Philippians, "did not count equality with God/ something to be grasped [*arpagmon*]" (Phil. 2:6 RNJB). Richard of Saint-Victor writes that what is true of kenosis or incarnation is true also of the Trinity itself. It is not that the Father, the Son, and the Holy Spirit are not "equal," far from it, but that the love of one for the other (the Father, for example, loving the Holy Spirit) does not impede love of the *third* (the Father also loving the Son, while neither the Son nor the Holy Spirit is "jealous" or "rivals" with regard to the love of the Father for the other). What is lived *in God*—a love for the loved other that is equal, indeed greater than, the love one receives oneself (con-dilection)—says nothing about and indeed is not lived, or is hardly ever lived, by humankind. One rarely finds children who are *absolutely not jealous* among themselves of their parents, or indeed children who desire that the love of their mother or their father for a sibling exceeds, indeed overflows, that by which they themselves are loved. But "things that are impossible by human resources, are possible for God" (Lk. 18:27 RNJB). Richard of Saint-Victor says in his *De Trinitate* that "we rightly speak of co-love [condilection] when a third [person] is loved by the two, in harmony and with a communitarian spirit." And "it is clear that not even divinity [*in ipsa divinatate*] would have *co-love* if only two persons were present and a third one [*tertia*] was missing."[3]

It would be easy enough to move directly to Richard among the Victorines, and to his "epitome of love," but to grasp his concept of the "third" is not so simple, and it cannot be fully understood without first undertaking a detour. Summarizing the "scholastic" point of view (Bonaventure and Thomas Aquinas) in the pages that follow is not a way of abandoning the "field of monastic experience" (Anselm, Hugh, and Richard of Saint-Victor; Aelred of Rievaulx and Bernard of Clairvaux): far from it. Counterpoints are sometimes necessary but not in order to reject them: nothing would be more absurd, as I see it, than to oppose the "monastic" (mystical theology) to the "scholastic" (pedagogical theology). My aim is rather to show through what they clarify retrospectively how their originality is deployed. With Richard of Saint-Victor (Chapter 6) and his brother theologian, Hugh of Saint-Victor (Chapters 4–5), we find a specific "canonical lineage" which is displayed here, allowing us to see to what degree the "book of experience" from the Middle Ages is one that we can still "revisit" today. If we cannot share it, then at least we shall not be ignorant of what was done in the past. Hans-Georg Gadamer, on the subject of his master and friend Martin Heidegger, wrote: "His progress through the history of philosophy was very like that of a *water-diviner*. Suddenly his diving rod stops: he has found it."[4]

§ 17. The Blind Alleys of Love, or the Limits of "Two"[5]

What seems clear in theology is not necessarily clear in the context of phenomenology. Thus we might consider the importance and emergence of the Third Party in the Trinity which, opening up the relationship of the "two" (Father and Son) to a "third" (the Holy Spirit), forbids any reduction of the relationship to a kind of duel ("between two"). A *theological* reading of this opening "to the third party" will point to structural identity, but that is very different from the philosophical exposition of alterity in Edmund Husserl's famous fifth *Cartesian Meditation* (1929). According to the founder of phenomenology there is no intersubjectivity without a "community of monads," such that an "analogue" is always necessary to establish a bridge between oneself and another, engaged in the same world. *I* do not simply know the other because *I* know him and *he* knows me, but in that *we* share a *common world*, a location of the one and the other in our recognition of humanity.[6] We could put this up against the theological tradition of the Trinity, in particular as developed by Anselm and Thomas Aquinas, where the philosophical questioning of the Third Party shows first of all *negatively* that, in order to constitute a Third Party in the loving divine community, it is not enough (a) to love oneself, (b) to love the self of the other, or (c) to love one's self in the other.[7]

Necessity and Insufficiency of the Love of the Self

All theologians, including those who would tend to privilege the love of the self over love of the other, agree that it is not enough for the divine persons to love themselves in order to justify God as three in one. Anselm insists in his *Monologion* that "the Father loves Himself [*se amat*], the Son loves Himself [*se amat*], and the Father and the Son love each other [*et alter alterum amat*]." And "since what loves and is loved is wholly the same for the Father and for the Son, it is necessarily the case that each loves Himself and the other in equal degree."[8] Love of the self, or reflexive love [*dilectio reflexa*], certainly necessary in itself, is necessarily accompanied by mutual love, or connective love, at least in the unity of a common love. The metaphysical setting up of an alterity identified as such makes the act of loving more than a simple ethical wish for love. One can certainly wish that we love one another, such that the other returns the love that one has for her or him. But in that case one still remains in the mode of an ethical reciprocity that neglects the metaphysical necessity of establishing the loved other as such—that is to say as "another than myself" [*ego alter*] and not simply as "another myself" [*alter ego*]. All true "declarations of love" always address an injunction "to someone" [*alicui*], in which the wish for *reciprocity* between recipient and donor does not await a reply in order to be formulated. Thomas Aquinas, in the *Summa Theologica*, talking of God's love, but by analogy also of human love, says, "To love anything is nothing else than to will good to that thing [*nihil aliud sit quam velle bonum alicui*]."[9]

If, then, at least two are necessary for love, whether it is a question of humankind or God, one's love is directed "to" or "for" another in the dative case, and not simply for the sake of the other in the ablative, or "because the other is" that other, in the accusative. Love is a "propensity toward" that is sufficient to itself but in the act of loving justifies opening up toward a third, at least so as not to be locked into the duality of a mutual love. Reflective love of oneself [*dilectio reflexa*] and connective love of the other for me and from me to the other [*dilectio connexiva*]—to take up and develop the categories formulated by Richard of Saint-Victor [§18]—seem thus to demand, speaking both theologically and philosophically, a "charitable love of a third" [*dilectio caritativa*] that alone would make sense of the expansion of love. Thus, we encounter the question of the Third Party. Can and should the "procession of the third" free itself from the simple mutuality of the relationship between the first and the second? Or, to put it another way: Can we suggest, following Anselm, complete identity between the "same love" [*omnino idipsum*] of Father and Son so that it constitutes the communality of their love as such, in the Holy Spirit?

To Love Love: Or Love of the Other in Itself

The question here is significant in that it opens up not simply an examination of the Trinity but also of alterity—in that the "third" appears precisely, and paradoxically, as the transcendental condition for the constitution of the "two." Everything comes in threes—or as the French saying has it, *there is never two without three*. And this is because the "two" itself always opens up toward a third. That is how the Trinity is, according to Anselm, where the identity of love of the self and love of the other makes up the trinitarian community of the third (the Holy Spirit seen as the act of loving one another with the same love). It is the same in the constitution of alterity for Husserl (all things being equal), where only the prospect of a "communal world" [*Vergemeinschaft*] can open up space for a meeting of the *ego* and *alter ego*, by virtue of which they are not driven into total alienation of one from the other.[10]

However, viewing the other in humankind (as Husserl does), like viewing the other in God (as Anselm does), comes down solely to "loving the other in oneself" *on the basis* of oneself—what Jean-Luc Marion condemns as "amorous autism."[11] It reduces the other to the lived experience of one's own consciousness (Husserl) or suggests that what the Father and the Son love, in love, is just the love of their own selves and their identical nature through the love of the other (Anselm). And it is always—for humanity as for the divine—*one's own* love that one loves: "I see not her [the other] but the sum of lived experiences, for which she [the other] is only the accidental cause and of which my consciousness is the real measure."[12] The loving subject and the subject's love of self are set up thus as an exclusive norm for all love, and this is in proportion to the subject's unique capacity for love:

> How great, then, is the Supreme Spirit's love—[a love] so mutual [*sic communis*] to the Father and the Son? If the Supreme Spirit loves itself to the extent that it remembers and understands itself, and if it remembers and understands itself in proportion to its essence ... then surely the Supreme Spirit's love [*amor eius*] is as great as this Spirit itself [*ipse*].[13]

Love of oneself—or rather of the self—loved in God is thus, according to Anselm, the sole norm of all love. Love "so mutual" [*sic communis*] of the lover and the loved finds its rationale in the capacity of the self to reflect upon itself and its own love [*amor eius*]. As we shall see later, following Thomas Aquinas, the Father and the Son love one another not through a common *attraction* toward an other or a third (the Holy Spirit) but solely, and primarily, through the *recognition* of their essence in common. The other is thus always reduced *to the same*, in the double sense of identity and of the banality of repetition, above all in only loving the other in oneself.[14] Neither in phenomenology (at least since Levinas), nor in trinitarian theology (substantiated by Richard of Saint-Victor, as I hope to show), can or should the other fall within the sphere of the same—that is to say it will never leave the sphere of "two," always reduced to a "one," because it is not thought of transcendentally on the basis of a "third." Thus we find a problem, seemingly paradoxical but nonetheless pertinent: if the difficulty in *escaping from the same* brings us back theologically to thinking of the sameness of a "same love" as *love of the other in herself or himself*, through loving a love that is "the same in every way" [*omnino idipsum*], is it enough *to love oneself in the other*, rather than to love the other in oneself? Should one favor the reflected image of "one's own love in the other," rather than the image of "the other enclosed in oneself"? The question of "consideration of the two" comes up before that of the "establishment of the three," starting this time from *the other*, as though an ancillary love (of the "two") must always, and falsely, precede charitable love (of the "three").

To Love Somebody or the Love of the Self in the Other

Before getting to Richard of Saint-Victor, and in order to pursue the detour that takes us toward "condilection" (co-love), or love of *the third*, we should note that neither for Thomas Aquinas nor for Anselm would it be enough to love love in loving oneself first of all, and then loving the other, in order to make up a community of intra-divine love. Love is always addressed in reality *to someone* (*alicui*), and nobody loves in this sense truly as long as, in a purely anonymous way, she or he only loves love—particularly when that love is in the form of a pure will ingesting its object in only loving herself or himself. Far from being an appropriation of the other in the self, then, divine love truly represents a priority for Thomas Aquinas: "The relation of the Father to the Son [*habitudo Patris ad Filium*], and conversely … that of the lover toward the beloved [*ut amantis ad amatum*]."[15] It would in this sense certainly be a mistake because of a rather arbitrary separation between the "static character of the peripatetic metaphysic" and the "dynamic character of the pseudo-Dionysian metaphysic" (see Théodore de Regnon),[16] to pass over the truly "ecstatic" dimension of the reciprocal love between the Father and Son in the Holy Spirit in the school of Aquinas. In this sense, there is no "two without three" for Aquinas, any more than there is for Anselm or Richard of Saint-Victor, even if the three will be constituted through a propensity to love by the first (Aquinas), through community of the same love for the second (Anselm), and through the non-competitiveness between the self and the other for the third (Richard of Saint-Victor).

This ecstasy [or *rapture*], opening up as a matter of principle toward the Third Party, has its wings clipped, however, by Aquinas, who deliberately dismisses any *conceptual* reciprocity between Father and Son of the *essential* love of the self which is always its basis: "The Father loves not only the Son [*non solum Filium*], but also Himself [*sed etiam se*] and us [*et nos*], by the Holy Spirit."[17] While Aquinas follows Bonaventure (and Pseudo-Dionysius the Areopagite) in identifying an ecstatic love of the Father and the Son, which as we shall see later can only lead to a Third Party, his gesture nonetheless always brings us back to the Anselmian gesture (the "same love"), the movement of ecstasy in the identification of the divine *persons* prioritizing love in their *essence*. To put it another way, and without agonizing here over the transfer of certain philosophical categories into theological style, we might say that the *autism* of love by which *I only love the other in myself* (Anselm) follows on from a certain auto-idolatry in which *I only love myself in the other* (Aquinas).[18] While the Father *essentially* loves the Son first of all through the Holy Spirit [*Pater et Filius se Spiritu Sancto*], he also loves himself, as we have seen (since loving is directed to someone [*alicui*], and not simply a matter of loving the identity and community of love [Anselm]). But he only loves the Son insofar as he first of all reflects upon his own essence [*essentia sua*] in the beloved: "If 'to love' … is taken essentially, it means that the Father and the Son love each other not by the Holy Ghost, but by their essence [*se essentia sua*]."[19] Because the "loved is said to be in the lover; as also the thing understood is in the one who understands [*amatum dicitur esse in amante sicut et intellectum in intelligente*]."[20] Love [*amor*] certainly points to the Holy Spirit but solely in that the two persons—the Father and the Son—recognize one another and love one another in him. The gift [*donum*] is the site of community of their love, as "the reason of donation being gratuitous is love [*ratio autem gratuitae donationis est amor*]," but the gift does not produce love.[21] The one and the other (the Father and the Son) love the one and the other in the other (the Father in the Son and the Son in the Father), simply in that they recognize the communality of their love, not because the Holy Spirit constitutes a veritable Third Party to love. The rapturous (ecstatic) love of "charitable dilection" (toward the "third") remains within the circularity of the connected dilection (of the "two"), always brought back to the power of the Aristotelian ontology of instinctive dilection (love of "oneself" or the principle of self-sufficiency).

Neither pure love of oneself (Aristotle), nor love of the other in oneself (Anselm), nor love of oneself in the other (Aquinas): none of these three modes of loving are able, at least from a trinitarian viewpoint, to constitute true access to a divine circumcession [reciprocal existence in each of the three persons] opening up onto a Third Party. The "three" of the Holy Spirit seems always to be superimposed on the "two" of the Father and Son, as though in order to "be two" it was really necessary to "be three," in order that the "relationship between the two" would be enough to set up a "third," independently of whether the third was lovable or to be loved. Making the Holy Spirit *someone* [*alicui*] "to whom" love is directed is not simply a question of loving oneself in the Holy Spirit, or loving the Holy Spirit in the love and with the love with which the "two," the Father and the Son, love. It is also above all letting the Holy Spirit be a "self as another" (Ricoeur), that is to say as someone [*quis*] who receives their own identity, albeit that of God, but who does not exist without the "me" of the Father and the Son, which finds "in the Holy Spirit" the true reason to love.

The phenomenological schema and the Judaic heritage of the Third Party in love (God himself), which both explain the reciprocity of loving (humankind as "brothers") [Levinas], find thus in Christianity a motif entrenched *in* God himself (the Third Party inscribed even in the structure of God: the Trinity) [my perspective]. As far as Richard of Saint-Victor and St. Bonaventure are concerned, in the "book of experience" or the "challenge of love" (as we shall see), it is not a question any more of seeing God "loving" (immanent trinity) or "loving us" (economic trinity). In the Christian system the Third Party of humankind is nothing other than the Third Party of the Holy Spirit that today gives us life. A philosophical query concerning the Third Party, as we have seen it at the start of this chapter, finds its most advanced conceptualization in theological consideration of the Trinity, precisely in that the "brother as third party," unlike the Jewish face-to-face of *Illeity* [Levinas], is never superimposed upon the "two" of humankind and God—and even less on the three of the Trinity (Father, Son, Holy Spirit). The relationship of human to human, and of God with his third *ad extra*, as we shall see at the close of this chapter, "is incorporated" in the relations of Father, Son, and Holy Spirit insofar as we are ourselves included in the second *ad intra* (the Son in whom we are contained (Col. 1:16-18). The Third Party of Love *in* God has priority in this sense over the Third Party of God's love, in that God does not simply love humankind in Christianity but loves Himself "as an other" in loving the human in Himself.[22]

§18. Condilection or the Third Party in Love

What needs to be said then, and to be accepted despite a certain psychologism, whose limitations will also need to be shown, is that at least if we think *positively* of the Holy Spirit as a co-Beloved [*condilectus*] of the Father and the Son (Richard of Saint-Victor), or perhaps better as the act of their "Love in common" (Bonaventure), the reflective pattern of trinitarian relationships does not leave reflective dilection (of "oneself") or connective dilection (of "two") in order to go toward charitable dilection (of a "third"). And phenomenological description, if it accepts drawing upon Christianity, will still not consider a true Third Party–that is to say, according to the traditional legal definition, not just a third person ("*tierce*") added on to a contract, but a third party ("*tiers*") brought into an affair in order to resolve it.[23] *Dilection* thus becomes *condilection* once the Third Party finally takes its place in the act of "loving in common" [*cum diligere*] of trinitarian theology; it awaits, however, the Holy Spirit as "friend" (Richard of Saint-Victor) becoming the "will to love" (Bonaventure).

Sharing with a Third Party

Condilectio, a neologism created by Richard of Saint-Victor, originally denoted a joy for God but also implicitly the extreme difficulty for humans to *share with a third* the mutual love that two enjoy for one another:

> When one feels love for someone else and he is alone in loving another, single one, he certainly has love [*dilectio*] ... We rightly speak of *co-love* [*condilectio*] when a third (person) is loved by the two, in harmony [*concorditer diligitur*] and with a communitarian spirit [*socialiter amatur*]. (We rightly speak of *co-love*) when the two (persons') affects are fused so as to become only one, because of the third flame of love.[24]

True love in God is no longer here pure love of the self (Aristotle), nor love of the self in the other (Anselm), nor a love of the other in the self (Aquinas); on the contrary it is an intersection of aims of love of the self and love of the other, such that their *sharing with a third* becomes an index of their common abundance. A thisness (*haeccity*) or a distinctive character of divine love in the divine persons, just as in human love and its need for alterity, is thus spelled out all the more in trinitarian theology because the Father and the Son, in the boundless rapture of their glory, put all their weight [*kabôd*] behind this sharing with a third.

Curiously, and probably in a paradigmatic fashion for the one who is the trinitarian Third Party in the condilection, the two who love one another (Father and Son) are no longer satisfied with "the crossing of two invisible gazes."[25] On the contrary, they share their love of lover and beloved, in accepting to expose the love of the friend who is co-loved [*cum-dilectus*] (the Holy Spirit) to their mutual play of gazes and counter-gazes in loving one another. Far from taking refuge in the exclusiveness of an *invisible* love that is visible only to the "two," the Father and Son make their *visible display* to a third (the Holy Spirit) the site and guarantee of their true love. God, according to an account that is at once Victorine and Franciscan, is "visibility," wonder in the world (Hugh of Saint-Victor), and proximity in the flesh (Bonaventure). God is all this, rather than, as I see it, invisibility, distance, and the consequence of glory in his reign, which is how he appears according to the pseudo-dionysian tendency (Pseudo-Dionysius the Areopagite). We not only love one another in Christianity; we love so that the love of the self (reflective dilection), as well as the love of the one for the other, and of the other for one (connective dilection), is entirely offered and returned through the love of a Third Party (charitable love). Only the sharing of love with a *third beloved* definitively removes all assumptions of egoism, either human or divine. The simple face-to-face of lovers, with their counter-intentionality, invisible to a Third Party, would not be enough to undo their heroicity. Using Martin Buber's term, and applying it to the Holy Spirit, we could say that what answers to the I-Thou of the Father and Son, or the simple inter-relation of lovers, is an *Us* of the Holy Spirit. This alone can provide a basis and can break through into a reciprocity with a third that is still and always contained within God himself.[26]

The Anthropomorphism in Question

We need to take care, however, not to jump too quickly from human love to divine love, in particular when we consider the "friend in common" and thus the status of the "third" [*tertius*] in the "harmony of condilection" (Richard of Saint-Victor). A caution against anthropomorphism is necessary (a) from the point of view of categories of humankind applied to God and (b) from the point of view of categories of God applied to humankind.

(a) First of all, as far as *categories of humankind applied to God* are concerned, St. Augustine, for example, quite rightly rejects a familial metaphor when speaking of the Trinity: "We speak of the Holy Spirit of the Father; but, on the other hand, we do not speak of the Father of the Holy Spirit, lest the Holy Spirit should be understood to be his Son. So we also speak of the Holy Spirit of the Son; but we do not speak of the Son of the Holy Spirit, lest the Holy Spirit should be understood to be his Father."[27] To put this in terms that we are concerned with here, we could say that the identification of the Third Party with a child, and the Son or the Holy Spirit with that Third Party, would make the Holy Spirit on the one hand something it is not (because it coexists through all eternity with the Father and the Son), and on the other hand, it would make Father and Son into spouses (which they are not) because language itself, and experience, would distinguish a father and mother on one side and a father and son on the other. The metaphor of the family applied directly to the trinitarian schema thus leads to incestuous aberrations (the Father and Son giving birth to the Holy Spirit) which are unworthy of a true consideration of the Third Party. It remains, however, and St Augustine also underlines this, that we need to speak of the Trinity "not that it might be spoken, but that it might not be left unspoken."[28] We can accept then, along with Richard of Saint-Victor, that one can speak with a certain exaggeration of Love or of the Holy Spirit as the fruit of divine nuptials [*amor*], as long as we recognize that a human child [*prolem*] is only beloved of her or his parents [*amatus*], and as long as we do not identify this love with what will be in the third person of the Trinity.[29]

(b) From the point of view of categories of God transferred to humankind, the application of the trinitarian condilectio that is divine love to a supposed human tri-unity of love could also evidently lead to disastrous consequences. It is not obvious how a "third," with her or his own visibility, could "play" a role in the display of love of "two," when they have their own specific visibility, without shading into a kind of pornography. We might recall in this context the gaze of a third party in Sartre's account of shame. As opposed to the situation in Sartre's *Huis Clos* [*No Exit*], it is particularly appropriate for Christian love to be exposed to God, even more than to other people. As far as the gift of the body is concerned, the visibility of lovers is in fact to Him who made his own body the key site of a loving donation: *accepite, hoc est corpus meum*—"Take; this is my body" (Mk 14:22). The Third Party of love in the human eros is not satisfied by an exclusive relation with the divine agape. The Christian quality of love awaits the specificity of the second [*agapê*] that it transforms so as to give meaning to the first [*eros*]. The conjugal Third Party that *is God* in the sacrament of marriage is so for all eternity and thus translates the fidelity of the vow into a "fidelity of the body" that spoken words alone would not be sufficient to guarantee. As when the Father and Son are exposed to the Holy Spirit in their mutual love, "we rightly speak of co-love [condilection] when a third [person] is loved by the two, in harmony and with a communitarian spirit."[30] The common friend [*cum-dilegere*] to whom man and woman expose themselves in their bodily fidelity amounts to God himself, incorporated in his incarnation, and not to some other pornographic witness of what really only belongs to the lovers in their intimacy. Nothing of what belongs to humankind is immaterial to God. And if one truly recognizes that God is made human one will accept in this sense that the "metamorphosis of the *eros* by the *agapê*" gives meaning to condilection. Condilection is not simply in God in an interrelationship in the Trinity (of the Third Party of the Holy Spirit); it is also for humankind in our relationship with God (the Third Party of God, and in particular the incarnate Son, as Third Party of their love exposed bodily).[31]

The accusation of anthropomorphism, so often brought up in relation to the theological trinity, finds its true rejoinder once one dares, to a certain degree, to think of God by starting off from human experience and transferring as a consequence to humankind what truly belongs to God. If the figure of "the child" [*prolem*], in going from human to God, is not appropriate as a way of speaking about the Holy Spirit as Third Party in relation to the Father and the Son, we can retain all the same "with a certain exaggeration" the idea of the nuptials or the fecundity of God. And if there is never a "two without three" even in God himself, as Richard of Saint-Victor suggests (condilection), it is difficult to see why, or how, humankind could be satisfied with the invisibility of the "two" without proposing visibility of a third (God incorporated in humankind). Boethius, in his treatise on the Trinity, says, "When these categories are applied to God they change their meaning entirely."[32] Might we not say then that they belong properly in this sense to the God of Christians? And is that not even more so when they are translated in a Victorine or Franciscan *experience* of being, and in the good sense of the term *anthropomorphized*, signifying through the trinitarian decision a Christ, alone among all the gods, truly in "human form" (Phil. 2:7)?

Nothing, in reality, would cut short the false accusations of anthropomorphism if the much-maligned argument of love shared with a "third" [*condilectio*], in humankind as in God, did not clarify from top to bottom a truth that is above all biblical before being theological or philosophical. The "book of experience" is an "experience of the book" that *is* God himself, here the Trinity, in whom we are "read" at the same time as "incorporated." We need certainly to leave *our* book (our world, our lives, our nuptials) in order to read the book of God (the Trinity and the mystery of the perichoresis [relationship of the three persons of the Trinity] or circumcession). But that we are included and incorporated in the book of God does not prevent us from reading *first of all* our own book *with God* and *in God*. At the end of our reading, as in each line of our existence, *our* pages will not in reality take on meaning unless they are inserted into *God's* work (in the double sense of "God's work"). God does not simply make us into a "library": on the contrary we await how God will convert *our* lives to *his* life and make of our "vellum," or our "volumes," the leaves of a true "book of life" [*liber vitae*]. "Another book was opened, the book of life. And the dead were judged according to their works, as recorded in the books (Rev. 20:12 NRSV).

The Anti-jealousy of God

According to Richard of Saint-Victor's formula, as we have seen, there is no co-love, or condilection, except "when a third [person] is loved by the two, in harmony and with a communitarian spirit."[33] And, "[f]rom this it is clear that not even divinity would have co-love if only two persons were present and a third one were missing."[34] In other words, the "three" are not simply derivative from the "two," as in the love of their own selves in Anselm (pp. 115–7) or the outpouring of the self in the knowledge of the other in Aquinas (pp. 117–8). The Third Party explains the "two" of Richard of Saint-Victor. Without the Third Party there is no "never two without three," at least "in the divinity itself." The structure of the divine requires the Third Party *in it* so that "nothing is lacking in it"—which is how in Christianity we have moved on from the face-to-face of humankind and God (Judaism), in order to think of the Third Party as the being itself of God, to integrate humankind into this "tri-unity." The justification for this is not simply logical or analytical, so that it is a great mistake as I see it to reduce the question of the Third Party to a simple problem of linguistic structure. The meaning of the Trinitarian Third Party is existential, theological, and at the same time phenomenological. Richard's teacher Hugh, as we know (chaps. 4–5), warned against all the dialecticians who, as we find in our contemporaries, could reduce the problem of the Trinity to a simple question of compatibility however scholarly it might seem to be: "Every day people [dialecticians] ask themselves what they should say and very rarely what they should do. They ask if such and such an expression is good, if it is acceptable, it if needs to be developed … They want to secure judgement, but they refuse the spirit, without which they cannot judge correctly."[35] The Third Party is not simply a question of numbers however important they are. It is a matter of life, and belongs to the Life, so much does the being itself of God depend upon in its structure, as well as in its union with humankind. Condilection, or the love of the Third Party in love, constitutes the being itself of God in that, this time, it inscribes *in God* the remedy for sin, which can certainly affect humankind, and could even affect God himself, in the ordeal he faced of temptation.

In fact, and below or beyond moralizing speculation, the prison of sin in Genesis derives entirely, and from the start, from the *jealousy* of the serpent: "I want to be God because God is defined as he who does not wish that I would be like him … It is a question then of *taking the place* of God after he has declared that he wants to occupy it on his own."[36] Because human sin can be defined as an incapacity, or perhaps a refusal, to share love with a Third Party, never mind if that Third Party is God himself, perfect charity *in* God (charitable dilection and not simply reflective or connective dilection) demands, by contrast, that "an *other* should be involved in the dilection that is being witnessed [*exhibitae sibi dilectionis consortem requirit*]" even in the structure itself— that is to say, the Holy Spirit. The Trinitarian God accepting and also desiring the Third Party thus *contains in the depths of its nature the antidote for the poison of sin*. In other words, its nature contains the sharing of love with a third as opposed to the rivalry of jealousy. Jealousy would occur when one of the parties tries to keep everything for themselves. It is greater and more difficult to wish that the being one loves supremely, and by whom one is supremely loved, loves as *an other* [*alium*] with an equal love, Richard states, than it is simply to love "he whom I love" because "I am loved by him."[37]

It is easy for us to love in a reflexive or connective dilection (to love each other, to love, and to be loved), but difficult or indeed impossible to show love in a charitable dilection (to love that the other should be loved as such, indeed more than we ourselves are loved.) And because of this God has placed the Third Party of the Holy Spirit at the heart of his structure, in the form of a remedy for sin, in that the Son "did not cling" jealously for himself "to his equality with God" (Phil. 2:6 JB) in his kenosis, and neither did he keep for himself the love of the Father, but loved that the Father loved as much, or more, the Holy Spirit. Thus he gave back the beloved Holy Spirit at the moment of committing his own exhausted spirit: "And when Jesus had cried out in a loud voice, he said, 'Father *into your hands I commit my spirit*.' With the words he breathed his last" (Lk. 23:46 JB).

The supreme greatness of the reciprocal love of the Father and the Son in their common donation to the Holy Spirit comes back then to God, according to Richard of Saint-Victor, not simply recognizing or suffering [*pati*] their community in love but also to accepting it [*suscipere*] or even desiring it [*ex desiderio requirere*]. We do not suffer from the Third Party in Christianity, we receive, and we share; indeed we require it for our own good. And it is the same, in an exemplary fashion, for Christ at Gethsemane, when keeping nothing for himself; he gives in the act of donation, an "aban-don," which designates specifically the other name of the Holy Spirit. If "the ability of accepting this [sharing]" of love is a great thing, Richard concludes, "accepting it, will be an even greater merit," and "the greatest thing of all will be to seek this [kind of sharing of love] specifically."[38]

There is still, however, the "friend" [*condilectus*]—because the Third Party thus objectivized, albeit with the desire of loving it, could become completely reified. To accept that the other should be so much loved, indeed more than we ourselves are loved, is to leave the other in an exteriority that the divine Trinity could never accept. The community of love, required by Anselm (the love of the other in oneself as love with the same love), and by Aquinas (love of oneself in the other through recognition or essential identification with the loved being), awaits being set into motion, or *perichoresis* [*peri-choreô*], when a loved Third Party (the Holy Spirit in the immanent Trinity) will correspond to the Third Party in the act of loving (the donation of God to humankind in the economic Trinity). The Third Party *in* love (Richard of Saint-Victor) becomes the Third Party *of* love (Bonaventure), once the fontal plenitude of the Father flows into his Son, in whom we are also contained, and from whom, with the Father, we receive the Holy Spirit. In this sense, but solely in this sense, the Third Party is theologically sufficient and complete, prohibiting any opening or diversion for the Trinity toward some kind of "quaternity," which might lead to a drift into an infinite series (condemned at the Fourth Council of the Lateran, 1215).

§19. The Act of Loving Together or the Third Party of Love

Co-well-Beloving or the Act of Loving in Common

To go from Richard of Saint-Victor (the love of the third—*condilectio*) to Bonaventure (the co-beloved—*condilectus*) is not to point to something lacking, or even less to an ineffectiveness, of the one as opposed to the other: far from it. On the contrary, taking this route, one sees how much the Victorine master was able to enrich thought in this field. *Experience* in the Middle Ages, as we have seen from the start of this book (§3), is not simply a question of living but also of conceptualizing—and then indeed of making from this conceptualization a mode of life. Just as the "world written by the finger of God [*liber est scriptus digito Dei*]" and the "three ways of seeing [*triplicem oculum*]" of Hugh of Saint-Victor were to be so fruitful in Bonaventure's thoughts on the "book of the world [*liber mundi*]," or on the divisions of theology (symbolic, illuminative and mystical) [§13], so "condilection" from Richard of Saint-Victor, like the "Third Party *in* love" [§19], was to lead Bonaventure to the act of "loving together," as "Third Party *of* love" [§20]. From the Victorines to the Franciscans there is an effective sequence. And we have sometimes lost a sense of the unity of the "book of experience" because we have forgotten what came to link them together.

It is thus hasty and wrong-headed to suggest that "it is just this notion of the co-beloved that Bonaventure would reject"[39]—as though the affective theology of the Franciscan could disregard Richard's concept of the Third Party necessary in love.

Even the expression "*ami commun*" [co-beloved] used in French translations of Richard is an attempt to transcribe his "*condilectus*," which is found several times in Bonaventure's work.[40] The reluctance to make this link is justified to some extent because Bonaventure's *condilectus* probably points less than Richard's to the beloved, or the one who is loved in common [*condilectus*], than to the *act* of loving in common of the Father and Son—their "co-Well-Beloving" (to infinity) or "loving-the-other-together" [*cum-diligere*]. *Condilectio* in Bonaventure's view is not envisaged independently of *diffusio* [the self-diffusive good of the Father]. The act of loving the third (the Holy Spirit) does not take place without a flowing from the source [*fontalité*] from the first (the Father), to the vessel of the second (the Son): "Unless [the loved and beloved] were present, there would not be the highest good here."[41] As opposed to the reduction of the love of the "third" to the love of love of the self in the other (Anselm), or the love of the other as someone in themselves in the notional community of the same love (Aquinas), Bonaventure replies not simply that the Third Party or "co-beloved" is a mode of love between the first and the second that is open to a third (Richard) but points to a way in which the third "stems from," or "arises from," the first two—in other words the theological doctrine of "spiration." In order that the Third Party should be *transcendentally* there from the start, along with two others (which simply defines the uncreated structure of the Trinity), it is necessary that it issues from the first two in the sense that they would be nothing independently of this spiration, which gives them breath, as it were their own respiration: "The Trinity is like a movement of the mouth [*oris mutatio*] where the Father is the mouth [*os*] from which issues the Son or the Word [*verbum*] and the Holy Spirit or the breath [*spiritus*]."[42]

Because the Trinity is then a movement or perichoresis of the three persons, in Bonaventure's view, the "three" of the "Holy Spirit" is not *added* to the "one" of the Father, and the "two" of the Son but entails transcendentally the open movement of the three of the Trinity. Bonaventure writes of the "conditions of pure love [*amor purus*]," a term that he attributes to Richard of Saint-Victor. "These 'conditions' do not represent a mode of loving with respect to love [*non dicunt modum amandi circa amorem*] but point to a mode emanating from or originating relative to persons [*sed dicunt modum emanandi sive originis circa personas*]."[43] In other words, according to Bonaventure, the Seraphic Doctor of the Church, there is no "two without three," not simply in that the "three" unites the "two," as we find in Anselm or Aquinas, or that it adds on to the "two" as in Richard, but because there are "two" in the movement of the "three." A "two without three" does not add "three" to "two" but makes inversely for their separation because it is solely in being "with three," or "insofar as three," that they are two. Bonaventure concludes in the *Breviloquium*: "He supremely communicates himself by eternally possessing One who is beloved [*dilectum*] and One who is Mutual Love [*condilectum*], so that He is both one and Trine [*Deum unum et trinum*]."[44]

As opposed to the double illusion of a substantifying which precedes the relationship or the individuality as condition of community, the Third Party or co-Beloved [*condilectum*] remains always there, transcendentally "with" the Father and Son. This is similar to the way that, in Heidegger's phenomenological terms, as we have already seen in relation to Hugh of Saint-Victor [§14], Being-with [*Mitsein*] others, "we do not mean everyone else but me … but those among whom one is too."[45] In other words, being in-common is at the heart of the human community (as in a divine community), not first of all in the sense that the community belongs to the beings who compose it, as one of their properties, but rather insofar as the community, and only the community, constitutes their specific mode of being. In phenomenology it is a question, as Jean-Luc Nancy suggests, of "the community of being" and not the "being of the community"[46]—just as it is, as I see it, in trinitarian theology.

The Impossible Quaternity

There is still a possible objection, however, that pushes the "Ricardian condilection" to its limits. If the Third Party of love (the Holy Spirit) also precedes transcendentally the two who love (Father and Son), as the transcendental condition of their act of loving, what is there in this of the act of loving for humankind? And what is the possibility, or the lack of a possibility, of becoming integrated in such love? If the "three" are the condition for the "two" not simply in their "mutual love" (Richard) but also in the act of "loving as co-well-beloved" (Bonaventure), why not go further to "four" and add on humankind to this Trinity, making up a new and original "quaternity"?

The suggestion is certainly tempting, and it was even purposefully proposed by Joachim of Fiore at the turn of the twelfth century but energetically disputed by Bonaventure. Joachim's famous theory of three ages in fact adds the Son to the Father, then the Holy Spirit to the Father and Son: "The age of the Father, from Abraham to John the Baptist; the age of the Son, from John the Baptist to today (end of the twelfth century); and the age of the Holy Spirit from today (1207 according to the Franciscan followers of Joachim) to the second coming on this earth."[47] The "two" (the Son) comes then from a "one" (the Father), and the "three" (the Holy Spirit) from a "one" and a "two" (the Father and the Son). To go on to suggest that a "four" is added on to the "three," not in order to make a new "age of humankind"—something that the Franciscan Joachim never maintained—but to make of the human a "new person," who is "superposed" as "fourth" on the three "divine persons" of the Trinity, seems to be only taking a further step. In other words, we could ask if the addition of "four" to "three" would not conclude the idea of a Third Party insufficient in itself. Because the Third Party *in* love—immanent Trinity: Father, Son and Holy Spirit—does not seem to make sense of the Third Party *of* love—the Economic Trinity. Why not add humankind to God?

But that is a leap into the unknown that, quite justifiably, Christian theology has always refused to envisage. It has been too attached to the Third Party of the Trinity to add on a fourth for humanity. Even if it is only *philosophically speaking* that the thought of the Third Party suggests adding a "quaternity" to the "trinity," such a suggestion implies that one has understood nothing about the Trinity. Just as, in the French language, "*second*" [used when there are only two objects in question] is not the same as "*deuxième*" [used to indicate the second when there are three or more], so the "Third Party" is not just the same as "third": it brings to a close enumeration of the "three." There is no "two without three" in Trinitarian theology, as we have seen, because the Third Party in love (the Holy Spirit) firmly ends the movement of the trinitarian circumcession. But neither is there "three with four," in the sense of the Holy

Spirit as a third waiting for a fourth—humankind. The profession of faith of the fourth Lateran Council (1215), directed explicitly at Joachim de Fiore, states: "There is only a Trinity, not a quaternity, since each of the three persons is that reality—that is to say substance, essence or divine nature."[48] We might say that to add a "four" of humankind to the "three" of the Trinity would be to make humans members of that substance that is God's self, which would be a radical denial of our state as creatures.

The Trinity of the Incorporation of Humankind in God

Is all this then to say that it is necessary to reject definitively the "four"—or rather that the Third Party *of* love according to Richard of Saint-Victor (humankind as an integral part of the trinity; the economic trinity) has nothing to do with the Third Party *in* love according to Bonaventure (the unity of the Father, Son and Holy Spirit: the immanent trinity)? Bonaventure provides the solution here, not in opposition to Richard, who had the great merit of inventing a concept ("condilection," or the love of the third), but to avoid *scholastically* speaking, drifting off into discussions where humankind no longer holds an appropriate place. Rejecting consideration of "two without three" is not to forget the "four"; on the contrary it is to integrate the "four" (humankind) in the "two" (the Son), in what he receives from the "first" (the Father), and in how he participates in the movement together along with the "third" (the Holy Spirit). "All things have been created through him and for him. He himself is before all things, and in him all things hold together" (Col. 1:16-16 NRSV). What does this mean if not that we are *in the Word for all eternity* and that we await nothing other from incorporation *in* the "two" (the Son) than to be received *with him* in the donation of the "one" (the Father)? We await participating all together in the movement of charitable dilection of the "three" (the Holy Spirit). The Father does not solely give the Holy Spirit to the world; he gives himself to himself in giving himself to the Son, in whom the world, and we ourselves, are always beforehand contained. Bonaventure outlines in a masterly way, taking to its limits the argument that I have called theophanic rather than ontological (chap. 2) how

> [t]his diffusion [*Diffusio*] is pushed to such a degree that the one who produces [*ut det producens*] gives all that he can [*quidquid potest*]. And the creature [*creatura*] cannot receive all that God can give … It is thus necessary that this diffusion according to all its power is *in someone* [*in aliquo*], who could not be thought any greater [*quo maius cogitari non potest*] …—in the Son [*in Filio*] whose production is in the Father [*sicut in Patre*].[49]

In this sense, and in this sense only, the Third Party is paradoxically never more open than when it is closed in upon itself and never as much an integrator as when it accepts a "terminal" movement. The Third Party is not the "three" because of that closure which makes monadology the very structure of God. Theology itself teaches us this in its trinitarian deployment, and philosophy would benefit also from taking on, at least in order to think through its essentials (anxiety, birth, love, death, etc.) that only the Trinity is capable of metamorphizing. As Hans Urs von Balthasar underlines, discussing Bonaventure, what "is said with a view to the creation, nevertheless … is true first of all in the inner life of God."⁵⁰

*

The triple act of "reading" (chap. 6), of "living" (chap. 7), and of "loving" (chap. 8), according to Hugh and Richard of Saint-Victor (part 2), thus takes over from the "coming of God to mind" (chap. 1), and the "theophanic argument" (chap. 2), as well as the "debt for the gift" (chap. 3) in Anselm's thought (part 1). The "experience in thought" (part 1) was transmuted into "experience of the world" through the triple challenge of interpretation, embodiedness, and alterity in God (part 2). The *book of experience* thus continues in a variety of forms at the heart of the monastic theology of the eleventh and twelfth centuries, holding together indissolubly, as we have already seen [§4], "theory" and "practice" in the sole act of contemplation. Hugh taught us this, and Richard follows suit: the *lectio divina* which becomes *lectio scolastica* cannot rely simply upon, or meditate simply upon, scripture, but it opens up, as a model of the whole presence of God in the world, deciphering God's presence in his "traces," or even better in his "symbols."

From this center—fixed among the Victorines, between the Benedictine Anselm of Canterbury and the Cistercian Bernard of Clairvaux—we move on now to the consequences or rather to the ripe fruit of Cistercian life: the act of "feeling oneself alive" for Aelred of Rievaulx (chap. 7), the "divine-human empathy" (chap. 8), and freedom defined as "openness" or *apérité*⁵¹ in Bernard of Clairvaux (chap. 9). Something new is produced in the Cistercian's work, which probably distinguishes it from that of the Benedictine and the Victorine: "Saint Bernard never speaks of experience *in relation to the world*" as Ulrich Köpf, in his exegesis of Bernard's work, comments.⁵² Not, certainly, that we do not have to read God "in the woods rather than in books" [§24], but a "turn to ourselves" [*ad vos ipsos*], or to "our own consciousness" [*conscientiam suam*], characterizes this specific reading of the "book of experience." No longer the epiphany of God in thought (Anselm), or the decipherment of God in the world (Hugh), but the descent, indeed the kenosis (if that word can be applied to humankind), that goes as far as "affects" ensuring how *ex-periencing* is linked this time, and definitively, to *affectivity* and *spirituality*. We might recall here the quotation from the start of Bernard's Sermon Three on *The Song of Songs* cited earlier in this book [§3]: "We shall read to-day in the book of experience [*Hodie legimus in libro experientiae*]." He goes on to say, "Turn your minds inward upon yourselves [*convertimini ad vos ipsos*], and let each of you examine his own conscience [*et attendat unusquisque conscientiam suam*] in regard to those things which are to be mentioned."⁵³

Part 3

Affectivity and Spirituality or *Experience in Affects*: Aelred of Rievaulx and Bernard of Clairvaux

Hodie legimus in libro experientiae—"We shall read to-day in the book of experience."[1] The formula, as we have seen [§3], comes from Bernard of Clairvaux, taking him back to "conceptualize" that which we are investigating here: experience itself. "Experiencing" in Cistercian terms is not simply "manifesting God in our thought" (Anselm: part 1), nor "deciphering God in the world in trinitarian terms" (Hugh and Richard of Saint-Victor: part 2): it is letting "God make a way through our affects" without in any way overlooking the human being that God is called upon to inhabit (Aelred of Rievaulx and Bernard of Clairvaux: part 3). "Experience in affects" (Bernard), which follows on here from "experience in thought" (Anselm) and "experience of the world" (Hugh and Richard), tries thus to descend to the heart of the human and to meet up with that which the capacities of language could not reach. A sort of "brute world," indeed a wild or "savage being," dwells in all humankind and in the world in general. Discourse is manifestly powerless to speak this, and yet it is really necessary for us to speak of it. The Cistercians, Aelred of Rievaulx (*Spiritual Studies*) and Bernard of Clairvaux (*Sermons on the Song of Songs*), knew this. And they can still today help in formulating it, according to a mode of affectivity that they were probably the first in the history of philosophy to have thematized to this degree. Merleau-Ponty asks, "[W]hether philosophy as reconquest of brute or wild being can be accomplished by the resources of eloquent language, or whether it would be necessary for philosophy to use language in a way that takes from it its power of immediate or direct signification in order to equal it with what it wishes all the same to say."[2]

Phenomenology of Affects

The return today to a phenomenology of affects is the proof, or at least the sign, that a simple analysis of the Being-there of humankind in terms of reason or consciousness is not sufficient to fully explain the constitution of our humanity. Contemporary phenomenology, indicting the idealist turn in Husserl's phenomenology; disbelieving, or no longer believing, in the great deconstruction of Heideggerian onto-theology; and seeking to question above all the other of thought (aesthetics, ethics, psychiatry, mysticism), has come back progressively toward the first love of the 1920s—the age during which the question of empathy or *Einfühlung* was on every tongue, as well as in all hearts: the age of Edith Stein's *On the Problem of Empathy*, Max Scheler's *The Nature of Sympathy*, and Hannah Arendt's *Love and Saint Augustine*.[3]

In this context monastic theology does not deserve to be put to one side. If it is the site where affect finds its corpus and a time when it is embodied, then it is very likely texts in the Cistercian tradition that are significant, above all those of the twelfth century. Affect is enough to create an "order" in the Middle Ages, and what depends upon this order is a way of seeing the world that can still have a clarifying effect for us.[4] It would not be enough simply to write a history of the process, although the task would seem to be essential. It is still necessary to reap the rewards of what was done, especially for our time. To read is also to interpret, indeed to embrace, and not simply to reiterate. Walter Daniel, the biographer and brother of Aelred of Rievaulx, in his *Letter to Maurice* writes magnificently: "Let those believe who will and let who will read, and let those who do neither reject both and despise what I, his son, have written about my Father."[5]

On the question of affect, Aelred of Rievaulx, following on from Bernard of Clairvaux, but using an even more didactic conceptualization (*Dialogue on the Soul, Spiritual Friendship, the Mirror of Charity*), gives us exemplary testimony. Corresponding to our contemporary search for empathy (*Einfühlung*) we find a description of the order of *affectus* in the Cistercian master's work that is still too little appreciated, but whose history is without parallel.[6] It will be agreed certainly, as I have already made plain [§2] concerning phenomenology and monastic theology, that the questions they explore are not the same (affective consciousness in phenomenology and the test of the heart in monastic theology), any more than are their answers (empathy in relation to the mode of immanence in phenomenology and concerning the third party of a transcendence in theology). We cannot simply shift the monastic *affectus* (Aelred) to the phenomenological *Befindlichkeit* (Heidegger) without damaging either the one or the other. As far as monastic theology is concerned, we would be playing around with contemporary categories that are totally independent of all mysticism. And as for modern phenomenology, we would be introducing a sense of the third party of the other in me (the Christ), which could not be introduced without becoming immediately religion-based.

But all the same, in our contemporary commitment to affect, something of Cistercian thought seems to have been found; it is as though the twentieth century has been "rediscovering" affect, even if it has been modifying it. The aim has been to produce a mode of philosophizing whereby the affects, or feelings, are not superimposed upon representations (as though it were necessary first of all to conceive something and then to hate or love it). They accompany and orientate the representation or indeed go toward making the representations themselves (I see or I conceive in hating or loving, and the mode of viewing this representation [affect, or the intentionality through which I see it] is as important, or even more important, than the representation itself"):

> We do not merely have a presentation with an added feeling *associatively* tacked on to it, and not intrinsically related to it, but pleasure or distaste *direct* themselves to the presented object, and could not exist without such a direction … Pleasure without anything pleasant is unthinkable … because *the specific essence of pleasure demands a relation to something pleasing.*[7]

To say in this sense that "all consciousness is consciousness of something" is not simply to return consciousness to the object in order to steer clear of a sheer void or a gap for the cogito: it is to show that the act of sighting something also constitutes the vision, even more (or at least as much as) the thing seen.

To continue in this phenomenological vein, we find that what is analyzed by Husserl in terms of the characteristics of "intentional feelings" becomes radicalized by Heidegger, in terms of affect (*Befindlichkeit*—"attunement") or affective tonality (*Stimmung*—mood). This is no longer the simple targeting of feelings that become critical, but the fact, even more fundamental, that we go into the world only *in* and *through* our affect. And our affect does not remain, or not simply, as acts of vision of the world but as a kind of transcendental prism through which we make the world. Heidegger says, "What we indicate *ontologically* with the term *attunement*

[*Befindlichkeit*] is *ontically* what is most familiar and an everyday kind of thing: mood, being in a mood. Prior to all psychology of moods, a field which, moreover, still lies fallow, we must see this phenomenon as a fundamental existential and outline its structure."[8]

Concluding this fundamental detour into *affect* in phenomenology, and thus recognizing that an affective tonality cannot simply be broken down in ontic or psychological terms, we could say, for example, of anxiety in Heidegger's work that he is not content with showing it as one feeling among others; it shows on the contrary the ontologic disposition or the fundamental affective tonality through which the world emerges, as finally questioning being and the emergence of nothingness: "Why are there beings at all instead of nothing?"[9]

If one can, or should, "feel oneself fully alive" (chap. 7) along with Aelred of Rievaulx, before linking up "experience and empathy" (chap. 8) and then "openness [*apérité*][10] and freedom" (chap. 9) in Bernard of Clairvaux, that is a way of bringing into view how much the Cistercian tradition is also a tradition of affectivity. Affectivity and spirituality stand linked together in the "experience of affects," in that the mode of experiencing [*affectus*] becomes the privileged site of contact with divinity [*spiritus*]. The "book of experience," if we return to its clarification in phenomenology, can, as we have seen [§2], certainly be deciphered as "self-confrontation" [experience—*Erlebnis*], but it is also a "passage of the self through the world" [*Erfahrung*], being in itself totally modified by this alterity. The "pages of the book" have thus not finished being turned since for the twelfth-century "living" is also allowing oneself "to affect."

7

To Feel Oneself Fully Alive

A Fundamental "Affection"

The comparison that we have seen continues to be illuminating. *Befindlichkeit*, or affect, represents for Martin Heidegger the heart of what is human, without however reducing the human to its "heart," or indeed to lived experience, as though that were separated from what is *also* human in the imagination or the reason. As far as the phenomenological mode is concerned, one does not see or think first of all (image or representation) and then go on to love or detest (affect or judgement); one sees or is self-presented *directly* in loving or detesting. Husserl famously tells us that "all consciousness is consciousness of something," which does not simply suggest that all intentions are linked to an object of representation (noetico-noematic correlation) but suggests that intentions are accompanied by diverse modalities of lived experience which cannot be reduced to a represented thing.[1] In phenomenology, as indeed in the context of Cistercian monastic theology, "affect" as a fundamental given does not refer to one faculty among others (like reason or sensitivity) but shows itself and is affected as the mode of every faculty. We neither think nor do we feel outside of affect, and this intentionality of the self and the world through affect is not in any way optional because it is what always directs the principle of all our world-making for us. A kind of homonymy of structure seems then to unite what these centuries of history have separated: a "secret force of affect" in the twelfth century (Aelred), and a "fundamental affection" [*Affektion*], for Heidegger in the twentieth century.

Affectus for Aelred of Rievaulx, like *Befindlichkeit* for Heidegger, cannot be broken down into simple terms for faculties. It marks the fundamental disposition by which the human subject "opens a world" shows a "mode in which the world appears" and deploys a "way of seeing and conceiving the world."[2] A triple journey in the corpus of Aelred's work allows us to demonstrate this. But the "force of affect" [§20], the "secret of affect" [§21], and the "expression of affect" [§22] are not just three stages in an itinerary that is, to say the least, stimulating; they are also a quest and a definitive proof that in the "book of experience" of monastic theology contemporary thought can truly find the means of renewing itself—to the extent that we should perhaps demand of all phenomenology, and even of all philosophy, that they should also decipher the book of experience, albeit when guided in order to penetrate the meaning and the secrets within it.

§20. The Force of Affect

If You Feel Yourself Alive

The treatise of Aelred of Rievaulx, unfinished and probably cut short by this death, entitled *Dialogue on the Soul* (*Dialogus de Anima*), poses in "philosophical" terms what Saint Augustine in his treatise *The Happy Life*, William of Saint-Thierry in his *On the Nature of the Body and the Soul*, and Isaac of Stella in his *Letter on the Soul* see in an essentially "theological" way. Certainly, Aelred's work, like those of his predecessors and contemporaries, concerns the connection between God and humankind with all our being, including our senses, but the "force of affect" [*vis affectus*] takes on a central, or indeed transcendental, role for Aelred, one that it had never before been accorded. The "force" of affect, or of being affected, is certainly gained from the world and its modifications that we are subjected to, but it also opens up a world since it is that "in which" we live. A *cogito of affect* originating with Aelred of Rievaulx could serve as premise, or at least prelude, for what would later be seen as auto-affection or self-affection (Michel Henry).

Thus, a question arises all at once at the heart of the *Dialogue on the Soul*, or perhaps we should say it comes back at the heart of a question put by Aelred to his Brother and disciple John in order to simplify and radicalize the discourse. The master says to his disciple first of all "tell me if you feel alive" [*si te sentis vivere*]. The monastic interrogation, in astonishingly modern terms, thus joins key preoccupations of phenomenology: those of affection, or "auto-affection" of the self by the self (Michel Henry), according to which living is not first of all a "feeling" (perspective of empirical experience as objectivity [*emperia*]) but a "being felt" (perspective of phenomenological experience as lived experience [*Erlebnis*]). Replying to the question in the *Dialogue on the Soul* then means, paradoxically and also anachronistically, already moving on from the abbot of Rievaulx to a kind of quasi-Cartesian *cogitatio*. The abbot says to Brother John:

> Look closely at your self thinking [*te ipsum inspice cogitantem*]. Suppose that you are in the dark, that you have closed your eyes and stopped up your ears, that your nostrils smell nothing, and that you feel nothing. Now turn your attention to what it is that, when all these senses are quiet, thinks of so many things, reflects on so many things, purposes and decides so many things ... When, therefore, you are aware of your soul thinking so strongly [*cum igitur animam tuam sentis vehementius cogitantem*], are you aware of any place in which it might be [*num aliquem sentis locum in quo sit*], or of any bodily mass that constitutes it [*aut aliquem molem quae ipsa sit*]?
>
> John [reply]. Not at all [*minime*].[3]

One could discuss at length this passage from the *Dialogue on the Soul*, which constitutes a unique, or almost unique, moment in the history of thought. As in the hypothesis of the "flying or floating man" by Avicenna,[4] the disciple in Aelred's *Dialogue*, deprived of sight (eyes closed), of hearing (ears blocked), of smell (nostrils not sensitive), of taste (palate unsolicited), and of touch (inactive), will no less perceive "with force" [*sentis vehementius*] that his soul is "in the process of thinking" [*cogitantem*]. Certainly, read in context, it is plain that it is not enough to localize the soul and then pass over it to the senses and insist that it is they that think. But the implied interpretation, paradoxically, would make us see that the soul "sees itself in the process of thinking" [*sentis cogitantem*] even though it does not use the senses for thinking. This "sees itself thinking" for Aelred is what makes his thought, not just the thought itself. And there is more, or better, here (in Aelred's work) than we find in Descartes that "French horseman who set out with such a good step" (Péguy). Or rather, what we see in Aelred—his "sees itself thinking"—is also found in Descartes—"It seems to me that I see" [*videre videor*]. It is the affect of the thought that will already determine, as it were in advance, every act of thought and will do so in a way more fundamental than the discovery of the cogito itself.[5]

A Hidden Force

The abbot of Rievaulx does not, however, just stick with thought. In addition, he identifies explicitly in terms of "affect" [*affectus*] what is the mainspring of all acts of thought, as well as all ways of feeling or being felt. Abbot Aelred asks his disciple Brother John, "Tell me if you are aware that you are alive." Brother John takes an Augustinian line, evoking a kind of "hidden force" [*vim aliquam occultam*], by which his soul receives from his parents and from their seed something that allows him to feel and be felt:

> [This hidden force] lies latent in the seed and although it is not a sense yet later on develops into a sense by means of which the rational soul is held within the body, so, by means of the same force or power another one, more subtle and even more powerful, issuing not from the flesh of the parents but emanating invisibly and incorporally from their affection [*sed affectu procedens*] resides in the seed; and this force or power, although it is not the rational soul, is nevertheless the material or source of its creation.[6]

Affect and Auto-affection

There is no room for doubt about originality: "The reference to the power of the *affectus*, in this case, is specific to Aelred; it is not found in St. Augustine."[7] Moreover affect is referred to by Aelred as a kind of "hinge" for the supposed "transfusion of the soul into corporal matter." It is a "spiritual dynamism, product of the union of parents, from which emanates the power of generation contained in the seed."[8] As far as the thorny problem of the generation of souls is concerned, and as a way of avoiding the notion of the pre-existence of souls (Neoplatonism), or simply the divine and non-corporal emanation of the soul (Manichaeism), the power of *affectus* or the "force of affection" plays in a sense the role of intermediary, or hinge, by means of which the door is opened to the sprit as well as to the body. Given by the parents at the height of their mutual love, and anchored in the seed while remaining nonetheless spiritual, affect marks the frontier or border zone where the soul is united to the body and "feels the effects of" its own body. To the question "are you aware that you are alive," John thus replies to Aelred that at least he is aware of his own power of feeling, which is none other than the faculty of auto-affection through which he experiences himself. Auto-affection, to take up Michel Henry's term, "is no longer anything foreign or external to me who am affected," even so far that being auto-affected, in God, is through God who is the "source" of all affection.[9]

Affect in this sense, and from its origin, possesses a language—or rather *is* the language that constitutes it. Given in the form of an original stratum of our constitution through which we go to ourselves and to the world (because we perceive *affectively* that we are in the process of thinking, or think ourselves, even when there is no sensible object of our thought), the "force of affect" (*Dialogue on the Soul*) contains a "secret" which it is barely permissible for humankind to speak of. It is the secret of the "person in Christ" described by St. Paul, who "was caught up into Paradise and heard things that are not to be told, that no mortal is permitted to repeat" (2 Cor. 12:4 NRSV).

§21. The Secret of Affect

A Thought Affected

The *affectus* discovered by Aelred as "connection" or *nexus* of body and soul on the one hand, and of feeling and consciousness on the other, becomes then more and more constituent of what we ourselves are, in our manner of being in the world as well as toward the other. For Heidegger, *Stimmung* [variously translated as "attunement" or "mood"] or affective experience is, as Éliane Escoubas tells us, "not a specific existential among the others, but preserves all the characteristics of a fundamental existential, which simultaneously has its sources in almost all the others, and reciprocally makes of all the existentials what they are: it is *Existenz* itself."[10]

The secret—that of Affect—comes down essentially to revealing ourselves and exhibiting ourselves to ourselves. Experience has its language and understanding that language is above all submitting to it. As we have already seen, following here Philippe Nouzille [§2] but this time applying what he says explicitly to Aelred of Rievaulx, "Monastic theology aims at a description of experience and the conditions of its possibility."[11] What experience implies, however, for Aelred, as for Bernard of Clairvaux and all the Cistercians, is not firstly the relationship between humankind and the world (empirical), but the relationship of subjects to themselves, to the other as well as to God (intersubjectivity). There is a need, then, in this Cistercian mode, not just to think but also to feel or be affected. Or rather, it is a need to feel what the other feels, albeit through thought, which, far from detaching itself from affect or feeling, commits itself as the site of an accession of the self to the self in a particular ordeal that is both subjective and mystical. According to Aelred of Rievaulx, one does not think on the one hand and experience on the other. Thought itself *is* and becomes a kind of test, or a quintessential mode of affect, in that thinking comes down above all to experiencing, and experiencing oneself. And it is in such experience—affective rather than just a matter of sentiment—that our identity speaks most strongly to us.

Aelred's act in writing a treatise on *Spiritual Friendship* (*De spiritali amicitia*) tells us how important this mode was to him. In the prologue, before embarking on a dialogue with Brother Yves, he says, "[Because I wished] … to love spiritually but [was] not able to [*cum volens spiritaliter amare nec valens*], I decided to write on spiritual friendship [*de spiritali amicitia scribere*] and to set down for myself rules for a pure and holy love [*dilection*]."¹² The writing, or the thought, becomes a means of loving, or rather it is in itself an act of loving, of affect, and of being affected. Only the knowledge of the "law of true friendship" [*verae amicitiae legem*] can ensure, according to the Cistercian monk, that we are not "wavering among various friendships."¹³ And the kind of method [*quamdam formulam*] that he mentions at the start of the treatise "to which I could recall my quest for many loves and affections" is none other than the "route" through which thought does not simply force affect but admits itself affective, in that it is that through which one is also oneself, and by one's self, auto-affected. Aelred's secretary, Walter Daniel, tells us that the saint meditated upon such realities as the Last Judgment: "he *meditated upon them and in them* day and night and turned his heart to them."¹⁴

To Think What One Feels and Feel What One Thinks

It was not enough simply to think, as Aelred saw it; one had to think what one feels and feel what one thinks. We can certainly make a distinction between those who think on the one hand, and those who feel on the other, or perhaps it should be between those who feel that they think and think that they feel, and those who do not feel that they think and do not think that they feel. "I fear that there is no way of explaining what I feel in this regard [*quid inde sentiam*]." Aelred says, in a sermon, somewhat perplexed before his community. "I shall say what I can so that you can at least conceive [*concipere*] what perhaps you also have experienced." And in the same sermon he goes on: "Have you understood [*intellexistis*]? Certainly, if you have experienced it [*plane si experti estis*]. And you have understood [*et intellexistis*]."¹⁵ It is important to read this carefully or even to live it carefully. To have understood [*intelligere*] is certainly to have experienced [*experiri*]. It is to read in the "book of consciousness" and connect it directly to the "book of experience." A monk listening to the whole sermon would not understand what "receiving the Holy Spirit" signified if he had not himself had the experience. And moreover, to have understood would also, and at the same time, be to have had the experience and to experience having understood [*experiri intelligere*]—which is what leads Aelred to the exclamatory repetition of "you have understood" [*et intellexistis*], implying "you have experienced understanding."

Blessed Obscurity

Certainly, it is above all experience of the visitation of God or the Holy Spirit that is shared with Aelred in his sermon on the purification of the Virgin Mary (*In purificatione sanctae mariae* [sermon 34]). But what one also comes to see is that understanding oneself is a kind of test, or an affect, through which one enters into lived experience, albeit of the thing itself in the mode of feeling; that is, one enters into its apprehension and reception according to the affect of the thought. "Understanding" [*Verstehen*] is transformed into a mode of "attunement" [*Befindlichkeit*—in French, "affection"],[16] in such a way that the opening up through affect is not superimposed on thought but constitutes the mode of thought itself. We understand certainly that there is such a thing as an affect that is lived (as in the visitation of the Holy Spirit in the liturgy, for example), but understanding this also leads one to living this understanding in the mode of affect. To put it another way, we could say that it is already also a *visit of the Holy Spirit and a* mode of affect when we come to understand in thought that God is given to us even in the heart. The *theophanic argument* (chap. 2) here becomes in a way *pathic* (chap. 7) in that what *appears* in the thought (Anselm) *is felt* in the consciousness (Aelred).

The "secret of the Affect" (*secretum affectus*) will consist then, paradoxically in Aelred, in not delivering up all its affects. There are three reasons for this: (a) First reason: Every affect has its own language, and not all Brothers would speak the same language (affective language), so that they could not share that which was not *already experienced*. In his sermon on the Feast of the Annunciation Aelred takes up the words of the evangelist: "Not everyone can accept this teaching, but only those to whom it is given" (Mt. 19:11 NRSV). *Fear* has its own language that only those who fear can truly understand: suffering has its language that is understood only by those who suffer. And thus *love* also has its language that is only understood by those who love.[17] (b) Second reason: The transmission of affects, or the mode of *empathy* (to use the phenomenological term), is not so easily accessible, in particular since it is a question of affecting or being affected, through feeling certainly, but also by thought. Aelred says,

> Whatever way one who suffers speaks, you do not understand *if you do not also suffer*; equally, whatever are the words by which one who is joyful expresses that joy, you do not understand *if you are not also joyful*. You will even laugh at the utterance of one who fears [or who loves] if, being safe on all sides, you fear nothing [or you do not love].[18]

(c) Third, and not the least, reason: All affect *keeps its secret* that it cannot and must not disclose fully to an other—being a "barrier that language is never able to cross." According to Aelred there are also spiritual experiences that one can certainly *feel*, "but in no way explain."[19] The point here is crucial and fundamental. The *secretum meum mihi*, or the utterances and affects that remain my secret, are to some extent the guarantee of my own depth in the face of the other, as opposed to the frequently reiterated ideal of the transparency of the ego (Merleau-Ponty's critique of Husserl), and make the *affectus* into an inexhaustible crucible upon which we draw in order to speak and also to think. Because the primordial base or the *Urgrund* of our affect is always in a way incomplete, all our spoken words will never fully deplete our affects, and will ensure that we cannot measure ourselves up simply by "the feeling of our affects."

§22. The Reflection of the Affect

The Excesses of Sentimentalism

One of the principal achievements of Aelred's *Mirror of Charity* (*De speculo caritatis*) is that "affect" is not identified with the "feeling of affect": prevention is better than the cure. To talk about Aelred's "test or ordeal of affects" is not to sink into a sentimentalism that would be as shameful as it is dangerous, measuring all experience of God, as also of the other, solely in the way that we feel it or feel the effects of it (an excess of sentimentalism rightly condemned, as we shall see, in the encyclical of Pius X, *Pascendi dominici gregis* of September 8, 1907).[20] If, as I have tried to show, *thought is a form of affect* (not simply being affected, but being affected as thought by the fact of understanding what it is that being affected means), *affect itself is then a form of thought* (not simply measuring up affect in terms of feelings but also measuring it in terms of its spiritual effectiveness, whether or not its effects were felt by me or for me). In what constitutes the heart of the *Mirror of Charity*, a kind of treatise for novices, rather like Hugh of Saint-Victor's *Training of Novices* (chap. 5: "To Live One's Body"), Aelred warns that

> [t]he person whose will is in harmony with God's will, that is, who patiently bears whatever God sends and accomplishes with fervor whatever he has commanded, must, without any hesitation, be said to love God. Otherwise, if our love had to be measured by those attachments, so that we would be said to love God or even another human being only when we experience attachments of this sort, we should by no means be said to love constantly but only during certain very rare intervals ... To feel those attachments [*affectus illos sentire*] is not so much to love God [*Deum amare est*], as you claim as at this gentle touch perceive in advance [*praesentire*] a drop of that sweetness offered to—or rather infused into—the mind, present there, as it were, to the inward palate.[21]

Enduring God

We need to be careful here. The true "experience of affects"—in the triple sense of their pathos, passage, and danger—is not found in the rapture of lived experience, even less in the force in which they are expressed (the "attachments" or "*élans sensibles*"). It is found wholly and solely in our capacity to "endure God" [*sustinere Deum*], being his screen [*écran*], as well as his jewel case [*écrin*], such that we can patiently reflect God as well as hold God hidden within us. If God is a "Mirror of Charity" it is not solely as such that the love or dilection of God is able and must speak through us. The *Speculum caritatis* (mirror of charity) does not just invite us to live some day, and sentimentally, an affective experience—not even of the highest and most desirable kind. The *Mirror of Charity* is above all a product and an act of thought or a "piece of work" through which thought itself secures effectivity as well as affectivity—an understanding (*Verstehen*) that is also a being-affected (attunement—*Befindlichkeit*). If a text leads us, or can lead us, to affection or to sentiment, it is thus solely insofar as it deploys the proper rigor of thought, something that a return to lived experience could not exhibit without some watering down. In his preface Aelred writes with an exhortation that recalls Bernard:

> I command you, then, in the name of Jesus Christ and in the spirit of God, to the extent that these things have been remarked to you in prolonged meditation, not to put off writing (something) down [*stylo adnotare*] on the excellence of charity, its fruit and its proper coloring. Thus in this work of yours let us be able to see as in a mirror [*in ipso opere tuo quasi in speculo agnoscamus*] what charity is, how much sweetness there is in its possession.[22]

The Mirror Book

The first *speculum*, or the mirror itself, remains a "piece of work" as such [*in ipso opere tuo*]. It is the monastic work in thought, the putting down on paper—or rather on parchment—not simply of that which was already thought, but of the effect and the affect of the work of thought. The "mirror book" [*liber speculum*] shows charity and "reflects" affect as a way of opening up to all existentiality. It is like that thought which, in the monastic mode and in Anselm's work, always holds together the liturgical and the speculative, the Abbey church and the Scriptorium (chap. 2: "The Theophanic Argument"). The study of affect as a "feeling of attachment," so well described in book 3 of the *Mirror of Charity*, does not pass over the body (physical attachment) moving to the spirit (loving attachment). In each case, as in all cases, it converts the attraction to the crucible of thought, not as dry rationality, but as the capacity to take on and transform *into thought* the experience of an affect in the process of being offered:

> Most beloved Father, these are my meditations on charity [*de caritate meditationes meae*] ... Not to obey one's superiors is a dangerous thing, but it is sweet and pleasant to converse in spirit [*in spiritu fabulari*] on this sort of thing with someone very dear who is absent. I thought it necessary for me to bind together [by the links of meditation (*meditationum vinculis*)] the wandering and useless digression of my [exuberant] mind.[23]

To feel, or to feel the effect, marks in this sense an "address" to the other, and not simply an anonymous "appeal." Anonymity of an appeal, like abstraction of the gift (chap. 3: "The Debt for the Gift"), could then very well make us lose all that there is singular in, and particular to, the rooted Christian community. God does not simply call to a *people* or arouse the *prophets* (Levinas); God addresses also his *disciples* explicitly convoked, whose assembly constitutes precisely a "community of brothers."[24] It is thus to "enjoy one another" [*invicem frui*] that *Spiritual Friendship* invites us, as do all the works of Aelred. One will be called then, and one will call, since it is a question of addressing God (vocative). One will also be addressed, and one communicates "toward" or "for" the Brother to whom one speaks (dative), in that the human and fraternal face-to-face constitutes the benevolent and indispensable basis of all charity, as also of all friendship—a basis that monastic theology would call "compassion" [*compassio*] and phenomenology "empathy" [*Einfühlung*]. Aelred's biographer and fellow monk remembered him at the hour of his death: "He so shared the generosity of his spirit that with him, before the abundance of his substance failed, the liberality of his heart, according to his own derivation of his name, always gave preference to the *dative* over the *vocative*. Are you streaming down my tears, or not?"[25]

8

Experience and Empathy

From Aelred of Rievaulx to Bernard of Clairvaux, or from "To Feel Oneself Fully Alive" (chap. 7) to "Experience and Empathy" (chap. 8), we have found a convenient sequence, though by rights it should be the other way around: the abbot of Clairvaux (Bernard, 1090–1153) precedes rather than follows his fellow monk at Rievaulx (Aelred, 1110–67). On the other hand, they knew one another and more importantly they read one another. Appointed third abbot of Rievaulx in 1147, and often referred to as the English Saint Bernard, Aelred was, along with William of Saint-Thierry, a worthy successor to the great preacher of the order. Having looked at how he establishes affect in *Dialogue on the Soul*, *Spiritual Friendship* and the *Mirror of Charity* (chap. 6), we move on in this book to see how it was developed by Bernard of Clairvaux in his *Sermons on the Song of Songs* (chap. 8). It is not that we can dispense with chronological order but the "things themselves" demand that we move through the *didactic* account of "force" (§20) to the "secret" (§21) and then the "reflection" (§22) of Affect, before setting out on the heuristic path that is consistent with the mode, or rather the "song," of the *Sermons on the Song of Songs*. Bernard, as I hope to show, does not "speak" of affects. But we can return to that imperative of Merleau-Ponty's already cited, an imperative for a type of discourse that sticks closely to what we experience and to what makes "the flesh of things" that we call a "brute world" or "savage being" (see part 3). And we can say that Bernard "gives life" to them. In this respect bringing in Bernard after Aelred is not devaluing him or making him depend upon Aelred; it is showing the astonishing proximity of the monastic *affectus* to the phenomenological *Befindlichkeit* that must be read also in the way in which they write, indeed in how they look for a type of language adequate for what is "asked about" [*Gefragtes*], "what is interrogated" [*Befragtes*], or what "is to be ascertained" [*Erfragtes*].[1] Bernard "describes" and "lives" while Aelred has already interpreted or constructed. Such is the richness of the monastic tradition, and especially of the Cistercian tradition, which is always experimenting at the same time as it is working out a theory of experience.

Empathy will thus become a form of experience, and experience a way of speaking empathy, in that we are already there, in the monastic mode as in the phenomenological mode, "in" the things, or "among things" (*inter-esse*), rather than just talking about them as "interesting" because they have been objectivized or made distant from us.[2] *As close as possible to our affects*—that could be the leitmotif of Saint Bernard's sermons, for which the Song of Songs serves as support in that it is sung, and thus all its discourse can "follow" or "describe" but never truly "explain" or "analyze" it without distortion. As Merleau-Ponty says in his famous preface to *Phenomenology of Perception*: "Phenomenology involves description, and not explaining or analyzing. This first rule—to be a 'descriptive psychology' or to return 'to the things themselves' … is first and foremost the disavowal of science."[3]

Noverim te, noverim me[4]

"Experience" and "empathy" (chap. 8) are thus two terms that orient at once the ambition of phenomenology and the examination of medieval mystical theology as a whole [*experientia et compassio*]. We can point to a key theme of this present work [§2] that what we find in our present is not without its roots in the past. We too easily forget this when we relegate things to the margins of a philosophy that seems to be lost and gone. We speak certainly of an "overcoming of the metaphysical by the mystical" as though the intuition of a frequently forgotten corpus continued to haunt us.[5] But the essential is no longer there, at least today. For a long time, at least as I see it, we have ceased to "cling" to a *sole* requisite in phenomenology, so that the so-called overcoming of the metaphysical has fizzled out, if one understands by that the notorious search for an "other discourse" that would disqualify the former discourse or would search simply in it for what suits us.[6]

Far from making a "choice," we shall turn then to Bernard of Clairvaux, not in the hope that he will "get us out" of metaphysics through mystical theology (as might have been believed or thought in the past), but because *in himself* he holds to a rare unity of the natural and the spiritual, the affective and the rational—to experience that does not give up on the conceptual. We shall not find in this sense any of the anti-rationalism or anti-philosophy in Bernard's work that, because of a misunderstanding of his dissension with Abelard or Gilbert de la Porrée, has been incorrectly attributed to it. On the contrary, a new and exemplary unity of the "knowledge of God" (mystical), and knowledge of the self (philosophy), establishes the "true philosophy." In a sermon that has recently been brought to light, Bernard recounts how "a saint prayed thus: God, he said, let me know you [*noverim te*] and know myself [*noverim me*]. It was a short prayer and a true one. That is in the fact the true philosophy [*vera philosophia*]."[7]

Relation to the other [*noverim te* (mystical)] is thus mediatized, or annexed, to the self [*noverim me* (philosophical)] in a true philosophy [*vera philosophia*]—and not the other way round: an astonishing reversal of St. Augustine.[8] In this sense, but in this sense only, there is no affective experience of the self for Bernard of Clairvaux [*noverim me*] beyond the empathic experience of the other [*noverim te*], whether he is talking about his fellows in the monastery, [*socius*] or his deceased sibling (Brother Gerard), or God himself (who affects but is not affected). Cross-reference between his *Sermons on the Song of Songs* and his treatise *On Loving God* makes this plain precisely in the "field of experience" where thought is moved to the *affectus* of compassion, as the most common form of Christian empathy. Thus, we can take seriously Rémi Brague's proposition, never fully developed, in the "anthropology of humility" that he finds in St. Bernard's work: "It could be suggested that the Bernardine endeavor can continue to help us rethink the essence of philosophy, and in particular might give birth to *possibilities that are undoubtedly still there in phenomenology*."[9]

§23. From the Experience of the Song of Songs to the Songs of Experience

The Experience of the Song of Songs

As with Anselm and his "illumination" of God as "that which no greater can be conceived," whose source we traced to the Aosta valley [§5], Bernard's experience is rooted in his own existence. In the opening of the third sermon on the Song of Songs we read:

> He alone ... who has received even once only, the spiritual kiss from the lips of Christ; him his own experience incessantly urges to obtain a renewal of that which he found so full of sweetness. It is my strong opinion that no one can comprehend what it is [*neminem vel scire possit qui sit*], save he who has experienced it [*nisi qui accipit*].[10]

It is lived experience that thus determines all discourse concerning the experience—that which now is strictly speaking the object. To receive [*accipit*] that which is to be experienced becomes the condition for having it [*habere*] or rather for comprehending it [*scire*]. In mystical theology, as in phenomenology, there is nothing that can be said *regarding the experience* [*experimentum*] independently *of the one who experiences* [*experior*] and who determines it throughout. The comprehension *of* the one who experiences is originally "experience *of* comprehension" (subjective genitive) and not comprehension *about* the experience (objective genitive). All the same it is distinctive of monastic theology and in particular that of Bernard of Clairvaux that it conceptualizes what had up to then simply been practiced [§3]. Before Bernard confides his originary experience of the birth of the child Jesus to us, his pure and simple reading of the Song of Songs is already the site and source of an experience—that of the transfer to another way of doing and living his *connection with the lived experience of the text* (spousal union of spouse and spouse) and not just a *lived experience of a connection with the text* (the meaning of Scripture and its interpretation).

The history of what happened to Bernard is a familiar tale. In 1124 William of Saint-Thierry, abbot of the Benedictine monastery of Saint-Thierry, and admitted later as a simple Cistercian monk to the monastery of Signy, fell ill. Under the orders of Bernard, he went to the sick-bay at Clairvaux, where it seems Bernard was now also suffering from a sickness that could not be shaken off. In William's *Life* of St. Bernard, we read:

> Once I myself was sick in our own house, and completely drained. The sickness was prolonged and went on and on for a very long time. Hearing about it, Bernard sent me to his brother Gerard, a man of happy memory. He pressed me to come to Clairvaux, and he promised me that I would either be soon cured or die.[11]

And he was certainly cured. Two sick brother monks: one at the bedside of the other: that is what constitutes the *originary experience* for Bernard, at the time when he had written more or less nothing (Bernard was 34 when he suffered this illness and only started to write out his famous letter on the love of God [to Guigues du Chastel, fifth

Prior of the Grande Chartreuse] in the following year, 1125).[12] Bodily weakness, or rather a spiritual detachment, is the point of departure for all mystical experience: Bernard attests to that here, but we find it as well with Francis of Assisi, Ignatius of Loyola, Teresa of Avila, or Saint John of the Cross. St. Bernard's famous theme is that "through humility [*humilitas*] we know that we are nothing [*quod nihil sumus*]; through humility we learn about ourselves and our *own weakness*."[13]

But there is more and better in the burden-sharing of the two abbots and in their common vulnerability. William of Saint-Thierry goes on to tell us how they "discussed for the whole day the soul's *spiritual physique* [*de spirituali physica animae*], that is, the remedies of the virtues against [sickness and] vices."[14] Everything happened thus as if the bodily physique caused by the sickness led necessarily to the "spiritual physique" or to a therapy for the soul, of the kind that made sure the second (the soul) did not fight against the first (the body), but on the contrary fed it and healed it through and through. The *proximity of the flesh* in the burden-sharing of physical suffering (Bernard and William in the sick-bay at Clairvaux) leads to an *interpenetration of hearts* in their mutual concern over the distress of the soul. The mystical and spiritual experience given to some (spiritual physique) is rooted in a philosophical and fleshly experience shared by both (bodily physique). There is neither a leap not a rupture between the two but simply a congruence and an impossibility of disconnection—despite the false accusations of spiritualism made concerning the abbot of Clairvaux. Bernard says in *On the Love of God*, "The flesh is a good and faithful *companion* to the good spirit. It helps it if it is burdened, or if it does not help, it relieves it."[15]

A Sharing of Experience

At the heart of this "spiritual physique" the Song of Songs serves as a common basis for the sharing of experience. William writes, "He then commented on the Song of Songs to me, explaining the moral meaning [*moraliter tantum*] to me during the time of my infirmity."[16] Certainly a text, and particularly the reading together of the same written material, was fruitful here in renewing the mystical theology and all theology in the future. It has been rightly emphasized that the *Commentary on the Song of Songs* by Origen was probably available to the two abbots and that they probably worked together on the topic (William of Saint-Thierry would write a short commentary on the Song of Songs: *Brevis commentatio in Canticum*, based on notes taken during his discussions with Bernard; and Bernard would write his sermons on the Song of Songs: *Sermones super Canticum canticorum*).[17] In short there is a hermeneutic at the base of the mystical, in particular because the theory of the meaning of scripture inherited from the Origenian corpus would not have been overlooked by these two authors.

But, what counts here, rather than the text, is the precise situation in which it is read and the experience to which it refers. The importance of this axis for Bernard is something wholly new (in comparison with Origen, for example). On the one hand we find his insistence on the moral sense [*moraliter tantum*], which indicates that nothing should be read or commented upon that is not first of all edifying. On the other hand, there is a strange match between what is read and what is lived in experience at the same time as it is shared: "Let him kiss me with the kisses of his mouth!" (Song

1:1 NRSV). What do those await who have in common the same weakness of the flesh (sickness), if not precisely a "kiss" that is every bit as fleshly as it is spiritual: a "kiss" of the Word that comes to heal their body and soul? Rarely in the history of philosophy has the act of reading and the shared experience of readers been so appropriate for the content of the message. There is no longer a holding on to a "hermeneutic," either of the world or of factuality, as in Hugh of Saint-Victor (chap. 4: God as an "Open Book"); with Bernard of Clairvaux one "writes as one lives," or writing itself sets out, transcribes, and imitates the act of "life." Fleshly suffering also awaits its fleshly transcription, and one does not simply seek to outstrip suffering with the spiritual in order to heal wounds.

In short, Bernard did not just communicate his thoughts to his friend William—never mind that they were both intelligent and could swiftly provide an appropriate commentary. He gave William, or taught him, his *way of doing*. That certainly included the "formula of his thought" [*sententias intelligentiae*], but also and above all the "meaning of his experience" [*sensus experientiae*], through which he communicated his *own mode* of being toward the world and toward God. And making the "inexperience" [*inexpertum*] of William into the springboard of a renewing of his own "experience" [*expertum*], Bernard gained from experiential sharing what is above all a tropological reading [i.e., a reading stressing moral metaphor] of the Song of Songs. No one could know these things except in "experiencing them themselves" [*nonnisi experiendo*], and it is exactly in this way that the master is said to "instruct" [*docere*] and open up a new world of conceptuality. William recounts how Bernard "used to expound [the Song of Songs] to me kindly and without any envy, to communicate his understanding of the text and his own meaning drawn from experience [*sensus experientiae*]. He brought light to his [instruction (*docere*) of my inexperience (*multa niteretur inexpertum*)] which would usually be discerned only through experience [*quae nonnisi experiendo discuntur*]."[18]

The Song of Experience

The *experience of the Song of Songs*, sharing the force of the text and the weakness of the body, shifts then progressively in Bernard's sermons into a *song of experience*. The introduction to the *Sermons on the Song of Songs* demonstrates this from the start (sermon 1). Readers could not expect here that Bernard, as Cistercian abbot, would provide an exegesis of the text in its linguistic content: historical, symbolic, critical, or hermeneutic. They learned from the abbot to remain silent or rather to speak differently. Certainly, they would be accustomed to singing the psalms, and Bernard underlines how that should be practiced every day. But he insists that what the Song of Songs is for him "by its excellence and incomparable sweetness, rightly surpasses those which I have mentioned [the psalms]," in that "it is itself the fruit of all others [*quia caeterorum omnium ipsum est fructus*]."[19] Certainly it could be said that the Song of Songs sings to us—as do the psalms. And moreover, it produces a kind of joy that the liturgy also tries to communicate. But it possesses something further that is particular to it: "It is not heard without, nor does it make a sound in public."[20] In other words, we return again to that phenomenological "suspension" of the exteriority of the world that brings us back to our "selfhood" [*égoïté*]. We might recall Husserl's famous conclusion to his *Cartesian Meditations*, where he cites the act of withdrawal demanded by Saint Augustine in his *On True Religion*: "*Noli foras ire, in te redi, in interiore homine habitat veritas* [Do not go outside, return into yourself. Truth dwells in the inner man]."[21]

There is more and better in the song of experience as it is performed by Bernard of Clairvaux because when it comes to a reading of the Song of Songs, "experience only makes the soul to be familiar with it [*sola addiscit esperientia*]," and only "those who have had experience of it know it well [*experti recognoscant*]."[22] What is at stake here, like the experience of eros, or even the learning of foreign languages, is something that can simply die when it is not practiced: "Jut as one who is unacquainted with Greek, or with Latin cannot understand a person who speaks in either of those languages, … so it is with the language of love."[23] The *spoken* (love or Latin) is nonetheless the *done* (love or Latin grammar). And one can always discuss the virtues of the Song of Songs, though as long as one has not been through the experience, nothing particular will happen. What happens when one truly goes through it, according to Bernard? Precisely nothing—or rather nothing like the usual linguistic exchange that enriches the liturgy with psalms. "[With the Song of Songs] it is not a cry from the mouth [*non strepitus oris*] but the gladness of the heart [*sed jubilus cordis*]; not the sounds of the lips [*non sonus labiorum*], but the impulse and emotion of joys within [*sed motus gaudiorum*]; not a concert of voices [*non vocum consonantia*], but of wills moving in harmony."[24]

It could not be clearer—this is radicalizing more and more the "book of experience." If a narrow definition of hermeneutics marks out a route of the transformation of the "reader" by the "world of the text" (Ricoeur), while phenomenology describes the field of passive data that precedes all conscious activity (Husserl), then the act of reading the Song of Songs that Bernard undertakes comes closer to the second (phenomenology) than to the first (hermeneutics). Moreover Bernard takes us to the "limits of the spoken" because he finds at the heart of the Song of Songs not simply the multiplicity of its linguistic meanings, all the more complex as they are more exposed: historic, tropological, allegoric, and anagogic (Origen); rather it is that "pure—and, so to speak, still dumb—experience," that awaits, as we shall see [§25], the utterance of "its own proper sense with no adulteration."[25] Concerning the song of the Song of Songs, Bernard specifies that "[o]nly she who sings, and He in whose honor it is sung, that is the Bridegroom and the Bride, hear the accents of that song"; when "the King has brought me into his storerooms (Song 1:4)."[26] The mystical experience touches the heart of intimacy and requires of philosophy that it question and renew its categories. The "nuptial song" [*nuptiale carmen*] does not deny the validity of the "cry from the mouth," the "sounds of the lips," or the "concert of voices." But it is also an invitation to an *affective experience* all the more profound because it has such proximity to the self and is for that reason probably more difficult to utter. It is "the gladness of the heart," "the impulse and emotion of joys within," and "wills moving in harmony." Max Scheler in due course understood this process, when he said: "The feelings can have a meaning, inherent to the experience itself that one is having, impossible to confuse with their causal origin and their purely objective usefulness in the lived economy."[27]

§24. A Knowledge of Experience

The Doctrine of Experience

It could be said, however, and perhaps correctly, that one cannot boil down the mystical to an experience that is all the more silent because it relinquishes speaking (a claim made against Bernard, suspected of "illuminism"[28]); nor should one suggest that the mystical confines philosophy to a sentimentalism so pure that it is definitively committed to the loss of the concept (a claim made against Max Scheler, mistakenly connecting him with Schleiermacher). The encyclical of Pius X, *Pascendi Dominici Gregis* (1907), as we have seen already in discussing Aelred and sentimentalism [§22], despite its radical condemnation, warned that not everything was to be rejected:

> [The Modernist Philosopher] recognizes as the object of faith, the *divine reality*, still this reality is not to be found in the heart of the Believer, as being an object of sentiment and affirmation; and therefore confined within the sphere of phenomena; but as to whether it exists outside that sentiment and affirmation is a matter which in no way concerns this Philosopher. For the Modernist Believer, on the contrary, it is an established and certain fact that the divine reality does really exist in itself and quite independently of the person who believes in it … Given this *doctrine of experience* [*doctrina experientiae*] … every religion, even that of paganism, must be held to be true.[29]

The caution against religious "sentiment(alism)" could not definitively discredit either sentiment or experience. The "book of experience" would not be erased simply because a "book of consciousness" had so completely redacted it that nothing remained to experience. On the contrary it is on the borderlands that concepts speak since it is exactly under the impulse of experience that they are able to shift without abandoning their regulatory function. Rather than opposing Bernard as an *experimentalist* it is necessary to give him credit: First, in that he says he *has had* the experience ("Believe in my experience" [letter from Bernard to Henry Murdach, and the narrative of the birth of the Word in *The First Life*]). Then in that he testifies to *going through it*, sometimes still going through the same experience, even if in another form ("I wish to tell you, as I have promised, how such events have taken place in me.")[30]

Believe in My Experience

We have come then to the heart, or even to the summit, of "experience," but also, and above all we have come to the conceptualization of the "book of experience" which runs through the whole of the monastic theology of the eleventh and twelfth centuries (Anselm of Canterbury, Hugh and Richard of Saint-Victor, Aelred of Rievaulx, and Bernard of Clairvaux). Bernard's words are famous and worth emphasizing. In order to persuade his friend Henry Murdach, theology teacher among the English (who will later become abbot of Vauclaire), to join the monks at the abbey of Clairvaux, Bernard refers explicitly to his own experience, telling Murdach to believe in it [*Experto crede*] and going on to say: "You shall find a fuller satisfaction in the woods than in books. The trees and the rocks will teach you that which you cannot hear from masters."[31]

We know certainly, from what William of Saint-Thierry wrote in his *First Life of St. Bernard*, that Bernard confessed how "whatever he gains from the Scriptures ... comes chiefly from the woods and fields, and he has no teachers beside the oaks and beeches."[32] But for Bernard that was not the main point. One does not find in his writings a kind of *song of the creatures*, in the style of St. Francis. What remains important for the Cistercian is a return to an ego-ity that suspends or "brackets" all positions of exterior-ity. For his respondent to believe in his experience—*experto crede*—requires that the respondent *gives credence*, without, however, having seen, or even lived through, the experience. But it is not, for Bernard, a question of renouncing books or reading them with an anti-intellectualism that would be as inappropriate for his thought as for his person. The "true philosophy" [*vera philosophia*], as we have already seen, does not deny the act of philosophizing; rather it requires that, knowing the other in oneself [*noverim te*], one should break through to the knowledge of oneself [*noverim me*]. What matters, in the eyes of the Cistercian, is that one's lived experience can both *speak itself* and *address itself* to an other, in an alterity directly and analogically constitutive of one's most characteristic self. If experience is always first "for me" as an other to all others [*ego alter*], to go back to a constant of late Husserlian phenomenology, it nonetheless projects itself in the other as an other self [*alter ego*], precisely in that it seeks to accomplish an "apperceptive transfer" that is as necessary to imagine as it is impossible fully to accomplish. In short, the experience *of* myself is not only *for* me in mystical theology and later in phenomenology.[33]

But if there is a true "knowledge" [*docere*], indeed a "science of a way of life" in Bernard of Clairvaux (see Étienne Gilson), it is no less rooted in an originary or intentional background [*Urgrund*] which determines it through and through.[34] Renouncing the simple notion of fitting a discourse to its object (objective truth), the Cistercian monk takes up here a *subjective process* involving his own coming to himself as he comes to God, a source location starting from which everything that he has experienced speaks, as well as everything that his brother monks have to live through. Far from sinking into the pure relativism of a norm that works only for himself, Bernard sets up, as a good Cistercian abbot, the intersubjective community of his monks as *guarantor* of an experience which is not just his own. It is not just his own since it needs to express itself, to be shared, and to regulate itself through others. What Bernard recommends to his monks in his famous sermon on the three rooms of the king is "to learn how to act as an inferior [*sub alto*], how to act as an equal [*cum alio*], and how to act as a superior [*super alium*] ... In the first you learn to be a disciple [*primo discipulus*], in the second to be a companion [*secundo socius*], in the third to be a master [*tertio et magister*]."[35]

Bernard relates his experience to William in the sick-bay at Clairvaux so as to operate more effectively the "transfer" to his brother monk, who is also called upon to face his own experience. Bernard's experience is like that of Anselm's childhood vision when he thought he should go up to the summit of the mountain in the Aosta Valley to the court of God [§5]—an experience that *he himself* had of God. In his youth, Bernard explains, he had a vision of the Word born on Christmas Eve.[36] We should note from the outset that visions of this kind were not yet commonplace in the twelfth century and that if it was *originary* in Bernard's life, it was no less *original* in the history of theology and piety in general. The move toward the figuration of the mystery of Christmas in a creche was only emerging with St. Francis, and the potential of the birth of the Word in ourselves, as Johannes Tauler or Meister Eckhart was to develop it, was still far ahead. For Bernard everything fits into a dream, or almost, in his initial vision:

> On the solemnity of the Lord's nativity ... Bernard was sitting there waiting [with the other faithful—*cum caeteris*] and his head drooped in sleep. Then it happened that the child Jesus revealed himself [*se revelans*] in his Holy Nativity to the little boy [*affuit illico puero suo revelans pueri Jesu sancta Nativitas*] ... Jesus appeared to him like the spouse coming forth from his chamber. He appeared to him before his eyes [*ei quasi iterum ante oculos suos nascens*] as the wordless Word ... being born from his mother's womb [*ex utero matris Virginis*].[37]

This narrative of experience says it all for us—no longer this time a shared experience with William in his sickness but testimony by Bernard himself of what happened and could perhaps happen again (a vision of God in himself). From the spiritual health or the soul therapy of the *Sermons on the Song of Songs* [§23] we move now to a "personal confession," indeed to the "mystical" as such, understood etymologically as the "experience of mystery" [*musterion*] [§24].[38] To talk of that experience of the self is then to *describe* it, tracing its contours so that their "exemplary originality" gives "rules" to the mystical, and never becomes "absurd," as sometimes the fine arts may do, in the art of genius (Kant).[39]

(a) First characteristic of this originary experience of Bernard's: Its *personal* character—though it is not given in an exclusively *individual way*. It comes about through the Church's divine service, and thus along with the Spouse to whom he holds, while the child is "waiting with the other faithful" [*cum caeteris*], his head "drooped in sleep." The liturgical community already, and once again, is the guarantor of the "mystical" experience—though there is a risk of validating under the term "mystical" everything that springs from the esoteric and goes beyond the philosophic.
(b) Second characteristic: The experience is that of a "holy infant" [*illico puero*] seeing the "infant Word" [*Verbum infans*]. It is significant that Bernard's originary experience is given to him from the start (perhaps because we ourselves constitute the world) in our own flesh and showing God "as a child" (Husserl). Moreover, the child "without speech" (*in-fans*) says nothing, not because he has nothing to say but because his language is not that of utterance; it is a language of affects experienced in his body through which first of all he expresses himself. In a remarkable passage, in sermon 67 on the Song of Songs, Bernard underlines that it is affect that speaks, not intelligence [*affectus locutus est, non intellectus*], and that is why he does not address the intelligence [*et ideo non ad intellectum*].[40]
(c) Third characteristic: The *encounter with the child* does not descend into *infantilism* in terms of the mystical. We need to find here the "second naïveté" in

phenomenology (Husserl), as in the spiritual domain (Bernard), that theology has sometimes wrongly neglected in its attempt to integrate itself too closely into philosophy. When the "holy child" sees in his dream "Jesus born," he is not simply dreaming of attending an ordinary birth. On the contrary, he gives the experience of the *flesh* all its due: his own flesh first of all because he speaks, and that of the Word, in that it is expressed in its own form in the incarnation. In his famous sermon on the divine kiss, prefaced by the quotation "Let Him kiss me with the kisses of His mouth" (Song 1:1), Bernard says:

> Observe: It is the Word become Incarnate [*Verbum assumans*], who is the Mouth who gives the kiss [*os osculans*]. It is the [flesh] which is assumed [*caro assumitur*] which receives it [*et osculato*]. The kiss, which is perfected equally by Him who gives [*ab osculante*] and Him who receives [*et osculato*], is that Person constituted of each nature [*persona ipsa scilicet ex utroque compacta*], the Mediator between God and men, the man Christ Jesus [*mediator Dei et hominum homo Christus Jesus*].[41]

(d) Fourth and last characteristic of Bernard's mystical experience, and not least important: What he sees is above all for him of the order of an "apparition" or a showing forth [*apparuit*], indeed a *revelation* of which he is the recipient [*se revelans*]. Something shows itself in the mystical experience independent of all judgment of the objective truth of that which is shown. It is not significant, in fact, for phenomenology or for mystical theology, whether the scene of the birth of the Word corresponds or not with what actually happened in Bethlehem on Christmas Day. What counts is simply the lived experience of the young child Bernard, brought on by the phenomena of a God who "appears to him," or "is shown" ("*Offenbarung*" to use a phenomenological term). In being born in himself, God gives birth in a sense to the world—the Cistercian abbot convincing us, as it were in advance, that nothing actually *is* in the world if it does not *give birth* to the world: "So persuasive to his mind was this moment that from then on, as he confesses, he believed he was at the very moment of the Lord's birth [*fuisse dominicae Nativitas*]."[42]

We can sum up then by noting that the phenomenological or descriptive characteristics of the mystical experience of the young Bernard on that Christmas Eve at the turn of the twelfth century were (a) personal but not individual, (b) affective and fleshly rather than linguistic [*in-fans*], (c) belonging to childhood but not infantile, and (d) appearances but not objective. The experiential event, which is given solely in its immediacy, deserves to be exploited over the long term. Nothing is worse than always confining an event to the past in which it took place—as though the evidence of one's transformation in the past were sufficient to exempt one from all later experience. One can say that things happen to me, indeed along with me [*mecum agitur*]—and to describe them, like Bernard of Clairvaux, I do not simply allow myself to be traversed and modified by what has happened [the experience of the Song of Songs or the vision of the infant Jesus]; I turn toward the originary interiority which ensures that nothing remains ephemeral [*Erlebnis*]. As Hans-George Gadamer says, "Something becomes an 'experience' [*Erlebnis*] not only insofar as it is experienced, but insofar as its being experienced makes a *special impression* that gives it *lasting importance*."[43]

How Things Happen in Me

The crucial point of the mystical experience does not then call upon, or does not solely call upon, a statement of "belief" in the lived experience of the other: *experto crede*. Its non-longevity is also important. To say that it leaves a "special impression" is not to deny its ephemeral character but to interpret it in a way that gives it meaning, despite its provisional and transient characteristics. *Transcendental conditions* of time and space belong to the mystical, as they do to the phenomenological. Thus, in order to "work" on the double relationship (a) with *time* (the non-realization of what had been expected in millenarianism), and (b) with *space* (the attractions of Jerusalem in the era of crusades), the abbot of Clairvaux based his discourse on a mystical experience that was not simply something to live but also to conceptualize.

(a) The failure of millenarianism had transformed all temporality. Since eschatology had not been fulfilled as was expected with the passing of the year one thousand, immediate experience had come to be seen differently. John's gospel tells us that Christ says, "In a little while you will no longer see me, and again a little while and you will see me again" (Jn 16:16 RNJB). But Bernard laments, "How canst Thou call the time in which I do not behold Thee 'a little while'? Saving the deference due to my Lord's word, it seems to me a *long* time [*longum est*] and even excessively long [*et multum valde nimis*]."[44] The famous Cistercian thesis of a *medius adventus*, a "middle coming" [or time of visitation] of the Word, does not arise here simply to join a new model of Christian temporality. Strictly speaking it resolves a paradox, for personal experience certainly, but also for the Cistercian monk and for ourselves, still waiting for the final fulfilment. The Resurrected One, clothed with "flesh" and "mortality" in his incarnation, and with "glory" and "majesty" in his Parousia, comes nonetheless *in me* in "spirit" and in "truth" in the present life.[45] The failure of millenarial predictions in their *exteriority* is converted here into the success of mystical experience in its *interiority*. It is precisely because the Word does not seem to be coming (returning) to the world that I constitute myself into a site for the coming of the Word in me. Confessing "how such events have taken place in me" [*quomodo mecum agitur in ejusmodi*] in this same sermon 74, Bernard makes the event of the visitation of the Word in the past (when he was a child) into a moment that has been many times repeated, with the entering of the Word into him in the present (now he is an adult).

> I confess then, though [it may be against modesty to say it] that the WORD has visited me [*mihi adventasse Verbum*] and even very often [*et pluries*]. But although He has frequently entered into my soul [*cum saepius intraverit ad me*] I have never at any time been sensible of the precise moment of His coming. I have felt that he was present. I remember that He has been with me; I have

sometimes been able even to have a presentiment that He would come; but never to feel His coming, nor His departure.[46]

Not just a matter of feeling, and very far from the hypothesis of a conversion of meaning held by Origen, Bonaventure, or Ignatius of Loyola, the encounter with mystery for Bernard is only recognized in retrospect—*a posteriori*—as is the case for the subjective event of all births. It is not a priori as it would be by contrast in an objective discourse on the conditions of the possibility of the experience. I become *myself* in my purest *egoïté*, the site of the espousal of the groom and bride, in the failure of an exteriority (millenarianism), which leads to a conversion to interiority (the union, at the heart of the personal, of the lived experience of the flesh): "If I have looked … within, He was at an inner depth still" [*se vero intus, et ipsum interius erat*].[47]

(b) It was not sufficient, this time from the point of view of *space*, to undertake those crusades, of which Bernard was a promoter, to search for the Resurrected One where he was born, at Bethlehem, rather than at Clairvaux, or to search for him in Judea, rather than simply in our own countries. Bernard can say that he *is himself* the site of an experience and of the birth of the Word in him—not like Meister Eckhart in the path of negation but rather, if we stick solely to Bernard, in the thick of his affectivity:

> You will ask then, how … I could know He was present? But He is living and full of energy, and as soon as He has entered into me [*moxque ut intus venit*] He has quickened my sleeping soul, has aroused and softened and goaded my heart, which was in a state of torpor, and hard as a stone. He has begun to pluck up and destroy, to plant and to build, to water the dry places, to illuminate the gloomy spots, to throw open those which were shut close, to inflame those with warmth which were cold, as also to straighten its crooked paths.[48]

Movement [*motus*] becomes for Bernard the site of affect [*affectus*] so that he testifies to recognizing the presence of the Word by the "revived activity [or movement] of my heart" [*ex motu cordis*]. "Instruction [*instructio*] renders men learned [*doctos*]," but only "feeling [or affect–*affectio*] makes them wise [*sapientes*]"—and this is the true meaning of the visitation of the Word in each of us: "There we are indeed instructed [*ibi instruimur quidem*], but here we are touched [*sed hic afficimur*]."[49] The true wisdom is not that which knows the Word theoretically, from his hypostasis [underlying state] and his communication in languages (although these things are also essential for Bernard of Clairvaux). In terms of experience, "wisdom" [*sapientia*] is "derived from 'sapor,' since it is, as it were, the seasoning of virtue; to which it gives taste and savour [*sapidam*]."[50]

In short, as one gathers, Bernard becomes through the Resurrection the theatre of the Word in himself, and any escape elsewhere (to the crusades or foreign pleasures) will bring him back *eventually* to his own interior (the wisdom of the Word in his own heart): "Taste has its seat in the palate [*sapor in palato*], but wisdom in the heart [*in corde est sapientia*]."⁵¹ In calling upon the Word to himself, like the spouse whose beloved is absent (Song 2:17), the Cistercian monk establishes his heart [*cor*] as the affective and liturgical dimension of a new mode of temporality and spatiality, which the monastic community in prayer will share with him—a site of waiting and renewal.

> After having, then, such an experience of the happiness derived from the indwelling WORD, what wonder that I should adopt for my own the language of the Bride [*vocem Sponsae*], who recalls Him when he has departed? ... As long as I live that utterance shall be in my mind, and I will employ, for the recalling of the WORD, that word of recall, which I find here in the word *Return* [*pro Verbi revocatione revocationis verbum, quod utique revertere est*].⁵²

In the tradition of scholarship devoted to St. Bernard some attention has been given to this, but it has not been discussed widely. Husserl's "*pure* and, so to speak, still *dumb*" experience awaits being "made to utter its own sense with no adulteration," as we have seen [§23], not in order to speak it but also to experience it, indeed also to formulate it. As far as the "book of experience" is concerned, affect [*affectus*] is no longer simply a language; in the work of Bernard of Clairvaux, it is "the" language—not posed against intellect but along with it; or rather it speaks as it, indeed often in its place: *affectus locutus est, non intellectus*—"it is affect that speaks, not understanding," and "that is why it does not address the intellect" [*et ideo non ad intellectum*].⁵³

§25. The Language of Affect

The rediscovery of affect [*Befindlichkeit*] is part of the basic methodology that defines phenomenology as such, and it is something to which other disciplines, not necessarily philosophical (in particular psychology) aim to return to today.⁵⁴ We can trace the roots of such considerations in Husserl's work, and it is closely debated by his followers who break away from Husserl's idealist perspective (Edith Stein, Max Scheler, Eugen Fink, Theodor Lipps): "While Husserl studies his *intellectual intentionality* in consciousness, Scheler focusses on his *emotional intentionality*."⁵⁵ The first "turning point" of phenomenology, affective rather than realist, initiated at least to some degree by Max Scheler's book on the nature and form of sympathy (a distinction between sympathy, affective participation, contagion and affective fusion), has, as I see it, its strongest confirmation in Cistercian mystical theology.⁵⁶

This is reflected in exemplary fashion in Bernard of Clairvaux's work: on the one hand in his firmly affective interpretation of the loving declaration of the bride to the bridegroom in the Song of Songs ("My beloved is mine and I am his" [Song 2:16; Sermon 67]); and on the other hand, in the paradox of a "commandment to love"—paradoxical because love seems impossible to command. This love transforms, however, into obedience if love itself is no longer able to move us (active charity and affective charity; Sermon 50: "Two Kinds of Charity"). The "book of experience" seems this time to *speak on its own* rather than to be read or made to speak. We have seen the *meditating* subject when God manifests himself in thought (Anselm: part 1), and the *interpreting* subject when God is given to us to be read in the world or in the body (Hugh and Richard of Saint-Victor: part 2). We move now to the *experiencing* subject when love itself becomes the language (Aelred of Rievaulx and Bernard of Clairvaux: part 3).

When Affect Speaks

Who indeed speaks? Or what faculty speaks, when the Bride declares her love to the Bridegroom in her loving embrace: "My Beloved is mine and I am his" (Song 2:16 JB) [*ille mihi, et ego illi*]? What Bernard notices first in this experience in common that the lovers share is a learned ignorance: we do not know, or "we do not comprehend what [the Bride] says, because we do not feel what she feels [*nescimus quid sponsa loquitur quia non sentimus quod sentit*]."[57] The discovery is sufficiently striking that it deserves to be emphasized. That impossibility to feel what the other feels [*non sentimus quod sentit*] positively enshrines the other's alterity, in the same way as in Merleau-Ponty's work the impossible "coincidence" of the "toucher-touching" establishes depth and irreducibility.[58] But, as in such crossing of flesh, Bernard does not remain in the muteness of love, which is sometimes so much of a fusion that it dies from being unable to speak. Egoism can very well lose itself in identity or "empathy" [*Einfühlung*], in an "affective fusion" [*Einsfühlung*], if the "me" [*ego*] becomes too much "to her/him" [*illi*] and she/he too much to me [*mihi*].[59] And thus we find the mystical theologian, Bernard, long before the phenomenological approaches, posing questions: "For thee is He [*tibi ille*], and for Him thou art [*tuque illi*]. But is He to thee that which thou art to Him, or does He stand in some other relation [*an aliud*] to thee? If thou speakest for us [*nobis*], and for our understanding, speak forth clearly thy thought [*evidenter quod sentis edicito*]."[60]

The phrasing here has accents that could enrich all our contemporary debates on the identification of love. One cannot indeed be "to the other" [*ei*] what "one is in oneself" [*idipsum*] without reducing the other to "another myself" [*alter ego*], and no more can the other be radically some other thing [*an aliud*] without falling into a strangeness that radically kills all alterity [*ego alter*]. In short it is obvious that the question of the generative constitution of the other on the basis of the self was already implicitly raised by Bernard of Clairvaux at the start of the twelfth century in a quasi-phenomenology of love.

But Bernard's reply to the question takes the opposite direction from intentionality, as though to speak of intention or counter-intention was already to be stuck in a pure conceptuality. It is necessary to resolve this question because with love it is always the same: "It is thus: [affect] has spoken, not the understanding [*ita est affectus locutus est, non intellectus*], and therefore what is said is scarcely understood [*et ideo non ad intellectum*]."[61] What then does the bride want to say [*qui est hoc quod dicit*]? Or rather, to what [*ad quid ergo*] is her affect addressed if it is not to understanding? The answer comes back in a flash: To nothing [*ad nihil*]. We should understand "nothing" here as nothing reasoned or reasonable.[62] It is as though, on the brink of defining the constitution of alterity on the basis of *égoïté*, all purely rational discourse had first of all to be rejected, which necessarily entailed making one abandon one's affectivity. One becomes in a way "auto-affected by oneself" (Michel Henry) to the extent of not being able to produce a discourse without losing the silent experience in which one is already engaged. To put it another way, and to return to a leitmotif that we have already used [§23. The Song of Experience], the "beginning is the *pure* and, so to speak, still *dumb*—psychological experience, which now must be made to utter its own sense" (Husserl); *affectivity* is the privileged site in which the Bride speaks, in another language, not truly what she feels (not to disarticulate her pathos into an articulate language) but at least that which she cannot silence without injuring her own flesh:

> Nor did she speak by way of expressing (her feelings) [*neque quod sensit ut exprimeret*], but in order not to be altogether silent [*sed ne taceret*]. Out of the abundance of the heart [*ex abundantia cordis*] the mouth speaketh ... The affections have their own language [*habent suas voces affectus*], in which they express themselves, even against their will [*etiam cum nolunt*].⁶³

Kinesthesis of the Body and *Pathema* of the Soul

It should then be clear: the kinesthesis of the body as well as the *pathema* [that which one suffers] of the soul, precisely because they are not always under control, speak our own truth or at least speak that identity from which we cannot distance ourselves. And that which we cannot keep silent [*nec taceret*] is not the spoken or articulated expression of our affectivity, as though there was a great deal to be said about what we feel, even if we never manage fully to do so. On the contrary, affect and flesh have "their own language" [*suas voces*], in which they overflow themselves and speak themselves—a bit like the eructation of an overfull stomach [*seu etiam saturatorum ructus*]—that which words try to hide. Such expressions,

> The lamentations of those who are in trouble, the sobs and sighs of mourners, the sudden and ungovernable screams and cries of those who are frighted or stricken ... are not the products of a deliberate purpose [*non nutu prodire animi*], but are caused by a sudden and unforeseen impulse [*sed erumpere motu*]. Thus burning and vehement love [*sic flagrans ac vehemens amor*] ... not being able to restrain itself, takes no heed of the order nor connection of the words it employs, nor even of their fewness, provided that it suffers no diminution of its vigour. Sometimes it does not seek for words [*nec verba*], nor even for articulate language [*nec voces*], but is content with the wordless [*solis ad hoc contentus suspiritis*].⁶⁴

As far as Bernard is concerned, there is a *language of affect* that is also the language of the body, and that nullifies any erroneous suspicion of "sentiment." Not that it is enough for the Bride simply to refer to it in order to put her trust in it (encyclical *Pascendi*, §24), but in that her feeling allows that to emerge in her which she could not restrain any more without fatal consequences:

Thus it is that the Bride, burning inconceivably with holy love ... takes no heed of what she speaks [*quid eloquatur*], nor of the way in which she speaks [*qualiter eloquatur*] ... but [breathes] forth the first words which come into her mind. And how should she not breathe out [*quidni eructet*] that with which she is so filled and so satisfied [*sic refecta et sic repleta*].[65]

With such a heightened experience there is also the possibility of a conceptual foundation of a "language of affect" whose translation *in via* would be to speak the paradoxical and imperious commandment to "love one's neighbor"—as if love, usually so resistant to any "command," could or should be enacted "upon order" in the Christian regime.

Love on Order

The *proposal of affect* is not in fact enough to constitute a *command to love*. The Bride recalls on the subject of her spouse: "He has set in order charity in me" [*ordinavit in me caritatem*].[66] Bernard returns to the formula of the second commandment of love: "You shall love your neighbour as yourself" (Mt. 22:39 RNJB). In both cases— the injunction to the spouse and the commandment of Christ—love seems first of all impossible because *all commands to love kill love*. Bernard asks, "How, then, has that been commanded, which can by no means, be fulfilled by us?"[67] The problem here is not simply one of the gap between being and being obliged to be—because if one can certainly *in actuality* confess one's incapacity to love, still it is necessary to find, in terms of *the commandments*, a mode of being of charity that does not auto-destruct when formulated as such. To put it another way, and to complete the paradox, one could ask on the one hand whether a love that has been commanded deserves to be called love, and on the other hand whether one could refuse the command to love without definitively obliterating the message of Christianity itself. A suitable reply is not obvious, and the questions put into play again the meaning of *affectus*—no longer this time in terms of language (sermon 67) but in terms of the realization of a mode of being that is true and permanent between the two spouses (sermon 50). We must establish here below [*in via*] a type of love that is capable of justifying and fulfilling the command of Christ, without suppressing the priority of affect, whose characteristics amount precisely to being never imposed or fully articulated.

A distinction between "actual charity" here below [*in via*], and an "affective charity" effectual only in an after-life [*in patria*], would then resolve the contradiction. On the last day we shall know that it is "not because of any works of righteousness we had ourselves done but in accordance with his own mercy" (Tit. 3:5 RNJB). But to know and say this today, as indeed on the first day of Adamic life, is to suggest we agree that affective charity "was command by a distinct law imposed upon us." And Bernard admits that this command to love "seems to refer the law rather to charity in act [*sed actuali in potius convenire*]."[68]

My purpose in this book is not to undertake an exegesis of a text that has often been brilliantly performed elsewhere.[69] My aim, in the context of a delineation of *affectus*, is very different—and comes down rather to a recognition that the double primacy of experience [§24] and affect [§25] cannot diminish the importance of the "rule" or the "commandment," whether it be divine, monastic, or simply moral. To call on this "commandment," in the form of a norm, as a trial of the self and its inner movements is not to fall into pure subjectivism, nor to militate in support of sentimentalism. As we have seen, the "I" is a privileged site for the visitation of the Word, best expressed by the will, but the "I" must nonetheless comply with the imperative to "love one's neighbor as one self," independently of all feelings of love or hatred toward the other. "Empathy" is not "sympathy," at least in the current French sense of the term, which includes union and fusion within a pathos of equals. Bernard says, "I have read, among the great and grave crimes, which the Apostle writes, that men commit, this enumerated, that they are *without natural affection* (Rom 1:31)."[70] And there is another crime even greater, at least for us here below, that is to be without rule [*sine ratione*] in our actions, when people no longer show the taste [*sapor*] nor the wisdom [*sapientia*] to affect or be affected. Bernard, longtime abbot of Clairvaux, knows this for himself and for his monks, who must all go through dry and arid times together. The rule or reason [*ratio*] that commands us to love, "steady but strong" [*sicca sed fortis*], is sometimes—indeed very often—necessary. The difficult proof of love for the one who commands [affective charity (wisdom)] has to include simple obedience to the command to love [charity of action (reason)]: "There is an affection ... which reason rules [*quam ratio regit*] ... (which) shows itself consentient to the Divine law [*consentientem legi Dei*] ... because it is good [*quoniam bona est*]."[71]

The abbot of Clairvaux is also and above all a theologian for a time of crisis. Far from being satisfied with the simple beatific joys of divine charity, he requires instead of his brother, as of himself, to love "through reason" (charity of action) what he could not, or can no longer, love by affection (affective charity)—a unique way of recovering passion.

> A certain charity of action, which, though it does not as yet refresh the soul with the sweetness of inward delight [of affective charity], yet probably contributes to fire it with the love of that love itself. Let us not love, says St. John, in word [*verbo*], nor in tongue [*neque lingua*], but in deed and in truth [*sed opera et veritate*]. (1 Jn 3:18)[72]

§26. Loving Empathy

Aimeric's request to Bernard in the Prologue to *On Loving God* that he tell him "why and how God ought to be loved [*quare et quomodo diligendus sit Deus*]" seems almost excessive in light of the difficulty of setting up a command to love.[73] In other words, while one could very well give reasons to love *in via*, by resorting to the rule of reason (charity in action), one could not provide evidence of love *in patria* without killing the impetus of love itself (affective charity). That probably explains Bernard's cautious statement at the start of *On Loving God*: "You usually ask me for prayers [*orationes*], not answers to questions [*quaestiones*]."[74] We need to be clear about what is happening here: There is a certain hesitation on the part of Bernard at the moment of producing his treatise on love. He knows this, and even feels this, paradoxically confining the philosophy to a kind of mutism that avoids the task ahead: "Accept from my poverty what I have, or I shall be thought a philosopher because of my silence [*ne tacendo philosophus puter*]."[75] But there is more because of the subject itself [*quaestio*] that makes the topic theologically *intractable*—in the double sense of the impossibility of its being analyzed and of its uncompromising nature for those who are exposed to it. Because, as far as true love (affective charity) is concerned, there are no reasons for it—we know this "in a thousand things" especially since Pascal's formulation ("the heart has it reasons of which reason know nothing").[76] But taking that too far we risk destroying what is unmistakable about love. And thus the sole response of the monk Bernard to the cardinal deacon Aimeric concerning this matter is both appropriate and well known: "I answer: the cause of loving God is God himself [*causa diligendi Deum, Deus est*]. The way to love him is without measure [*modus, sine modo diligere*]."[77]

The Mode of a Love without a Mode

"The way to love … is without measure": The Bernardine formula has been so often overused that its meaning has become completely obscured. The phrase from *On Loving God* is frequently, if not always, interpreted in the sense of "excess" [*sine modo*] or of an excess of divine love and of that which we should render God—as if the difference were above all *quantitative* and not *qualitative*. Such an exegesis certainly seems justified and even confirmed by what follows in the text: "'He first loved us' [1 Jn 4:10]. He loved—with such love, and so much and so generously—us who are so insignificant … something infinite (for God is both immense and infinite [*infinitus et immensus*]) who, I ask, ought to draw a line to our love [*finis vel modus*] or measure it out?"[78] In short *modus sine modo diligere* does mean, at least at first reading, that the "way to love him is without measure."

But, as I see it, the famous formula must also be read in another way; the essential question here is not simply that of a *quantitative excess* of the divine over the human, but of *qualitative otherness* to the way of being of human love, in comparison with divine love. Aimeric's question does not refer to the limits or the extension of the love of humankind for God, even though that would also be included in Bernard's reply to him but relates to the cause and modality of the love. "Why [*quare*] and how [in what way (*quomodo*)] God ought to be loved."[79] To put it another way, the problem is not to know *how much* God loves us and ought to be loved (*quantitative reason*) but *how* he loves us and how we have to show him (*qualitative mode*). Thus I propose a literal translation that may seem unnecessary but is nonetheless appropriate for Bernard's formula: the mode for us to love God [*modus diligendi Deum*] is to love him without a mode [*sine modo diligere*].[80] If we adopt this new formulation, which is a reinterpretation but closer to the original language (with respect to *modus*) it is the actual meaning of "book of experience" that is transformed—passing definitively from a series of syntagma (that is, a sequence of words in a particular syntactical relationship) that have to be deciphered (a hermeneutic), to a "modality of being," or a "field of personal experience" that has to be inhabited (phenomenology) [§3]. Every degree of the love of humankind for God demonstrates this—introducing in every case a *qualitative* difference where one might have thought, quite wrongly, that it would be quantitative: (a) the love of oneself for one's own sake, (b) the love of God for one's own sake, (c) the love of God for God's sake, and (d) the love of the self for God.

(a) The Love of Oneself for One's Own Sake

In the first degree of love as "love of oneself for one's own sake" we see above all and without meeting any objections that it is not a question of the other or of God—at least that is what the section heading of *On Loving God* implies: "The first degree of love [*de primo gradu amoris*]: When man loves himself for his own sake [*quo diligit homo se propter se*]."[81] The loving subject is not in fact egoistic but simply egocentric—and in this Bernard shows an astonishing modernity: "Man is driven by necessity to serve nature first. This results in bodily love [*amor carnalis*], by which man loves himself for his own sake [*propter seipsum*] … 'First came what is animal, then what is spiritual' (1 Cor. 15:46). This love is not imposed by rule [*non praecepto indicitor*], but is innate in nature [*sed naturae inseritur*]."[82]

The fleshly character [*carnalis*], indeed the "animal" [*animalis*] character of love, that has been mistakenly interpreted as "the sickness of nature and of the natural *affection*" (Delfgaauw), should rather be understood as "the first step of a natural evolution" (Blanpain). I have tried to show elsewhere (*The Wedding Feast of the Lamb*) that "the beast is not the animal, and bestiality marks precisely the descent of animality below the animal—a descent of which, paradoxically, only human beings show themselves capable."[83] That one finds the same sense in Bernard of Clairvaux of the flesh [*carnalis*], or the animal [*animalis*], in humankind is not to show a fault in human nature—rather the contrary—so long as one distinguishes it from the sinful or bestial. There is an unusual *taking into account of the human* in "the (Cistercian) love of oneself for one's own sake." And we can take a lesson from this, while being astonished that in the "book of experience" the medieval had already seen so much.[84]

But there is more, and better, than simple "fleshly love" of oneself when the imperative to "love oneself for oneself'" [*propter se*] is transformed into the imperative of the gospels to love the other, or "*You shall love your neighbour as yourself*" (Mt. 22:39 RNJB). The "as" that we are to love [*sicut*] points in fact positively to one who "shares (or fraternizes) with my nature" [*consors naturae*]—not as a sinner like me but as one of humankind like me. "[A man] can indulge himself as much as he likes as long as he remembers to show an equal [*aeque*] tolerance to his neighbor [*proximo*]."[85] In short, empathy or "affective understanding"[86] has a basis that is above all *human* in the work of Bernard of Clairvaux, not simply in solidarity with the other who is suffering (ethical point of view), but also in that while conceiving myself first of all as my self, I cannot conceive myself independently of the other (metaphysical point of view). The other appears in fact *in me*, and for Bernard the other appears even as I constitute myself, serving at once as a brake to my covetousness or desire (like shame for Sartre), and as indicative of my humanity (like, for example, the face-to-face for Levinas):

[Remember] to show an equal tolerance to [your] neighbor. O man, the laws of life and discipline impose restraint to prevent you chasing after your desire ... share nature's goods with your fellow man, that is, your neighbor ... Then will your love be sober and just [*temperans et iustus*], when you do not deny your brother what he needs from the pleasures you have denied yourself.[87]

Bernard's notion is that "in this way bodily love is shared when it is extended to the community [*sic amor carnalis efficitur et socialis*]."[88] And, setting aside all problems of anachronism, we might say it works in the same way as Husserl's inter-monadic community that has its basis in each monad, or Husserl's statement that "the alter ego becomes evinced and verified in the real of our transcendental ego."[89] The genesis of the other [*socius/alter ego*] on the basis of the self [*seipsum/ego*] is astonishingly similar from one to the other, even if for fundamentally different reasons—mystical on the one side (the access to the self through the other and thus through God), and philosophical on the other (the constitution of the world through the other). In both cases, and despite the supposed objectivism and moralism of medieval philosophy, empathy is not ethical but metaphysical, not axiological but gnoseological.

Nonetheless, according to Bernard, my neighbor on his own could not satisfy my nature. Because sharing it with him risks stripping me of it (affective fusion), if it is not also given to me by another. Bernard asks, "What are you to do, if when you share with your neighbor [*dum communicas proximo*], you yourself are left without something you need [*defuerint et necessaria*]?"[90] At this point precisely, compassionate *empathy* becomes also Christian, and self-love, like the other in the self (fleshly love and social love) becomes a mode [*modus*] of love of the human "in" God (charitable love), through which we embrace *qualitatively* his manner of being: "How can you love your neighbor with purity if you do not love him in God?"[91] In fact what characterizes Bernard of Clairvaux, following on from Richard of Saint-Victor [§18] is not the rejection of humanity but its insertion in the Trinity. Not that a properly human study of the *erotic phenomenon* did not take place—we have seen how Bernard competed in this field (description of affects)—but simply in that he found in God, and in his divine *agapê*, his justification as well as his transformation: "He who does not love God cannot love in God [*in Deo*]. You must first [*prius*] love God, so that *in* him [*in Deo*] you can love your neighbor too [*et proximus*]."[92]

The formula here is exemplary and makes the monadological the basis of the psychological, indeed of the phenomenological. One does not love the self, then God, in Bernard's writing; one loves God, then the self, and the neighbor *in* God [*in Deo*]. In other words, the "love of oneself for one's own sake," at the first level of love [*diligit homo se propter se*], says so little of God and one's neighbor that not only does humankind discover God and our neighbors in our own selves (generative phenomenology of alterity); we discover ourselves held and included *in God* and the neighbor *with us* (monadologic theology of the Trinity).[93]

Bernard's shift in sermon 50 from *love of one's neighbor* to *love of the enemy* is in this respect instructive; it establishes probably what is specific to Christianity as opposed to certain psychological tendencies. The "neighbor" [*proximus*] is certainly the person with whom one "share(s) nature's goods" according to *On Loving God*, or "he is that which you are" [*quid id est quod tu*] according to the end of sermon 50 (charity in action and affective charity).⁹⁴ And this accords with the laws of a phenomenology that is generative of alterity (*alter ego* and *ego alter*). But to love your neighbor "as yourself" [*sicut teipsum*] (Mt. 22:39) is not simply to love him because he is himself [*ipse*] like you [*tibi*] in a simple community of nature or of monads. It is for me to love the neighbor as I love God, or rather *am loved* (by God), or even better to love him *because he loves the one I love* (God himself). This is close to the Victorine condilection or "The Anti-Jealousy of God" [§18]. "You love yourself only because you love God [*nisi quia diligis Deum*]," Bernard states, and he draws a coherent conclusion: "It follows that you love as yourself [*diligis tamquam ipsum*] all those who love God as you love Him [*omnes qui similiter diligunt eum*].ˮ⁹⁵

If we are to grasp the implications of this statement in full it must be taken at face value in three progressive stages. First, the abbot of Clairvaux does not simply say that I love myself and that I love the other also for that reason. He suggests that I do not love myself *only* because I love God [*quia diligis Deum*]. It is thus through the love of God that I come to love myself, and not the other way around. Second, to love the other or neighbor does not come back simply to loving that the neighbor loves me (or detesting that he detests me), but to loving that he loves, similarly [*similiter*], the God that I love. What is important is not the love of the other for me but the love that the neighbor *himself* has for God, who is *also* the object of my love. Third, I do not directly love the other; my love is *mediated* because the neighbor loves the God that I love. I love the neighbor "because the neighbor loves" [*diligere quia diligit*] the One whom I love, and not because the neighbor loves me. These three steps in the *love of the friend*—love of the self through God, love of God in common with the other, and love of the other loving God—characterize a monadologic theology of the insertion of humankind in God (loving through and in God who loves us) where generative phenomenology will free up a privileged access (the engendering of the loved *alter ego* starting off from the loving *ego*).

But there are further implications in *loving one's enemy* that are particular to Christianity and that disqualify any approach to the other that is unilaterally metaphysical or ethical. One could certainly think here either that the other had no need for God or myself in order to be (an ontology based on the *ego*) or that I could myself attempt to love an unamiable other (ethic of the good life). But these two perspectives, however justifiable in themselves, are nonetheless irrevocably dismissed by Bernard precisely because the *eros* is nothing apart from the divine *agapê* that gives it meaning and is its foundation:

> As for an enemy, he is, as it were, nothing [*quoniam nihil est*], since he has no love for God; you cannot, therefore, love him as yourself, who do love God, but you will love even him that he may learn to love God [*diliges tamen ut diligat*]. For it is not the same thing to love a person so that he may love God [*ut diligat*], and to love him because he does this [*quia diligit*].⁹⁶

Here again, but this time in the shift from *friend* to *enemy*, we need to undertake a close reading that goes through three stages. First, the enemy is "nothing" for me [*nihil est*], not in that he does not love me, but because "he has no love for God." The perspective here is generative and constitutive and not axiologic. The other being nothing does not mean that the other "is worth nothing," in some sinful disparagement;[97] but above all that he has cancelled his own being because he no longer depends upon the One who keeps him in existence: "What could not have come into existence without [God] cannot continue in existence without him [*ne sine ipso valeat subsistere*]."[98] Here "to love" is not *to be* or *to subsist* in the scholastic sense of a "substance," a notion that is absent from the Bernardine corpus and that would not be useful for it; it is, conversely, to escape from the nothingness of non-being in the Augustinian sense of the term or to avoid the loss of the self if it does not continue in God. The "is nothing" in relation to the other is thus not my doing vis-à-vis him (that I do not love him), nor of his doing vis-à-vis me (that he does not love me); it is of the other's own doing vis-à-vis God (that he does not love the God that I love). Second, the incapacity in which I am as regards loving my neighbor in the way in which I am loved—"as myself," that is to say according to the divine mode of loving him that gives me access to my inherent love of myself [*modus (sine modo) diligere*]—does not prohibit, and indeed demands, that I love him *so that* he loves, not me, but the way that I am loved. While I may love a *friend "because* he loves" [*quia diligit*], in that he loves the God I love, I cannot love an enemy unless it is "*so that* he loves" [*ut diligat*]—that is to say, so that I can bring him also into the love of the loving God. And that is why, third, I do not look for love of me by the other but for love of God by the other—a love of which I shall be again and immediately the beneficiary if the other comes to love the God that I love: "[A person] loves [her or his] enemy as one who may perhaps at some time in the future turn to the love of God."[99]

These three points in relation to *love of the enemy*—nothingness of his being outside the love of God; love of God perceived (so that he loves), rather than shared (because he loves); and love of himself by me on the strength of the possibility of his love for God some day in the future—break definitively with all the illusions of reciprocity in love but without abandoning, as I see it, the sense of "recognition" (chap. 3). It is legitimate that I might not love my enemy, not because he is not lovable in himself but because he does not respond to the modality of my love for God. I shall, however, be called upon to love him, not because he loves *me* but so that he loves *the God* that I love—my enemy then becoming my friend, not through me (that I love him), nor through himself (that he loves me), but *through* God (that he is loved), *in whom,* in return, and in an asymmetrical fashion, he stands along with me. The *mystical* route of the incorporation of humankind in the Trinity takes precedence over the *psychological* dimension of an introspection of the self by the self, which all too often, starting off from humankind, forgets God as the source and dimension of all love: "If you love those who love you, what reward do you have? Do not even the tax collectors do as much? And if you save your greetings for your brothers and sisters, are you doing nothing exceptional? Do not even the gentiles do as much? You must therefore be perfect, as your heavenly Father is perfect" (Mt. 5:46-48 RNJB).[100]

What remains then is to define the "mode" that is specific to this divine love "without mode." The three outstanding degrees of the love of God are what counts here in a search for a *qualitative* difference, where the first degree has shown that the love "of oneself for one's own sake" [*seipsum propter se*] is only fully realized "in God" [*in Deo*], in whom oneself and the neighbor continue to be included in—or are waiting for—divine love itself.

(b) The Love of God for One's Own Sake

The difficulty of this route we have taken remains that of defining the "mode" of "love without a mode," which points, as I see it, rather to the qualitative modality of divine love than to its quantitative excess. Bernard's second degree of love shows us a way forward. The love with which humankind "loves God for ourselves and not for God" [*propter se non propter ipsum*] does not represent a "dominance" over God, far from it. According to the generative mode of alterity already defined it comes back on the contrary to Bernard of Clairvaux to show *how* "when man loves himself for his own sake" (first degree of love), this gives birth to "when man loves God for his own good" (second degree of love). Humankind, conceived and, we might almost say, carried maternally in God, with our neighbors (or perhaps we should say on standby), becomes aware, with the other, that we cannot love one another, or love God, simply with a natural love—as in this way the love of God would become superfluous: "The wise man ought to know what he can do by himself [*quid ex te*] and what he can do only with God's help [*quid ex Dei adiutorio*]; then you will avoid hurting him who keeps you from harm."[101]

"Learning through suffering," or "knowledge by test or trial"—*Tô pathei mathos*—as we have already seen [§1] reminds us of our dependence on God, though all the same one would hardly crave for such dependence in order to be saved. Bernard's psychological realism shows here how an *appeal to the supernatural* takes place within the *limits of the natural*, or that the *recognition of dependence* goes along with the insufficiencies of *independence*—and at the same time there is the necessity of achieving salvation: "If a man has a great many tribulations [*si frequens ingruerit tribulatio*]," Bernard insists, using a conditional that needs to be emphasized; then in this sense, and in this sense only, the tribulations can provoke him "frequently [to turn] to God" [*frequens ad Deum conversio fiat*] and ensure that in some way he "frequently experiences God's liberation" [*et a Deo aeque frequens liberatio consequatur*].[102] In other words in the "resort to God" we need his "help," although tribulations are not to be desired as a necessary pathway to deliverance. But while the transit through experience may achieve such deliverance, when it comes about, the faithful discover, through their experience, that autonomy as independence and subsistence of the self for one's own sake does not belong and has never belonged to the mode of divine love. The "mode" [*modus*] of our love for God is then a love "without mode" [*sine modo*], in the sense, already *negative* according to Bernard, that it refuses the sinful mode of being or the mode of being of pride, such as would be found in a false independence of humankind with regard to God. Heteronomy and not simply autonomy lie behind the modality of the love of humankind for God so that the "love of God for one's own sake" (insofar as that is what delivers us) leads progressively, and in a way that is always generative, to the "love of God for God's sake." And in this respect humankind may "love God not only for his own benefit [*non propter se tantum*], but *for* [God's self] [*sed et propter ipsum*]."[103]

(c) The Love of God for God's Sake

Along with the third degree of love, the "love of God for God's sake [and no longer simply for one's own sake]" [*Deum propter ipsum*] there emerges, *positively* this time, the distinctive modality of divine love—not love "without a mode" [*sine modo*], sinfully independent, but love "with a mode" [*cum modo*] sanctified by a disinterested recognition: "He who trusts in the Lord not because he is good to him [*non quoniam sibi bonus est*] but simply because he is good [*sed quoniam bonus est*] truly loves God for God's sake and not for his own."[104]

A familiar distinction has been made between the action of grace (to love God for that which he gives us) and that of praise (to love God for what he is), and we should not forget such a distinction in the passage from the second to the third degree of love. But Bernard implies more here—much more. It is not enough to claim that one must love God "in himself," or "for himself," and not simply "for oneself" in order to justify loving him: even less can one claim that one has succeeded in doing so. It is only the mode of divine love that can lead us there: a mode which paradoxically makes its strongest modality that of "dis-interestedness" [i.e., not lack of interest, but impartiality or lack of self-interest]. The text suggests that the love of God is very acceptable because it is dis-interested or "given freely" [*quia gratuitus*].[105] Chaste or pure love [*amor purus*] is freely given love [*amor gratuitus*] according to Bernard, not simply in the sense that it releases humankind from our pernicious inclinations or our curvature toward ourselves, but in that it learns and receives from the One who lives his love in this mode (of disinterestedness) what it is to live without a mode (of self-interest). The modality of love is what makes its beingness here, much more than a simple excess or an overflowing.

The third degree of love (love of God for God's sake), and the last stage of loving that is truly accessible to us here-below, thus allows us to see qualitatively *how* God loves us [*quomodo*] so that we ourselves are able to love him *as* he loves us [*sic amat*], that is to say in a disinterested way [*gratuitus*]. We do not just see quantitatively [*quantum*] or how far [*usque*] God loves us but come to see the vastness of his love.

> He [who] truly loves God [*veraciter*] ... loves what is God's ... [His love] is just because it gives back what it has received [*qualis suscipitur*]. For he who loves in this way loves as he is loved [*quam amatus est, amat*] ... [he] loves for God's sake and not for his own [–a love that is in his interest because it is dis-interested (*gratuitus*).][106]

(d) The Love of Oneself for the Sake of God

The fourth degree is completed with the *rendering of love for love*—or, we could say, a passing across [*transire*] of the mode of the love of humankind for God ("where man loves himself only for God") into the mode of the love of God for man ("to lose yourself as though you did not exist ... to be emptied out of yourself, belongs to heavenly, not human, love.")[107] In this way, and solely in this way, a specifically Christian mode of empathy of humankind, one for another, is born, of the kind that we find in exemplary fashion in the sermon given by Bernard on the occasion of the death of his own brother Gerard (sermon 26).

With the fourth degree of love, "man loves himself only for God's sake" [*ne seipsum diligat homo nisi propter Deum*].[108] The psychological and Bernardine spiritual realism forces us to realize, as I have already emphasized with reference to "affective charity" [§25], that such experience is not, or is seldom, found in this mortal life [*in hac mortali vita*], except at "rare" moments [*raro interdum*], or even once only [*vel semel*], indeed just in passing [*raptim*], or hardly "a single instant" [*unius vix momenti spatio*].[109] In short, what is the summit of love is probably not one of those achievements that we can realize here-below [*in via*]. But the nonaccessibility of the experience *in fact* does not prevent us describing it *legitimately* or at least as it could be. And this seems to lead us, at least initially, to a strict analogy between the Cistercian path and Rhineland mysticism. Bernard concludes that no longer loving except for the sake of God leads you "to lose yourself as though you did not exist" [*perdere tamquam qui non sis*], to "have no sense of yourself" [*et omnino non sentire teipsum*], indeed to be "almost annihilated" [*ex paene annullari*].[110] In other words there is no difference, at least at first sight, between the exclusive love of God as a renunciation of the self in Bernard's account and "detachment" as the search for nothing [*Abgeschiedenheit*] in the work of Meister Eckhart.[111] The "love of oneself for the sake of God" (fourth degree of the love of God) seems thus to accomplish a kind of "dissolution" in itself and of the self—a way of saying that nothing remains of "the affected self" that we have seen before and of saying how the self must exist in front of and *face to face* with God to survive and to be transformed.

After this journey, and the description of "the mode of a love without a mode" according to the four degrees of *On Loving God* [the Love of Oneself for One's Own Sake, the Love of God for One's Own Sake, the Love of God for God's Sake, and the Love of Oneself for the Sake of God], nothing seems left of the human except the divine in which the human is lost [*perdere*], or indeed annihilated [*annullari*], in order to love better. In the "book of experience" the "experience of affects" (part 3) tends, at least at first and according to some interpretations, to dissolve all that the "experience in thought" (part 1) and "experience of the world" (part 2) had of substance and consistence in monastic theology. With respect to the "phenomenological practice of medieval philosophy" [§2] the *theological* question of the dissolution of the subject in the experience of God (medieval debate in Bernard of Clairvaux and Meister Eckhart) joins here, in the same vein but from a different perspective, the *philosophical* dispute over the necessary distinction between "empathy" and "affective fusion" (phenomenological debate in Edith Stein and Theodor Lipps).

Deification and Annihilation

There is a shade of difference that is far from insignificant in the texts cited above by Bernard of Clairvaux (on loss of the subject in God [*perdere*] and on reduction to nothing [*annullari*]) which definitively separates Bernard's Cistercian vivacity from Rhineland annihilationism. Bernard does not demand of his brother monks that in *losing their personalities* they should not exist or that they should *forget themselves* so far as to detach themselves from everything, from themselves as well as God. He recommends them on the contrary, as we have seen, to go forward "in a way *as though* [*tamquam*] one did not exist." He underlines precisely that in this supreme condition humankind will be "*almost* [*paene*] reduced to nothing" and thus not totally or entirely dissolved into the divine. As Étienne Gilson justly and brilliantly pointed out, this is "to eliminate from oneself all that prevents one from being truly oneself. It is not that man *loses himself*, but that he *finds himself*."[112] This is important, in my opinion, because it rids Christianity conclusively of all the mysticism of "nothingness" or the "void," including that found in the Asian tradition (Buddhism, for example), but also sometimes in Christianity (in particular under the influence of the Eckhartian revival). Putting aside all anachronism, St. Bernard's warning here is salutary and deserves to be recalled today when we consider how the Resurrection is not an annihilation but a transformation.[113] Certainly the deification [*deificari*] of humankind is like "a drop of water [that] seems to disappear completely in a great quantity of wine, taking the wine's flavor and color" without being totally lost.[114] What is expected, in this fourth degree of love, is not detachment, or the *forgetting of the self* in everything, or in the deity, but a transformation or a *metamorphosis of the self* in the Trinity.

We could say, in phenomenological terms this time, that the "love of oneself for the sake of God" as last degree of the love of God) does not come down to losing oneself in an "affective fusion" in God (*Einsfühlung*: Theodor Lipps); rather it is entering into a true "empathy" with God (*Einfühlung*: Max Scheler, Edith Stein). The "I" remains oneself without denying that one can "transform oneself" or "become other." In the course of her intense debate with Theodor Lipps, Edith Stein says, "I am not one with the acrobat [in the circus] but only 'at' him. I do not actually go through his motions but *quasi* ... I do not outwardly go through his motions. But neither is what 'inwardly' corresponds to the movements of his body, the experience that 'I move,' primordial; it is non-primordial for me."[115]

This was precisely Bernard's view; though certainly he was writing at a different time, and in another place but above all, with a different overall perspective (theological and not phenomenological), he does not "lose" or "dissolve" the lived human experience in the lived experience of God. "Affective fusion" (*Einsfühlung*) in phenomenology (Lipps), like "detachment" (*Abgeschiedenheit*) in theology (Eckhart), would *annihilate* the personality, or the egoism, something that Bernard already warns against in his absolute preservation of identity: "[Human nature] remains [*manebit quidem substantia*], but in another form [*sed in alia forma*], with another glory [*alia gloria*], another power [*alia potentia*]."[116]

Passion and Compassion[117]

Such a "divine-human empathy," with its surprising modernity at the heart of an ancient discourse (the fourth degree of love: the love of oneself for the sake of God), is fully realized in the terms of an "apperceptive transfer" for which Bernard of

Clairvaux and William of Saint-Thierry seemed to share the premises: "There will be a time when he will cause everything to conform [*conformet*] to its Maker and be in harmony [*concordet*] with him. In the meantime, we make this our desire [*in eumdem nos affectum transire*]"[118] This is a remarkable statement that is worth underlining. "Affective participation" as intentional mode of empathy ("a directing of feeling toward the other's joy or suffering")[119] finds here its most exemplary illustration—that is a "transfer of affects" (*nos affectum transire*). Bernard gives us the outline of this in *On Loving God* and Saint Paul gives the basis in his hymn at the heart of his Letter to the Philippians: *hoc enim sentite in vobis, quod et in Christo Jesu*, "Let the same mind be in you that was in Christ Jesus" (Phil. 2:5 NRSV). What is stressed by Saint Paul, and developed by Bernard, if not a transfer of characteristics between man and God, is at least an *affective transport* which ideally makes the experience of humankind into the experience of God, the second "making other" the first (*in alia forma*), though always maintaining it in its original form (*manebit quidem substantiam*). The "conforming" (*conformatio*) or the "harmony of hearts" (*concordet*) is accomplished only as a result of a "transfer" (*transire*), through which the sentiments (*affectus*) that are in humankind (*nos*) become progressively those that are in God (*in eumdem*), in that God transforms them, not to dissolve them but to give them back to us in some way purified. Deification (*deificari*), for Bernard, is not a dissolution of the human into the divine, but on the contrary an "affection" (*affici*) or even "liquefaction" (*liquescere*) such that the human affect—like the "transfer of fluxes" in Husserl—flows into the divine affect without being suppressed or annihilated: "To love in this way is to become like God [*sic affici, deificari est*] ... In those who are holy, it is necessary for human affection to dissolve in some ineffable way [*ineffabili liquescere*] and be poured into the will of God [*atque in Dei penitus transfundi voluntatem*]."[120]

Since in Bernard's *book of experience* to love or "be affected" [*affici*] is to become like God or "be deified" [*deificari*], does that mean that God himself is affected when we are transformed in him? The question comes up since a God without affect would be in some way, and logically, contrary to his nature that is divine and thus deifying. We might recall in this context Origen's famous hypothesis, taken over by François Varillon [*La Souffrance de Dieu*]: *Ipse Pater non est impassibilis*—"The Father himself is not impassable."[121] Though a direct dialogue with Origen's *Homilies on Ezekiel* is impossible to prove,[122] Bernard seems in fact to correct Origen's formula in his *Sermons on the Song of Songs*. His funeral elegy (sermon 26) given by Bernard sometime after the death of his own brother, Gerard, in 1138 is perhaps the most moving and beautiful of the *Sermons on the Song of Songs*:

> He that is joined unto the Lord is one spirit (1 Cor. 6:17) with Him, and is transformed [*mutator*], into a certain feeling of the Divine presence [*in divinum affectum*] ... Although God is impassible [*porro impassibilis est Deus*], He is not incapable of compassion [*sed non incompassibilis*], and it is his especial attribute always to have pity and to spare.[123]

Certainly, it is true that humankind is transformed by God (*patitur*) in a transfer of affects (*affectum transire*), by which deification is produced (*deificari*) without dissolution (*manebit quidem substantia*). But it could not be the same for God. That would suggest (in an anthropological reduction), submitting God to our affects and reducing him to our humanity. Bernard takes care to emphasize and to sustain, the thesis of *divine impassibility* in line with medieval philosophy and theology in general—avoiding the heresy of theopaschism or the notion that God could suffer. God is impassible—*impassibilis est Deus*—at least in the sense that he does not suffer necessarily from *that which* we suffer and *as* we suffer. But such a conception of impassibility does not prohibit a certain form of "compassibility" or "compassion." On the contrary, *non est incompassibilis*—"he is not incapable of compassion." Briefly then, the thesis of the *impassibility* of God is not contrary to his "compassibility." And it is certainly to the credit of the Cistercian abbot to have made this distinction in his subtle description of "experience in affects" (part 3). The impassibility of the Father, that is necessarily maintained because he is not one of humankind and so does not suffer like us (as is possibly implied in Origen's thesis), requires, however, in its stead a form of "compassion" [*non est incompassiblis*] which renders him so evidently close to man that one is no longer able to accuse God of some sort of *indifference* with regard to the spectacle of human misery.[124]

The exemplary definition of God that Bernard gives in *On Loving God*: "*non est affectus Deus, affectio est*" could be translated as "God is not affected, he is affection." God is "not affected" because the affect of humankind [*affectus*] is almost always exterior or received from the outside: we receive our affects without choosing or deciding to undergo them. But he is nevertheless "affection" [*Deus affectio est*] in that the active love that he shows [*affection*] is always interior and deliberate: he makes the choice of compassion for that which we ourselves suffer.[125] The exclusion of affect in God [*affectus*] preserves his impassibility, and the necessity of his love or affection for us [*affectio*] makes possible his "compassibility" or "compassion." The God who is, in Bernard, "impassible ... [but] not incapable of compassion" is a valid development of Origen's "Father [who] is not himself impassable." Not that Bernard needs at all costs to maintain the impassibility of the Father, but Bernard realized that his passibility ought not to be identified simply with human sensibility, though God is not unfeeling, theologically speaking: "On the one hand, in order to avoid the anthropomorphic representation of a God submitted to his passions, it is necessary to recognize the impassibility of God. On the other hand, this impassibility ought not to be understood as insensitivity because, in God also, suffering is characteristic of love" (Emmanuel Housset).[126]

It Has to Come Out ...

From the experience of the Song of Songs we pass then ultimately to the "song of experience." We have already seen, though we might now formulate it in another way, that with regard to the "*pure* and, so to speak, still *dumb*—psychological experience" as well as the "language of affect" [§25], *it is useless to speak if it is not in order to experience it*. When an event (tragic or happy) occurs, one finds the whole horizon overturned. The death of his brother Gerard in 1138, while he was working on the Song of Songs (sermon 26), was not an event *in* the world but an event *of* the world—which went so far as to modify its structure. It is events (ontologic and not ontic) that produce an "advent," unanticipated because their coming must, or should, change our capacity of seeing the world or of constituting it. An event is not "created," as in the fashionable formula which maintains that it can only be caused, "found," or "discovered." Human beings are "the ones to whom something happens" because only the human being is "capable of events" in the sense that only humans are beings with destinies.[127] Leaving suddenly the transports of the lovers that he had emphasized from the start of these sermons ["Let him kiss me with the kisses of his mouth" (Song 1:1)][128] the abbot of Clairvaux makes us see how, when our neighbor is close, or indeed *very close* (and Gerard was Bernard's actual brother), the *abrupt* experience of *death* may put an end to the songs of joy, bringing the one who is affected by sadness and mourning into his grief. Bernard wonders what he has to do with the Song of Songs, and says to his brother monks: "My grief, and the pain which I am enduring, compels me to come to an end."[129]

Tô pathei mathos—"Learning through suffering," or "knowledge by test or trial" [§1]. The phenomenological definition of experience [§2] as a "passage" and "transformation" of the self (*Erfahrung* [Heidegger, Maldiney]), and not simply as "lived experience" or "experience of the self by the self" (*Erlebnis* [Husserl, Gadamer]) reaches its highest point here. We can reject any suspicions of a flight from the intelligible by Bernard; he makes plain once more how he lives through, and himself inhabits, his own existence—the *affectus* that he has always declared, in other places and at other times, as the "compassionate" base of God himself. Because it is not enough to *speak of* the challenge of experience, as he does in his fine sermons [*dicere*], it is still necessary to "make his way through" [*ex-perire*], to the point of reaching true wisdom [*sapientia*]. Bernard is not exempt from traversing this experience, he explains, some time after his bereavement and, as it were in confidence, when the illusion of all mastery of himself in his suffering has ceased ("I am overcome"), and with the choking sense in his inner self of one who cannot express himself openly, ends ("it must come forth"):

> I was able to command my tears [on the day of the funeral] but not my sorrow … [But now] I am overcome [*fateor, victus sum*], I confess, and what I suffer inwardly [*foras quod intus patior*] must come forth into the light [*exeat*]. Let it come forth, then, to the eyes of my children, who, knowing the greatness of my loss, will pardon the excess of my grief, and be the more moved kindly to console me.[130]

The confession here is such that it underlines once again how these great figures, or at least these great saints, show their true strength in an admission of weakness. It is not solely a spiritual question but simply a human one. We do not conquer our passions in just accepting them but in expressing them and offering them up to one another—to fellow human beings or God—who are capable of accepting them.[131] But the Christian who is caught up in the turmoil of suffering says more or speaks differently: in spite of his tears, Bernard does not convert his bitterness into the last word of a *Treatise on Despair*. On the contrary, in his belief in the communion of saints, he asks for "mercy" from his dead brother, who has *himself also* become, through his union with "Merciful God" [*qui inhaeres misericordi*], "impossible … [but] not incapable of compassion."[132]

What is true of God becomes thus also true through the participation of humankind since the latter are themselves fully within the former. The "conveying of feelings" from human to God ["Let the same mind be in you as was also in Christ Jesus" (Phil. 2:5 RNJB)] is transformed into a "transfer of affects" from one human being to another—one standing *in* God "with" the other or beseeching *in via* compassion of the deceased, who is now *in patria*. The *human-divine empathy* of a God "impassible ... [but] not incapable of compassion" forms and transforms the *humano-human empathy* for those who recognize themselves, through him and in him, as also capable of compassion. The *properly human affection* [*affectus*] of the deceased Gerard united with God is not in this sense "diminished" according to Bernard [*imminutus*], as we could imagine if there was a supposed indifference of those who stand in glory toward those still steeped in their misery. It is on the contrary "metamorphosed" or "transformed" [*immutatus*]—that is to say it becomes possible in the hereafter, through compassion [*compassio*], or love [*affectio*], to give that which his passion [*passio*], or his affect [*affectus*], did not know how to offer here-below, when he could not surrender himself without suffering as a result:

> It must necessarily be that you, my dear brother, should be pitiful [*esse misericordem*], because you are joined unto Him who is Pity itself [*qui inhaeres misericordi*] [and from now are delivered from misery]. Although you can no longer feel any unhappiness, although you can no longer suffer [*qui non pateris*], yet you can still feel for the suffering of others [*compateris tamen*]. Your affection, then, is not diminished [*non est imminutus*], but [transformed] [*sed immutatus*].[133]

He fears to say too much and thereby to undo what he has been describing, so it is necessary above all to keep quiet, to let "*affect speak* and not the understanding" [*affectus locutus est, non intellectus*]. At the end of the sermon Bernard says "tears put an end to my words" [*finem verborum incidunt lacrymae*] and he shows his own feelings, their transfer to God, and the silent experience they bear.[134] But such an exposure of his suffering flesh does not make him any less human, far from it. Flesh so injured, at least when all this is consensual and transformative rather than just spoken, allows us to see the human qualities that would otherwise be hidden. One is never more human than when one recognizes affects [*affectus*] and discovers God there precisely in our own language as love or "affection" [*affectio*]. Bernard, as he brings his troubles to mind, and tries to put an end to all this ("O Lord, impose a limit to my tears, and bring them to an end"), goes beyond a simple avowal of powerlessness. He moves purposefully into a site of dependence—all the more human because it does not fly off directly into the spiritual:

> I have confessed my great affliction, and deny it not. Someone has called this carnal [*carnalem quis dixerit*]; I do not deny that it is human [*ego humanum non nego*], just as I do not deny that I am a man [*sicut nec me hominem*]. If that does not suffice, then I shall not deny that it is carnal [*se ne hoc sufficit, nec carnalem negaverim*] ... Far from being insensible to [suffering] I shudder at death, I confess, for myself and for those who are dear to me.[135]

But so that the affect speaks [*affectus locutus est*], and because one cannot reduce it to silence, it is still important to "allow it" to speak, indeed to make it speak—in the sense that one opens up the possibility of affecting and being affected. In linking up affectivity and spirituality (part 3), one can certainly "Feel Oneself Fully Alive" (chap. 7) and join together "Experience and Empathy" (chap. 8). But all the more it is necessary to have the experience of *freedom* understood here as openness or "*apérité*" (chap. 9).[136] In Bernard's works, in a way that is probably unique and original in philosophy, it is not simply a question (or no longer a question) of "free will" or deliberate choice, but rather of "freedom" as an act of "turning toward" what is happening. *Grace* [*gratia*] as an "appearance" and "visitation" in theology is what we call an *event* [*Ereignis*], as "monstration" (showing) or "appropriation" in phenomenology. "Experience," understood as *Erfahrung*, as we have seen at the start of this book, in taking place comes over us, "reaches us and falls on us" [*über uns kommt*], indeed overturns and transforms us [§3].[137]

One does not "decide" to live in God or to "enter" into him, any more than one "chooses" to rejoice in the joy of another or "chooses" to suffer from an other's suffering. Empathy or the "transfer of affects" is something that is received rather than decided upon, including when it comes to welcoming God. All the same, we should engage in empathy or at least not refuse it. There is one way of having an experience that is "to refuse all experience." A *decision of closure* would refuse all *openness*. This was well understood by Bernard before phenomenology made it a leitmotiv of a freedom defined as "openness" (*apérité*) and not simply defined as the "power to decide." To be free as "to open up" and "to prepare oneself for" [*apero*] is in this sense no expansion at all of the "field" or "book of experience" of monastic theology. On the contrary, it establishes the limits of that theology, or declares its apogee, through what was already given at the start (chap. 1: "The Theophanic Argument") or by the act of allowing God to show himself in our thoughts (Anselm). And it finds its meaning through the condition of its final reception: freedom as "openness" (chap. 9: "Openness [*apérité*][138] and Freedom" (Bernard of Clairvaux)].

9

Openness [*apérité*] and Freedom

Going through Freedom

"What I suffer inwardly [*foras quod intus patior*] must come forth to the light [*exeat*]."[1] Such are, or were, Bernard's last words at the time of his brother Gerard's death in sermon 26 on the Song of Songs. If it is still a question here of "freedom," which will be the subject of Bernard's *Concerning Grace and Free Will*,[2] it is not so much a matter of choosing as of recognizing that one does not have choice. Or, we might say that to choose is first of all to open up (*apérité*) rather than to decide (free will). We often suggest concerning freedom that it is a "faculty," like the intellect, like the will, like the feelings and other powers of the soul or the body. Thus, Descartes identifies free will in an exemplary fashion as "the power of choosing to do a thing or not to do it."[3] Kant sees it as a "faculty of beginning a series of successive things or states" or "autonomy of pure practical reason, i.e., freedom."[4] Hegel sees it as a superseding and reconciling of opposites.[5] These definitions are all worthwhile, though one could not easily compare or indeed identify Cartesian free will, Kantian autonomy, and Hegelian supersession. In all these cases freedom is defined as a *mode of action*, a "power" [*potentia*], or a "faculty" [*facultas*], according to which, in the words of Thomas Aquinas, "a power [*potentia*] as such [*secundum illud quod est potentia*], is directed to an act [*ordinatur ad actum*] … Wherefore we seek to know the nature of a power from the act to which it is directed [*accipi ex actu quem ordinatur*]."[6] In the same way that our sight is organized by color, hearing by sound, and touch by tangible objects, the faculty of feeling aims at the perceptible, that of thinking toward the intelligible and that of acting toward the transformation of oneself and the world. According to Marie-Joseph Nicolas, the editor of Aquinas, "[i]n the language of St. Thomas, the 'powers' of the soul correspond to what these days we would call 'faculties.' It is a question here of *active powers*, not of the power to receive a form, or undergo an action, but the power to produce an action or an operation."[7]

§27. The Amphibology of Freedom

It is not surprising that we come back again to Thomas Aquinas—as we did for the definition of "love of the self" in relation to Richard of Saint-Victor's "condilection"

[§17]—because his perspective allows us as an indirect consequence to clarify what St. Bernard is saying. Not that Aquinas simply serves as a foil, on the contrary; I have emphasized elsewhere his importance as the only one to have pushed his thought to the "threshold" and as the precursor in considering the question of "finitude."[8] But here what is significant is that his definition of freedom as faculty *closes* and *thinks otherwise* what was previously "openness" or *apérité*. In the *amphibology* (or duality of meaning) of freedom, we do not find a simple opposition of genres but differences in thinking that spread over a century (from the twelfth to the thirteenth century), where it is the world itself that has profoundly changed. There is nothing to regret here, and indeed the change can be welcomed, but the "book of experience" so beloved of monastic theology will come to be closed or at least will not be read with the spontaneity of those who had only just learned what it was that "to read," and thus "to decipher," seemed to want to say.

The Faculty or the Power of Action

What then do we find concerning free will in Aquinas? On free will he is canonical: his definition of freedom will be very different from that given by Bernard, but it will come to determine the whole history of philosophy in the future. Aquinas is stern and doctrinal: "The free-will is indifferent to good and evil choice [*indifferenter se habet ad bene eligendum vel male*]: wherefore it is impossible for free-will to be a habit [*impossibile est quod sit habitus*]. Therefore it is a power [*relinquintur ergo quod sit potentia*]."[9] Two characteristics thus define free will in the eyes of Aquinas and will constitute the norm of all later reflections on freedom: indifference with respect to oppositions [of good and evil choice] and its power of action rather than its "habitus" or disposition. To be free is to have the choice to act on the basis of the choice. The "faculty" [*facultas*] is "a power ready for operation" [*potestatem expeditam ad operandum*] according to Aquinas, while the habit of freedom according to Bernard of Clairvaux, who is explicitly cited by Aquinas in his discussion, is reduced and taken as "a certain aptitude by which a man has some sort of relation to an act [*habitudinem ad actum*]."[10]

What has happened is obvious enough: Bernard's concept of freedom as *habitus animi* or "disposition of the spirit" has been directly transposed to freedom as *potentia animi* or "power of the spirit" by Aquinas. This is an important decision and will remain important in terms of its historicity since it determines a way of thinking about the freedom of humankind that continues as far as today. From Aquinas to Hegel, including Descartes and Kant, freedom remains understood as a "power" [*potentia*], or a "faculty" [*facultas*], either as a mode of action through which it comes down to the subject to decide, according to given alternatives (the moment of choice) and to act in consequence (the moment of effectuation). That was not, however, how Bernard saw it in the twelfth century nor, paradoxically, how it was seen by Martin Heidegger in the twentieth century.

In fact, despite the insistence of Aquinas, and a good number of medievalists influenced by him, Bernard—as far as the content of what he is saying is concerned— resists retrospective interpretation through the Thomist formula or through

Cartesianism. In whatever way we take the famous revival by Descartes of the image of God in humankind in terms of the infinity of the will ("the mark of the workman imprinted on his work"),[11] and despite the insistence of many commentators on his anticipation of Descartes, Bernard is much further from Descartes than is usually supposed.[12] Bernard says, "I do not speak of willing what is good, nor of willing what is evil, but merely of willing [*sed velle tantum*]"; but the "self-determining" of free will, or the discovery of pure "will" independently of that which is willed, is only ever found by default in Bernard's work.[13]

Thus, we find a central thesis in *Concerning Grace and Free Will* that it is important for us now to try and recover: in Bernard's work the capacity of choosing is a matter of openness (*apérité*), rather than a "faculty" (power). And it is only because of what is *lacking* in free will (the pure will), of being always preceded by grace (the freedom of grace in the face of sin) and summoned by glory (the freedom of glory in the face of misery), that free will comes to be satisfied with a position of neutrality or with its simple power of opposition. In other words, the freedom of free will for Bernard does not indicate a simple alternative according to which the subject "receives [or refuses] salvation" insofar as he "recognizes himself free to [decide] on his own by his will" (Jean-Luc Marion). Nor does it indicate a kind of topsy-turvy reconstruction in which "all our history *starts with this free decision*," that is to say of an "intentional being [who] can *accept* or *refuse* such and such an object, say *yes* or *no*, and that from the simple fact that he is gifted with will" (Étienne Gilson).[14] To start off with a "choice" between alternatives, taking from that a definition of freedom as "action" is, as I see it, to read Bernard's *Concerning Grace and Free Will* the wrong way around. Bernard does not go from freedom to grace, or from a "neutral faculty of deciding upon the gift" to the "reception of the gift"—readings that depend directly on the identification of freedom as an "active power" in Thomas Aquinas or a "power" of "determining oneself to one of the other of two contraries" with Descartes.[15]

To return to the "book of experience" as it was lived and described in the twelfth century is to turn directly, and to depend upon, an otherness. The *experience of affects*, or the link between affectivity and spirituality (part 3), is not just a hollow expression from an epoch that is now long passed. The *spiritus* unites with *affectus* in that the one and the other are forms of "openness." We say of a being or of an individual that they are "spiritual" even today, in a language like French, not in that they "decide" or "think" but in that they "aspire to" [*spiro*] what happens to them. "*Apérité*," as a form of openness (*apero*: I open) does not then withdraw from deciding, rather the opposite. All the same it knows that the first decision is not one of "choosing" but of "turning to the right side" to open up (or not to open up) toward choice.

Apérité or the Capacity to Receive

As we can see from the title of Bernard's small book, *Concerning Grace and Free Will*, divine action (grace) precedes and is in contrast with human action (free will). Freedom is in reality, in his eyes, nothing less than "consent" to the gift—that is to say it is an "active passivity" in which subjects make ready to receive what has been assigned to them: "None can grant [salvation] save God alone, nothing can receive it save the free will."[16] Free will, considered positively and spiritually, "welcomes" or develops the capacity [*capacitas*] to receive the gift of salvation, far more than it operates the choice of accepting or refusing. It is only where it is in some way "switched off" from grace (freedom of grace) and glory (freedom of glory) that it is experienced wrongly as a simple freedom of choice ("free will" in the modern sense of the term) independently and irrespective of any motive for the choice: "It hath, I think, been sufficiently shown that this freedom of wills is yet in certain fashion held captive [*captiva tenetur*], so long as the other two kinds of freedom [grace and glory] scarcely at all, or only in small measure, accompany it."[17] It is not then by default or *a posteriori*, and not owing to an excess or *a priori*, that humankind is defined by free will in Cistercian thought. Freedom does not describe for Bernard firstly and originally the essence of humankind, as we shall go on to see [§28]. Quite simply, the *philosophical* freedom of choice that lies behind free (intentional) will (reason) always comes second relative to the primary *theological* freedom of the welcome for a divine gift. Right at the start of his treatise Bernard says authoritatively, "What ... doth free will do? I answer in a word: It is saved."[18] And there is no question of deciding, or it being decided, "for" or "against" salvation.

Under all the "metaphysical history of freedom" defining free will as the power of an independent stance between opposing choices, and as the faculty of action starting off from the subject's self (from Aquinas up to and including Hegel), there stands a mystical identification, that philosophy has come very close to forgetting, of the free act as a "reception of the gift" and "consent." Martin Heidegger does not explicitly cite St. Bernard but was able to rediscover the "essence of freedom" under the phenomenological concept of openness or *apérité* [*Offenständigkeit*][19]—which Bernard's treatise helps us in turn to clarify afresh. If, on the one hand, "disclosedness [openness] belongs essentially to the constitution of Dasein," as Heidegger says in *Being and Time*, and if, on the other hand, "the essence of truth belongs in the context of freedom," and that freedom is, as Heidegger states in his lecture *The Essence of Truth*, "unhiddenness" (the letting be of being and the opening up of openness), then it is a safe bet that *mystical* identification of freedom as an opening up to God (Bernard of Clairvaux) also had a part to play in the *phenomenological* identification of *ek-sistence* as "the ex-position of the question of being" (Heidegger). Heidegger thinks (and no doubt the Cistercian would have signed up to his formula) that freedom before anything else, before being "negative" or "positive," is a surrender to the unhiddenness of being as such.[20]

Certainly, what is revealed (unhidden) is not the same: Being on the one hand (Heidegger); God on the other (Bernard). Moreover, those who do the revealing have nothing in common: Heidegger is a phenomenologist and Bernard a mystical theologian. All the same, the attitude or disposition (*habitus*) is the same. As we hardly need to repeat here, medieval philosophy has much to say to phenomenology, and phenomenology has much to say to medieval philosophy. The Bernardine *identification* of "free will" as "consent of the will" and "self-determination" corresponds in another schema to the Heideggerian *designation* as "unhiddenness (*Offenständigkeit—apérité*)" and "exposition of ... being."[21]

In this openness of being, or openness to the other, "There Is No Choice," or, as I have tried to show elsewhere, we do not have the choice whether or not to have choice.[22]

The requirement of a "philosophy of decision" in fact calls on us not so much to choose "this or that" (free will) or to take on "that which has been chosen" (responsibility), as to "choose ourselves in choosing" (*apérité* or openness). Kierkegaard, successor in this respect to Bernard of Clairvaux, and precursor of Heidegger, says: "What takes precedence in my *Either/Or* is, then, the ethical. Therefore, the point is still not that of choosing something; the point is not the reality of that which is chosen but the reality of choosing."[23] To choose the reality of choosing, or to be open rather to make a choice of this or that, is then today an existential perspective (to choose choosing) and a phenomenological perspective (*Dasein*), but its foundation lies in a spiritual and monastic quest (consent). *Apérité* (and) freedom, as I have placed them in the heading to the present chapter (chap. 9), form a "connection" initiated in the twelfth century (Bernard of Clairvaux), but which awaited the nineteenth century (Kierkegaard) and the twentieth century (Heidegger) to be reactivated or oriented afresh.

The *book of experience* conceptualized from the start within the framework of a monastic community—"experience of thought" (Anselm of Canterbury: Benedictine), "experience of the world" (Hugh and Richard: Victorines), "experience of affects" (Aelred of Rievaulx and Bernard of Clairvaux: Cistercians)—was not simply to be confined within the context of medieval philosophy. It opened up on the contrary a perspective that I should like to call "*philosophy of religious experience*", which is not at all the same as "philosophy of religion." It is time in fact to rediscover a philosophy in which the "criterion of belief"—whether philosophical or religious—is not disclaimed (Pascal, Kierkegaard, Nietzsche …) without necessarily limiting access to those who can, or say they can, adhere to it.[24] To "converse" or "dialogue" is certainly worthwhile [*loquente*], but always according to a manner of "acting," which is above all a way of "being disposed" [*habitus*], rather than making a choice to favor one side over the other. At the opening of his *Concerning Grace and Free Will*, Bernard says:

> It happened once that, while I was publicly commending the grace of God towards me that in any good work I both recognized [the kindness of God] and felt that I was being furthered and hoped for full attainment, by its means, one of the bystanders demanded: What then is thine own work in the matter, or what recompense or reward dost thou hope for, if so be that God doth it all?[25]

What Then Is Thine Own Work?

Quid tu ergo? What about you then? [or, in the Eales translation "What then is thine own work?"] One of those present, or one of those listening to Bernard's appreciation of the work of grace in him, asks, "What … dost thou hope for, if so be it that God doeth all?" The argument here evokes the quarrel over Pelagianism, dealt with briskly by St. Augustine.[26] In his *Retractions* St. Augustine recalled, "Those persons [Pelagians] … defend free will in such a manner as to deny the grace of God by affirming that it is bestowed according to our merits."[27] In short, in too earnestly divesting oneself of Pelagianism one can fall into an "excess of grace" or the sentiment that "God does everything" [*totum facit Deus*] without leaving any place for humankind. According to a lesson that Descartes would later recollect, directly inheriting from Bernard,[28] the question of freedom is first of all a matter of *experience* in Bernard's *Concerning Grace and Free Will*. It is not a question here of an abstract debate on the subject of the power of humankind confronted by God in a metaphysical quasi-rivalry between power and counter power (absolute power and conditional power). What counts is the description, part mystical but, as we shall see, well supported by argument [§28], of the "consent of the human will" [*consensus voluntarius*] of the believer in relation to our Savior, to whom the believer remains open rather than having made a choice.

The treatise *Concerning Grace and Free Will* is unique among Bernard's works (apart from Letter 174 on the Immaculate Conception) in that it was written on his own initiative, not in response to a request from others. At the same time its existential intensity is considerably increased when we learn that it is confidentially addressed to William, abbot of Saint-Thierry, who is invited to "amend" or correct it, and that it is also addressed to the "charity of the reader."[29] It is far from being a discourse *in abstracto* because, as far as Bernard was concerned, one could not discourse upon freedom except *in concreto*, to the extent that he preferred the "giver of the good" [*dator boni*] to the simple "teacher" [*doctor boni*] and preferred those who "aid" [*iuvari*] to those who "instruct" [*doceri*]. To introduce his thesis Bernard explains that "one thing it is to lead the blind and another thing to carry the weary" [*ac fesso praebere vehiculum*]. To the first, the "blind," one simply shows the way [*ostendit viam*]: to the second, the weary man, one "giveth the wayfarer food for his journey" [*praebet viaticum itineranti*]. The teacher can certainly clarify things, but the "giver of the good" acts and does what is right, indeed does good. Those who just give lessons give nothing unless they are capable of putting into practice what they preach. And that is what is at stake with regard to freedom, as with free will in general: not simply to want to do it but to "perform the same."[30]

Velle adiacet mihi, perficere autem non invenio—"The will is present with me, but [I cannot accomplish it]" (Rom. 7:18).[31] This quotation from St Paul's Letter to the Romans, slightly modified in Bernard's own version, serves as a leitmotiv throughout the treatise. Freedom is not satisfied simply by the will (free will), although certainly it holds firmly to it; it strives also to will the good that it knows ("freedom of counsel") and to "perform the good" that it wishes (freedom according to one's own pleasure). Bernard does not try to use the Pauline tension between "will" and "power" [*velle* and *posse*] that we have already seen [§27] to disengage pure will as a power operating between contrasting choices (free will as such). Rather he makes us see how a freedom that is not directed (by freedom of counsel and freedom according to one's own pleasure) is already powerless as freedom. One can reject then what we find in discussions of Bernard by many medievalists—a direct link between "image and metaphysical freedom," and the identification of freedom with the simple "possibility of saying 'yes' or 'no.'"[32] In Bernard's thought everything starts with (creative) grace and returns to (salvific) grace—and outside this circle nothing remains of freedom simply as nature or pure will, other than by default.

The rallying cry of freedom as vocation and essence of humankind [§28] leads then to a call *to* the freedom, in that freedom held "captive" in its neutrality paradoxically needs to be set free in order to be redirected. Philosophically reduced to an "image," or to free will that is simply a "faculty" or "power of choice," freedom awaits *theologically* being liberated in order to find its "likeness" as "*apérité*." The essence of freedom is "openness"—to the other in general and to God in particular. What medieval philosophy in reality initiated (St. Bernard) has, as we have seen, only recently been rediscovered in phenomenology (Heidegger).

§28. The Summons of Freedom

The Response to the Summons

Speaking about the summons *of* freedom does not imply making a summons *to* freedom. If, as we shall see [§29], it is really and ironically necessary, according to St. Bernard, to "free up free will," the first call is not to give it up, nor to redo it (in linking it afresh to grace and salvation); it is to welcome it or rather to confirm it as the act of acceptance or being saved: "Take away free will and there remaineth nothing to be saved [*tolle liberum arbitrium, non erit quod salvetur*]; take away grace and there is no means by which it can be saved [*tolle gratiam, non erit unde salvetur*]."[33] Grace and freedom respond to one another without ever breaking the circle: what is threatened, on the contrary, is that a break between them would be the site of sin. "This work of salvation cannot be wrought without two factors; the one [grace], that by which it is wrought, and the other [free will], that for which or in which it is wrought."[34]

Human subjects, as recipients and destination of grace, do nothing in their freedom but welcome it and do not choose it: freedom is *apérité* rather than faculty. Moreover, free will is such that it singularizes whoever has received grace. The question is not, or is no longer, like an interlocutor or an assistant asking, "what about you?" or "what are you doing?" It is that posed by Bernard himself, addressing himself all the more as he modifies the question: "What therefore, thou askest, doth free will do?" [*quid igitur agit, ais, liberum arbitrium*].[35] The point here is not who makes the individual's freedom (I/Thou), but rather the free will that makes *me* and defines *me* myself. I am never as free through my freedom as when *I am made* by it, that is to say when I allow myself to be defined as the one "for whom" [*cui*] and "in whom" [*in quo*] grace is realized. Allocated by an other (grace or all other forms of alterity) and committed to a potential welcome (vessel or screen), my freedom singularizes me out, makes my individuality, and defines me as myself. *I* am not then sum of my acts (Sartre), nor my power to accept or refuse contraries (Descartes): *I* am principally the one who makes ready to receive the gift that is grace, in an openness or *apérité* that makes my freedom, and thus my singularity.

Theologically, and in the most ordinary human way, we do not distinguish ourselves from one another through our decisions, no matter how important they are but through our capacity to make ourselves the recipients, or receptors, of alterity— here the created grace. Emmanuel Levinas emphasizes "Here I am, just that," "Without referring myself directly to [God's] presence."[36] And St. Bernard keeps insisting upon this, demonstrating on this topic a rare originality and moreover distancing himself from Saint Augustine. What differentiates humankind from animals in his view is not simply *reason*, which would, for the Cistercian, reduce the category of *apérité* once more to a faculty: it is salvation itself and the capacity to consent to it. What counts, for the abbot of Clairvaux, is not first or all a supposed superiority of the nature of humankind over animals, even though that could not be denied: it is the suitability for salvation through which the human being, like the angels, is originally summoned by grace to the opening up of our freedom. "The spirit of a brute can in no wise receive such salvation [*pecoris spiritus salutem huiuscemodi minime capit*], for it lacketh the faculty of free consent whereby it may submissively obey the God that saveth it [*salvanti placide obtemperet*]."[37] The summons to freedom by grace *can be read then in a way through its response*, in that respondents show at once the grace that maintains openness and their singularity in their freedom. What is at issue here is freedom, of the kind we see in the figure of St. Matthew painted by Caravaggio in "The Calling of St. Matthew," in which Christ is saying "Follow me" (Mt. 9:9). Among the people shown in the painting, as Jean-Luc Marion rightly points out, "Only Matthew reads a call therein because he alone took it for himself ... 'This is mine? This is for me?' ... Matthew received the call of his calling by taking it upon himself—and this taking it upon himself already constituted his first response."[38] The original freedom, as Christianity understands it, does not consist in replying "yes" or "no" to an alternative or choice that the creator granted first of all to his creatures. It comes down, above all, to being "always 'Yes'" in the Son, open to him and identifying for oneself, according to "God's promises," as St. Paul writes to the Corinthians, that "each in him is 'Yes'" (2 Cor. 1:18-20 RNJB). The final *amen* of the glorious Resurrection (salvific freedom) is always linked to the *amen* of the originary creation (creative freedom)—and according to St. Bernard is unblemished before sin.

The mistake or the misconception of a purely philosophical reading of Bernard's treatise *Concerning Grace and Free Will* derives from reading it at cross-purposes or back to front: from free will to grace and not from grace to free will, as opposed to what the title explicitly states (in Latin: *De gratia et libero arbitrio*). Moreover, one misses the meaning of freedom if one reduces free will to the autonomy of pure will, forgetting that at the start it was there in order to be oriented and receptive to the gift of God. As far as Bernard is concerned, creative grace (free will) cannot be understood independently of "salvific grace" (freedom of good counsel and according to one's pleasure), paradoxically even before original sin. Humankind does not have first of all a created nature (free will), only then to receive a kind of over-nature (freedom of good counsel and according to one's pleasure). Such a conception of an addition, or *superadditus*, which according to Henri de Lubac constituted "a revolution in the conception of man and of his relationship with God" in the mystical perspective of the thirteenth century, is totally absent from the mystical perspective of the twelfth century.[39] The "addition" [*additamentum*] of salvific grace (freedom of good counsel and according to one's pleasure) to creative grace (free will) has nothing to do with such an "add-on" or "complement" of an over-nature to nature [*superadditus*]. "The terms fear and love ... signify affections, but with the addition [*cum additamento*] [of God] they signify virtues; so also is it one thing to will and another thing to will what is good ... [the addition comes from grace]."[40] The "addition" [*additamentum*] is not simply a complement or the actualization of a power by Bernard [*superadditus*]; it is the excess or, as in the title of Jean-Luc Marion's book, the "In Excess,"[41] by which grace saturates nature and entirely overflows it. Nature, or free will, can never be understood independently of the freedom of grace. The reduction of freedom to a simple faculty risks sinking into sin and forgetting *apérité*.

In this sense, according to Bernard, the gift of salvation comes to redress Adam's original sin so that free will would be reduced simply to "the power to sin or not to sin" [*posse peccare aut non peccare*]. And this implies that free will can no longer hold its place as an indisputable image of God (St. Augustine).[42] The freedom coming from good counsel and according to one's pleasure rooted solely in God (salvific grace) allocates and calls up a free will that has been there *from the start* (creative grace), a free will that would have gained even more ground if it had not fallen into sin. Free will is not, or is not solely, that *by which* humankind fell, according to Bernard (the power of opposition); it is that *in which* the believer is anchored in order to receive the proffered gift (*apérité*). Bernard says, in a tone reminiscent of Irenaeus, "[Free will] was given to [mankind] not in order that he should accordingly sin [*non ut perinde peccaret*], but in order that, if he did not sin when he was able to have sinned, he might appear more glorious [*sed ut gloriosior apparet*]." (And not sinning was possible because "while devils and angels both sinned, good angels did not: not because they were not able to sin, but because they did not will to sin.")[43] In short, the summons of freedom through grace is a response or an "orientation toward the other" that is launched toward me and not a call *for* freedom of the kind that, while supposedly being something one decides, always remains a "claim for oneself." The first response does not arise from a "yes" or "no" in a decision by the person faced with salvation; it is the *display* of "consent" of the created being to the "excess" of grace that comes to us. "To consent is to be saved" [*consentire enim salavari est*].[44]

All the same the human subject should not just do nothing. One might then face the accusation that one has let go one's freedom ("What, therefore … doth free will do?"). But what does "do" imply here if it is not potentially a question of us welcoming in ourselves that which is *done*? We are not incapable; we are "capable"—but capable solely, or above all, of receiving God. The *capax Dei*[45] in the operation of salvation comes down to welcoming (passive sense of capacity), rather than choosing (active sense of capacity); to making ourselves the container of He who has no other content than to be poured out; it is not opting for a salvation in which freedom carries sole responsibility. "God is the author of salvation [*Deus auctor salutis*]; free will is *merely* receptive thereof [*liberum arbitrium tantum capax*]."[46] The person "capable of experience," the monk or the disciple, shifts here into someone who has experience of what they are capable. Far from this being a passage from culpability to capability, as though "fallibility" was always found upstream from "capacity" (Ricoeur),[47] grace paradoxically precedes sin in the monastic theology of the twelfth century, as does the dependence of the creature on the creator with regard to the avowal of sin. The *book of experience* is translated afresh here into an *experience of the book*—not in virtue of wrongful conduct to be corrected but through the life flow (*flux vital*) that the text examines. For Bernard, the "capable" subject is not guilty or "culpable." As the title of the treatise indicates, *Concerning Grace and Free Will* only sees "choice" in an opening up of choice and "free will" in a "reception of grace."

A Capable Subject

It is certainly difficult for us today to conceive what there is in such a capacity. The change that was made from free will as "passivity in *apérité*" (Bernard) to an "activity of the faculty" (Descartes) is such that we no longer know how to think of freedom as *apérité*. As Jean-Luc Marion states: "The concept of *capacitas/capax* has tended to undergo semantic shifts; it now no longer involves receiving God (*capax Dei*), but rather the exercise of a power (*capax domini*)."[48] Bernard, the Cistercian, is very clear on this point: what makes the will is above all that it is " capable of blessedness or of misery" [*miseriae sive beatitudinis capax est*];[49] that is to say, its mode of reception of salvation and not its power of choice, in the active modern sense of "capacity" understood as power and faculty. And if, inadvertently, free will comes to point to a pure will in the sense that "it maketh us neither able [freedom according to one's pleasure], nor wise [freedom of good counsel] but simply willing [*sed tantum volentem*],"[50] it is in this alone, as we shall see [§29], that free will as power of choice, "the will to will," remains when humankind, having sinned, has precisely lost the capacity to welcome what was originally given to us. An active capacity of the will, or free will as a choice between opposing alternatives (Descartes) only shows, if we follow Bernard's reasoning, a lack *a posteriori*, or the failings of freedom as passive capacity to receive grace, humankind having forgotten how to make ourselves containers and becoming ourselves our own content. "Simply" to wish is not necessarily to wish for the good rather than for evil, to be indifferent to the problem of choosing between opposing alternatives. But what it reveals is that the "wish for the good" (freedom of good counsel) and the "power for the good" (freedom according to one's pleasure) have been lost.[51]

The theme of *capax Dei* is, obviously, not just the prerogative of St. Bernard. Its source is essentially in St. Augustine, though a false opposition has been suggested by its interpreter, Jean-Luc Marion, between the static character of the image in St. Augustine and the dynamic character in St. Bernard.[52] St. Augustine moreover bears witness to this in his *On the Trinity*, where he says that the image of God must be found in the human mind: "For it is his image in this very point, that it is capable of Him [*quo ejus capax est*], and can be partaker of Him [*ejusque particeps esse potest*]."[53] What principally distinguishes St. Bernard from Saint Augustine is not then, as I see it, the famous "image of God" in the "intellectual cognition" for the one and in "freedom" for the other (Étienne Gilson); nor is it the supposed static characteristic of *capacitas* for the one and the dynamic for the other (Jean-Luc Marion).[54] What fully constitutes their difference is the *mode* according to which this image or this capacity is achieved in its initial consent: that is, through participation according to St. Augustine [*ejusque particeps*], and through cooperation according to St. Bernard [*cooperari*]. "Accordingly free will is said to co-operate [*cooperari*] with the grace which worketh salvation, when the free will consenteth [*dum consentit*], that is to say, is saved [*hoc est dum salvatur*]."[55] Consent and cooperation are thus, according to St. Bernard, the two characteristics that determine the *capax Dei*.

Consent or agreement [*consensus*] accorded to this capacity of welcome thus defines us in a proper sign of the sole and unique response possible from the recipient to the donor: "Even as it [salvation] cannot be wrought without the consent of the receiver [*absque consensus accipientis*], so cannot it be wrought without the grace of the giver [*quam absque gratia dantis*]."[56] Who consents receives, consents to receive, and makes this consent the privileged mode of reception. Just this once, the "capable subject" cannot be reduced simply to the passivity of an acceptor or a container but must also, in some hard work over the self, rather than choosing between possible alternatives, devote herself or himself to "consent," and thus "may submissively obey the good that saveth it."[57] Human beings, "capable" and "consenting," *receive* and *act* at the same time, in that they do everything to keep up such openness. Freedom comes down, not so much to deciding when there are contrasting alternatives, as to keeping up the original *apérité* in which humankind was created, "co-operating" in the salvation for which they were "destined." We are coadjutors of God "in the case of those who consent … With them God expressly shareth the work which He hath in hand."[58]

We should not get this wrong: the cooperation of free will and grace, as far as Bernard is concerned, has nothing to do with the cooperation of the secondary and primary causes that Aquinas was later to discuss. When Aquinas and his followers define God as "the cause of operation for all things that operate" [*causa operandi omnibus operantibus*], they are referring simply to a cooperation between action and causality.[59] Bernard on the contrary, and in a purely retrospective fashion, sees rather in the act of being a cooperator [*cooperari*] an association through consent and a simply capacity of welcoming:

> When Paul … saith: "Not I, but the grace of God which was with me" (1 Cor. 15:10). He might have said, "by means of me [*per me*]," but, because that would have been too little he preferred to say "with me" [*mecum*]; representing himself to be not only a minister of the work by giving it effect [*ministrum per effectum*], but also, by giving his consent, in a fashion a partner of Him that worketh it [*operantis quodammodo socium per consensum*].[60]

God is "with me" or "with us" [Emmanuel], for Bernard of Clairvaux and all the monastic theology of the eleventh and twelfth centuries, rather than acting "through me" [*per me*] to work providentially at the heart of the created. To cooperate is certainly to devote oneself to work, but the essence of this labor sits at the heart of our interior beings in order to re-orientate them, rather than in the world to transform it. Mystical theology is distinct from scholastic theology in that the will is only a *modality* for the one (Bernard) and for the other is the *power to act* (Aquinas).

Reading what precedes *Concerning Grace and Free Will* (by Augustine), and what follows (by Aquinas), leads us to recognize that Bernard has divested himself as much of "capacity through participation" (Platonic: Augustine) as "cooperation through causality" (Aristotelian: Aquinas). His originality is to define a form of freedom where the "capable subject" consents to salvation or an "openness" to divinity, not to a choice of salvation or a faculty of decision. Thus, for Bernard, free will is not, or is no longer, or is still not, a "power of the spirit" [*potentia animi*] (Aquinas); it is a "disposition" or *habitus* where the believers reveal themselves to themselves, paradoxically dissociating themselves from self, even their own selves. It is necessary to "divest oneself of egotism," and this is done in order to feel or to consent in another way. To lose oneself is always to find oneself at the same time; to deconstruct is at the same to reconstruct. As we have seen with Bernard's "four degrees of love," or the "mode of a love without a mode," the "me" is never denied, and even less is it in some way dissolved—it remains in its singularity, since the difference between the created and the uncreated can never be eliminated internally [§26. Deification and Annihilation].

A Disposition toward the Other

The "willing consent" through which the believing subject remains open to God by way of "spontaneous assent of the will" [*nutus est voluntatis spontaneus*] appears thus, according to Bernard's own words, like a disposition or "habit of the mind, self-determining" [*habitus animi, liber sui*].[61] According to Bernard, "consent" and "freedom" are first of all a disposition of the self or of one's own mind, that is to say a "manner of *being* of the will" rather than a power of the soul—and that is what the later tradition would, quite rightly, retain from Bernard. We read in Aquinas: "Bernard says the free-will is 'the soul's habit of disposing of itself.' Therefore it is not a power [*non est potentia*]."[62] When Aquinas concludes that for Bernard free will is not a power, this marks precisely the turning point for freedom in the thirteenth century, and in this sense it seems appropriate to call Bernard the "last of the Fathers," as it does to call Thomas Aquinas the "master of the scholastics." It changes nothing that the radical opposition of "disposition" and "power," of *habitus* and *potentia*, is presented in the *Summa Theologiae* in the form of an objection. Bernard never uses the word "power" [*potentia*] to speak of freedom in his treatise, and "faculty" [*facultas*] comes up rarely, for example, in the context of what *remains* when Adam's original sin is accomplished: "He converted to the use of sinning the faculty [*facultatem*] which he had received for the glory of not sinning."[63] The *habitus* of free will is not then some kind of disposition to act [*habitudinem ad actum*], as Aquinas makes it after rereading Bernard: it is a disposition of the mind [*habitus animi*] in the form of a reopening of one's own freedom to one's initial *apérité*.

As "manner of being," "disposition of the mind," or *habitus animi*, willing consent that makes for freedom is thus a *modality* for Bernard rather than a faculty. Just as for Heidegger "*Dasein is its disclosedness*" [*ist sein Erschlossenheit*], and "the expression 'there' [of 'being-there'] means this essential disclosedness," Bernard's capable subjects *are* here their capacity [*capax*], that is to say their being and their mode of receptivity.[64] Far from being reduced to a possible modality of the will, Cistercian freedom, like Heidegger's "being there" *is* the modality itself, the "there" of its "openness" through which the world defines a horizon rather than being a site of decision. In short, Heidegger's defining freedom as *apérité* (in an ex-position to being), and Bernard defining it as consent to God, is a way of de-substantializing that which should never have been reified into a simple "faculty." Free humankind is defined in a "manner of being" in the form of openness [*quomodo*] rather than in an "objectivity" as driving force at the origin of their acts or their decisions [*quid*].[65] Authenticity [*Eigentlichkeit*] is what defines freedom in *Being and Time*.[66] But as I see it one could not trace this back to Bernard, in that free will would then be free "to decide itself through its will" and " would anticipate thus what the analytic of Dasein seems truly to capture …: that human beings are defined less by representative understanding than by absolutely free decision in their choice" (Jean-Luc Marion).[67] It seems likely, however, following in this respect the route toward inauthenticity traced by the interpreter himself, that only the definition of "freedom" as "openness" in later Heidegger (*On the Essence of Truth* [1954]) matches up with Bernard's view of free will. It is not that of "the Authentic Potentiality-for-Being-a-Whole of Dasein" in *Being and Time*, which is always caught in the nets of a subjectification of freedom, reducing it into a simple "power" of the will. Evidence of an immensely significant turning point can be found in the letter Descartes wrote on November 20, 1647, to Queen Christina of Sweden, where he says: "Now free will is in itself the noblest thing we can have, since it makes us in a way equal to God and seems to exempt us from being his subjects."[68]

Bernard seems to have taken from Anselm, rather than from Augustine, the notion that freedom is a modality, indeed *the* modality, of the being of humankind. And this is something we have already encountered in looking at *Proslogion* (chap. 2: "The Theophanic Argument") and *Cur Deus Homo* (chap. 3: "The Debt for the Gift"). Saint Augustine discusses freedom principally as ability or power to sin or not to sin [*posse peccare, posse non peccare*] and indeed as "unable to sin" [*non posse peccare*]. Anselm (in this respect a precursor of Bernard) replies to this in his *De Libertate Arbitrii*, that freedom resides less in the grounds of choice than in openness to the will of God— an openness that Anselm calls here "uprightness" [*rectitudo*]: "Accordingly, since all freedom is (a power) [*potestas*], that freedom of choice [*libertas arbitrii*] is the (power) to keep uprightness-of-will for the sake of this uprightness itself [*potestas servandi rectitudinem voluntatem ipsam rectitudinem*]."[69] Although Bernard was to abandon the juridical character of uprightness for the mode of being of will [*rectitudo*] as well as the insistence on "power," preferring to talk of will [*posse/velle*], he nonetheless retained from Anselm the exemplary idea of a freedom that was to be defined less as a *choice between possible alternatives* and more as a *disposition of the subject* or *will itself*: *rectitudo* for Anselm and *habitus* for Bernard.[70] Freedom as a "disposition of mind" [*dispositio animi*] in Bernard's work is thus very far from its identification as "faculty" or "power of the soul" in the work of Aquinas [*potentia animi*]. In the monastic theology of the eleventh and twelfth centuries, then, everything is done to encourage the free being in an "openness to God" which defines par excellence the *apérité* that characterizes believers in their created being.

But it goes almost without saying that it is not enough just to stay "open." It is still necessary to identify what this disposition consists of—*liber sui*, "free of the self." According to *Concerning Grace and Free Will*, "Voluntary consent … is a habit [disposition] of the mind, [free of oneself]."[71] Bernard's discussion is helpful, to say the least, in showing the sense that he grants to such freedom in relation to subjectivity. Is *liber sui* then a matter of "freeing *the* self" in order to bring to light in humankind the disposition of one's own being through the will (freedom as faculty)? Or does one need, conversely, to be "freed *from* oneself" to make a place for God, who is alone what fills freedom (freedom as apérité)? To put it another way, we might ask, is one "free *of* oneself" in the sense that one is "oneself free," consecrating subjectivity? Or is it on the contrary in the sense that "one does not rely any more on the self" in the recognition of an alterity that always takes precedence? Everything depends, in reality, on the significance that one gives to the genitive of freedom [*liber sui*]. Is it (a) objective genitive where freedom frees the self and affirms the will? Or (b) subjective genitive where the freedom is freed *of* the self, welcoming an alterity? It is here that interpreters of Bernard differ from the Bernardine conception of freedom—and thus of the "experience" related to it.

(a) First alternative: The identification of freedom with the "self that wills" (objective genitive). Jean-Luc Marion says, "This identification of the man himself with his will inscribes it as the horizon of his freedom, or rather represents freedom as man's very specific horizon. Freedom signifies here: *the horizon where selfhood (ipséité) is revealed only in the willing self*."[72] This has at least the merit of bringing to light freedom as a "power of choice" and "commitment of the subject to freedom." But such an interpretation, at the heart of an argument that is forceful even though it may seem modest, springs above all from Cartesianism and its "power between contrasting alternatives," rather than the Cistercian conception of free will as total "openness" to God. Michel Corbin has pointed out (specifically addressing Jean-Luc Marion's argument): "This position of the will as a condition where there is a possibility of consent, as a prerequisite, is very far from the Bernardine discourse in which everything depends upon grace, including consent and its conditions."[73] In the heat of this argument one point emerges: it is important to let go of the "subject" ("free of the self"), something that has been spotted by the first (Jean-Luc Marion) but not by the second (Michel Corbin). I would moreover affirm, as least *negatively* and to maintain the coherence of the Bernadine text, that to be "free of the self" [*liber sui*] for the "disposition of the spirit" [*habitus animi*] that is free will does not imply either "to free the self" (Marion) or "to deny the self" (Corbin). The abbot of Clairvaux is *too much of a theologian* to accept the first (freedom of the willing self) and *enough of a philosopher* not to affirm the second (negation of all subjectivity).

(b) The second and more positive alternative is to bring back "subjectivity" to the act of "humility," to ask what the role of the "self" is truly in Bernard's notion of freedom. St. Bernard, in proposing what is strictly speaking (according to Rémi Brague), "a new model of the me," makes a distinction between an *anthropology of humility* and an *anthropology of humiliation*: "Humility is double: on the one hand it stems from knowledge, on the other affection ... Through the first we know that we are nothing [*nihil sumus*]. We learn this by ourselves, by our own weakness (Gal. 6:3). Through the second we *tread at the feet of the glory of the world*. We learn it from the One who emptied himself, taking the form of a slave (Phil. 2:7)."[74] The *humility of truth*, which teaches us to know ourselves in what we are, that is to say "nothing" [*nihil*], is distinguished here from the *humility of severity* which, referring to our being sinners, must also lead to a sense of humiliation. The first type of humility (of truth) sends us back to the *humus* of our created being as we are ourselves in our weakness; while the second (of severity) relates to the loss of the straight and narrow path from which we have deviated.

Such is then, as I see it, what is signified here by the *freedom* or *disposition of the spirit*—free of the self, *liber sui*. Not only is freedom as *habitus* ("disposition") the modality of our being defined as "openness" or "*apérité*" (humility of severity in the face of sin); in addition, freedom truly reaches its "me" when it is "released *from* self" [*sui*]—that is to say "*from the* self" (humility of truth as an act of nothingness). To be "free from self" [*liber sui*] is not to free one's "self" in an act of willing, or indeed "authentic" power; it is on the contrary to free oneself "from the self," to make a place for the other. Bernard impressively states that "they, who willed to be their own possession [*voluerunt sui esse*] ... did not belong only to themselves [*non tantum iam sui*], they belonged to the devil also [*sed et diaboli*]."[75]

There is a paradox here that should be emphasized: the wish to "be oneself" or to be one's own master [*sui esse*] is, for Bernard, precisely the best way of "no longer being oneself" [*non iam sui*] and becoming the property of another—here the devil—in that he turns the will away from its *apérité* to dwell solely in the one faculty: "In truth it is our own will, and not the power of God, which delivereth us over to the devil: it is *God's grace*, and not our own will, which maketh us subject to God."[76] The Fall and the rehabilitation of humankind are asymmetric here. We fall "through our own will" and not through the devil's: to suggest otherwise would be to attribute too much power to the devil. But we recover "through God" and not by ourselves: to suggest that would be to predetermine our power and to fall into Pelagianism. "Our will" [*nostra voluntas*], uncoupled thus from grace, is enough to make us fall. This does not, however, imply that the will is bad "in itself," but only that the reduction of freedom to a pure "faculty" (free will in the strict sense) always strips it in advance of its *apérité* (free will of grace and freedom of glory). The personal desire for the appropriation of the self is thus paradoxically what makes us lose all sense of ownership of it or even of identity. One never becomes so much other (subject to the "power of the devil") as when one thinks one is acting *only* for oneself (independently of God).

Nonetheless the resistance to losing the self in wanting to be oneself does not imply a caution and protection of the self in order to stop it becoming other, far from it. Rather than *expropriating the self through appropriating* the self (becoming the property of the devil in wishing to become one's own property), it is important above all, according to Bernard, to *appropriate oneself through expropriating* the self (becoming property of God in handing back to Him the property of our selves.) As opposed to the mistaken readings of a "pure will" and a positive will "through nature" in Bernard's work (a reading back of the Thomist or Cartesian view of free will onto Cistercian freedom) we can point out that "to be oneself," vis-à-vis God this time, is not—is not at all—"to be for oneself" in a pure willing. It is solely accepting oneself in an opening up to the other, in such a way that nothing would be worse than to wish to continue to be one's own master or to remain in one's own substantiality. "Better were it for us not to have existed at all [*non fuisse*] than for us to remain always our own possession [*quam nostros permanere*]."[77] One can then be other, or it is always appropriate to be *Oneself as Another* (Ricoeur), while knowing nonetheless "of whom" one is the property because it is there that true freedom lies: "Free will maketh us our own [*nos facit nostros*]; evil will maketh us the devil's [*mala diaboli*]; good will maketh us God's [*dona Dei*]."[78]

And if, by some twist or withdrawal into the self [*incurvatio*], the self ends up trusting too much "in oneself," it will certainly remain (an image that cannot be lost), but not enough to console us for a freedom that has lost its *apérité*: "Whether we belong to God or to the devil, we do not cease to belong to ourselves [*nostri*] also. Indeed, free will remaineth to us [*manet libertas arbitrii*]."[79]

There is a consistency throughout the whole of monastic theology of the eleventh and twelfth centuries with regard to the *Book of Experience*—from Anselm of Canterbury to Bernard of Clairvaux. One does not will "what one wants and when one wants" if one is a free being as Benedictine monk or a Cistercian keen to respect the rules and obey one's abbot (the hypothesis simply by default of a pure will [the residue of nature]). One wishes solely and above all that God will act in us, so that we will wish for the same thing that God wishes out of our own will (the hypothesis of "excess" or the addition of freedom as *apérité* [opening up to grace]). *Obedience* is not servitude, and nor is freedom the power to liberate oneself. "To wish for what God wishes"—such is the paradigm of the monastic or religious vocation in the period, not first of all to *transform the world* outside the monastery (a secondary cause for Thomas Aquinas), but to *work on oneself* in the cell of one's heart (consent). Anselm emphasizes that "[n]o will is just except one that wills *what God wills that it will* [*velle quod Deus vult illum velle*]."[80] And, no less judiciously, Bernard says: "He [God] made him [Paul] His fellow-worker [*coadiutorem*], when he made him His willing worker, that is to say consentient with His will [*voluntati consentitientem*]."[81]

In the book of experience then "the summons *of* freedom" [§28] can be broken down into a "summons *to* freedom" [§29] that will never be, at least in the monastic mode, a way of claiming autonomy. There is first of all a response to a summons (injunction, opening up, singularizing); then there is a capable subject (capacity, consent, cooperation); and finally, there is a disposition toward the other (habitus, relationship to the self, unity of wills). The *chain of wills* "open to God" is thus clearly established as long as it is not broken by sin. Independently of "original sin" free will has a "right to exist" because to be free is to "obey" or "listen" (power of obedience) and not "to free oneself" (power of choice between alternatives): "Where, therefore, there is consent, there is an act of will [*ubi consensus, ibi voluntas*]. Moreover, where there is an act of will, there is freedom [*libertas*]. In this sense it is that I understand the term free will [*liber arbitrium*]."[82]

How has divine logic now become lost or fractured to this extent? What has humankind done to shake off God and thus affirm our freedom as power or faculty, independently of all *apérité*? When free will is detached from grace, what remains of freedom must be understood as such. Nature, according to Bernard, is not the bedrock, existing in its own right, of a supernature that awaits perfection or actualization. (As Aquinas says, "grace does not destroy nature but perfects it [*cum gratia non tollat naturam sed perficiat*].")[83] Nature is simply "what remains"—it is simply what is left over when we seem to be cut off from grace. Cistercian thought never goes from nature to the supernatural; it goes from the supernatural to nature, to the extent that it sees a certain inevitability in the natural (an image of the divine through freedom of nature or faculty) in default of the supernatural (the similitude through freedom of grace or *apérité*). What we mistakenly take as *first* (the autonomy of nature) is always *second* for Bernard, and what we place *second* (openness to grace) must always remain *first*: "There remained to him [mankind] only freedom of choice, and that subject to punishment [*sola remansit ad poenam*], in that by its means he lost the other kinds of freedom [freedom of grace and freedom of glory]. But it [freedom of nature] he should not lose [*amittere non potuit*]."[84]

In the form of the "mark on Cain" (Gen. 4:15) free will as *faculty*, "pure will," or "given by nature," is not bad in itself. That goes almost without saying (one would not want falsely to accuse creation of a malediction). But free will does not remain in humankind as the "immovable image of God," above all in that it loses a similitude to God [*similitudo*] and *then* finds itself in the solitude of an image [*imago*]: "The two former [grace and glory] should be held to be the divine likeness [*similitudini*], and the latter [nature] the divine image [*imagini*]."[85] The *metaphysic* of freedom in a pure state (faculty or power over contrasting alternatives) marks thus, first of all, the loss of its *theological* character (*apérité* or openness to grace). Can humankind get over this? We cannot rule out such an outcome but only insofar as the summons *of* freedom (vocation to the self through reception of grace) responds to the summons *to* freedom (liberation of the self through the deliverance of an other).

§29. The Summons *to* Freedom

What Is Left of the Will

"There remained [*remansit*] to him [mankind] only freedom of choice ... by its means he lost the other kinds of freedom."[86] That is, we have taken free will for granted without fully defining it. There are three meanings of freedom for St. Bernard in *Concerning Grace and Free Will*: their order and linkage are instructive: "As may have occurred to us, there is set before us a threefold freedom [*triplex sit proposita libertas*] that from necessity [*a necessitate*], that from sin [*a peccato*], that from misery [*a miseria*] … Let us then call that which is first in development the freedom of nature [*libertas naturae*], that which is second, the freedom of grace [*gratiae*], and that which is third, the freedom of life or of glory [*vitae vel gloriae*]."[87]

The heuristic order adopted here—*prima* (of nature), *secunda* (of grace) and *tertia* (of glory)—is not then the didactic order of the creative project. This order for us [*pro nobis*] and not of God [*de Deo*]—nature, grace, glory—is appropriate here simply in that having totally lost the glory (the resplendent body), partially lost the grace (the innocence of Adam), what remains for us today [*remansit*], as it were by default, is only nature in the form of a common base for our freedom: free will. If we cannot "will the good" [*bonum velle*] (freedom of grace) or put it into practice [*bonum perficere*] (freedom of glory), we can at least just "will": "I do not speak of willing what is good, nor of willing what is evil [*velle bonum aut velle tantum*], but merely of willing [*velle tantum*]."[88]

The "pure will" or "faculty" [*velle tantum/facultas*] is then what "remains" [*remansit*], as we have seen: it is there when all the rest has gone or remains only in part. The will is within my reach, we read in the Letter of Paul to the Romans, commented on by

Bernard: "I can will what is right, but I cannot do it" (Rom. 7:18 NRSV). But the brilliant discovery of Bernard that has been neglected throughout the history of philosophy is that, in any event, I do not cease to "do" [*facere/agere*], nor to "will" [*volere/nolere*], even when "I do not do the good I want [*non enim quod volo bonum, hoc facio*]," and "the evil I do now what is what I do" [*sed quod non nolo malum, hoc ago*]" (Rom. 7:19 NRSV). In other words, "will power" is still there, independently of motives, or orientation, and of the execution of free will, and thus also of original sin. When I sin, I do not cease to will—sinning or not sinning. "[Man] has—not, indeed, equal facility in [choice] [*non quidem aequaliter in electione facilitas*] but—equal freedom in willing [*sed in voluntate libertas*] the one or the other."[89]

There is a great temptation, given that "will of the will" whose empowerment independently of any uncreated grace (from Spinoza to Nietzsche), is well known, to relate Bernard's "equal freedom in the will" [*(aequaliter) in voluntate libertas*] to the free will as "we can either do or not do something" in the fourth book of the *Meditations* of Descartes ("*vel facere vel non facere ... possimus*").[90] But that is to neglect what I see as the essential point in their divergent views: what is *first* for one (Descartes sees free will as image of the divine) is just the *last* for the other (Bernard sees free will as image of the divine solely insofar as it is that which "remains" when the double resemblance of the freedom of grace and freedom of glory is, at least in part, lost). We start off from humankind to go to God with one (Descartes): we are received by God and then go on to explore humankind with the other (Bernard). The *book of experience* ceases to be "experience of God" and becomes "experience of humankind." To cite Descartes again: The "will ... which I experience [is] so great [*quam tanquam in me experior*]," that it is "mine" before the "work" and "reception" of God in me. *Metaphysics* will not take precedence over the *theological* except in that freedom as *apérité* (Bernard) has now become effaced by freedom as faculty (Descartes).

In order to prevent such a misunderstanding, as it were in advance, Bernard is careful to distinguish orders—in effect distinguishing what will later be seen as the order of the *metaphysical* from the order that belonged to his own time of the *theological*:

> Accordingly, I think that this free consent of the will [will as innate freedom], upon which (as aforesaid) every act of judgment is founded, is not unsuitably wont to be called, as we have already defined it, free choice, the word "free" having reference to the will, and the word "choice" to the reason. Yet [*sed*] it is not necessarily with that liberty of which the Apostle speaketh: "Where the Spirit of the Lord is, there is liberty" (2 Cor. 3:17). This is that freedom from sin.[91]

Bernard is very clear: the freedom of the Apostle, inspired and received from the Holy Spirit (a resemblance to the divine through freedom of grace and freedom of glory), shares nothing with the kind of free will of humankind that remains in our nature if we rid ourselves of the supernatural (an image of the divine through free will). Bernard draws this conclusion, relying anew on a quasi-Pascalian separation of metaphysical and theological: "Of this [freedom] free choice can, I think [*opinor*], by no means [*nequaquam*] rightly be said to be possessed."[92] To think that free will (natural freedom) could be substituted for the freedom of *apérité* (of grace and glory) would be to fall into an inappropriate Pelagianism since it would then be up to "pure will" or to freedom as a "faculty" to show itself capable of responding by itself for its own errors.

In order to emphasize the precedence of "openness" over "faculty," Bernard brings out, at the end of his treatise, a "hierarchy" or "degrees of freedom," much like the "degrees of the love of God" that we have already seen [§26]. This hierarchy clarifies things so that a reading against the grain, or backwards, of *Concerning Grace and Free Will* is not really possible. First of all, according to Bernard, it is always grace that starts things and controls things, in such a way that free will must rightly accompany it and cooperate with it: "Grace worketh [*operator*] with free choice in such a manner that, while in the first instance [*primo*] it only [anticipates] it; and afterwards it accompanieth it; indeed it [anticipates] free choice, to the very end that it may co-operate with it."[93]

Secondly, the true order of freedom (a resemblance to the image of the divine) is always restored when it is a question of salvation and not as the simple remains of "free will or the faculty": we have already seen how "the two former [freedom of glory and freedom of grace] should be held to be the divine likeness, and the latter the divine image [here a natural freedom]."[94]

Thirdly, and going back to the heuristic order rather than a didactic order, resemblance becomes more important than an image of the divine, to the extent that the "high point of joy" (glory) and of "virtue" go before us in our "honor" (free will) and tower over us in their summons to us: "Thus the first freedom [free will] hath great honour, the second [freedom of grace] hath more abundant virtue, the last [freedom of glory] hath super-abundant delight."[95]

If we accept these three degrees, freedom always starts off from God (grace) and arrives at God (glory). The fact that there is, meanwhile, a *first* freedom called "free will," a *second* called "of grace," and a *third* called "of glory" does not mean, and has never been a question of signifying, that free will would exist independently of grace and glory. Rather the opposite: the freedom seen logically as *last*—freedom called "of glory" and considered here as the "highest" or "the most full" [*novissima*]—is in reality ontologically the *first*, in that glory comes down to humankind in its condescension rather than pulling us up to its elevation, opening up humankind to its freedom rather than waiting for some compensation.

Error and Sin

How is it then that we do not stick to freedom of a free will that is oriented in such a way—that is to good will as "*apérité*" and not to freedom as a "faculty"? Or, to put it otherwise, and in the same terms as Bernard of Clairvaux, how has humankind been able to convert "to the use of sinning the faculty [*facultatem convertit in usum peccandi*] which he had received for the glory of not sinning [*quam acceperat ad gloriam non peccandi*]"?[96] The abuse of free will finds its rationale here—in that sin does not just use it but is happy enough with it, indeed is happy to use it badly, that is to say in disconnecting it from grace or other types of freedom (freedom of grace [in the face of sin] and of glory [in the face of misery]):

Of the three kinds of freedom, therefore, which he has received, [mankind] by the abuse of that which is called freedom of choice [*abutendo illa quae dicitur arbitrii*], deprived himself of the rest [*reliquis ses privavit*]. But he abused it [*abusus est*] by the fact that, when he had received it for his glory, he made of it his disgrace [*convertit sibi in contumeliam*].⁹⁷

This still needs to be underlined. It is not free will as such that is being indicted here but the fact that it is "deprived" [*privavit*] of its "true nature" when it contents itself with "the" nature; it is "deprived" of an opening to grace in believing that it can attribute more consistency or substance to its own being. One "deprives" oneself of freedom, as far as Bernard is concerned, not solely in that freedom is shackled (free will confronted with necessity), but also in that it is etymologically unchained (from freedom of counsel confronted with sin and freedom of pleasure confronted with misery). The matter of freedom with regard to sin or "error," as we shall see later, is not any longer its manner of "depending upon" (freedom depending on grace); it is also its way of "no longer depending" (autonomation of free will). The *freeing of freedom* as emancipation of the subject, and not as "openness to the other," will continue to be indicted by Bernard, the Cistercian abbot, to ensure that the *experience of free will* does not turn into "misuse of freedom." The three links of freedom (to glory, to grace, and to nature) are eternally linked among themselves, and to wish to separate them is to lose the unity that alone can lead us to happiness. "The elect of mankind, who shall at length prove by the happy experience of a threefold freedom [*triplici libertatis felici experientia*] 'what is that good, and acceptable, and perfect, will of God.'"⁹⁸

Experience of free will and *image of freedom*. The proximity of Descartes is certainly obvious again and is indeed tantalizing. In Descartes's fourth *Meditation* we read: "I am conscious of will so ample and extended as to be superior to all limits ... And it is this wrong use of the freedom of the will in which is found the privation that constitutes the form of error."⁹⁹ And the complicity between Descartes and Bernard is reinforced in that Descartes points, like Bernard, to the idea of an unrestrained free will: "We so act that we are not conscious of being determined to a particular action by any external force [*nulla vi externa nos ad id determinari*]." He talks of the infinite character of the will: "It is chiefly my will which leads me to discern that I bear a certain image and similitude of Deity [*imaginem quandam et similitudinem Dei*]." For his part Bernard insists that "freedom from necessity, however, belongeth to all reasonable creatures, whether evil or good, equally and indifferently with God."¹⁰⁰

There is nonetheless a token of their difference in that the "abuse of free will" for Bernard is not at all the same as Descartes's "wrong use." Free will is defined as "pure will" by Bernard and "power to choose between contrasting alternatives" by Descartes. Unlike the philosopher, the Cistercian monk never maintains that simply through free will we carry in us "the image and similitude" of God. On the contrary, Bernard continued to insist—as we have seen—on freedom of choice as a remainder: "There remained to [man] only freedom of choice, and that subject to punishment, in that by its means he lost the other kinds of freedom."¹⁰¹ According to Bernard, we are in the image of God through free will and in similitude through the freedom of grace and of glory, but we are not in the image and similitude of God solely by free will, as in Descartes.

The monk of Clairvaux in his abbey and the philosopher from the Touraine who slept in an oven-heated room (the famous "*poêle*" of Descartes) were not targeting the same thing. They saw "sins" on the one side (Bernard) and "error" on the other (Descartes). The Cartesian formula is famous—*ex magna luce in intellectu sequitur magna propensio in voluntate* ("great clearness of understanding was succeeded by strong inclination in the will").[102] What tips the balance for Descartes, even if there are still things that need to be "weighed up" in free will, is not the light of God but that of understanding. Error, for Descartes, as will flowing out over understanding, has nothing in common with sin for Bernard, which is a curving in toward the self and refusal of God. Where philosophy aims at the restoration of the faculty (good use of free will), mystical theology seeks the restoration of *apérité* (recovery of similitude). It is thus in breaking the chain of freedom that one becomes a sinner in Cistercian thought (freedom of nature, freedom of grace, freedom of glory) and in the misuse of free will that one commits error in Cartesian thought (the infinite choice of a finite thought not fully enlightened).

Thus, we find the paradoxical formula in Bernard's work that would be almost impossible for Descartes: "Free [will] needeth a liberator" [*liberum arbitrium liberatore indigere*].[103] Free will is not freed by itself. If one could correct one's errors by oneself, one would never arrive at breaking free from sin and even less at recovering glory. Free will that allows us the image of God, and that is totally dissociated from false or inadequate post-Cartesian readings of *Concerning Grace and Free Will*, awaits then freedom itself, or rather the *One who alone* is free: Jesus Christ. Only then can we be freed from a false satisfaction in our own freedom as faculty (power of choice) and recover the original sense of freedom as *apérité* (openness and consent to God): "From neither of which [sin and misery] could [free will] at all be set free, save only by means of Him [*nisi per illum*] who alone of man was made free among the dead; free that is to say, from sin, yet living in the midst of sinners."[104]

Metamorphosis of Freedom

It is certainly a paradoxical formula that we must "free the free will": "free will needeth a liberator" [*liberum arbitrium liberatore indigere*]. From the summons of freedom [§28 (response to a vocation, the capable subject and disposition to the other)] we move on, in the form of ultimate stage of the *Book of Experience*, to the summons *to* freedom, or rather to the liberator [§29]. In fact, despite the immense virtue of the freedom of choice which "belongeth equally to all who have the use of reason" [*cunctis pariter ratione utentibus convenit*], we need nonetheless to recognize, in Bernard's words, that "this freedom or will is yet in certain fashion held captive [*captiva tenetur*], so long as the other two kinds of freedom scarcely at all, or only in small measure, accompany it."[105] Free will pays here, in a sense, its tributary penny. In remaining alone, or in uncoupling itself from the freedom of grace and the freedom of glory, it certainly becomes *positively* aware of its character as irremovable, infinite, and universal (indestructible in the divine image and shared by all). But at the same time, in situating itself alone, it cannot but feel, *negatively* this time, an inadequacy relative to the lost similitude with the divine and an *apérité* that needs to be recovered: "The defect of ours of which the Apostle speaketh, saying: 'So that ye cannot do the things that ye would' (Gal. 5:17). To will indeed belongeth to us in virtue of free choice, but not also in the power to do what we will [*posse quod volumus*]."[106]

Thus, in order to be free with a true freedom, we need to "know" (freedom of counsel) and also to "be able" (freedom according to one's pleasure) and not simply to "will" (free will). Immovable in its "will," freedom is not in "knowing" or in "being able." We find an internal tension in our will that was so skillfully negotiated by Saint Augustine on the day of his conversion and then orchestrated conceptually by St. Bernard in preparing his treatise. Augustine writes in his *Confessions*:

> If I tore my hair, if I struck my forehead, if I intertwined my fingers and clasped my knee, I did that because to do so was my will [*quia volui, feci*] ... [Mind] is mind, and hand is body. The mind orders the mind to will. The recipient of the order is itself, yet it does not perform it. What causes this monstrosity and why does this happen? Mind commands, I say, that it should will, and would not give the command if it did not will, yet does not perform what it commands [*et non facit quod imperat*].[107]

According to Bernard, if it is "soul and body" then knowledge and power are in accord. If it is "soul and soul" then knowledge and power enter into disaccord. God alone will come, Bernard says, to bring together what sin has separated. "It needeth that He Who by thy mouth giveth me much counsel, Himself give me by His Spirit help whereby I may [put into practice (*implere*) that which you counsel]."[108]

Should we then settle for the pure will of our faculty (free will) before wandering in search of orientation (freedom of counsel) and realization (freedom according to one's pleasure) for our free will—something that is delivered to us and to our judgment? Or, quite the contrary, do we accept and will that an Other—the liberator—comes precisely to free this free will, which is "unleashed" because it did not know how to maintain the "golden chain" of freedom? The "power of contrasting alternatives" although we cannot lose it (free will), at the same time brings us to see, as it were deep inside it, that there is a *choice that is less than the power of choice,* as we have seen ("there is no choice"). It is the choice of subjecting ourselves, of opening up ourselves and consenting with the other as first response to the summons that has been made to us (freedom of grace and freedom of glory).

All this has not been sufficiently understood, obviously in philosophy but also in mystical theology, in particular the true relationship in which God stands with humankind. Free will, reduced to the self and enjoying its "divine image," can die of its "solitude," however hard-won. Having lost similitude and broken the chain of freedom, it looks more like a stone effigy than a conquering hero—although that is quite often, and quite wrongly, the figure that is attributed to it. Bernard asks himself, "What wonder is it if one that lieth prone [or thrown to the ground—*iacens*] be not able of himself to rise again [*per se resurgere*], seeing that when standing upright he was unable by any effort of his own to advance to a better position?"[109]

The vocabulary employed here by Bernard on the subject of free will is eschatological and not metaphysical: "lieth prone" and "thrown to the ground" for sinning; "rise again" and "standing upright" as in the Resurrection. For the Cistercian monk freedom is not first of all *philosophical*, but *theological*—or rather it is philosophical in that it is at the same time Christological: "In a word, my philosophy is this, and it is the loftiest in the world: to know Jesus, and Him crucified."[110]

That through which humankind has fallen (free will) is not then and never will be that through which we are raised up (consent), though we must be careful not to fall into a Pelagianism that should be avoided at all costs. "Though [man] fell by an act of will [*lapsus ex voluntate*], he hath it not equally in his power to rise again [*resurgere*] free from sin ... For not so easy is it to get out of a pit as it is to fall into it."[111]

It is like this when we "just can't any longer" or "can't take it any more" (by dint of attempting on our own to find an impossible deliverance). Those are times when we still "will" (to get out of the pit [free will]) although we cannot "know how" (freedom of counsel) and even less are we "able" (freedom according to one's pleasure).[112] That is when, precisely, what comes up is the necessity of "He" [*illum*] who came to deliver us—not simply in pulling humankind out of the pit into which we have fallen but in restoring and metamorphizing our free will in such a way that it could once more "consent" to the Resurrected One.

Only the "Savior" [*salvator*] in fact possesses "in full these three kinds of freedom: the first ... in virtue both of His divine and of His human natures [*ex humana et divina*], and the rest in virtue of His divine power [*ex divina potentia*]."[113] We must, however, be careful; Bernard does not reduce free will to "human nature," or the double freedom (of grace and glory) to "divine nature." A misinterpretation of this kind, often repeated, would commit free will to a faculty independent of all *apérité*. On the contrary, the divine characteristic of free will is very exactly specified (nature both human and divine at *the same time*), so as to leave to the two other freedoms an obligation which could not fall upon us: to free up a "power" [*potentia*].

If freedom is a "power" for Bernard, paradoxically it is not power of humankind or of the soul [*potentia anime*] (Thomas Aquinas: §27); it is a "divine power" [*divina potentia*] or a "power of God" [*potentia Dei*]. Freedom is positively defined by Bernard as "power" but unconnected to the autonomy of terrestrial realities in so far as it is in the jurisdiction of God and not humankind. The characteristics attributed to freedom by Thomas Aquinas [§27], that "a power as such is directed to an act" and not to receiving a form or undergoing an action, are such as belong only to the divine in his Resurrection, according to Bernard, and not to humankind in our supposed powers of transformation.[114] Free will, not having the power to "rise again" by itself [*per se resurgere*], will then be "drawn" and "put on its feet" [*stans*] by an Other: "man therefore hath need ... of Christ" who is "the power of God and the wisdom of God (1 Cor. 1:24)."[115]

Supposedly free, but having still "need for a liberator" [*liberatore indiget*], we will expect from the One who comes to free us that He [*illum*] possesses both knowledge for deliverance (freedom of grace that draws us out of sin) and "power of liberation" (freedom of glory that delivers us from misery). He will not be content, as far as we are concerned, with our "simple will" [*velle tantum*] (free will): "Free choice maketh us possessed of will [*volentes*]; grace maketh us possessed of good will [*gratia benevolos*]."[116]

A final question remains if free will is not to be deprived of the whole of the Trinity which is alone capable of raising us up. If Christ the liberator "frees," and thus saves the free will, in offering that he himself will not be locked into the solitude of his pure will, then is the *liberum arbitrium* suppressed in order that we shall be saved? Or, to put it another way, if freedom of choice is always what remains independently of sin (irremovable divine image), is it also that which is maintained in salvation (recovery of similitude)?

Bernard's reply on this point is clear. He brings in the figure of the transformative Father after that of the liberator Son: "The loving Father [*begnitus Pater*] ... while He changeth the will from evil to good, He doth not take away its freedom but [transforms] it [*transferat*]."[117] There is a significant point to note here: the salvation of free will in the Cistercian world does not come simply from the liberator Son, who certainly possesses the "purpose" of delivering us [*liberum arbitrium liberatore indigere*] but also from the transformative Father, who in his power of resurrection, comes to transform, indeed to metamorphose us. Thus two operations have their place in the paternity of God in relation to our freedom—confirming what I have described elsewhere as *The Metamorphosis of Finitude* or at least the metamorphosis of our sin: (a) a "change of will" [*mutat voluntatem*] in going from evil to good and (b) its "transformation" or "transfer" [*transferat*].

(a) Our will has been changed [*mutat*] in going from "evil to good" [*de malo in bonum*] and it is the second freedom—confronted with sin (freedom of grace or of good counsel)—that is concerned here. Remaining in the neutrality of pure will, or having fallen captive to the other (the devil) in wishing to belong only to oneself ("Error and sin"), we necessarily expect from free will that something will change in it, so that it will be delivered to us. In this change, or according to the mutation of the will, the intention of the Father is not to "save us against our will" [*non salvet invitos*] but on the contrary to make us willing to be saved [*ut faciat voluntarios*].[118] What is at stake here is not that we have lost our will to will because on the contrary only the "simple will" defines the irremovable image of God in us: it is simply that our free will rediscovers its *apérité* (openness to grace) in no longer being satisfied with the simple faculty of will (power in choosing between contrasting alternatives): "Paul was led by the hand to Damascus, that is to say consenting to his own will] [*hoc est suae voluntati consentientem*]."[119]

The call of freedom (free consent [§28]) under the resurrectional power of the Father shifts thus to a call *to* freedom in the act of fully recovering our will (transformation of the self [§29]). God has created "without us," capable of himself, but will not save us "without Him," nor "in spite of us," only "with us" [*nobiscum*]: "Whereas the creation hath been wrought also without us [*sine nobis*]; that alone, which on account of our free consent is in a certain manner wrought with us [*nobiscum*], namely, our reformation [*reformatio*], will be reckoned unto us as meritorious."[120] The true action of freedom, as I have tried to emphasize, does not come down for Bernard to something that works through causality but solely in submitting oneself to God through consent—whether it is a question of creation, or still more clearly, of redemption. "What then? Is this, therefore, all that free choice doth in the matter? Is this its sole merit, to consent [*quod consentit*]? Certainly, it is [*est prorsus*]."[121]

(b) Our will is "to be transformed" or rather "transferred" [*transferat*], in fully resurrecting. And as it is the third freedom that is the aim here, confronted with misery (the freedom of glory or of free good pleasure). Freedom cannot be content, according to Bernard, with being "in the image of God" through free choice and "in his likeness" through grace. It is also necessary, paradoxically, to become like the "image of the image." As the abbot of Clairvaux reminds his brother monks, the "Son of God … is the effulgence of the Father's glory, and the essential form of His very being."[122] And thus there is already iconic reference to his paternity in him. "Form that re-forms us," the Word is itself form in the image of which we are reconfigured. Bernard, with a surprisingly Irenean accent says: "He came, therefore, the very essential form (of God) to Whom the free choice of man had to be conformed [*cui conformandum*]: for, in order that it might receive again its original form [*ut pristinam reciperet formam*], it needed to be reformed from the same source [*ex illa erat reformandum*] from which it had been formed [*ex qua fuerat et formatum*]."[123] One should not say, then, that free will is "in the image of God," but rather "in the image of the image" of God in humankind, in that solely the Son is the true "image" of the Father. As Étienne Gilson says, "[o]nly the Word is this image itself, because he only is an adequate and subsistent expression of the Father."[124]

Image imaging rather than *image imaged*, the true "image" or "figure" belongs to the Son as liberator, icon of the Father. And as for free will, it only awaits this new con-formation, that is to say his Resurrection. "The conformation consisteth in the image doing that work in the human body [resurrection] which the form doth in the whole world (incarnation)."[125] The *metamorphosis of freedom*— that is to say its "transformation"—"transfers" [*transferat*] our image into the image of the Son so that the duality of wills corresponds to a unity of the same affect. By Grace of Wisdom "we may be conformed [*conformemur*] unto Him, and be 'transformed [*transformemur*] into the same image'"[126]—"whole being somehow [transformed] [*mutatur*] into a movement of divine love [*in divinum affectum*]."[127]

But so that such a "transformation" or "power" can be operated (the Father) and so that in that "image of the Word" we shall be "freed" (the Son), it is still necessary that we should be "drawn into" (the Holy Spirit). The *whole* of the Trinity is thus at work in Bernard's *Concerning Grace and Free Will*. "Freedom" or rather "consent" is such for the Cistercian that the "Holy Spirit" manages to open us up toward the openness of God (grace), making *apérité* as it were the name itself of the *third* person of the Trinity. "We may be conformed unto Him, and 'transformed in the same image … by the Spirit of the Lord [*tanquam a Domini Spiritu*]' (2 Cor. 3:18)."[128] St. Bernard is following and adapting St. Augustine's words, that "the blessing of so desirable a *transformation* is conferred upon us by the *grace of God*."[129]

The Spiritual Attraction

"If it be by the Spirit of the Lord [*ergo si a Domini Spiritu*] that this is brought about," we should then conclude, as it were in a final flourish along with St. Bernard, that "it is no longer by free choice … [that we are] conformed unto Him, and … transformed into the same image from glory to glory [freedom of glory]" and "no longer … the servant of sin [freedom of grace]."[130] Bernard comes out with the formula and insists upon it: "And thus salvation is not wrought by man's free will, but by the Lord [*non liberii arbitrii sed Domini*]"[131] The avowal of grace seems such here that, once more, nothing seems to belong in the same way to freedom. We need to return to the initial question that St. Bernard records the bystander making to him: "What then is thine own work in the matter [*quid tu ergo operaris*], or what recompense or reward dost thou hope for, if so be that God doeth all?"[132]

The reply of the saint, in the terms of his treatise, comes precisely and with authority: *everything is grace*, or better *everything is gift*, at least in Christianity. We possess nothing that we have not received: "What has thou which thou didst not receive [*quid enim habes quod non accepisti*]" (1 Cor. 4:7).[133] However we cannot just stay doing nothing or waiting for God to do things in our place. We should work, on the contrary, in everything that he does for us, for in that our freedom resides—less in the "action" than in "consent"; less in the faculty (power of choice between contrasting alternatives) than in *apérité* (openness to God). What is implied by "gift" [*munera*], according to Bernard, is not receiving presents or abstracting from the gift. The true gift comes down rather to rendering oneself "worthy of the gift"; that is to say converting the gift into what is deserved, in that one consents through one's own will. And because it is certain that these things are wrought in us by the Spirit [*divino in nobis actari Spiritu*], they are the gifts of God [*Dei sunt munera*]: yet because they are accompanied by the consent of our will [*cum nostrae voluntatis assensu*], they are also our due: "'For,' saith He, 'it is not ye that speak, but the Spirit of your Father that speaketh in you'" (Mt. 10:20).[134]

When the Holy Spirit speaks to us, it is interior, and it is at the heart of this subjectification that the true work of donation is carried out, understood here as "liberation" (the work of the Son), transformation (work of the Father), and openness to grace (gift of the Holy Spirit). *The gift comes back then to receive the gift*, not simply as a "non-reciprocity," or "withholding" of the gift, as we have already seen in Anselm's theory of "satisfaction" (chap. 3: "The Debt for the Gift"), but above all in the "recognition" of donation as a partnership with the given which is precisely what makes for the "merit" of freedom. What responds then to the Son who "frees us from free will," made captive by his neutrality, and to the Father who "takes on" and "transforms" our will, in order to integrate it into the image of the Son, is *for us today* the Holy Spirit, who accompanies us in this disposition [*habitus*] and changes the gift [*donum*] into what is merited [*meritum*]. Thus we shall be definitively "tied" to the God through the Holy Spirit, in this "link" or *nexus* of the creature to the Creator, through which we become his "co-operators": "Hence it is that we presume to be God's fellow helpers [*coadiutores Dei*], fellow-labourers with the Holy Spirit [*coopertores Spiritus*

Sancti] meritorious of the kingdom, because, in fact, by consent of will [*consensum voluntarium*] we are joined unto the divine will [*divinae voluntati coniungimur*]."¹³⁵

Freed *in* the Son, transformed *through* the Father and accompanied with the Holy Spirit, the Cistercian monk in the trinitary sense of his freedom will not then first of all seek to "merit" his salvation by any low or useless acts. But neither will he *do* nothing because salvation is not nothing, and to attribute everything to God is really just to "empty" it, as though humankind did not have to "cooperate." It is then by virtue of a "willing consent" [*consensus volontarium*] that believers desire to "be dissolved" *into* God, without losing, as I have tried to show [§26], their personality. They enter, or allow themselves to be drawn into, the "bridegroom's chamber" [*in cubilicum sponsi*], that precisely in which He will come to visit: "She was indeed most willing," says the treatise *Concerning Grace and Free Will*, taking up the theme from the *Sermons on the Song of Solomon* (sermon 92): The bride says, "Draw me (after you) [*trahe me post te*]: because of the savour of thine ointments we will run after thee."¹³⁶

The "spiritual attraction" of the Holy Spirit, accepting what is most "mystical" in freedom, does not seek then, according to Bernard, to be "raised" toward God [*ascendere*] but rather allows itself to be "at-tracted" by him, or indeed pulled along [*trahere*], toward more openness or *apérité*. It is necessary *first of all* to pass through a "knowledge of experience" [§24] or a "language of affect" [§25], which ensures that the "knowledge" is not necessarily or identically "power." It is not in fact "the same thing," as Bernard himself makes plain, to lead "the blind" [knowledge] or to help out someone who is "weary" [power] [§27]. But at the end of the road for the *Book of Experience*, as also for that of our own existence, we have to learn that nobody will accede to the divine unless they recognize *finally* that all knowledge and power are united in God, in that only God truly wills that we will what he wills: "His purpose is to make them willing to be saved."¹³⁷ *Consummatum est*—"It is accomplished" (Jn. 19:30 JB)—not simply in the sense that the monk or the disciple has reached the same place, simply it is that the *whole* of experience—"experience in thought" (Anselm), "experience of the world" (Hugh and Richard of Saint-Victor), and "experience in affect" (Aelred of Rievaulx and Bernard of Clairvaux)—was recapitulated *in God*, in the unique "openness to the Holy Spirit" by which Bernard was drawn: "Neither the blind, nor the weary are saddened for being led or borne [*nec contristatur cum trahitur*]."¹³⁸

Epilogue: Hold Fast to Humankind

Yesterday [*heri*] in the monastic theology of the eleventh and twelfth centuries, we were "reading" in the *Book of Experience*: "today [*hodie*]" we decipher the book and still "live" it, at least those who know how to move there and come back, certainly to the great benefit of "spiritual theology," but also to that of contemporary philosophy, in particular philosophy in the form of "phenomenology." The great transit going from the "theophanic argument or the *experience in thought*" (Anselm), to the "relevance of hermeneutic and phenomenology in the *experience of the world*" (Hugh and Richard of Saint-Victor), and as far as the ultimate dimension of "affectivity and spirituality in *experience through affect*" (Aelred of Rievaulx and Bernard of Clairvaux), is not one that aims in fact to prove things but simply to make us see or at least to show us things *otherwise*. The choice of these writers, the signs along the road, and the aim of the journey were not simply accidental but the result of a careful reflection over a long period of time. One does not read, or frequent, writers, in particular those of the stature of the medievals, without being oneself transformed. It is a matter, as one grows older, of exposing oneself, of contemplating more deeply, or perhaps of becoming more modest with regard to one's will to master everything. There is in the "style" of the *Book of Experience* (not only in the book but also in what it sends us back to) a manner of being, or a mode, that we do well not to forget. Whether it is a question of "thought" or of the "world," or of "affect," through the book one becomes in all respects what one did not even know existed. One is not simply fulfilling what one always believed one had to be or become.

Anyone who goes through a *Book of Experience*, through reading, through writing, through the thing itself, responds first of all—along the lines of, or indeed in the image of, the God of Exodus—to the summons "to be what he becomes" ("I AM WHO I AM," or "I AM WHO I SHALL BE" [Exod. 3:14]), rather than to "become what he is" ("Become such as you are" [or "who you are"] [Pindar]).[1] "Become what you are. You have only to become it," Henri Maldincy tells us.[2] History is not written in advance, and "man is the animal *whose nature has not yet been fixed*" (Nietzsche).[3] What holds here for humanity is significant for each one of us in our initial singularity. *Pathei mathos*, "Learning through suffering," or "knowledge by test or trial" is, as we have seen [§1], the primary meaning of experience as a "passage through the self" or an "endangering"—*ex-per-iri* [§2]. It is thus that the *Book of Experience* has transformed our triple experience—of "thought," "world," and "affect"—in that this God who is so "great" that one cannot think of him (Anselm) allows himself at the same time to be "deciphered" in the book of the world through the Trinity (Hugh and Richard) and "felt" in ourselves to the point of affecting us (Aelred and Bernard).

There have been several harbingers of this monastic turn in my previous writings, or at least of this step or pause, turning to the "mystical"—in particular discussing the primacy of the allegorical over the tropological in the four meanings of Holy Scripture (in *Crossing the Rubicon*[4]) or again in insisting on the Anselmian vein, beside Franciscan inspiration and Ignatian roots (in *Parcours d'embûches: S'expliquer*[5]). Should we rejoice in this, regret it, or just be surprised by it? Never mind our reaction; what "is there" is the book *in* the book, or the book *on* the book—*The Book of Experience*. It stands not as a monument but as an avowal or confession representing a particular moment. But what then was to come of it afterward? Or what would follow it? Nobody could know, least of all the author, whose "figure" also "has not yet been fixed." One can wish to construct and even anticipate or build up, but what is given *after the fact* always spills over whatever one has conjectured or programmed *beforehand*.

After a long acquaintance with St. Bonaventure (see my *Saint Bonaventure and the Entrance of God into Theology*[6]), the Church Fathers and the medievals were to accompany me for long years (see my *God, the Flesh, and the Other*[7]). The monastic theology of the eleventh and twelfth centuries began at this stage to surprise me and nourish me with its astonishing contemporaneity (*The Book of Experience*). One finds in such theology simply a field, that of "medieval philosophy," that is not to be confused directly either with "phenomenology" or the "philosophy of religious experience"— different domains that I was to explore elsewhere according to "triptychs" appropriately arranged.[8] In crossing disciplines, and drawing upon sources in texts that are still alive for those who know how to read them, one renews *for today as well* what there is in the "book of experience," if not to transmit it, at least to teach ourselves how to decipher it.

It would not be a question of asking *everyone* to write—perhaps that is only necessary for some people; though for them certainly it might be a summons and a demanding task. But *anybody* was able to read it once the parchment, goat's skin, or book was published and thus "open to debate" before a *public*. Afterward it no longer belongs to its author but becomes the property of its readers. Books have a history and a life, which is not that of their biographer as soon as they are published. To recognize this is not to lament or necessarily to celebrate: it is to give credit to the "lived experience" on the basis of which a book is begotten. The inspiration and structure of the *Book of Experience*, I should perhaps confess (?), became evident for me in the form of an "inner conviction" when I was visiting the abbey of Vézelay, an important center for monastic theology during the twelfth century, in Burgundy. A true "spiritual complicity" was then established in my work on the "monastic mode" of life and thought—connected to a Franciscan, Dominican, and Jesuit lineage that I have discussed elsewhere.[9] In this sense I am grateful for what was given to me and grateful toward Him *by whom* I could believe, or at least could think, that I was granted the power, the perseverance, and the vocation to accomplish what I had set out to do.

Homo es, sistere in homine—"You are man, *stand firm as man*."[10] With this key sentence from Charles de Bovelles, Canon of Noyon in the fifteenth century, a new era, or a new epoch, is opened up, at least as far as historical studies are concerned (Patristic, Medieval or renaissance), which can be put beside phenomenological work

(*Combat amoureux*), work based on religious experience (*Triduum philosophique*), and indeed work based on the relation between philosophy and theology (*Crossing the Rubicon*). It is characteristic of the renaissance in its first period that it discovers the importance of "mankind"—not against or independently of God, but in that it returns to mankind because God made man. Studies of the topic have, however, apart from a few exceptions, neglected this, dedicating their work to the supposed act of "rebirth," seen as a quasi-declaration of liberation and emancipation from the past.[11]

Coming back to this crux, then, or at least posing questions about it, points to a program whose completion is, as I know by experience, uncertain. But it is at least worth considering, and I would like to emphasize as a final statement that there remain authors whose work deserves to be re-examined in this context: Charles de Bovelles certainly but also Jean Gerson, Nicholas of Cusa, and indeed Pico della Mirandola could perhaps mark out various stages for us. We cannot really "predict," in particular as far as the "intellectual life" is concerned, how much would prove worthwhile in light of such encounters or what we would find of a *culture* on which we could draw to refresh our contemporaneity. But these "*Theologies of the Renaissance*" would then lead us and would certainly permit a "displacement" or at least a "shake up" because the "times" (the fifteenth century this time) are no longer the same, and the way in which we relate ourselves to them is different. I have said elsewhere that "the passage (in every sense of the term) through the Holy Scriptures, marks a journey of the self into an 'other than the self' insofar as its *pathos*, or its 'suffering,' relocates us rather than just confirming our ideas."[12] I hope to go on taking up the challenge, sure that gratitude will sustain our hopes, in that only "what has been done" (*The Book of Experience*) can reassure us that there will still one day remain something more to be done (the experience of a book).

Notes

Opening

i [Trans.—see *The Metalogicon of John of Salisbury* [1159], trans. Daniel D. McGarry (Berkeley: University of California Press, 1955), 167: "Bernard of Chartres used to compare us to dwarfs perched on the shoulders of giants."]

ii [Trans.—Biblical quotations are taken from the *New Revised Standard Version* (Oxford: Oxford University Press, 1989, 1995) [NRSV], the *Jerusalem Bible* (London: Darton, Longman and Todd, 1974) [JB], or the *Revised New Jerusalem Bible* (London: Darton, Longman and Todd, 2018) [RNJB], depending on the text that is closest to the French translations used by the author.]

Introduction

1 Hans-Georg Gadamer, *Truth and Method*, trans. Joel Weinsheimer and D. G. Marshall (1960; London: Continuum, 2006), 341.

2 Ludwig Landgrebe, "The Phenomenological Concept of Experience," in *Philosophy and Phenomenological Research*, trans. Donn C. Welton, September 1973, vol. 34, no. 1, 1–13. Quoted in Natalie Depraz, Francisco Varella and Pierre Vermersch, *À l'épreuve de l'expérience: Pour une pratique phénoménologique* (Bucharest: Zeta Books, 2011), 58.

3 See my debate with Yann Schmitt "Objectiver le vécu. Réponse à Emmanuel Falque," in *L'Expérience religieuse: Approches empiriques*, ed. Anthony Feneuil (Paris: Beauchesne, 2012), 290–6.

4 See the pioneering work in this respect (and note the evocative title) by Renaud Barbaras, *Le Tournant de l'expérience* [The Experiential Turn]: *Recherches sur la philosophie de Merleau-Ponty* (Paris: Vrin, 1998). Also, the book by Natalie Depraz, Francisco Varella and Pierre Vermersch, *On Becoming Aware: A Pragmatic of Experiencing* (Amsterdam: John Benjamin, 2002), especially chap. 6. As far as this development is concerned I fully subscribe to Natalie Depraz's statements in *Comprendre la phénoménologie: Une pratique concrète* (Paris: Armand Colin, 2012), 9: "(1) Phenomenology profits from relying on other disciplines: it derives from them an internal renewal, a guarantee of vitality." And, "(2) Before being the reading and interpretation of a text phenomenology is first of all an experiential challenge as well as the descriptive record by a single subject." The return toward a practical phenomenology resting upon experience is shared by a number of phenomenologists of the same generation (myself, Claude Romano, Natalie Depraz, Renaud Barbaras, Jérôme de Gramont, etc.), who follow the tradition of Merleau-Ponty rather than that of Heidegger or Husserl. See on this point the diagnosis argued in my interview with Tarek R. Dika and William C. Hackett, "The Collision of Phenomenology and Theology," in *Quiet Powers of the Possible: Interviews in Contemporary French Phenomenology* (New York: Fordham, 2016), 211–27.

5   Aeschylus, *Agamemnon*, line 177. Quoted and analyzed by Gadamer in *Truth and Method*, 350-1: "If we want to quote another witness for this third element in the nature of experience, the best is Aeschylus. He found the formula—or, rather, recognized its metaphysical significance as expressing the inner historicality of experience—of 'learning through suffering' (*pathei mathos*)." See Also Henri Maldiney, *Regard, Parole, Espace* (Paris: Éditions du Cerf, 2012), 71: "At the most moving ['*pathique*'] moments the words of Aeschylus fully apply '*pathei mathos*.' Being tested teaches us. Not through our reason, but by our sense." And Maldiney's *Penser l'homme et la folie* (Grenoble: Jérôme Million, 1997), 386. See likewise the discussion by Claude Romano (but without reference to Gadamer or Maldiney) in Claude Romano, *Event and World*, trans. Shane Mackinlay (New York: Fordham, 2009) Part 3 and note 11.
6   [Trans.—see Immanuel Kant: "If cinnabar were sometimes red, sometimes black, sometimes light, sometimes heavy, if a man changed sometimes into this and sometimes into that animal form … my empirical imagination would never find opportunity when representing red color to bring to mind heavy cinnabar." *Critique of Pure Reason*, trans. Norman Kemp Smith (Basingstoke: Palgrave Macmillan, 2007), A101, 131.]
7   See my *The Wedding Feast of the Lamb*, trans. George Hughes (New York: Fordham University Press, 2016), §3-4, 18-30. "Mass of sensations" is from Kant; "region of what can no longer be said" from Heidegger.
8   Ibid. §24: 166-72, "The Gaps of the Flesh."
9   [Trans.—The term *Ereignis* here is from Heidegger. See Martin Heidegger, *Identity and Difference*, trans. Joan Stambaugh (New York: Harper and Row, 1969), 14: "The event of appropriation (Ereignis) is a word belonging to common language and means 'event.' But Heidegger's use of it is more (1) 'abstract' … and (2) 'concrete' … thus to catch sight of, to see with the mind's eye, to see face-to-face."]
10 Hans-Georg Gadamer, *Truth and Method* [1960], trans. Joel Weinsheimer and Donald G. Marshall (London: Bloomsbury, 2004), 365 (my emphasis).
11 [Trans.—"Saturated phenomenon" is Jean-Luc Marion's term. See Shane Mackinlay, *Interpreting Excess: Jean-Luc Marion, Saturated Phenomenon, and Hermeneutics* (New York: Fordham University Press, 2010), 1: "A saturated phenomenon is one that cannot be wholly contained within concepts that can be grasped by the understanding. It gives so much in intuition that there is always an excess left over, which is beyond conceptualization. Thus, it is saturated with intuition."]
12 See my comments on altarpieces that open the three parts of my "Triduum philosophique": Grünewald's Isenheim Altarpiece in *The Guide to Gethsemane*, trans. George Hughes (New York: Fordham University Press, 2019), the Ghent Altarpiece of the van Eyck brothers in *The Wedding Feast of the Lamb*, and Rogier van der Weyden's Beaune Altarpiece in *The Metamorphosis of Finitude* (New York: Fordham University Press, 2012).
13 "Companions in my searching were the young Luther and the paragon Aristotle, whom Luther hated. Impulses were given by Kierkegaard, and *Husserl opened my eyes*." Martin Heidegger *Ontology—The Hermeneutics of Facticity*, trans. John van Buren (Bloomington, IN: Indiana University Press, 199), 4.
14 [Trans.-"Theophany": direct communication or appearance of God to human beings.]
15 For the importance of art which not only "allows one to see" but also "shows," see my *Parcours d'embûches: S'expliquer* (Paris: Éditions franciscaines, 2016), §29: 248-50, "Faire voir."

16 *God, the Flesh, and the Other*, trans. William Christian Hackett (Evanston, IL: Northwestern University Press, 2015), 11.
17 See the declension of experience in its various stages given by Jean Greisch, *Vivre en philosophant: Expérience philosophique, exercices spiritual et thérapies de l'âme* (Paris: Hermann, 2015).
18 "La prise" [The Hold] in Henri Maldiney, *Qu'est-ce que l'homme? Hommage à Alphonse de Waelhens* (Brussels: Publications des Facultés universitaires Saint-Louis, 1982), 135–57.
19 [Trans.—"Ethology" is concerned with core values of individuals or groups. According to Gilles Deleuze, "Studies … which define bodies, animals, or humans by the affects they are capable of, founded what is today called ethology," in *Spinoza: Practical Philosophy*, trans. Robert Gurley (San Francisco: City Lights Books, 1988), 125.]
20 [Trans.—Latin, present active infinitive of *experior*.]
21 Maldiney, *Qu'est-ce que l'homme?*, 135–57. In particular pp. 136–48 on the root "*per*." Maldiney's form of analysis was taken up by Claude Romano (though without citing Maldiney) in *Event and World*, 143–88: "The Primary Phenomenological Meaning of Experience." See especially 145.
22 Maldiney, *Qu'est-ce que l'homme?*: "La prise," 144–5. See also Romano, *Event and World*, 195–6.
23 Ibid., 197.
24 Hans-Georg Gadamer, *Truth and Method*, trans. Joel Weinsheimer and Donald G. Marshall (London: Bloomsbury Academic, 2013), 56. On the history of the word *Erlebnis*, 55–8. On the concept of *Erlebnis*, 58–64. As for the late appearance of the concept of *Erlebnis* (lived experience) which makes it a secondary formation in comparison to *Erfahrung* or the crossing [*traverse*] of the self, see 55: "It is surprising to find that, unlike the verb erleben, the noun Erlebnis became common only in the 1870s … The word appears suddenly with some frequency in the seventies." It is used by neither Schiller nor Goethe but by Dilthey, Schleiermacher, and of course Husserl.
25 See Edmund Husserl, *Ideas: General Introduction to Pure Phenomenology*, trans. W. R. Boyce Gibson (London: Routledge, [1931], 2012), §1: 9–10, "Natural knowledge and experience." A distinction is made here between the "'natural experience [*Erfahrung*] and the primordially given experience *Erlebnis*].'"
26 See my *Wedding Feast of the Lamb*: Introduction, 1–4, "The Swerve of the Flesh."
27 See my "Y a-t-il une chair sans corps," in *Le Combat amoureux* (Paris: Hermann, 2014), 197–238.
28 See René Descartes, *Meditations on First Philosophy*, trans. Elizabeth S. Haldane and G. R. T. Ross (Cambridge: Cambridge University Press, 1911), Meditation II: 10–11, "But it will be said that these phenomena are false and that I am dreaming … let it be so: still it is at least quite certain that it seems to me that I see light [videre videor], that I hear noise and that I feel hear. That cannot be false; properly speaking it is what is in me called feeling [*in me sentire*]; and used in this precise sense that is no other thing than thinking" [*cogitare*]. See also the interpretation by Michel Henry who reads in "what is in me called feeling" the greatest certitude of the human being in our "auto-affection" *Généalogie de la psychanalyse* (Paris: PUF, 1985), 17–52: "videre videor."
29 [Trans.—The "pathic" mode refers to a sensing of phenomena that is immediate and nonverbal, a primary internal sensation before any intentional project is formed. Important here is "the core principle of the 'pathic' dimension described by Viktor

von Weizsäcker, who famously wrote 'Life is not only an event that happens—but also something that is suffered.' See Hartwig Wiedebach, 'Some Aspects of a Medical Anthropology: Pathic Existence and Causality' in Viktor von Weizsäcker," *History of Psychiatry*, vol. 20, no. 3 (2009): 360–76.]

30   Michel Henry, *The Essence of Manifestation*, trans. G. J. Etzkorn (The Hague: Martin Nijhoff, 1973): Meister Eckhart is seen here as an "exceptional thinker" (p. 309), in that it is only in his work that we find "Clarification of the Concept of Phenomenon Transcendence and Immanence" (Section II, p. 135). Parts §39, §40, and §49 of Henry's book are explicitly concerned with Meister Eckhart. See also Yves Meessen, *Percée de l'Ego: Maître Eckhart en phénoménologie* (Paris: Hermann, 2016), §10: 129–14, on "Internal structure of the absolute" and the limits, or the reverberation from the thought of Meister Eckhart on intentionality in Husserl, or the primacy of auto-affection in the work of Michel Henry. §31: 392–402 ["*vivo ego, iam non ego*"]: "The Eckhartian counterblow to Husserlian phenomenology strikes head-on the conception of liberty hampered by an inscrutable complicity with radical evil" (Michel Henry, 392).

31   We can compare, along the lines of an implicit debate, Hans-Georg Gadamer in *Truth and Method* (§75: 60, "Every experience has something of an adventure about it,") with Claude Romano in *Event and World* (174: "With the irruption of suffering, a human adventure as a whole suffers a crisis and is submitted to a metamorphosis"). Romano defines humankind as adventurous beings "capable of experience" (52), "to whom events must happen" (52). And we might add Henri Maldiney: "The real is always *what one didn't expect*" (my emphasis) in *Penser l'homme et la folie* (Grenoble: Éditions Jérôme Millon, 2007), 230.

32   See Pierre Hadot, *Qu'est-ce que la philosophie antique?* (Paris: Gallimard, 1995), "Les écoles hellénistique," 145–226.

33   Philippe Nouzille, *Expérience de Dieu et théologie monastique au XIIe siècle. Étude sur les sermons d'Aelred de Rievaulx* (Paris: Éditions du Cerf, 1999), 22. I would like to underline here the importance of this work. Without it my *Book of Experience* might have never found its basic insights nor seen the light of day. The author is witness to a monastic (Benedictine) tradition that he lives in, belongs to, and shares with his readers. I would like to express my thanks here both for his writings and for the loyal friendship I enjoy with him.

34   Jean Leclercq, O. S. B., *The Love of Learning and the Desire for God: A Study of Monastic Culture* (New York: Fordham, [1957] 1982).

35   *Life and Works of Saint Bernard, Abbot of Clairvaux*, vol. 4, *Cantica Canticorum: Eighty-Six Sermons on the Song of Solomon*, trans. Samuel J. Eales (London: John Hodges, 1893), sermon 3:1, 17.

36   Aelred of Rievaulx cited in Nouzille, *Expérience de Dieu et théologie monastique au XIIe siècle*, 249, note 1: "'No one knows except the one who receives it' (Rev 2:17). Read, let me ask you, in the book of experience." See also *Aelred of Rievaulx: The Liturgical Sermons: The Second Clairvaux Collection*, ed. Domenico Pezzini (Collegeville, MN: Cistercian Publications, 2016), x: "The first book from which [Aelred] draws his sermons is the Bible, the second and no less important is what St. Bernard calls the book of experience."

37   See the article by J.-G. Bougerol ed., on "Liber," in *Lexique Saint Bonaventure* (Paris: Éditions Franciscaines, 1969), 91–2. We find here mention of the book of scripture [*liber scripturae*], book of the world [*liber mundi*], book of life [*liber vitae*], book of wisdom [*liber sapientiae*], book of Christ [*liber Christi*], book of the Virgin Mary

[*liber Virginis*], book of the conscience [*liber conscientiae*], book of the cross [*liber crucis*], book of nature [*liber naturae*], and book of the creature [*liber creaturae*]. No mention of the book of experience [*liber experientiae*] probably because it belongs to the monastic rather than the scholastic period, although it nonetheless certainly falls within the scope of Franciscan "wisdom" [*sapientia/sapor*].

38 Martin Heidegger, *Gesamtausgabe* [*Collected Works*], vol. 60. Part 3. *Die philosophischen Grundlagen der mittelalterlichen Mystik*, ed. C. Strube (Prepared notes and introduction to an undelivered course 1918/19), 1995, XIV.
39 This is confirmed by Rémi Brague in *Saint Bernard et la philosophie* (Paris: PUF, 1993), appendix 2, 184–6, citing an oral communication by Otto Pöggeler of June 1989 and a letter from F.-W. von Hermann dated March 27, 1990: "Heidegger (1889–1976) had also read Saint Bernard. That is at least what we have to conclude from the existence of extracts from his works (Third Sermon on the Song of Songs) contained in notes put together for a course at Freiburg but actually taught at Marbach."
40 Martin Heidegger, *The Phenomenology of Religious Life*, trans. Matthias Fritschard and Jennifer Anna Gosetti-Ferencei (Bloomington, IN: Indiana University Press, 2010). "On the *Sermones Bernardi in canticum canticorum* (Serm. III), 252." [The manuscript carries the date September 6, 1918.]
41 Bernard of Clairvaux, *Selected Works*, Sermon 3, p. 221 (Text adapted).
42 Michel Foucault, *The Hermeneutics of the Subject: Lectures at the Collège de France, 1981–82*, trans. Graham Burchell (New York: Palgrave Macmillan, [2001] 2005), 211.
43 Michel Foucault, "About the Beginning of the Hermeneutics of the Self: Two Lectures at Dartmouth," *Political Theory*, vol. 21, no. 2 (May 1993): 198–227. "The modern hermeneutics of the self is rooted much more in those Christian techniques than in the Classical ones. The *gnothi seauton* is, I think, much less influential in our societies, in our culture, than it is supposed to be."
44 Heidegger, *The Phenomenology of Religious Life*, 252.
45 Bernard of Clairvaux, *Selected Sermons*, 3:1 (p. 221).
46 Heidegger, *The Phenomenology of Religious Life*, 253.
47 Maldiney, "La Prise," 197.
48 Heidegger, *The Phenomenology of Religious Life*, 253.
49 Heidegger's *On the Way to Language*, as reproduced and modified in Romano's *Event and World*, 144–5.
50 Philippe Nouzille, "Manger le livre" in *Lettre de l'Abbaye de Saint Martin de Ligugé*, no. 286 (October–December 1998), 14–15. Nouzille cites St. Jerome's *Commentary on Ecclesiastes* from *Patrologia Latina*, col. 1039.
51 Ibid. See also the thought-provoking chapter by Jean Leclercq, "Jésus livre et Jésus lecteur," *Regards monastiques sur le Christ au Moyen Âge* (Paris: Desclée, 2010), 25–39.
52 [Eugène] Guillevic (1907–97), *Art Poétique* (Paris: Gallimard, 2001), 94. Quoted and commented upon by B.-J. Samain (monk in the Cistercian abbey of Orval), writing on "Guillevic, le ruminant" in "Lire le Christ: L'amour des mots et le désir du Verbe," in *Renaissance de Fleury*, no. 186 (June 1998), 23–4.
53 *Dieu, la chair et l'autre: D'Irénée à Duns Scot* (Paris: OUF, 2008). Published in translation as *God, the Flesh, and the Other*, trans. William Christian Hackett.
54 *Saint Bonaventure and the Entrance of God into Theology*, trans. Brian Lapsa and Sarah Horton (St. Bonaventure University: Franciscan Institute Publication, 2018).
55 St. Augustine, *Confessions*, trans. Henry Chadwick (Oxford: Oxford University Press, 1991), VII, x (16), p. 124.

Part 1

1 Étienne Gilson, "Sens et nature de l'argument de saint Anselme," *Archives d'histoire doctrinale et littéraire du moyen âge*, vol. 9 (1934), 5.
2 Anselm, *Proslogion*, in *Complete Philosophical and Theological Treatises of Anselm of Canterbury*, trans. Jasper Hopkins and Herbert Richardson (Minneapolis: Arthur J. Banning Press, 2000), 88. Retrieved on February 25, 2020, jasper-hopkins.info. [Trans.—In the French version of this book, Emmanuel Falque prefers to use the translation by Alexandre Koyré (Paris: Vrin, 1930), with occasional modifications from more recent translations. This translation uses the Hopkins and Richardson translation of Anselm's works into English throughout.]
3 [Trans.—See Henri Bergson, *The Two Sources of Morality and Religion*, trans. R. Ashley Audra and Cloudesley Brereton (London: Macmillan, 1935), 1: "The remembrance of forbidden fruit is the earliest thing in the memory of each of us, as it is in that of mankind."]
4 For a reading that avoids argument and excludes all interpretations other than the purely theological one, see Michel Corbin, "Une longue frequentation d'Anselme," *Revue Transversalités* (January–March 2005), 162: "If the text that I have read is a great one, it is because it has dispossessed me of any illusion of possession or mastery. If someone then points out by way of objection that there are many ways to read a text I can only reply once more that there is a text here that is able to reiterate in dialectical fashion the Word that the Holy Scripture speaks as narrative, and concerning that text we cannot just say anything we please. If that were not the case the good words of truth would simply be amiable pleasantries." As for the diversity and legitimate riches of differing interpretations of the argument, it is worth consulting the monograph by Paul Vignaux, "Saint Anselme, Barth et au-delà," *Les Quatre Fleuves*, no. 1 ("Dieu connu en Jésus-Christ") (1973), 84–95.
5 See Henri Bouillard, who finds the premise of a "natural theology" in the philosophical form of the argument (*The Knowledge of God*, trans. Samuel D. Femiano [New York: Herder and Herder, 1967]), and Étienne Gilson, who chooses a third way, supposedly that of "reason" between philosophy and theology ("Sens et nature de l'argument de Saint Anselme," 5–51.
6 R. W. Southern, *Saint Anselm: A Portrait in a Landscape* (Cambridge: Cambridge University Press, 1993), 441. Quoted by Ludovic Viallet, "L'huître et la perle: saint Anselme dans la vie intellectuelle de son temps," in *Cur Deus homo. Atti del Congreso Internationale*, May 21–23, 1998 ed. Paul Gilbert, Helmut Kohlenberger and Elman Salmann (Rome: Pontificio Alenero S. Anselmo).
7 [Trans.—Anselm, writing in Latin, uses the term "*insipiens*" for his imagined opponent, citing Psalm 14:1 (Vg 13:1) "*dixit insipiens in corde suo non est Deus*" ("It is the fool who says in the heart,/'There is no God'"). Translations into English of *Proslogion* often refer to this opponent as "the Fool," though we should be clear that Anselm's Fool is not a court-jester or Lord of Misrule. He is rather a *non-sapiens*. Thomas O'Loughlin in "Who Is Anselm's Fool," *The New Scholasticism*, vol. LXIII, no. 3, (Summer 1989), 313–25, points out that biblical references such as those cited by Anselm paint the Fool as morally degenerate, while St. Augustine "apparently believes that some of the biblical *insipientes* are in the category of genuine searchers" (321). Falque goes on to explore the problem of the Fool's belief and understanding in depth (§7), using the French term "*insensé*" for fool. *Insensé* is etymologically

derived from the ecclesiastical Latin "*insensatus*" and has the advantage of allowing Falque scope for wordplay on the *insensé* and his reasonable sense (*sens sensé*).]
8   [Trans.—See Husserl on "meaning-fulfilment": "The sounded word is first made one with the meaning-intention, and this in its turn is made one ... with its meaning-fulfilment" Edmund Husserl, *Logical Investigations*, vol. 1, trans. J. N. Findlay (London: Routledge, 1970), 192].
9   [Trans.—Asymptotic—"a line that approaches a curve but never touches." See Karl Rahner, "The Experience of God Today," in *Theological Investigations*, vol. xix (New York: Crossroads, 1988), 169–77.]
10 See Emmanuel Levinas, *Of God Who Comes to Mind*, trans. Bettina Bergo (Stanford, CA: Stanford University Press, 1998).
11 [Trans.—Biblical quotations are taken from the *Revised New Standard Version* (Oxford: Oxford University Press, 1989, 1995) [RNSV], the *Jerusalem Bible* (London: Darton, Longman, and Todd, 1974) [JB], or the *Revised New Jerusalem Bible* (London: Darton, Longman, and Todd, 2018) [RNJB], depending on the text that is closest to Falque's French version.]

Chapter 1

1   *Proslogion*, in *Complete Philosophical and Theological Treatises of Anselm of Canterbury*, trans. Jasper Hopkins and Herbert Richardson (Minneapolis: Arthur J. Banning Press, 2000), chap. 2, 94. [Trans.—modified in line with Falque's translation.]
2   Étienne Gilson, "Sens et nature de l'argument de saint Anselme," *Archives d'histoire doctrinale et littéraire du Moyen Âge*, 1934, 26.
3   *Of God Who Comes to Mind*, trans. Bettina Bergo (Stanford, CA: Stanford University Press, 1998), xv: "God-coming-to-the-idea, as the life of God."
4   *Proslogion*, chap. 2: 93.
5   See Eadmer, *The Life and Times of St. Anselm Archbishop of Canterbury and Primate of the Britains*, trans. Martin Rule (London: Kegan Paul, Trench and Co., 1883).
6   William Kent, "St. Anselm," in *The Catholic Encyclopedia* (New York: Robert Appleton Company. New Advent: Retrieved 12, 2018, on http://www.newadvent.org/cathen/01546a.htm
7   Levinas, *Of God Who Comes to Mind*, foreword, xv.
8   Eadmer, *The Life and Times of St. Anselm,* The Palace of God, 13. Retrieved April 15, 2018, on archive.org
9   Edmund Husserl, *Husserliana*, vol. xiv, 58. Quoted and translated by Didier Franck in *Flesh and Body: On the Phenomenology of Husserl*, trans. Joseph Rivera and Scott Davidson (London: Bloomsbury, 2014), 81. My emphasis.
10 [Trans.—Offered or displayed itself.]
11 *Proslogion*, 88.
12 Eadmer, *The Life and Times of St. Anselm*, 2: 7, 196.
13 Ibid., 96.
14 Anselm's preface to *Monologion*, trans. Jasper Hopkins and Herbert Richardson, *Complete Philosophical and Theological Treatises of Anselm of Canterbury* (Minneapolis: Banning Press, 2000).
15 Eadmer, *The Life and Times of St. Anselm,* 2: 7, 196. [Trans.—Martin Rule's note explains that this was not "in the night watches" as previous translations had it, but "during the office of matins," which comprised the night vigil.]

16   See St. Bonaventure, *The Journey of the Mind into God*, trans. anonymous (Veritatis Splendor Publications: CreateSpace Independent Publishing Platform, [1259] 2013).
17   [Trans:—According to Rule's notes on Eadmer's *Life* (1: 2, 21), Anselm was not taught to write on parchment with a pen but with a "style" upon "a slate of wood," or perhaps ivory, covered with wax, referred to as a "tablet." Eadmer employs the verbs "*dictare*" and "*scribere*." "*Dictare*" refers to writing on "tablets"; "*scribere*" to writing out on parchment or copying what has been corrected on the wax tablets.]
18   Eadmer, *The Life and Times of St. Anselm*, 2:7, 197–8.
19   Umberto Eco, *The Name of the Rose* (1980), trans. William Weaver (New York: Vintage Classics, 2004). Eco sets the narrative puzzle in his novel in the early fourteenth century and period of the Inquisition rather than in the Benedictine Abbey of Bec in the twelfth century. Nonetheless, the situation could have been much the same: a manuscript lost and found, or newly put together; a faithless brother; an argument perhaps inspired by the devil; the so-called ontological argument rather than laughter as specific to humankind, etc.
20   *Proslogion*, Preface, 88.
21   See Jacques Le Goff, *Les intellectuels au Moyen Âge* (1957) (Paris: Éditions du Seuil, 1985), 67. [Trans. Petrus Comestor (1100–78) was famous in his lifetime as a bookworm. Chancellor of theological school at Paris and author of a biblical history for students in 20 books that draws on a large range of profane authors.]
22   Michel Corbin, *Saint Anselme* (Paris: Éditions du Cerf, 2004), 8.
23   Ibid.
24   [Trans.—The author of the treatise *On the Divine Names*, who was writing around 485–528 CE. He presented himself as St. Dionysius the Areopagite and as disciple of St. Paul but is generally accepted to have lived much later. In French he is usually referred to as Denys or St. Denys.]
25   [Trans.—"Apophatic" is the practice of describing something by stating characteristics it does not have. "Apophatic" or "negative" theology attempts to approach God speaking only in terms of what he is not, or what cannot be expressed, rather than what he is.]
26   Olivier Boulnois, "Les preuves fatiguent la vérité. Michel Corbin et l'argument anselmien," *Revue Transversalités*, January–March 2005, 176.
27   Ibid, note 5, p. 176. As far as Marion is concerned it is nonetheless worthwhile to consult his masterly chapter on the argument: "Is the Argument Ontological?" in *Cartesian Questions: Methods and Metaphysics*, trans. Jeffrey L. Kosky (Chicago: University of Chicago Press, 1999), 139–60.
28   See on this question and as a starting point, Paul Gilbert, *Le Proslogion de saint Anselme, Silence de Dieu et joie de l'homme* (Rome: Universita Gregoriana, 1990), 68–9: "Understanding God imposes a negative on thought, a route made negative by *limitation* … This to something [*aliquid*] is not nothing [*nihil*] in worldly terms: it differs thus completely from experience and we can assert it solely through this *difference*" (my emphasis).
29   Textual and historical references for Anselm's argument can be found in the additional note to the French edition of St. Augustine's *La Doctrine chrétienne* (*De Doctrina Christiana*) in *Œuvres de saint Augustin* (Paris: Institut d'études augustiniennes, 1991), B. A no. 11/2 pp. 468–71: "la définition de Dieu" (for Plotinus, Cicero, Augustine); and in Gilbert, *La Proslogion de saint Anselme …*, 67 (for Boethius and Seneca).
30   Plotinus, *The Enneads*, trans. Stephen Mackenna and B. S. Page (London: Faber and Faber, 1956, 2nd edition), V.3.15; p. 396.

31 St. Augustine, *On Christian Teaching* (*De Doctrina Christiana*), trans. R. P. H. Green (Oxford: Oxford University Press, 1997), Bk 1, 7, p. 11.
32 St. Augustine, *On the Free Choice of the Will, on Grace and Free Choice and Other Writings*, trans. Peter King (Cambridge: Cambridge University Press, 2010), Book II, 6.14.56–58, p. 43.
33 Anselm, *Monologion*. Preface, 1.
34 Cicero's *Tusculan Disputations*, trans. C. D. Yonge (New York: Harper Brothers, 1877), xxvi, 37.
35 *The Natural Questions of L. Annaeus Seneca: Addressed to Lucilius*, trans. John Clarke (London: Macmillan and Co., 1910), Preface, Bk 1. "Here at last the soul comes to learn what it has long sought, it begins to know God."
36 *Proslogion*: Preface, p. 88.
37 *The Consolation of Philosophy* by Anicius Manlius Severinus Boethius, trans. W. V. Cooper (published by the Ex-classics Project, 2009: Retrieved August 10, 2020, on http://www.wxclassics.com) Bk. III, Prose X., p. 36.
38 [Trans.—"Saturated phenomenon" is Jean-Luc Marion's term. See Shane Mackinlay, *Interpreting Excess: Jean-Luc Marion, Saturated Phenomenon, and Hermeneutics* (New York: Fordham University Press, 2010), 1: "A saturated phenomenon is one that cannot be wholly contained within concepts that can be grasped by the understanding. It gives so much in intuition that there is always an excess left over, which is beyond conceptualization. Thus, it is saturated with intuition."]

Chapter 2

1 Eadmer's *Life of Anselm*, quoted in R. W. Southern, *Saint Anselm and His Biographer: A Study of Monastic Life and Thought 1059–c.1130* (Cambridge: Cambridge University Press, 1966), 58.
2 *Proslogion*, trans. Jasper Hopkins and Herbert Richardson (Minneapolis: The Arthur J. Banning Press, 2000), chap. 1, p. 93.
3 Paul Ricoeur, preface to Rudolf Bultmann's *Jésus* (Paris: Éditions du Seuil, 1968), 18: "Here Bultmann is perfectly in agreement with Karl Barth, when the latter says in his *Commentary on the Epistle to the Romans* that 'understanding is led by the object of faith.' But what distinguishes Bultmann from Barth is that the former has perfectly understood that the primacy of the object, this primacy of sense over understanding, is only exercised through using understanding itself, through the business of exegesis … That is why there is a *circle*: for me to understand the text I have to believe what the text tells me; but what the text tells me is given nowhere else but in the text" (my emphasis).
4 *Proslogion*, chap. 4: 95 (my emphasis).
5 Karl Barth, *Anselm: Fides Quaerens Intellectum: Anselm's Proof of the Existence of God in the Context of His Theological Scheme*, trans. Ian W. Robertson (London: SCM Press, 1960), 171.
6 *On Behalf of the Fool by Gaunilo: What Someone, on Behalf of the Fool, Replies to These [Arguments]* in *Complete Philosophical and Theological Treatises of Anselm of Canterbury*, trans. Jasper Hopkins and Herbert Richardson (Minneapolis: Arthur J. Banning Press, 2000), 2.

7 See respectively Henri Bouillard, *Connaissance de Dieu* (Paris: Foi vivante, 1966), 125 and Paul Vignaux, *La Philosophie au Moyen Âge* (Paris: Vrin, 2004), 121.
8 St. Augustine, *Sermons II*, 20-50. On the Old Testament, trans. Edmund Hill (New York: New City Press, 1990). Sermon 43§9, 242-3. (See also Augustine's *On the Profit of Believing*, chap. X). The Hebrew text of Isaiah 7, translated directly into Latin by Jerome as "*si non credideritis, non permanebitis* (if you do not believe you will not endure)" revised the earlier Latin translation of *non intellegetis*, based on the Greek Septuagint and used by Augustine. [Trans.—Latin editions of St. Augustine use the spelling of the verb "*intellegere*" while editions of Anselm give "*intelligere*." Thus editions of Augustine give "*intellegam*" and those of Anselm "*intelligam*." I should like to express my thanks here to the anonymous reader for Notre Dame University Press who (in a long list of very helpful corrections and suggestions) pointed out this difference.]
9 St. Augustine, *Sermons II*, 43§4, 240.
10 Ibid. 43§7, 241-2.
11 [Trans.—An "epileptic demoniac" RNJB.]
12 St. Augustine, *Sermons II*, 43§9, 242.
13 Ibid.
14 Ibid.
15 Ibid. 43§8, 242. My emphasis. [Trans.—There are two spellings of the verb *intelligere* or *intellegere*. The edition of Augustine's sermons uses *intellegam*, whereas that of Anselm uses *intelligam*.]
16 Ibid. 43§9, 242-3. My emphasis.
17 Paul Ricoeur, *The Symbolism of Evil*, trans. Emerson Buchanan (Boston: Beacon Press, 1969), 351.
18 Ibid., 352.
19 *Proslogion*, chap. 2, 93.
20 See the note to Ps. 13:1 in the *Traduction Œcuménique de la Bible* (Paris: Éditions du Cerf, 1975).
21 Paul Vignaux, *Philosophy in the Middle Ages: An Introduction*, trans E. C. Hall (New York: Meridian Books, 1959), 42.
22 Ibid., 44.
23 See Henri Gouhier, *Essais sur Descartes* (Paris: Vrin, 1937), 163: "The malicious demon [*malin génie*] is a creation as disingenuous as it is artificial. There is no presumption of its existence, and its essence is no secret from me as I am its author." See also Gouhier's *La Pensée métaphysique de Descartes* (Paris: Vrin, 1962), 113-21. The evil demon is an "epistemological scarecrow," 117, a "methodological artifice,"121.
24 St. Augustine, Sermon 43 §9 [Falque's translation].
25 On this overlap between philosophy and theology, rather than the notion of a rupture between the two, see my *Crossing the Rubicon: The Borderlands of Philosophy and Theology*, trans. Reuben Shank (New York: Fordham University Press, 2016), chap. 5, "'Tiling' and Conversion," 121-36.
26 *Proslogion*, chap. 3: 94.
27 Barth, *Anselm: Fides Quaerens Intellectum*, 104.
28 René Descartes, *A Discourse on the Method of Correctly Conducting One's Reason and Seeking Truth in the Sciences*, trans. Ian Maclean (Oxford: Oxford University Press, 2006), Part I, 5.

29 See Immanuel Kant, *Critique of Pure Reason*, Book I, section II, "Of Transcendental Ideas," trans. Paul Gayer and Allen W. Wood (Cambridge: Cambridge University Press, 1998). On transcendental experience see Karl Rahner, *Foundation of Christian Faith: An Introduction to the Idea of Christianity*, trans. William V. Dych (New York: Seabury Press, 1978).
30 *Proslogion*, chap. 2: 93.
31 [Trans.—"Gnoseological": relating to the basis and limits of knowledge.]
32 *Proslogion*, chap. 2: 93.
33 Ibid., chap. 2: 93–4.
34 Anselm, *Cur Deus homo*, trans. Sidney Norton Deane (Chicago: The Open Court Publishing Company, 1903), chap. 2. I owe this important parallel to Paul Vignaux, *Philosophie au Moyen Âge*, 120.
35 Michel Foucault, *The Order of Things: An Archaeology of the Human Sciences* (London: Routledge, 1989), 346. See part 2, 9-III, 340–46: "The analytic of finitude." See also my *The Metamorphosis of Finitude*, trans. George Hughes (New York: Fordham University Press, 2012), in particular chap. 3, "Is There a Drama of Atheist Humanism?" 30–40.
36 *Proslogion*, chap. 2: 94.
37 See Étienne Gilson, "Sens et nature de l'argument de saint Anselme," *Archives d'histoire doctrinale et littéraire du Moyen Âge*, 1934, 10–11, and Kurt Flasch, *Introduction à la philosophie médiévale*, French translation by Janine de Bourgknecht (Paris: Cerf, 2010), 64.
38 Kant, *Critique of Pure Reason*, chap. 3, section 4: "On the impossibility of an ontological proof of God's existence" (A596/B624). Example of the hundred dollars: "The actual contains nothing more than the merely possible. A hundred actual dollars do not contain the least bit more than a hundred possible ones" (567: A599/B627).
39 Barth, *Anselm: Fides Quaerens Intellectum*, 86.
40 *Proslogion*, chap. 2: 93 [Trans.—Modified in line with Falque's translation.]
41 Henri Bergson, *The Two Sources of Morality and Religion*, trans. R. Ashley Audra and Cloudesley Bereton (London: Macmillan, 1935), 44–5: "It might be said, by slightly distorting the terms of Spinoza, that it is to get back to *natura naturans* that we break away from *natura naturata*. Hence, between the first morality and the second, lies that whole distance between *repose* and *movement*. The first is supposed to be immutable … But the second is a forward thrust, a demand for movement; it is the very essence of morality" (my emphasis).
42 Barth, *Anselm: Fides Quaerens Intellectum*, 74.
43 Jean-Luc Marion, *Cartesian Questions: Method and Metaphysics* (Chicago: University of Chicago Press, 1999): "Is the Argument Ontological?" 68.
44 Paul Gilbert, *Le Proslogion de S. Anselme, Silence de Dieu et joie de l'homme* (Rome: Universita Gregoriana, 1990), 68.
45 Ibid., 68–9 (my emphasis). I agree with Gilbert that we can thus distinguish three modes of the *via negativa*: a negative route taken by surpassing (Dionysius), one by manifestation (John Scotus Eriugena) and one by limitation (Anselm of Canterbury).
46 See Edmund Husserl, *Ideas Pertaining to a Pure Phenomenology and to a Phenomenological Philosophy*, trans. F. Kersten (The Hague: Martinus Nijhoff, 1983). The example of the different ways in which we see a table while walking round it. §41: 86–7.
47 *Proslogion*, chap. 4: 95.

48 See Anselm, *De Grammatico: How (an) Expert-in-Grammar Is Both a Substance and a Quality*, trans. Jasper Hopkins and Herbert Richardson (Minneapolis: J. Arthur Baring Press, 2000): "The common term [*communis terminus*] of a syllogism must be common not so much in verbal form [*in prolatione*] as in meaning [*in sententia*]. For just as no conclusion follows if it is common in verbal form but not in meaning [*et non in sensu*], so no harm is done if it is common in meaning [*in intellectu*] but not in verbal form [*et non in prolatione*]. Indeed, the meaning [*sententia*]—rather than the words—determines a syllogism" (chap. 4: 136). For the sources of signification in Anselm, see Jean Jolivet, *Arts du langage et théologie chez Abélard* (Paris: Vrin, 1982). As for the link with the theory of signification as premise of Husserlian phenomenology, see Edmund Husserl, *The Shorter Logical Investigation*, trans. J. N. Findlay (London: Routledge, 2001): "We must go back to the 'things themselves.' We desire to render self-evident in fully-fledged intuitions that what is here given in actually performed abstraction is what the word-meaning in sur experience of the law really and truly stands for" (88).
49 Anselm, *The Incarnation of the Word*, trans. Jasper Hopkins and Herbert Richardson (Minneapolis: Arthur J. Banning Press, 2008), I: 269.
50 For the different types of knowledge that recall Anselm's *Proslogion*, see Benedict de Spinoza, *The Collected Works,* trans. Edwin Curley (Princeton: Princeton University Press), vol. 1: *The Ethics*, part 2, "Of the Nature and Origin of the Mind," Proposition XL, note 2.
51 *Proslogion*, chap. 4: 95.
52 Ibid., chap. 3: 94.
53 [Trans.—*Hexis*: stable arrangement or disposition.]
54 *Proslogion*, chap. 3: 94.
55 Ibid., chap. 3: 94.
56 Edmund Husserl, *The Idea of Phenomenology: A translation of Die Idee der Phenomenologie, Husserliana II*, trans. Lee Hardy (Dordrecht: Kluwer Academic, 1999), 27: "Rather, the critique of knowledge seeks to clarify, to bring to light, the essence of knowledge and the legitimacy of its claim to validity, a claim that belongs to its essence. And what else can this mean than to bring the essence of knowledge to direct self-givenness." Self-givenness is a translation of *Selbstgegebenheit*, a term which indicates *who* is given in person as well as the *character* of being given in person.
57 Martin Heidegger, *Being and Time*, trans. John Macquarrie and Edward Robinson (New York: Harper Perennial, 2008), §7:36, p. 60.
58 See Robert Poulet, *La Rectitudo chez saint Anselme. Un itinéraire augustinien de l'âme à Dieu* (Paris: Études augustiniennes, 1964), 78: "These principles of rectitude, expressed in *De veritate*, find their natural application in chaps. 2, 3 and 4 of *Proslogion*."
59 *Proslogion*, chap. 3: 94 (Modified in line with Falque's translation—Trans.)
60 See Alexandre Koyré's translation of Baruch de Spinoza, *Traité de reforme de l'entendement* (Paris: Vrin, 1938): "God's intellect, insofar as it is conceived to constitute God's essence, is really the cause both of the essence and of the existence of things."
61 *Proslogion*, chap. 2: 93.
62 Ibid., chap. 4: 94–5.
63 Hans Urs von Balthasar, *The Glory of the Lord: A Theological Aesthetics*, vol. II: *Studies in Theological Style: Clerical Style*, trans. Andrew Louth, Francis McDonagh and Brian McNeil (San Francisco: Ignatius Press, 1984), 233.

64 Gaunilo, *Liber pro Insipiente* [*In Defence of the Fool*], translation modified. [Trans.—Gaunilo's "Lost Island" refutation of Anselm's argument argues that if Anselm's proof of the existence of a greatest conceivable being were sound, then we should also be able to give proof of the existence of a greatest conceivable island. But we cannot do this, so Anselm's proof is unsound.]
65 *Monologion and Proslogion with the Replies of Gaunilo and Anselm*, trans. Thomas Williams (Indianapolis: Hackett Publishing Company, Inc., 1995), 132.
66 Paul Gilbert, *Le Proslogion de saint Anselm, Silence de Dieu et joie de l'homme* (Rome: Universita Gregoriana, 1990), 70.
67 *Proslogion*, chap. 3: 94.
68 Ibid.
69 Ibid., my emphasis.
70 [Trans.—Agathology: the science or doctrine of the good.] See Jean-Luc Marion, *Cartesian Questions: Method and Metaphysics*, trans. revised by Jeffrey L. Kosky (Chicago: University of Chicago Press, 1999), 152: "Is the Argument Ontological?" "The passage to the maximum limit of the *cogitatio* would lack an operational criterion; hence the argument would remain abstract, without the interpretation of *majus* on the basis of *melius* ... God surpasses essence through the same gesture that frees Him from the concept—because He can only be thought as He offers Himself, as sovereign good, as sovereign insofar as He is the good, rather than as Being."
71 *Proslogion*, chap. 1: 93.
72 *The Rule of St. Benedict*, Preface by W. K. Lowther Clarke (London: SPCK, 1931), chap. 7: Concerning Humility.
73 Barth, *Anselm: Fides Quaerens Intellectum*, 160: "The *insipiens* [Fool] thinks and speaks as one who is not saved by the grace of God. That is the reason of his perversity."
74 Jacques Paliard, "Prière et dialectique, Méditation sur le *Proslogion* de Saint Anselme," *Dieu Vivant*, no. 6 (1948), 57.

Chapter 3

1 Paul Ricoeur, *Memory, History, Forgetting*, trans. Kathleen Blamey and David Pellauer Chicago: University of Chicago Press, 2004), 480, 482. See Jacques Derrida, *Given Time: 1. Counterfeit Money*, trans. Peggy Kamuf (Chicago: University of Chicago Press, 1992) and Jean-Luc Marion, *Being Given: Towards a Phenomenology of Givenness*, trans. Jeffrey L. Kosky (Stanford, CA: University of Stanford Press, 2002).
2 Marcel Henaff, "Don ceremonial, Dette et reconnaissance," in *Le Don de la dette*, ed. M. M Olivetti (Rome: Archivio di Filosofia, 2004), 24. See also *Le Prix de la vérité. Le don, l'argent, la philosophie* (Paris: Éditions du Seuil, 2002) chapter 4: "L'énigme du don ceremonial."
3 See my *Saint Bonaventure and the Entrance of God into Theology*, trans. Brian Lapsa, Sarah Horton and W. C. Hackett (St. Bonaventure University, NY: Franciscan Institute Publications, 2018), Part 3, §10 "Toward an ontology of poverty."
4 See my *Metamorphosis of Finitude*, trans. George Hughes (New York: Fordham University Press, 2012), §5 "The Preemption of the Infinite," 16–19.
5 Aquinas, *Commentary on the Sentences of Peter Lombard*, Book 1, d.8, q.1, a.2, c.2. For a commentary on this see my *Crossing the Rubicon: The Borderlands of Philosophy*

and *Theology*, trans. Reuben Shank (New York: Fordham University Press, 2016), chapter 6, §19 "From the Threshold to the Leap," 139–47. Also see my article, "Limite théologique et finitude phénoménologique chez Thomas d'Aquin," *Revue des sciences philosophiques et théologiques,* colloque de Centenaire (July–September 2008), 527–56.

6 Louis Bourdaloue, "Premier Sermon sur la passion de Jésus-Christ," in *Œuvres complètes*, vol. 4 (Metz: Rousselot, 1864), 218–20. Cited by Bernard Sesboüé in *Jésus-Christ l'unique Médiateur* (Paris: Desclée, 2003), vol. 1, 72–3. For an exhaustive commentary on this text see L. Mahieu, "L'abandon du Christ sur la croix," *Mélanges de science religieuse*, vol. II (1945), 234–5.

7 Louis Bouyer, *Le Fils éternel* (Paris: Éditions du Cerf, 1974), 414–15 (my emphasis).

8 Hans Urs von Balthasar, *The Glory of the Lord: A Theological Aesthetics* II, *Studies in Theological Style: Clerical Style*, trans. Andrew Louth, Francis McDonagh and Brian McNeil (San Francisco: Ignatius Press, 1984), 249. The contrast between Balthasar and Louis Bouyer is discussed in Michel Corbin *L'Œuvre de S. Anselme de Cantorbéry* (Paris: Éditions du Cerf, 1998), vol. 3: 17–23.

9 Emmanuel Levinas, *Totality and Infinity: An Essay on Exteriority*, trans. Alphonso Lingis (Dordrecht: Kluwer Academic Publishers, 1991), 196. Michel Henry, *Incarnation* (Paris: Éditions du Seuil, 2000), 26. Jean-Luc Marion, *Being Given. Toward a Phenomenology of Givenness*, trans. Jeffrey L. Kosky (Stanford, CA: Stanford University Press, 2000). On these three analyses see also my *Le Combat amoureux, Disputes phénoménologiques et théologiques* (Paris: Hermann, 2014), chapter 3: "Le visage sans visage" (Levinas), chapter 5 "Y a-t-il une chair sans corps?" (Henry), and chapter 5: "Phénoménologie de l'extraordinaire" (Marion).

10 Marco M. Olivetti, *Le Don et la dette* (Rome: Archivio di Filosofia, 2004), 13 (my emphasis).

11 Paul Gilbert, "Violence et liberté dans le *Cur Deus homo*," in *Cur Deus homo, Actes du congrès de Rome*, ed. Paul Gilbert (Rome: Studia Anselmiana, 1988, no. 128), 692 (my emphasis). A perspective that opposes, or at least differs from, the very Dionysian view of the "surplus" developed by Michel Corbin in his interpretation of Anselm. See Corbin, *L'Œuvre de S. Anselme de Cantorbéry*, vol. 3: 46, "Un movement de négation et d'outrepassement"—which precisely cites Pseudo-Dionysius with reference to Anselm.

12 Martin Heidegger, *Being and Time*, trans. John Macquarrie and Edward Robinson (New York: Harper Perennial, 2008), §58: "Understanding the Appeal, and Guilt," 325–35.

13 Henri Declève, "Christologie et philosophie dans le *Cur Deus homo* de saint Anselme," *Cur Deus homo, Actes du congrès de Rome,* 492.

14 Anselm, Preface to *Cur Deus Homo* in *Complete Philosophical and Theological Treatises*, trans. Jasper Hopkins and Herbert Richardson (Minneapolis: Arthur J. Baring Press, 2000), 296. [Falque uses the translation of *Cur Deus homo* by Corbin in *L'Œuvre de S. Anselme de Cantorbéry,* vol. 3. He also refers readers to the introduction, translation, and notes in René Roques, *Anselme de Cantorbéry, Pourquoi Dieu s'est fait homme* (Paris: Éditions du Cerf, 1963)—Trans.]

15 See René Roques, *Anselme de Cantorbéry, Pourquoi Dieu s'est fait homme*, 48–51.

16 Eadmer's Life of St. Anselm in Rev. Alban Butler, *The Lives of the Saints*, vol. 4 (Dublin: James Duffy [1866]; New York: Bartleby.com, 2010). For the definition of Being-guilty as being struck with "nullity" see Heidegger, *Being and Time*, §58: 285,

331: "Dasein as such is guilty, if our formally existential definition of 'guilt' as 'Being-the-basis of a nullity' is indeed correct."
17 *Cur Deus Homo, Commendation of This Work to Pope Urban II*: "The understanding which we acquire in this life is a middle-way [*medium*] between faith and sight [*inter fidem et* speciem]," 295.
18 *Cur Deus Homo*, trans. Jasper Hopkins and Herbert Richardson, 295.
19 *The Virgin Conception and Original Sin* in *Complete Philosophical and Theological Treatises of Anselm of Canterbury*, trans. Jasper Hopkins and Herbert Richardson (Minneapolis: Arthur J. Baring Press, 2000), 428.
20 For the important role of Boso in *Cur Deus Homo* see René Roques, *Anselme de Cantorbèry, Pourquoi Dieu s'est fait homme*, 51–3.
21 *Cur Deus Homo*, trans. Jasper Hopkins and Herbert Richardson, 295–6.
22 Ibid., 1, 6: 306.
23 For the reduction of the gift to pure donation, indeed for the debate between Derrida and Marion (and the radicalization of the former effected by the latter), see Derrida, *Given Time I*, 14: "At the limit, the gift as gift ought not to appear as gift, either to the donnee or to the donor." See also Marion, *Being Given*, 84: "Reducing the gift to the givenness and givenness to itself therefore means: thinking the gift while *abstracting* from the threefold transcendence that affected it heretofore—by the successive bracketing of the transcendence of the *givee,* the transcendence of the *giver* and finally the transcendence of the *object exchanged*" (my emphasis).
24 *Cur Deus Homo*, trans. Jasper Hopkins and Herbert Richardson, 1, 7: 308.
25 [Trans.—*Epokhé*—term from phenomenology meaning the setting aside of biases and assumptions in order to explain phenomena in terms of their own inherent meaning.]
26 Heidegger, *Being and Time*, §58: 284, p. 329 (emphasis in original).
27 Paul Ricoeur, *Oneself as Another*, trans. Kathleen Blamey (Chicago: University of Chicago Press, 1992), 351.
28 Marcel Mauss, *The Gift: The Form and Reason for Exchange in Archaic Societies* (London: Routledge, 1990), 50.
29 Anselm comments on the passage in *Cur Deus Homo*, 1, 7: 308.
30 I am drawing here on the old but very useful study by Jean Rivière, *Le Dogme de la rédemption* (Paris: Librarie Victor Lecoffre, 1905), part 5, 373–486.
31 Origen, *Homilies on Genesis and Exodus* in *The Fathers of the Church*, vol. 71, trans. Ronald E. Heine (Washington, DC: Catholic University of America Press, 1982), *Exodus Homily* VI, 9: 296.
32 Origen, *Homilies on Jeremiah*: in *The Fathers of the Church*, vol. 97, trans. John Clark Smith (Washington, DC: Catholic University of America Press, 1998), *Homily on 1 Kings 28*, p. 162.
33 Origen, *Exodus Homily* VI, 9: 296.
34 *The Fathers of the Church: Seven Exegetical Works*, vol. 65, Ambrose of Milan, *Jacob and the Happy Life. Joseph*, trans. Michael P. Hugh (Washington, DC: Catholic University of America Press, 2003), 201.
35 St. Augustine, *On the Trinity*, book 13: chapter 12:16 in *Nicene and Post-Nicene Fathers, First Series*, vol. 3, trans. Arthur West Haddan, rev. and ed. Kevin Knight (Buffalo, NY: Christian Literature Publishing Co., 1887). Retrieved November 4, 2019, on www.newadvent.org
36 Ibid., book 13: chapter 14:18.
37 Ibid., book 13: chapter 13:17.

38 St. Augustine, *On the Free Choice of the Will, on Grace and Free Choice, and Other Writings*, trans. Peter King (Cambridge: Cambridge University Press, 2010), book 3, p. 96.
39 *Cur Deus Homo*, trans. Jasper Hopkins and Herbert Richardson, 1, 7: 306.
40 *De casu diaboli* [*The Fall of the Devil*], in *Complete Philosophical and Theological Treatises of Anselm of Canterbury*, trans. Jasper Hopkins and Herbert Richardson (Minneapolis: Arthur J. Banning Press, 2000), chapter 11, 234.
41 *Cur Deus Homo*, trans. Jasper Hopkins and Herbert Richardson, 1, 7: 307.
42 Ibid.
43 On the authentic sense of donation as gift of the gift see in particular Jean-Luc Marion, "Esquisse d'un concept phénoménologique de don," Filosofia della Rivelazione, in *Archivo di Fiolosopia*, 1994, no. 1–3, 78: "The formula 'if you only knew the gift of God' can serve here as paradigm (not theological) for all phenomenology of gift-giving: the recipient *does not know* and *does not have to know* what gift is being made, precisely because a gift can and should *go beyond all clear awareness*" (my emphases).
44 See *De casu diaboli*, chapter 10: "How evil seems to be something" [*quomodo malum videatur esse aliquid*], 214.
45 *Cur Deus Homo*, trans. Jasper Hopkins and Herbert Richardson, 1, 7: 308.
46 Heidegger, *Being and Time*, §58: 283, p. 328. [The translation of Heidegger used by Falque gives "dette" [debt] where Macquarrie and Robinson's translation gives "guilt."—Trans.] The absence of any reference to Anselm is noted in Robert Petkovsek, *Heidegger-Index (1919–1927)* (Ljubljana, 1998), 215–44 [*Namenregister*].
47 *Cur Deus Homo*, 1, 11: 318.
48 Ibid.
49 The paradox is underlined by Anselm himself: "I see on the one hand a necessity for a reward, and on the other it appears impossible" *Cur Deus Homo*, book 2:19, in *Works of St. Anselm* (1903), trans. Sidney Norton Deane (Peru, IL: Open Court Publishing Company, 1962). See *The Catholic Primer*. Retrieved November 10, 2019, on www.catholicprimer.org.
50 *Being and Time*, §58: 252, p. 328.
51 *Cur Deus Homo*, trans. Jasper Hopkins and Herbert Richardson, 1, 11: 318.
52 *De veritate: On Truth* in *Complete Philosophical and Theological Treatises of Anselm of Canterbury*, trans. Jasper Hopkins and Herbert Richardson (Minneapolis: Arthur J. Banning Press, 2000), chapter 12, 184.
53 *Cur Deus Homo*, 1, 11: 318 (translation modified).
54 Emmanuel Levinas, "Philosophy and the Idea of the Infinite," in *To the Other: An Introduction to the Philosophy of Emmanuel Levinas*, ed. Adrian Peperzak (West Lafayette, Indiana: Purdue University Press, 1992), 110. For the opening to the other as obligation and breaking of the circle of the self, see Levinas, *En découvrant l'existence avec Husserl et Heidegger* [1949] (Paris: Vrin, 1998), 172.
55 *Cur Deus Homo*, trans. Jasper Hopkins and Herbert Richardson, 1:20, 338. [Trans.—modified in line with Falque's translation.]
56 Claude Bruaire, *L'être et l'esprit* (Paris: PUF, 1983), 59–61 (emphasis in original).
57 *Cur Deus Homo*, trans. Jasper Hopkins and Herbert Richardson, 1:11, p. 318.
58 Ibid., 1, 9: 313.
59 Ibid., 1, 9: 314.
60 Ibid., 1, 10: 316.
61 Ibid., 1, 11: 318: "What sinning and making satisfaction for sin are."

62 Ricoeur, *Oneself as Another*, 351.
63 *Cur Deus* Homo, trans. Jasper Hopkins and Herbert Richardson, 1, 19: 336.
64 *Being and Time*, §58: 287, p. 333.
65 Bruaire, *L'être et l'esprit*, 60.
66 *Cur Deus Homo*, trans. Jasper Hopkins and Herbert Richardson, 1, 23: 342–3.
67 Ibid., 1, 24: 341.
68 Ibid., 1, 21: 340.
69 Ibid., 1, 22: 342.
70 Ibid., 1, 23: 343.
71 Ibid., 1, 24: 344.
72 Ibid., 1, 21: 341.
73 Ibid., 1, 20: 337; 1, 11: 319.
74 Ibid., 1, 9: 314.
75 Ibid., 1, 20: 337.
76 *Proslogion*, chapter 2: 93. "God truly exists"; *Cur Deus Homo*, 1, 21: 341; 1, 13: 322. On this point see the introduction to the French edition of *Cur Deus Homo* by Michel Corbin (*Pourquoi un Dieu-homme* in *L'Œuvre de S. Anselme de Cantorbéry* [Paris: Éditions du Cerf, 1998], vol. 3, 291), which centers on the name of God as "great" or as surplus of the gift over the debt.
77 Sesboüé, *Jésus-Christ l'unique Médiateur*, vol. 1, 328 (my emphasis).
78 *Cur Deus Homo*, trans. Jasper Hopkins and Herbert Richardson, 1, 7: 308 [Trans.—modified in line with Falque's translation.]
79 Ibid., 1, 12: 319–20.
80 Ibid., 1, 12: 320 [Trans.—modified in line with Falque's translation.]
81 Ibid., 1, 20: 339 [Trans.—modified in line with Falque's translation.]
82 Ricoeur, *Memory, History, Forgetting*, 466.
83 *Cur Deus Homo; St. Anselm*, trans. Sidney Norton Deane, 2, 19: 85.
84 Ibid.
85 Ibid., 2, 19: 85–6.
86 Emmanuel Gabellieri, "Un don sans retour? Pour une analogie et un catalogie du don," in *Le Don, théologie, philosophie, psychologie, sociologie*, ed. J.-N. Dumont (Lyon: Éditions de l'Emmanuel/Le collège supérieur, 2001), 78–9 (my emphasis).
87 *Cur Deus Homo*, trans. Jasper Hopkins and Herbert Richardson, 1, 24: 346.
88 *Cur Deus Homo; St. Anselm*, trans. Sidney Norton Deane, 2, 20: 87.
89 See my *Crossing the Rubicon*, "The Illusion of the Leap," 142–5.
90 Thomas Aquinas, *Contra Gentiles*, trans. Vernon J. Bourke (New York: Hanover House, 1955–7), book 3, chapter 67. Retrieved March 11, 2020, on www.dhspriory.org/thomas/ContraGentiles.htm
91 See my *Saint Bonaventure and the Entrance of God into Theology*, chapter 1(b): "The *Breviloquium*: a *summa* of revealed theology."

Part 2

1 Emmanuel Falque, *Crossing the Rubicon: The Borderlands of Philosophy and Theology*, trans. Reuben Shank (New York: Fordham University Press, 2016).
2 Ibid., chapter 1: "Is Hermeneutics Fundamental?": "In addressing Ricoeur's theological claim, I argue in a Catholic mode that the text or the book of scripture

(*liber scripturae*) does not necessarily overshadow the book of the world (*liber mundi*)—rather, the opposite is the case," 43.

3   Hugh of Saint-Victor, Prologue to *On the Praise of Charity* [*De Laude caritatis*] in *On Love*, ed. Hugh Feiss (Hyde Park, NY: New City Press, 2012), 159 [*Patrologia Latina* (LP), 176, 971A].

4   The origin of the wordplay in Latin is found in St. Augustine's, *Confessions*, trans. Henry Chadwick (Oxford: Oxford University Press, 1991), XIII, 18, 283: "They read, they choose, they love. They ever read, and what they read never passes away." [*Legunt, eligunt et diligunt, semper legunt et nunquam praeterit quod legunt.*]

5   [Trans.—The School of Saint-Victor was based in the Abbey of Saint-Victor in Paris, founded by William of Champeaux, where the theologian Hugh of Saint-Victor started to teach, around 1115-20. Other Victorine theologians associated with the school are Achard of Saint-Victor, Andrew of Saint-Victor, Richard of Saint-Victor, Walter of Saint-Victor, and Godfrey of Saint-Victor.]

6   See on this point the fascinating interview of Anthony Grafton with Roger Chartier, "De la page à la Toile: une rupture essentielle?" *Critique*, no. 785 (October 2012), 854-65.

7   See Claude Romano, *Au Coeur de la raison, la phénoménologie* (Paris: Gallimard, 2010), 873-906: "La phénoménologie *en tant qu*'herméneutique."

Chapter 4

1   Jean Leclercq, *L'Amour des lettres et le désir de Dieu* (Paris: Éditions du Cerf, 1990), 21. There is further confirmation of the practice of the abbey of Saint-Victor in Jean Chatillon's *Le Mouvement canonial au moyen âge* (Brussels: Brepols, 1992), "La culture à l'école de Saint-Victor au xii siècle," 332: "In the daily routine of the monastery, a large place was in fact given to private reading. As a result, certain works were left permanently at the disposition of the religious in the cloister. Others could borrow from the library which the *armarius* (librarian) had in charge. Private reading was done in the cloister, and in silence. It was however very *much a relative silence*, as many religious, for their personal convenience, *read in a low voice*" (my emphasis).

2   See my *Crossing the Rubicon,* trans. Reuben Shank (New York: Fordham University Press, 2016), chap. 1, "Is Hermeneutics Fundamental?" §4 "The Hermeneutical Relief," 31-40.

3   *Deutsche Mystiker des vierzehnten Jahrhunderts*, vol. 2, *Meister Eckhart* (Leipzig: Pfeiffer, 1957), 599. Cited in *Maître Eckhart et la mystique rhénane* (Paris: Éditions du Cerf, 1999), 25: "Master Eckhart says, 'A *master of life* is worth a thousand *masters of reading*, but to read and live in God is something that nobody can achieve. If I had to search for a master of the Scriptures, I would look for him in Paris, in the great schools there, to [learn] his high science. But if I wanted to consider the perfect life, I would not know what to say. Where would I go? Nowhere but in a *naked and free nature*: that which would be able to teach me if I put the question to it.'" See the comments on this passage in Yves Meessen, *Percée de l'ego, Maître Eckhart en phénoménologie* (Paris: Hermann, 2016), 27-8.

4   [Trans.—"sensible world": i.e., the world as perceived, as opposed to the intelligible world.]

5   Hugh of Saint-Victor, *De diebus tribus* [*Des trois jours de la lumière invisible*] (Patrologia Latina [PL], 176, 814B), taken here from the translation into French by Alain Michel in *Théologiens et mystiques au Moyen Âge* (Paris: Gallimard, 1997), 345.
6   Jos Decorte, "L'art de lire au Moyen Âge," in *Le Vaste Monde à livres ouverts, Manuscrits médiévaux en dialogue avec l'art contemporain* (Tielt: Lannoo, 2002), 95.
7   Hugh of Saint-Victor, *De diebus tribus* (PL, 176, 814B), trans. Boyd Taylor Coolman, cited in "'In Whom I Am Well Pleased': Hugh of St. Victor's Trinitarian Aesthetics" in *A Journal of Catholic and Evangelical Theology*, vol. XXIII, no. 3 (Summer 2014), 348.
8   Ivan Illich, *In the Vineyard of the Text: A Commentary to Hugh's Didascalicon* (Chicago: University of Chicago Press, 1996), 68.
9   From Jean Leclercq, *The Love of Learning and the Desire for God: A Study of Monastic Culture*, quoted in Ivan Illich, op. cit., 56.
10 Hugh of Saint-Victor, *De diebus tribus* (part not translated by Alain Michel).
11 "On Earth Dwelling Every Creature" [*Omnis mundi creatura*], trans. John Lord Hayes, in *Corolla Hymnorum Sacrorum* (Boston: John Wilson and Son, 1887), 59. (Revisions on the basis of the French—Trans.) Cited and translated by Gilbert Dahan in *L'Occident médiéval lecteur de l'Écriture*, in *Cahiers Evangile*, supp. No. 116, 2001, text 43, 60 (from which I have also borrowed the formula of nature as a "second language").
12 Hugh of Saint-Victor, *De diebus tribus* (PL, 176, 814B).
13 Hugh of Saint-Victor, *Didascalicon*, bk. 3, chap. 12: 127 in *The Interpretation of Scripture Theory, a Selection of Works of Hugh, Andrew, Godfrey and Richard of St. Victor and Robert of Melun*, ed. Franklin T. Hawkins and Frans van Liere (Turnhout: Brepols, 2012) (PL 176, 773C).
14 Ibid., Preface, 82.
15 See Luce Giard, "Hugues de Saint-Victor; cartographe du savoir," in *L'Abbaye Parisienne de Saint-Victor au Moyen Âge*, ed. Jean Longère (Turnhout: Brepols, 1991), 253–69. The focus is on the theological aim of such a cartography underlined by the author (see in particular p. 258), which takes *Didascalicon* not simply as the "first encyclopedia" but also as a "recapitulative mapping" (a term I use here), in the sense that nothing can or should escape from the assumption of the cosmos by the Word incarnate.
16 *Didascalicon*, bk. 3, chap. 7: 124. (PL 176, 771C).
17 Ibid.
18 Ibid. (my emphasis).
19 Michel Lemoine, introduction to *Didascalicon* (Paris: Éditions du Cerf, 1991), 19.
20 Gilduin (second abbot of the order under which Hugh taught), *Liber ordinis*. See Roger Baron, *Hugues et Richard de Saint-Victor* (Brussels: Bloud et Gay, 1961), 13.
21 [Trans.—Falque's term here is "*parole*" which can mean in French "speech" or "utterance." In §12 *parole* is discussed in relation to Hugh of Saint-Victor's *La parole de Dieu* (*De Verbo Dei—On the Word of God*).]
22 Hugh of Saint-Victor, *La parole de Dieu* in *Six opuscules spirituels, sources chrétiennes* 155, ed. Roger Baron (Paris: Éditions du Cerf, 1969), I, 1: 61.
23 See Louis-Marie Chauvet, "Sacrament," in *Dictionnaire critique de théologie*, ed. Jean-Yves Lacoste (Paris: PUF, 2002), 1030: "L'élaboration de sacramentum au xii siècle."
24 On this argument, the so-called enchanted quarrel (in particular the debate between Berengar of Tours and Lanfranc), see my *The Wedding Feast of the Lamb*, trans. George Hughes (New York: Fordham University Press, 2016), §27. "The Dispute over Meat," 188–95.

25 Hugh of Saint-Victor, *La parole de Dieu,* chap. 2: 63–5.
26 Ibid., I, 2, 61.
27 Ibid.
28 Ibid., V, 1, 75. As far as the capacity of humankind to receive the ark of speech is concerned, I am drawing on the work of Jean-Louis Chrétien with that title: *The Ark of Speech,* trans. Andrew Brown (Oxford: Routledge, 2004), Introduction (the figure of Adam). See also my comments in *Le Combat amoureux, Disputes phénoménologiques et théologiques* (Paris: Hermann, 2014), 239–62: "*Adam ou l'arche de la chair*."
29 Hugh of Saint-Victor, *La parole de Dieu,* I, 2, 63 (my emphases).
30 See my *Crossing the Rubicon,* chap. 2: 55–77: "For a Hermeneutic of the Body and the Voice."
31 Hugh of Saint-Victor, *La parole de Dieu,* I, 1, 61.
32 Ibid, I, 2, 61–3.
33 Hans Urs von Balthasar, *The Glory of the Lord,* vol. 1: *Seeing the Form,* trans. Erasmo Leiva-Merikakis (San Francisco: Ignatius Press, 1982), "The Spiritual Senses," 356–425. "God brings man to a halt by confronting him through his Incarnation *in the midst of the sphere of the senses ... Flesh speaks to flesh*; the Word chose this *unmistakable* language in order to overtake and encounter from below the sinner who had lost his spirit" (my emphases), 397.
34 Jacques Derrida, *Voice and Phenomenon: Introduction to the Problem of the Sign in Husserl's Phenomenology,* trans. Leopold Lawlor (Evanston, IL: Northwestern University Press, 2011), 79–80.
35 Hugh of Saint-Victor, *La parole de Dieu,* I, 2, 63.
36 Ibid., I, 3, 63.
37 Ibid., I, 2, 63 (my emphases).
38 *The Works of Saint Augustine, Sermons 273-305 (III/8) On the Saints,* trans. Edmund Hill (New York: New City Press, 1994), "On the Birthday of John the Baptist," 150.
39 Hugh of Saint-Victor, *La parole de Dieu,* V, 2, 77.
40 Ibid.
41 Ibid.
42 Ibid.
43 See my *Saint Bonaventure and the Entrance of God into Theology,* trans. Brian Lapsa and Sarah Horton (St. Bonaventure University, NY: Franciscan Institute Publications, 2018), Part 3 "The Manifestation and Naming of God."
44 See Illich, *In the Vineyard of the Text: A Commentary to Hugh's Didascalicon.* In this book Illich limits himself to a reading of *Didascalicon,* but the author himself recognizes the necessity of opening up to other works and other perspectives belonging to Hugh of Saint-Victor (see the Introduction).
45 See, for the distinction between negative or apophatic theology and positive or cataphatic theology, my *Saint Bonaventure and the Entrance of God into Theology,* chapter 1, "Toward a Descriptive Theology." As for the distinction between the "book of the world" and the "world of the book" see also my *God, the Flesh, and the Other,* trans. William Christian Hackett (Evanston: Northwestern University Press, 2015), "Saint Francis, or the Language of the Flesh," 169–75; "Saint Dominic, or the Flesh of Language," 175–9. My three volumes on medieval topics, mentioned in the introduction, could be said to have as their framework the quest for a "common visibility."
46 Hugh of Saint-Victor, *Exposition sur la Hiérarchie céleste* [*Expositio in hierarchiam coelestem*], LP 175, 926D, trans. R. Baron, *Hugues et Richard de Saint-Victor,* 77–8: "deux théologies."

47 Dominique Poirel, *Hugues de Saint-Victor et son école* (Brussels: Brepols, 1991), 60.
48 Hugh of Saint-Victor, *Exposition sur la Hiérarchie céleste*, LP 175, 926D-927A, 78.
49 See my *The Metamorphosis of Finitude*, trans. George Hughes (New York: Fordham University Press, 2012), 15: "We have no other experience of God but human experience. When I experience God, what sustains me is, at least first of all, God made human. No access opens toward the nonhuman—God, angel, beast, or demon—other than precisely through the human that I am."
50 Immanuel Kant, *Critique of Pure Reason*, trans. Paul Guyer and Allen W. Wood (Cambridge: Cambridge University Press, 1998), 129.
51 See my *Crossing the Rubicon*, §19, 142-7: "The Illusion of the Leap."
52 See Blaise Pascal, *Pensées*, trans. A. J. Krailsheimer (London: Penguin, 1966), L. 308/B. 793, on the "three orders": "The infinite distance between *body* and *mind* symbolizes the infinitely more infinite distance between *mind* and *charity*, for charity is supernatural" (my emphases), 123.
53 Hugh of Saint-Victor, *La parole de Dieu (De verbo Dei)*, IV, 2, 73.
54 Ibid. "The *eye of the flesh* [*oculus carnis*] sees only the exterior of bodies, and the *eye of the mind* [*oculus mentis*] the exterior of the heart; the *eye of God* [*oculus Dei*] sees the interior. The eye of the heart is interior in relation to the eye of the flesh, exterior in relation to the eye of God. And just as the eye of the flesh does not grasp what the eye of the heart grasps, the eye of the heart does not grasp what the eye of God grasps. But the eye of God grasps what is grasped by the eye of the heart. Consequently the eye of the flesh grasps only what is exterior to the body; the eye of the heart, the exterior and the interior of the body, but only the interior of the heart; the eye of God is at once exterior and interior to the heart, as well as to bodies." This triple movement where the lower order is observed by the upper order, but not the other way around is exactly repeated by Pascal: "The greatness of intellectual people [*gens d'esprit*] is not visible to kings, rich men, captains, who are all great in a carnal sense [*grands de chair*]. The greatness of wisdom, which is nothing it if does not come from God, is not visible to carnal or intellectual people. They are three orders differing in kind." *Pensées*, L. 308/B. 793, 124. A "triple eye" [*triplicem oculum*], or "triple view," is explicitly taken up by Bonaventure in his *Breviloquium*, II, 12, "On the completion and ordering of the whole world after creation": "For this triple vision [*triplicem visionem*], man was endowed with a triple eye [*triplicem oculum*], as explained by Hugh of St. Victor: the eye of flesh, or reason, and of contemplation: the eye of flesh [*oculum carnis*], to see the world and what it contains; the eye of reason [*oculum rationis*], to see the soul and what it contains; the eye of contemplation [*oculum contemplationis*], to see God and that which is within Him." Bonaventure, *Breviloquium*, in *Works of St. Bonaventure* trans. José de Vinck (Paterson NJ: St. Anthony Guild Press, 1964), vol. 9: II, 12, 5. With many modifications that should be noted this passes from one author to another: the substitution of the eye of the mind by the eye of reason and the eye of God by the eye of contemplation in passing from Hugh of Saint-Victor to Pascal; the substitution of "carnal people" for the eye of flesh, "intellectual people" for the eye of reason, and "wisdom" for the eye of contemplation in passing from Bonaventure to Pascal. There is a move from the "view" (Bonaventure) to a division into classes of "people" (Pascal) which enshrines a "separation into orders" that had precisely been absent in the monastic theology of the twelfth century. Separation of the "three orders" in Pascal has been analyzed brilliantly in Jean-Luc Marion's *On Descartes: Metaphysical Prism*, trans. Jeffrey L. Kosky (Chicago: University of Chicago Press, 1999), "The Distance between

the Orders," chap. 23. See also V. Carraud, "Des concupiscense aux ordres des choses," in Martin Pécharman, "Les Trois Ordres de Pascal," *Revue de Métaphysique et de Morale,* March 1997 (but without any reference to Hugh of Saint-Victor or Bonaventure which would, however, justify the theological source and the philosophical modification).

55 Hugh of Saint-Victor, *La parole de Dieu (De Verbo Dei),* IV, 3, 75.
56 Hugh of Saint-Victor, *Homélies sur l'Ecclésiaste (In Salmonis Ecclesiasten Homeliae)* PL 175, 142A-B, this quotation is taken from the French translation in Patrice Sicard, *Hugues de Saint-Victor et son école* (Turnhout: Brepols, 1998), 241.
57 Maurice Merleau-Ponty, "Eye and Mind," in *The Merleau-Ponty Aesthetics Reader: Philosophy and Painting,* trans. Michael B. Smith (Evanston: Northwestern University Press, 1993), 141–3. See also "Cezanne's doubt," in *Sense and Non-Sense,* trans. Hubert L. Dreyfus and Patricia Allen Dreyfus (Evanston: Northwestern University Press, 1964), 12: "[Cezanne's] painting was paradoxical: he was *pursuing reality without giving up the sensuous surface [la sensation],* without following the contours, with no outline to enclose the color, with no perspectival or pictorial arrangement" (my emphasis).
58 See for example the graphics in color of Noah's ark reproduced by Patrice Sicard at the end of *Hugues de Saint-Victor et son école,* plate V1, 294, which could almost be of abstract paintings by Mondrian, or again the complex geographical map of the world in the *Descriptio mappe mundi* de Hugues de Saint-Victor (ed. Patrice Gautier Dalché, Ph.D. thesis, Bibliothèque Mendès France, Paris).
59 Martin Heidegger, *Being and Time,* trans. John Macquarrie and Edward Robinson (New York: HarperCollins, 2008), §7:30, 54.
60 Hugh of Saint-Victor, *De diebus tribus,* PL 176, 819B, translated into French by Alain Michel in *Théologiens et mystiques au Moyen Âge* (Paris: Folio, 1997), 346.
61 Edmund Husserl, *Logical Investigations* (1901), vol. 2, §1, "Complex and simple, articulated and unarticulated objects." See also Jean-Luc Marion, *Reduction and Givenness: Investigations of Husserl, Heidegger and Phenomenology,* trans. Thomas A. Carlson (Evanston: Northwestern University Press, 1998), 12: "On the one hand, intuition serves as a foundational presentation for an act of individual intention—we aim at a *particular* house, or a particular shade of red, a particular little patch of yellow wall and not another, according to a singularity that is so irreplaceable that in order to reach it one must go 'directly to the model' ['*sur le motif*'] … On the other hand we can also aim … at *the* house as the essence of any empirically possible or impossible house, the universal color red which no shade among the reds of the world could exhaust or approach" (emphases in original).
62 Hugh of Saint-Victor, *Des trois jours de la lumière invisible* [*De diebus tribus*], trans. Alain Michel in *Théologiens et mystiques au Moyen Âge* (Paris: Gallimard, 1997), 346. This is reminiscent of the celebrated fragment by Pascal, and his example of the "mite" and the "Milky Way" (not far from the "midge" [infinitely small] and the "thigh of an elephant" [infinitely large] in Hugh of Saint-Victor): proof, if there is need—after the "three orders"—of the influence of Hugh of Saint-Victor over Pascal of Port-Royal. See Pascal, *Pensées,* 199/H9, 89: "But, to offer him another prodigy equally astounding, let him look into the tiniest things he knows. Let a *mite* show him in its minute body incomparably more minute parts, legs with joints, veins in its legs, blood in the veins, humours in the blood, drops in the humours, vapour in the drops: let him divide these things still further until he has exhausted his powers

of imagination, and let the last thing he comes down to now be the subject of our discourse ... I want to show him a new abyss" (my emphasis).

Chapter 5

1. Patrice Sicard, *Hugues de Saint-Victor et son école* (Turnhout: Brepols, 1991), 189. (An important work of reference, not just for its numerous translations of texts fully documented, but also for its general presentation of Hugh of Saint-Victor.) For a general introduction to Hugh of Saint-Victor there is the exemplary and precise synthesis by Dominique Poirel, *Hugues de Saint-Victor* (Paris: Éditions du Cerf, 1998), as well as Roger Baron's succinct *Hugues et Richard de Saint-Victor* (Brussels: Bloud et Gay, 1961).
2. Martin Heidegger, *Being and Time*, trans. John Macquarrie and Edward Robinson (New York: HarperCollins, 2008), §118: 154. See also §15, "The Being of the entities encountered in the environment" and §26, "The Dasein-with of Others, and everyday Being-with."
3. Hugh of Saint-Victor, *In Ecclesiasten Homiliae* 141D-143A, modified from the translation into French in Sicard, *Hugues de Saint-Victor et son école*, 241–3.
4. See my *God, the Flesh, and the Other: From Irenaeus to Duns Scotus*, trans. William Christian Hackett (Evanston: Northwestern University Press, 2015), chap. 6: "The conversion of the flesh," 179–81 and "The symbolic or the Good use of the Sensible," 180–2.
5. Dominique Poirel, Introduction to *De Institutione novitiorum*, in *L'Œuvre de Hugues de Saint-Victor* (Turnhout: Turnhout Brepols, 1997), vol. 1: 7. I should like to express my appreciation here for the excellent translation into French and exegesis in this volume.
6. Hugh of Saint-Victor, *De Institutione novitiorum*, §10: 49.
7. Ibid.
8. Ibid.
9. On the celebrated distinction between *intus* and *foris* as constitutive of the Victorine corpus itself, see Dominique Poirel, introduction to *De Institutione novitiorum*, 108 n. 65: "Hugh proposes to educate the body simultaneously and progressively by the spirit, and the spirit by the body. This dialectic of *intus* and *foris* is typical of Hugh's thought. It is not simply based on his anthropology but also on his sacramental theology, indeed upon his theology of revelation."
10. Hugh of Saint-Victor, *De Institutione novitiorum*, §8: 45.
11. For the status of the "examination of conscience" in the twelfth century see Irénée Noye, "Examen de conscience," in *Dictionnaire de spiritualité*, vol. 4: *Moyen Âge et temps modernes* (Paris: Beauchesne, 1961), 1807–31. For Epicureanism and Stoicism See Pierre Hadot, "La philosophie comme mode de vie," in *Qu'est-ce que la philosophie antique?* (Paris: Gallimard, 1995), 178–215.
12. Maurice Merleau-Ponty, *Phenomenology of Perception*, trans. Donald A. Landes (Abingdon, Oxon: Routledge, 2012), IV: 150.
13. Hugh of Saint-Victor, *De Institutione novitiorum*, §12: 73.
14. See Saint Bonaventure, *Itinerarium Mentis in Deum* [*Journey of the Mind into God*], trans. Philotheus Boehner (Saint Bonaventure, NY: Franciscan Institute, Saint Bonaventure University Press, 1956), 1: 7. "[Jesus Christ] has taught the knowledge

of truth in its threefold theological sense [symbolic, literal and mystical] so that through symbolic theology, we may rightly use sensible things, through literal theology, we may rightly use intellectual things, and through mystical theology, we may be rapt to ecstatic experience."

15 Hugh of Saint-Victor, *De Institutione novitiorum*, §12: 73.
16 Ibid., §12: 49. "The discipline [*disciplina*] is a way of living [*conversatio*] good and well proven, for those who think it no great thing to avoid doing wrong, but who are watchful, even in what they do for the good, to appear [*apparere*] blameless in everything." For what follows from the double critique by Merleau-Ponty of behaviourism and Gestalt theory because of his recognition of signifying intention, see Merleau-Ponty's *The Structure of Behavior* (1942), trans. Alden Fisher (Boston: Beacon Press, 1963).
17 On the changes in the sense of *disciplina* in Hugh of Saint-Victor's work, going from pedagogy and material for study to the norms or rules of conduct, see Jean Leclercq, *Dictionnaire de spiritualité* (Paris: Beauchesne, 1957), vol. 3, "Discipline," 1291–302.
18 Hugh of Saint-Victor, *De Institutione novitiorum*, §10: 49.
19 Ibid., §11: 51.
20 Ibid., §11: 51–3.
21 Ibid., §11: 53.
22 See the text discovered and translated by Dominique Poirel, "Un *De institutione novitiorum* victorin inédit," in *L'Œuvre de Hugues de Saint-Victor*, vol. 1, appendix 2:312.
23 Hugh of Saint-Victor, *De Institutione novitiorum*, §7:43. The image of the "seal" was used repeatedly in the twelfth century for the moral life and in particular by Abelard in relation to the Trinity (the signet ring metaphor). See Jean Jolivet, *Abélard ou la philosophie du langage* (Paris: Éditions du Cerf, 1994), 162–6.
24 Ibid., §7: 41.
25 Ibid.
26 Ibid., §1: 23. For instruction through discipline as teaching, for example, see the opening of *De Institutione novitiorum* (19–23). See also C. W. Bynum, "*Docere Verbo et Exemplo*: An Aspect of Twelfth Century Spirituality," *Harvard Theological Studies*, vol. xxxix (1931): 1–8.
27 See C. W. Bynum, *Jesus as Mother: Studies in the Spirituality of the High Middle Ages* (Berkeley: University of California Press, 1982), 42–3.
28 Hugh of Saint-Victor, *De Institutione novitiorum*, §6: 39.
29 Heidegger, *Being and Time*, §12: 78–86.
30 Edmund Husserl, *Cartesian Meditations: An Introduction to Phenomenology*, trans. Dorion Cairns (Dordrecht: Kluwer Academic Publishers, 1999), §44.
31 Hugh of Saint-Victor, *De Institutione novitiorum*, §12: 69: "Since we have described the vices of gesticulation [*vitia gesticulationum*], good order requires that we now define what is, for every gesture [*in omni gestu*], the disciplinary measure [*modus disciplinae*]."
32 See Jacques Le Goff, cited in Jean-claude Schmitt, *La Raison des gestes dans l'Occident médiéval* (Paris: Gallimard, 1990), 14.
33 Schmitt, *La Raison des gestes*. See especially the introduction (13–31), and the chapter entirely consecrated to Hugh of Saint-Victor's *De Institutione novitiorum*: "la discipline des novices," chap. 5: 173–207.
34 Maurice Merleau-Ponty, *Phenomenology of Perception*, trans. Donald A. Landes (London: Routledge, 2014), 140.

35 Hugh of Saint-Victor, *De Institutione novitiorum*, §12: 59.
36 Ibid.
37 Schmitt, *La Raison des gestes*, 177.
38 "On Loving God," in Bernard of Clairvaux, *Selected Works*, trans. G. R. Evans (New York: HarperCollins, 2005), 49: "The cause of loving God is God himself. The way to love him is without measure."
39 See Dominique Poirel, Introduction to *De Institutione novitiorum*.
40 See Edith Stein, "La signification de la phénoménologie comme conception du monde" (1932), in *Phénoménologie et philosophie chrétienne* (Paris: Éditions du Cerf, 1987), 1–18.
41 On the full interpretive debate concerning the "definition of gesture" in Hugh of Saint-Victor, see Dominique Poirel's Introduction to *De Institutione novitiorum*, in *L'Œuvre de Hugues de Saint-Victor*, vol. 1: 7–17, as well as notes 80–92, on pages 110–11. This is a remarkable publication as far as the translation and its critique are concerned. Without such a volume in French no real study of the Victorine master would be possible.
42 See Marcel Jousse, *Anthropologie du geste* (Paris: Gallimard, 1974), vol. 1: 10. "I went down from mechanism to mechanism and I arrived at the language of gesture that is the origin of human expression … that is the overall method of the research that I pursue." Jousse is an author who is well worth revaluing today, not simply in terms of his anthropological aims (which are his own) but in terms of a perspective that is strictly speaking metaphysical (the setting up of a world through gesturality as such).
43 Hugh of Saint-Victor, *De Institutione novitiorum*, §1: 23.
44 See Laurent Pernot, "Lieu et lieu commun dans la rhétorique antique," *Bulletin de l'association Guillaume Budé*, vol. 1, no. 3 (1981): 253–84. "The list of *peristaseis* or 'constitutive parts of the situation' in rhetoric is simple. The most common includes six places: *person, action, place, time, manner cause*. Philosophers sometimes add a seventh: *matter*" (263).
45 See Charles Péguy, *Note conjointe sur M. Descartes et la philosophie cartésienne* (July 1914 [posthumous]) in *Œuvres en prose complètes* (Paris: Gallimard, 1992), vol. 3: 1307: "There is something worse than having an evil thought. It is to have a thought *ready-made*. There is something worse than to have an evil soul or even to become an evil soul. It is to have a *ready-made soul*. There is something worse even than having a perverse soul. It is to have a habituated soul." See also Maurice Merleau-Ponty, "Bergson in the Making," in *Signs* trans. Richard C. McCleary (Evanston IL: Northwestern University Press, 1964), 182–91.
46 Hugh of Saint-Victor, *De Institutione novitiorum*, §3: 25.
47 Jean-Luc Marion, *In Excess; Studies of Saturated Phenomena*, trans. Robyn Horner and Vincent Berraud (New York: Fordham University Press, 2002): "The Event or the Happening Phenomenon," 31–7.
48 Hugh of Saint-Victor, *De Institutione novitiorum*, §3: 25.
49 Ibid., §4: 25.
50 Ibid.
51 Ibid.
52 Ibid., §4: 28.
53 Ibid., §5: 29.
54 Ibid.
55 Ibid., §12: 59.

56 Schmitt, *La Raison des gestes*, 178. In this context I would also recommend consulting the three tables showing the categorization of gestures according to Hugh of Saint-Victor, 180–3.
57 Hugh of Saint-Victor, *De Institutione novitiorum*, §12: 71.
58 Ibid., §4: 27.
59 Emmanuel Levinas, *Ethics and Infinity: Conversations with Philippe Nemo*, trans. Richard Cohen (Pittsburgh: Duquesne University Press, 1985), 86.
60 Hugh of Saint-Victor, *De Institutione novitiorum*, §12: 71.
61 Ibid., §12: 67.
62 [Trans.—"Hylomorphism": Aristotelian theory that suggests being is a compound of matter and form.]
63 Hugh of Saint-Victor, *De Institutione novitiorum*, §12:75.
64 Ibid., §12: 75.
65 Ibid., §12: 69.
66 See Rudolf Burnet, *Conscience et existence, Perspectives phénoménologiques* (Paris: PUF, 2004), pt. 2, chap. 4, 229–33: "Le regard de l'autre chez Sartre et Lévinas."
67 [Trans.—See Emmanuel Levinas, *Otherwise than Being: Or Beyond Essence*, trans. Alphonso Lingis (Dordrecht: Springer Science+Business Media, 1991), 5–8.]
68 This lies behind the concrete character of the "face," or rather the "figure," in Hugh of Saint-Victor's work, which is very far from the "abstract," or face without a face, in Levinas. See my *Le combat amoureux, Disputes phénoménologiques et théologiques* (Paris: Hermann, 2014), chap. 3, 124–7: "Le visage et la figure."
69 Hugh of Saint-Victor, *De Institutione novitiorum*, §12: 71.
70 Merleau-Ponty, *Phenomenology of Perception*, IV: 152.
71 Husserl, *Cartesian Meditations: An Introduction to Phenomenology*, §16.
72 See Carla Casagrande and Silvana Vecchio, *Les péchés de la langue. Discipline et éthique de la parole dans la culture médiévale*, trans. from the Italian by Ph. Baillet (Paris: Éditions du Cerf, 1991), 69–73 on Hugh of Saint-Victor's *De Institutione novitiorum*.
73 Casagrande and Vecchio, *Les Péchés de la langue*, 69.
74 Hugh of Saint-Victor, *De Institutione novitiorum*, §14: 81.
75 Ibid., §17: 89.
76 Merleau-Ponty, *Phenomenology of Perception*, VI: 185 (my emphasis).
77 Hugh of Saint-Victor, *De Institutione novitiorum*, §13: 77 (my emphasis).
78 See Jean Longère, *L'Abbaye parisienne de Saint-Victor au Moyen Âge* (Paris: Bibliotheca victorina, 1991), introduction.
79 Hugh of Saint-Victor, *De Institutione novitiorum*, §14: 77–9.
80 Ibid., §14: 79.
81 Casagrande and Vecchio, *Les Péchés de la langue*, 71.
82 Hugh of Saint-Victor, *De Institutione novitiorum*, §16: 85.
83 Jean-Louis Chrétien, *The Ark of Speech*, trans. Andrew Brown (Abingdon, Oxon: Routledge, 2004): "The hospitality of silence," 39–76.
84 Hugh of Saint-Victor, *De Institutione novitiorum*, §17: 89.
85 Ibid., §12: 59 and §10: 51.
86 Ibid., §17: 89.
87 Ibid.
88 Ibid.
89 Hugh of Saint-Victor, *La parole de Dieu (De Verbo Dei)* in *Six opuscules spirituels, sources chrétiennes 155*, ed. Roger Baron (Paris: Éditions du Cerf, 1969), I, 2: 63.

90 Jacques Derrida, *Voice and Phenomenon: Introduction to the Problem of the Sign in Husserl's Phenomenology,* trans. Leonard Lawlor (Evanston: Northwestern University Press, 2011), 52–4, 65.
91 See Paul Claudel, *The Eye Listens,* trans. Elsie Pell (Port Washington, NY: Kennikat Press, 1969).
92 See "*Omnis mundi creatura*," cited in G. Dahan, *L'Occident médiéval lecteur de l'Écriture,* supplement to *Cahiers Evangile* no. 116 (Paris: Éditions du Cerf, 2001), text no. 43, 60.
93 See my *God, the Flesh, and the Other*: chap. 7, "Community and Intersubjectivity (Origen)"; chap. 8, "Angelic Alterity (Thomas Aquinas)"; chap. 9, "The Singular Other (Duns Scotus)."
94 Hugh of Saint-Victor, Prologue to *On the Praise of Charity* [*De Laude Caritatis*] in *On Love,* ed. Hugh Feiss (Hyde Park, NY: New City Press, 2012), 159. [Patrologia Latine (LP), 176, 971A].

Chapter 6

1 Emmanuel Levinas, *Of God Who Comes to Mind,* trans. Bettina Bergo (Stanford, CA: Stanford University Press, 1998), 82.
2 Ibid.
3 Richard of Saint-Victor, *On the Trinity* [*De Trinitate*], trans. Ruben Angelici (Eugene, Ore: Cascade Books, 2011), 19: 132.
4 Hans-Georg Gadamer, "Heidegger et l'histoire de la Philosophie," in *Heidegger, Cahiers de l'Herne* (Paris: Grasset, 1983), 124. See my *God, the Flesh and the Other,* trans. William Christian Hackett (Evanston: Northwestern University Press, 2015): "*Fons Signatus*: The Sealed Source," 3–19, for analysis and discussion of how "to pass in a new way from phenomenology to medieval philosophy" (15).
5 I return here [§17–§19], with some profound modifications, to certain ideas in my *Saint Bonaventure and the Entrance of God Into Theology,* trans. Brian Lapsa and Sarah Horton (St. Bonaventure University, NY: Franciscan Institute Publications, 2018). See §9: "The condilection or anti-jealousy in God." My discussion of Richard of Saint-Victor, initially placed in a consideration of Bonaventure's thought, finds its proper place here—that is to say, among the Victorines in a quasi-monastic perspective (*The Book of Experience*), rather than in a scholastic one (the debate on the Trinity).
6 Edmund Husserl, *Cartesian Meditations,* trans. Dorion Cairns (The Hague: Martinus Nijhoff Publishers, 1960), §55. "Establishment of the Community of Monads. The first form of Objectivity: Intersubjective Nature."
7 I am transposing here, in a theological and trinitarian context, the categories of the autism of love ("to love the other in myself") and of the auto-idolatry of love ("to love oneself as the other"), developed by Jean-Luc Marion in "The Intentionality of Love (Homage to Emmanuel Levinas)," in *Prolegomena to Charity,* trans, Stephen E. Lewis and Jeffrey L. Kosky (New York: Fordham University Press, 2002).
8 *Monologion* in *Complete Philosophical Treatises of Anselm of Canterbury,* trans. Jasper Hopkins and Herbert Richardson (Minneapolis: Arthur J. Banning Press, 2000), 48: 63.
9 Thomas Aquinas, *The Summa Theologica: Documenta Catholica,* trans. Fathers of the English Dominican Province: question 20, "God's love": article 2. Retrieved December 8, 2019, on www.documenta-catholica.eu/d_1225-1274-ThomasAquinas.

10 Edmund Husserl, *Cartesian Meditations*, trans. Dorion Cairns (The Hague: Martinus Nijhoff Publishers, 1960), §55: 125: "It is implicit in the sense of my successful apperception of others that their world, the world belonging to their appearance-systems, must be experienced forthwith as the same as the world belonging to my appearance-systems, and this involves an identity of our appearance-systems."
11 See "Amorous Autism" in "The Intentionality of Love," Jean-Luc Marion, *Prolegomena to Charity*, trans. Stephen Lewis (New York: Fordham University Press, 2002), 75–80.
12 Ibid., 77.
13 *Monologion*, 52: 65.
14 See the critique of metaphysics in the well-known categories of Levinas. *Totality and Infinity* (Dordrecht: Kluwer Academic Publishers, 1991): "The Same and the Other," 33–102.
15 Thomas Aquinas, *The Summa Theologica*, Question 37: "Whether 'Love' is the proper name of the Holy Ghost?" Article 1, Reply to Objection 3.
16 Théodore de Regnon, *Études de théologie positive sur la sainte Trinité* (Paris: Éditions Victor Retaux, 1892), vol. 2, 448–51: "Métaphysique statique et métaphysique dynamique." Regnon's book, in spite of its date and its simplifications, remains still a mine of information in relation to trinitarian theology.
17 Thomas Aquinas, *The Summa Theologica*, Question 37, Article 2, Reply to Objection 3.
18 For the identification and meaning of "auto-idolatry" as love of the self in the other, see "The Intentionality of Love" in Jean-Luc Marion, *Prolegomena to Charity*.
19 Thomas Aquinas, *The Summa Theologica*, Question 37, Objection 3, Answer.
20 Ibid., Question 37, Article 1, Answer.
21 Ibid., Question 38, Article 2 "Whether 'Gift' is the proper name of the Holy Ghost," Answer. On this exemplary reversal of the primacy of the gift over love in Bonaventure, through Aquinas (where the continuing love has priority this time over the gift), see the very valuable analysis by Jean-François Bonnefoy, *Le Saint-Esprit et ses dons selon saint Bonaventure* (Paris: Vrin, 1929), 28–33. Also see my *Saint Bonaventure and the Entrance of God into Theology*, §7.
22 Out of respect for Emmanuel Levinas and his relation to Judaism I think we should not translate *his* categories directly into Christian theology. On the necessary "difference," and fidelity to the thought of Levinas himself, see my *Le Combat amoureux, Disputes phénoménologiques et théologiques* (Paris: Hermann, 2014), 113–36: "Le visage sans visage [Levinas]."
23 See *Dictionnaire encyclopédique*, Quillet (1934), 4730: *Tiers*: "a person outside a contract called upon in order to resolve it." *Tierce personne*: "simply refers to a person adjunct or assistant."
24 Richard of Saint-Victor, *On the Trinity*, trans Ruben Angelici (Cambridge: James Clarke and Co., 2011), III, 19: 132–3. For the origin of the neologism see the French edition of *De Trinitate* (Paris: Éditions du Cerf, 1958), 192, note 2: "The word condilectus which seems to be a creation of Richard's."
25 See Jean-Luc Marion, *Prolegomena to Charity*, trans. Stephen E. Lewis (New York: Fordham University Press, 2002), "The Intentionality of Love." Marion argues that two invisible gazes cross and renounce their invisibility: "We will try to argue that the crossing of the visible gazes becomes visible only for the parties involved, because they alone undergo an experience without recognizing an object in that experience" (87–8).

26 See Martin Buber, *I and Thou*, trans. Ronald Gregor Smith (New York: Charles Scribner's Sons, [1923] 2010), as well as the critique by Emmanuel Levinas, who insists on the necessary opening up of the I-Thou toward a You as figure of the other completely surpassing man: "Martin Buber and the Theory of Knowledge" in Levinas, *Proper Names*, trans. Michael Smith (Stanford, CA: Stanford University Press, 1997), 29. Without rejecting this necessary opening up of the two (I-Thou) for a Third (You), and very much in line with the view of Richard of Saint-Victor, Christian trinitarian theology possesses something specific that it incorporates in an Us, that is to say in God himself, the human who is always situated in the figure of the Word. For a precise and careful application of a Buber-style dialogic structure of the Trinity see Hans Urs von Balthasar, *Theo-Logic*, vol. 2 *Truth of God*, trans. Adrian J. Walker (San Francisco: Ignatius Press, 2014).
27 St. Augustine *On the Trinity*, trans. Arthur West Haddan in *Nicene and Post-Nicene Fathers*, first series, vol. 3 (Buffalo, NY: Christian Publishing Co, 1887), bk. 5, 12:3. Retrieved July 2, 2019, on www.newadvent.org/fathers/1301/htm, ed. Kevin Knight. For the limits of this familial metaphor see also Bertrand de Margerie, *La Trinité chrétienne dans l'histoire* (Paris: Beauchesne, 1975), 367–90.
28 St. Augustine *On the Trinity*, bk. 5, 9: "When the question is asked, what three? human language labors altogether under great poverty of speech. The answer, however, is given, three 'persons' [*tres personae*], not that it might be spoken, but that it might not be left unspoken [*non ut illud diceretur, sed non taceretur*]."
29 St. Bonaventure, *Sententiae*, 1, d. 10, a. 2, q. 1, concl. "If that child had been produced solely by the harmony of will, he would be Love [*amor esset*]; but in reality he is just the beloved [*nunc vero est amatus*], unless we say Love with a certain exaggeration [*nisi dicatur amor per emphaticum loquendi*]."
30 Richard of Saint-Victor, *On the Trinity*, III, 19: 132.
31 On this necessary "metamorphosis of *eros* by *agapē*" which cannot be limited either to "pure univocity" or "simple equivocity" see my *The Wedding Feast of the Lamb*, trans. George Hughes (New York: Fordham University Press, 2016), §23 "Desire and Differentiation," 154–66; and my article "Dieu charité" in *Communio*, no. XXX, 5–6, (September–December 2005), 75–87.
32 Boethius, *The Trinity Is One God Not Three Gods*, trans. E. K. Rand and H. F. Stewart, bk. 4, Retrieved December 12, 2019, on www.logoslibrary.org>boethius>trinity. There is a commentary on this in Alain de Libera, *Métaphysique et noétique, Albert le Grand* (Paris: Vrin, 2005), 145. See also my *God, the Flesh and the Other*, chap. 1: "Metaphysics and Theology in Tension (Augustine)," 25–46.
33 Richard of Saint-Victor, *On the Trinity*, III, 19: 132.
34 Ibid., 19: 133.
35 Hugh of Saint-Victor, *On the Sacraments of the Christian Faith (De Sacramentis)*, cited and translated by Patrice Sicard, *Hugues de Saint-Victor et son école* (Turnhout: Brepols, 1991), 51.
36 Paul Beauchamp, *L'un et l'autre Testament* (Paris: Éditions du Seuil, 1990), vol. 2, chap. 3: "l'homme, la femme, le serpent," 143–4.
37 Richard of Saint-Victor, *On the Trinity*, III: 7.
38 Richard of Saint-Victor, *On the Trinity*, III, 2, 126 (trans. modified).
39 B. de Margerie *La Trinité chrétienne dans l'histoire*, 419–20. (No specific reference is given to Bonaventure's work and thus there is no textual justification for this statement.)
40 Se Bonaventure, *Sententiae* I distinction 10; *Collationes in Hexaemeron* XI, 12; *Breviloquium* I, 2; *Itinerarium* VI, 2. All these references to *condilectio*, or the

friend in common, have their roots in Richard of Saint-Victor's *De Trinitate*, III, chap. 11: "Those who are—and are worthy to be—supremely loved seek with the same desire someone else to be included in their love and [seek] to possess [him] in absolute concord, according to [that very] desire [of theirs] [*ut pari voto condilectum requirat*]." Given these several occurrences, it is surprising that the article on *dilectio* in the *Lexique de saint Bonaventure*, ed. J.-G. Bougerol (Paris: Éditions franciscaines, 1969), 55 does not refer back to Richard's *condilectio*.

41   Bonaventure, *The Journey of the Mind to God*, trans. Philotheus Boehner (Indianapolis: Hackett Publishing Company, 1993), V, 2: 33.

42   Bonaventure, *Sententiae*, Proem 1: 3. See on this point my article "Le *Proemium* du *Commentaire des Sentences* ou l'acte phénoménologique de la *perscrutatio* chez saint Bonaventure," *Archivum franciscanum historicum* (July–December 2004), 275–300.

43   Bonaventure, *Sententiae*, Book I, distinction 10, article 1, questions 3, and 4 (I. 99a).

44   Bonaventure, *The Breviloquium*, vol. 2 *The Works of Bonaventure*, trans. José de Vinck (Paterson, NJ: St. Anthony Guild Press, 1963), 36.

45   Martin Heidegger, *Being and Time*, trans. John Macquarrie and Edward Robinson (New York: HarperCollins, 2008), §26: 118, 154.

46   See Jean-Luc Nancy, *The Inoperative Community*, trans. Peter Connor et al. (Minneapolis: University of Minnesota Press, 1991), part 4 (an essay in reinterpretation of the Heideggerian "being-in-common").

47   See Henry Mottu, *La Manifestation de l'Esprit selon Joachim de Flore* (Neuchatel: Delachaux-Niestlé, 1977), 77–123: "La théorie du système herméneutique" (a reconsideration of chap. 5 of *Exposition sur l'Apocalypse*). See also my contribution to the debate: "La posterité spirituelle de Joachim de Flore ou le principe d'immunité chez Henri de Lubac," *Revue des Sciences Religieuses*, no. 2 (April 2003), 183–98.

48   Fourth Lateran Council (1215). On Papal Encyclicals Online: Retrieved July 28, 2019, on papalencyclicals.net.

49   Bonaventure, *Les Six Jours de la création* (*Hexaëmeron*) (Paris: Desclée/Éditions de Cerf, 1991), XI, 11 [V, 382a]), 282–3. Translation modified. As I am unable in the context of the present book to develop the Bonaventurian sense of the trinitarian redesigning of Anselm's argument (in light of a diffusive "donation" of the self), I would suggest reference to my commentary in *St. Bonaventure and the Entrance of God Into Theology*, §11.

50   Hans Urs von Balthasar, *The Glory of the Lord; A Theological Aesthetics*, trans. Andrew Louth et al. (San Francisco: Ignatius Press, 1984), vol. 2, *Studies in Theological Style: Clerical Styles*, 290.

51   [Trans.—The French word "*apérité*" has been used in French phenomenology as a translation of the German "Offenständigkeit," which has been variously translated into English as "openness," "being-open," "standing-open," or "open disponibility." See also Jacques Derrida, *Conversations of Friendship and Philosophy*, trans. Pascale-Anne Brault and Michael Naas (New York: Fordham University Press, 2014), 76: "The distinction Heidegger makes between *Offenbarung*—the place of biblical, historical revelation—and *Offenbarkeit*, that is the possibility of opening (*apérité*), the *possibility* of this *Offenbarung*, a *possibility* that Heidegger of course says is more originary."]

52   Ulrich Köpf, *Religiöse Erfahrung in der Theologie Bernhards von Clairvaux*, in *Beiträge zur historischen Theologie*, no. 61 (Tubingen, 1980), 54–5. Cited and commented upon in Lode van Hecke, *Le désir dans l'expérience religieuse, L'homme réunifié, Relecture de saint Bernard* (Paris: Éditions du Cerf, 1990), 38: "The world [*mundus*] is

first of all the ensemble of the things we perceive in the senses. Köpf remarks that *in this context*, Bernard never speaks in terms of experience" (my emphasis).
53 *Life and Works of Saint Bernard, Abbot of Clairvaux*, vol. 4, *Cantica Canticorum: Eighty-Six Sermons on the Song of Solomon*, trans. Samuel J. Eales (London: John Hodges, 1893), sermon 3:1, 17.

Part 3

1 *Life and Works of Saint Bernard, Abbot of Clairvaux*, vol. 4, *Cantica Canticorum: Eighty-Six Sermons on the Song of Solomon*, trans. Samuel J. Eales (London: John Hodges, 1893), sermon 3:1, 17.
2 Maurice Merleau-Ponty, *The Visible and the Invisible*, trans. Alphonso Lingis (Evanston: Northwestern University Press, 1968), 102–3. See also my *Le Combat amoureux, Disputes phénoménologiques et théologiques* (Paris: Hermann, 2015), chap. 2 "Une pensée du sous-sol" (Merleau-Ponty), 67–112, and chap. 6 "Le Dieu sauvage," 107–8.
3 Edith Stein, *On the Problem of Empathy*, trans. Waltraut Stein (Dordrecht: Springer Science+Business Media, 1964); Max Scheler, *The Nature of Sympathy*, trans. Peter Heath (London: Routledge, 1970); Hannah Arendt, *Love and Saint Augustine*, ed. Joanna Vecchiarelli Scott and Judith Chelius Stark (Chicago: University of Chicago Press, 1996). On the renewal of interest in contemporary phenomenology of affect, see in particular Eliane Escombas et al., *Affect et affectivité dans la philosophie modern et la phénoménologie* (Paris: L'Harmattan, 2008).
4 See Damien Boquet, *L'Ordre de l'affect au Moyen Âge, Autour de l'anthropologie d'Aelred de Rievaulx* (Caen: CRAHM, 2005), 17: "The order of affect with which this study is concerned prioritizes the analysis of the rules of organization of a religious discourse around the words *affectus* and *affectio*, while recognizing that this order of discourse underpins an orderly conception of Christian man."
5 Walter Daniel, *The Life of Aelred of Rievaulx and the Letter to Maurice*, trans. F. M. Powicke (Kalamzoo, MI: Cistercian Publications, 1994), 149. See also the excellent biography by Pierre-André Burton (commenting on Daniel), *Aelred de Rievaulx (1110–1167), Essai de biographie existentielle et spirituelle* (Paris: Éditions du Cerf, 2010).
6 We cannot neglect in this context, the pioneering work already cited, of Philippe Nouzille, *Expérience de Dieu et théologie monastique au XIIe siècle, Étude sur les sermons d'Aelred de Rievaulx* (Paris: Éditions du Cerf, 1990).
7 Edmund Husserl, *Logical Investigations*, trans. J. N. Findlay (Abingdon, Oxon: Routledge and Kegan Paul, 2001), vol. 2: 108 (emphasis in original).
8 Martin Heidegger, *Being and Time*, trans. Joan Stambaugh (Albany, NY: State University of New York Press, 2010), §29, "Dasein as Attunement." [Trans.—The French translation of Heidegger used by Falque gives *Befindlichkeit* as "*affection*."]
9 Martin Heidegger, "The Fundamental Question of Metaphysics," in *Introduction to Metaphysics*, trans. Gregory Fried and Richard Polt (New Haven: Yale University Press, 2000), 1.
10 [Trans.—On "apérité" see Chapter 6, note 51.]

Chapter 7

1 See Edmund Husserl, *Cartesian Meditations: An Introduction to Phenomenology*, trans. Dorion Cairns (The Hague: Martinus Nijhoff Publishers, 1960), 71–2: "Every conscious process is, in itself, consciousness of such and such, regardless of what the rightful actuality-status of this objective such-and-such may be … The house-perception means a house—more precisely, as this individual house—and means it in the fashion peculiar to perception; a house-memory means a house in the fashion peculiar to memory; a house-phantasy, in the fashion peculiar to phantasy. A predicative judging about a house, which perhaps is 'there' perceptually, means it in just the fashion peculiar to judging; a valuing that supervenes means it in yet another fashion; and so forth. Conscious processes are also called *intentional*" (emphasis in original).
2 Characteristics of *Befindlchkeit* clearly analyzed by Éliane Escoubas in "Heidegger, Topologie de la *Stimmung*," in *Affect et affectivité dans la philosophie moderne et la phénoménologie*, ed. Éliane Escoubas and Laszio Tengelyi (Paris: Harmattan, 2008), 267–92 (particularly 270–5).
3 Aelred of Rievaulx, *Dialogue on the Soul*, trans. C. H. Talbot (Kalamazoo, MI: Cistercian Publications, 1981), 48–9.
4 Avicenna (Ibn Sina), *On the Soul* [*De Anima*], quoted in L. E. Goodman, *Avicenna: Arabic Thought and Culture* (London: Routledge, 2013), 155: "One of us must suppose that he was just created at a stroke, fully developed and perfectly formed but with his vision shrouded from perceiving all external objects—created floating in the air or in space, not buffeted by any perceptible current of the air that supports him, his limbs separated and kept out of contact with one another, so that they do not feel each other. Then let the subject consider whether he would affirm the existence of his self. *There is no doubt that he would affirm his own existence* although not affirming the reality of any of his limbs or inner organs, his bowels, or heart or brain or any external thing. Indeed, he would affirm that *existence of this self of his* while not affirming that it had any length, breadth or depth" (my emphasis).
5 Michel Henry, "*Videre videor*," *Généalogie de la psychanalyse* (Paris: PUF, 1985), 28–9: "Yet I certainly seem to see—*at certe videre videor* … it is thus in this feeling that Descartes deciphers the original essence of appearance expressed in the *videor* and interpreted as the ultimate basis … Descartes unceasingly affirmed that we feel our thought, we feel what we see, what we hear, what warms us up. And it is this primitive feeling, insofar as it is what it is, that is the pure appearance, identical with itself and with the being that defines itself here. I feel what I think, therefore I am."
6 Aelred of Rievaulx, *Dialogue on the Soul*, 62–4.
7 Pierre-Yves Émery, Introduction to *Dialogue sur l'âme* (*Dialogue on the Soul*) (Oka, Quebec: Abbaye Notre-Dame-du-Lac, 2007), 10.
8 Damien Boquet, *L'Ordre de l'affect au Moyen Âge, Autour de l'anthropologie d'Aelred de Rievaulx* (Caen: CRAHM, 2005), 147–9.
9 Michel Henry, *I Am the Truth: Toward a Philosophy of Christianity*, trans. Susan Emmanuel (Stanford, CA: Stanford University Press, 2003), 105. [Trans.—"Auto-affection" or "self-affection" is a term from phenomenology referring to self-experience. It is important for Husserl and has been deconstructed by Derrida in his reading of Husserl. Michel Henry's translator prefers to use "self-affection," but the French term is "*auto-affection*" and it has been widely translated as "auto-affection," especially in discussions of Derrida.]

10 Escoubas, "Heidegger, Topologie de la *Stimmung*," 275.
11 Philippe Nouzille, *Expérience de Dieu et théologie monastique au XIIe siècle. Étude sur les sermons d'Aelred de Rievaulx* (Paris: Éditions du Cerf, 1999), 22.
12 Aelred Of Rievaulx, *Spiritual Friendship*, trans. Lawrence C. Braceland (Collegeville, MN: Liturgical Press, 2010), 54.
13 Ibid., 53.
14 Walter Daniel, *The Life of Aelred of Rievaulx: And the Letter to Maurice*, trans. F. M. Powicke (Kalamazoo, MI: Cistercian Publications, 1994), 104 (my emphasis).
15 Aelred of Rievaulx, *Sermon pour la purification de la Vierge Marie*, Sermon 34. From the translation into French by Philippe Nouzille in *Expérience de Dieu et théologie monastique au XIIe siècle*, 247.
16 [Trans.—Heidegger's term *Befindlichkeit* is given as "state-of-mind" in the Macquarrie and Robinson translation of *Being and Time*, and as "attunement" in the Stambaugh translation.]
17 Aelred of Rievaulx, *Sermon T4, pour la fête de la Présentation*, cited and translated in Philippe Nouzille, *op. cit.*, n.3: 248.
18 Ibid., 299.
19 Ibid. See also Aelred of Rievaulx, Sermon 76, 47 (T20, p. 142), cited and translated by Nouzille, n.3: 248.
20 See §24: "A Knowledge of Experience": "Believe in My Experience" (concerning Bernard of Clairvaux).
21 Aelred of Rievaulx, *The Mirror of Charity*, trans. Elizabeth Connor (Kalamazoo, MI: Cistercian Publications, 1990), 201–2.
22 Ibid., 71 (translation modified).
23 Ibid., 301 (translation modified).
24 For the sense of "singularity" or thisness so fundamental in Christianity—and avoiding the danger of the "neutrality of the other"—see my *God, the Flesh, and the Other*, trans. William Christian Hackett (Evanston, IL: Northwestern University Press, 2015): "Desiring the Singular," 275–7.
25 Daniel, *The Life of Aelred of Rievaulx*, 143. The tears here are paradoxically, in contrast to how we feel about them today, not so much to be rejected, or even prompting consolation, but desired. "Are you streaming down, my tears?" is asked not in the sense that it would be best to restrain them, or that they are shameful, but because of the memory (and joy?) of the "generosity" of heart of Brother Aelred. Because, starting from the Middle Ages, and according to a tradition later and sadly largely abandoned, a "positive meaning of tears" was strongly claimed. The Benedictine Jean of Fécamp (990–1078) was probably one of the first to start this, in his treatise *Pour obtenir la grâce des larmes par la consideration des péchés* (a text falsely attributed to Anselm, to be found in the collection *Patrologia Latina*, PL 158, col. 892–4 [as well as under the title of a *Liber méditationum* wrongly attributed to St. Augustine PL, 40 cap 36, col. 930–2]). On this point there is an excellent article by Piroska Zombory-Nagy, "Le don des larmes, Un usage des pleurs dans le christianisme médiéval," in *Nouvelle revue de psychanalyse*, "La Plainte," Spring 1991, no. 47: 153–69: "In the Middle Ages also tears were thought to be more sincere than words, but a true communication by tears was still possible. Even better, to cry could prove the success of a full exchange, engaged in with the Absolute that presided in the heart of the believer" (154).

Chapter 8

1. See Heidegger's celebrated distinction between the "asked about" [*Gefragtes*], the "interrogated" [*Befragtes*], and "what is to be ascertained" [*Erfragtes*]. The first points to "what is asked," the second to the person for whom one is searching, and the third to the reason or meaning that we search for. Martin Heidegger, *Being and Time: A Translation of Sein und Zeit*, trans. Joan Stambaugh (Albany, NY: State University of New York Press, 1996), §2:4–5. "The Formal Structure of the Question of Being." See also the commentary by Jean Greisch in *Ontologie et temporalité, Esquisse d'une interpretation intégrale de Sein und Zeit* (Paris: PUF, 1994), §2: 76–80. "La structure fondamentale de la question de l'être."
2. See Martin Heidegger, *What Is Called Thinking*, trans. Fred D. Wieck and J. Glenn Gray (New York: Harper and Row, 1968), 5: "Nobody will deny that there is an interest in philosophy today. But—is there anything at all left today in which man does not take an interest, in the sense in which he understands 'interest'? Interest, *interesse*, means to be *among* and *in the midst of* things, or to be at the center of a thing and *to stay* with it. But *today's interest* accepts as valid only what is interesting. And interesting is the sort of thing that can freely be regarded as *indifferent* the next moment, and be *displaced* by something else, which then concerns us as little as what went before" (my emphasis).
3. Maurice Merleau-Ponty, *Phenomenology of Perception*, trans. Donald A. Landes (London: Routledge, 2012), lxxi.
4. See St. Augustine's prayer: *Domine Jesu, noverim me* [Lord Jesus, Let me know Myself].
5. See, for example, Olivier Boulnois's preface to the French translation of Bonaventure's *Hexaemeron, Les Six Jours de la création* (Paris: Desclée, 1991), 10: "The discourse which these debates call upon, their ordering and their incarnation in our life constructs a new discipline: a *logic of the mystical* which is at the same time an *overcoming of the metaphysical*" (my emphasis).
6. See my *Crossing the Rubicon: The Borderlands of Philosophy and Theology*, trans. Reuben Shank (New York: Fordham University Press, 2016), §18. "Of Conversion or Transformation," 131–6.
7. *Sermo de diversis* 5, 5 in *Sancti Bernardi Opera*, vol. 8 (Rome: Éd. Cisterciennes, 1957–77), SBO VI/1, 104: (The text was discovered and added by Dom Jean L. Leclercq to the critical apparatus of the new Latin edition of the complete works.) This important formula, which on the one hand rescues a part of philosophy from a pseudo-condemnation and on the other hand reverses Augustinian priorities, can also be found in the book by Jean Leclercq (not the Cistercian abbot this time but the professor of the Catholic University of Louvain with the same name), entitled *Maurice Blondel lecteur de Bernard de Clairvaux* (Brussels: Lessius, 2001), 79. I would like to take this opportunity to underline the intelligence and brilliance of Professor Leclercq's book, both from the point of view of studies on St. Bernard and Blondel and their interconnections.
8. St. Bernard has radically reversed the formula found in St. Augustine's *Soliloquies*, trans. C. C. Starbuck in *Nicene and Post-Nicene Fathers*, vol. 7 (Buffalo, NY: Christian Literature Publishing Co., 1888), bk. 2, 1 R3: "God, always the same, let me know myself, let me know You." For the implications of this reversal, see Leclercq, *Maurice Blondel lecteur*, 79–80 (on Bernard) and 133 (on Augustine and

Blondel). The hypothesis of a reversal has also been contested by Philippe Nouzille in "Saint Bernard et l'épreuve de soi," in *L'Actualité de saint Bernard* (Paris: Collège des Bernardins, 2010), 149–64 (in particular p. 151, note 7). It could be said that this reversal, or inversion, from the "knowledge of the other through the self" to the "knowledge of the self through the other" makes sense overall and defines what is specific to Christianity and should be noted all the same that certain modes of its formulation are first found in St. Augustine not in Bernard of Clairvaux. As for the theme of knowledge of the self, and possible analogies with the medieval period (St. Augustine, St. Bernard, Hugh of Saint-Victor) in contemporary philosophy (Husserl, Sartre, Merleau-Ponty), see Brian Stock, *Bibliothèques intérieures* (Grenoble: éd. J. Million, 2005), chap. 5, 88–106: "la connaissance de soi au Moyen Âge."

9 Rémi Brague, "L'anthropologie de l'humilité," *Saint Bernard et la Philosophie* (Paris: PUF, 193), 152 (my emphasis). Apart from the work of Jean Leclercq already cited (*Maurice Blondel lecteur de Bernard de Clairvaux*), it is worth noting, with regard to the realization and actualization of St. Bernard in relation to phenomenology, the important contribution of Guillaume de Stexhe, "Entre le piège et l'abîme: l'ambiguité du discours de l'amour," in *Qu'est-ce que Dieu, Hommage à l'abbé Daniel Coppetiers de Gibson (1929–1983)* (Brussels: Facultés universitaires de Saint-Louis, 1985), 415–54. (A direct presentation of Bernard of Clairvaux along with Heidegger, Merleau-Ponty, Levinas, Ricœur, etc.)

10 *Life and Works of Saint Bernard, Abbot of Clairvaux*, vol. 4, *Cantica Canticorum: Eighty-Six Sermons on the Song of Solomon*, trans. Samuel J. Eales (London: John Hodges, 1893), sermon 3:1, 17–18. [Trans.—Falque explains that he quotes throughout from the old bilingual edition of the sermons in *Œuvres complètes* of Bernard (Paris: Vivès, 1873), which has the merit of being complete, rather than the newer, and still incomplete, edition of the works by Éditions du Cerf, 1996–2003.]

11 William of Saint-Thierry, *The First Life of Bernard of Clairvaux*, trans. Hilary Costello (Athens, OH: Liturgical Press, 2015), 61: 59.

12 On this chronological point see Claudio Stercal, *Bernard de Clairvaux, Intelligence et amour* (Paris: Éditions du Cerf 1998), 123–9.

13 See *De Adventu domini*, IV: 4, cited and commented upon in Rémi Brague, "L'anthropologie de l'humilitie," *Saint Bernard et la philosophie*, 149. See also Jean-louis Chrétien, *Le Regard de l'amour* (Paris: Desclée de Brouwer, 2000), 33–54. In particular 46–7 concerning the link between experience and oblation in the act of humility.

14 William of Saint-Thierry, *The First Life of Bernard of Clairvaux*, 62 (text modified).

15 *On Loving God*, trans. G. R. Evans, in *Bernard of Clairvaux: Selected Works* (New York: HarperCollins, 2005), 82.

16 William of Saint-Thierry, *The First Life of Bernard of Clairvaux*, 62.

17 For the connection with Origen see in particular J.-P. Bouchot, "La bibliothèque de Clairvaux" and Paul Verdeyen, "Un théologien de l'expérience," in *Bernard de Clairvaux, Histoire, mentalités, spiritualité* (Paris: Éditions du Cerf, 1992), 564–93 on the discovery of Origen's work on the *Song of Songs*.

18 William of Saint-Thierry, *The First Life of Bernard of Clairvaux*, 62 (text modified).

19 *Life and Works of Saint Bernard, Abbot of Clairvaux*, vol. 4, sermon 1:11, 11.

20 Ibid., 12.

21 St. Augustine, *De vera religione*, 39, n72. Quoted by Edmund Husserl, *Cartesian Meditations*, trans. Dorion Cairns (The Hague: Martinus Nijhoff Publishers, 1960), 157.

22 *Life and Works of Saint Bernard, Abbot of Clairvaux*, vol. 4, sermon 1:11, 11.
23 Ibid., sermon 79:1, 484.
24 Ibid., Introductory Essay, xv.
25 Husserl, *Cartesian Meditations*, §16, 38: "Its beginning is the *pure* and, so to speak, still *dumb*—psychological experience, which now must be made to utter its own sense with no adulteration" (my emphases). See also my *Crossing the Rubicon*, "Toward a Phenomenality of the Text," 50–7.
26 *Life and Works of Saint Bernard, Abbot of Clairvaux*, vol. 4, sermons 1:11, 23:1.
27 Max Scheler, *Sur le sens de la souffrance* [posthumous work] (Paris: Aubier-Montaigne, 1954), 2–3. See also Husserl, *Experience and Judgment*, trans. James S. Churchill and Karl Ameriks (Evanston, IL: Northwestern University Press, 1973), §16 "The field of passive data and its associate structure."
28 [Trans.—Illuminism: Belief or claim to a special personal enlightenment not available to humankind in general.]
29 *Pascendi Domini Gregis* (1907), Encyclical of Pope Pius X on the Doctrines of the Modernists, §14. Retrieved December 27, 2019, on vatican.va (emphasis added). For a nuanced and well-argued judgment of this encyclical and the meaning of the condemnation of the "doctrine of experience" see Pierre Colin, *Modernisme* (Paris: Desclée de Brouwer, 1996).
30 *Life and Works of Saint Bernard, Abbot of Clairvaux*, vol. 1, Letter to Henry Murdach, Letter 106, 353; vol. 4, Sermon 74, 456–7.
31 Ibid., vol. 1, Letter 106, 353.
32 William of Saint-Thierry, *The First Life of Bernard of Clairvaux*, trans. Hilary Costello (Collegeville, MN: Liturgical Press, 2015), I:23, 27.
33 See Husserl, *Cartesian Meditations*, §53–54.
34 In addition to his reference to the intentional background [*Urgrund*] which supports a life-world [*Lebenswelt*] (see Edmund Husserl, *The Crisis of the European Sciences and Transcendental Phenomenology*, trans. David Carr, 132), I agree here with Étienne Gilson, who recognizes in St. Bernard a true "science of a way of life" (referring as I see it to experience), denying however that it would also be a question of truly "systematic" thought in the Cistercian. See Étienne Gilson, *The Mystical Theology of St. Bernard* (Kalamazoo, MI: Liturgical Press, 1990).
35 *Life and Works of Saint Bernard, Abbot of Clairvaux*, vol. 4, sermon 23:6, 134.
36 Geoffrey of Auxerre, *Fragmenta de vita et miraculis sancti Bernardi*, AB, 50 (1932), 91. And William of Saint-Thierry, *The First Life of Bernard of Clairvaux*, II:4, 7. See also the commentary on this in Paul Verdeyen, *Œuvres complètes de saint Bernard* (SC380), 563–4.
37 William of Saint-Thierry, *The First Life of Bernard of Clairvaux*, I:4, 7.
38 For the identification of the mystical and its meaning today, see my article "Mystique et modernité. Aspirations spirituelles et mystique chrétienne," *Études* (June 2001), 785–92.
39 Emmanuel Kant, *The Critique of Judgment*, trans. Werner S. Pluhar (Indianapolis, IN: Hackett Publishing Company, 1987), §46. "Fine Art Is the Art of Genius" (on absurd originality and exemplary originality).
40 For this sense of infancy as constituting the world "without utterance" and by "the flesh" (Husserl), see the conclusion of my *The Guide to Gethsemane*, "the In-Fans [without-Speech] or the Silent Flesh," trans. George Hughes (New York: Fordham University Press, 2019), 107–9. [Trans.—Falque explains in his note that he disagrees with the French translation of Bernard's "*affectus*" as "*cœur*" ("heart") in the Vivès

edition. He thinks it goes too far into the affective and distorts the symmetry between affect and intelligence, changing it into an opposition. He further considers the translation into French of "*et ideo non ad intellectus*" mistaken. Vivès gives it as "one can hardly understand." Falque gives it as "that is why he does not address the intellect." The Eales translation in English gives: "the affection has spoken, not the understanding, and therefore what is said is scarcely understood" (sermon 67:3, 419)].

41   *Life and Works of Saint Bernard, Abbot of Clairvaux*, vol. 4, sermon 2:2, 13–14.
42   Ibid., 1: 4, 7. On the topic of birth as a mode of being in the world of God, and thus also of the resurrection, see my *The Metamorphosis of Finitude*, trans. George Hughes (New York: Fordham University Press, 2012).
43   Hans-Georg Gadamer, *Truth and Method*, trans. Joel Weinsheimer and Donald G. Marshall (London: Bloomsbury, 2013), 56 (my emphasis).
44   *Life and Works of Saint Bernard, Abbot of Clairvaux*, vol. 4, sermon 74:4, 456.
45   See sermon 74, 454–61, On this point, and on St. Bernard in general, see Philippe Nouzille, *Expérience de Dieu et théologie monastique au XIIe siècle*, 61–9: "le *medius adventus*: un avènement traditionnel?" and "description du *medius adventus*."
46   *Life and Works of Saint Bernard, Abbot of Clairvaux*, vol. 4, sermon 74:5, 457 [Trans.—translation modified.]
47   Ibid., sermon 74:5, 457. A reference here to St. Augustine's "You were more inward than my most inward part" [*Deus interior intimo meo*]. St. Augustine, *Confessions*, trans. Henry Chadwick (Oxford: Oxford University Press, 1991) III, 6: 11, 43. The difference between them is less in the discovery in himself of the presence of God (as in St. Augustine) and rather in the coming of the Word in the heart of the personal that imposes such a quest (Bernard).
48   *Life and Works of Saint Bernard, Abbot of Clairvaux*, vol. 4, sermon 74:6, 457.
49   Ibid., sermon 23:14, 140.
50   Ibid., sermon 85:8, 521.
51   Ibid., sermon 28:8, 181.
52   Ibid., sermon 74:7, 458. The double liturgical dimension of spatiality and temporality is very impressively developed by Jean-Yves Lacoste in *Expérience et absolu, Questions disputées sur l'humanité de l'homme* (Paris: PUF, 1994), 7–27: "topologie et liturgie," and 67–93 "l'avenir absolu: anticipation et conversion."
53   It is less a question, as I see it, of an "opposition between love and reason," as in William of Saint-Thierry, for example, but one of accepting a different translation by the affect of that which cannot be expressed by the intellect. [Trans.—Falque gives here the translation of sermon 67:3 from the Vivès edition, vol. 4, 482, translated here into English. The Eales translation in English of the same passage is: "the affection has spoken, not the understanding, and therefore what is said is scarcely understood" (sermon 67:3, 409).]
54   See, for example, Bernard Granger and Georges Charbonneau, *Phénoménologie des sentiments corporels* (Paris: Le cercle herméneutique, 2003), vols. 1–2.
55   Pierre Klossowski, foreword to Max Scheler, *Le Sens de la souffrance* (my emphasis). The opposition made between "intellectual intentionality" and "emotional intentionality" by Scheler needs, however, to be nuanced after the publication of the Husserl manuscripts on intersubjectivity [Hua x-xv]. See Natalie Depraz, *Transcendance et incarnation. Le statut de l'intersubjectivité comme alterité à soi chez Husserl* (Paris: Vrin, 1995), section 1, 45–192: "Égologie et Einfühlung." As for the primary and important return to fundamental affect [*Befindlichkeit*]

at the heart of phenomenology, see Heidegger, *Being and Time*, §29 "Da-Sein as Attunement."
56 Max Scheler, *The Nature of Sympathy*, trans. Peter Heath (New Jersey: Transaction Publishers, 2008. [Trans.—The title of the French translation used by Falque is closer to the original German and could be rendered in English as *Nature and Form of Sympathy*.]
57 *Life and Works of Saint Bernard, Abbot of Clairvaux,* vol. 4, sermon 67:3, 409.
58 Maurice Merleau-Ponty, *The Visible and the Invisible*, trans. Alphonso Lingis (Evanston, IL: Northwestern University Press, 1968), 147–8: "My left hand is always on the verge of touching my right hand touching the things, but I never reach coincidence; the coincidence eclipses at the moment of realization … But this incessant escaping … this is not a failure."
59 See the dispute with Theodor Lipps in Max Scheler's *The Nature of Sympathy*, where he cites Edith Stein discussing the question of empathy in *On the Problem of Empathy*, trans. Walter Stein, *Collected Works of Edith Stein*, vol. 3 (Washington, DC: ICS Publications, 2016).
60 *Life and Works of Saint Bernard, Abbot of Clairvaux,* vol. 4, sermon 67:3, 409.
61 Ibid., sermon 67:3, 409 [Trans.—translation modified in line with Falque's translation.]
62 Ibid. I follow here the most literal translation in "Sources chrétiennes," avoiding however translating *affectus* as "heart" and *intellectus* as "intelligence" (as in "it is the heart that has spoken not the intelligence.") I do this as the terms "heart" and "intelligence" do not sufficiently mark out the philosophical distinction of faculties (affect/understanding).
63 Ibid., sermon 67:3, 409–10. See Michel Henry, *Généalogie de la psychanalyse* (Paris: PUF, 1985), 39 on "auto-affection": "*Affectivity of thought* … should be understood as that essence, and as its most interior possibility, as *auto-affection* in that the thought reveals itself immediately to itself and is felt itself in itself as it is … As the ultimate possibility of thought, affectivity prevails over all its modes and secretly determines them." Also Husserl, *Cartesian Meditations*, §16, 38, on "dumb … experience": "Its beginning is the *pure* and, so to speak, still *dumb*—psychological experience, which now must be made to utter its own sense with no adulteration."
64 *Life and Works of Saint Bernard, Abbot of Clairvaux,* vol. 4, sermon 67:3, 409.
65 Ibid. [Trans.—translation modified in line with Falque's translation.]
66 Ibid., sermon 50:1, 303 (citing Song 11:4).
67 Ibid., sermon 50:2, 303.
68 Ibid., sermon 50:3, 303.
69 See in particular Étienne Gilson, *The Mystical Theology of St. Bernard*, trans. A. H. C. Downes Sheed (Kalamazoo, MI: Liturgical Press, 1990), chapter 3, "schola caritatis."
70 *Life and Works of Saint Bernard, Abbot of Clairvaux,* vol. 4, sermon 50:3, 304.
71 Ibid. [Trans.—translation modified in line with Falque's translation.]
72 Ibid.
73 *On Loving God*, 49.
74 Ibid.
75 Ibid. Note the reference to Boethius here: "I should have [seen that you were a philosopher], had you kept silence [*si tacuisse, philosophus fuisse*]," *The Consolation of Philosophy* by Anicius Manlius Severinus Boethius, trans. W. V. Cooper, bk.2 prose 7, p. 26, trans. (published by the Ex-classics Project, 2009: Retrieved August 10, 2020, on http://www.exclassics.com). See J. Chatillon, "Note pour l'interprétation de la

preface du *De diligendo Deo* de saint Bernard," *Revue du Moyen Âge latin*, 20 (1964), 98–105. Bernard's refusal to be a philosopher when it is a question of the other corroborates the interpretation of Jean-Luc Marion of a "forgetting of love" (more than of being) in the whole philosophical tradition. See Jean-Luc Marion, *The Erotic Phenomenon*, trans. Stephen E. Lewis (Chicago: University of Chicago Press, 2007), 1: "Philosophy today no longer says anything about love, or at best very little … One would almost doubt whether philosophers experience love, if one didn't instead guess that they fear saying anything about it."

76 Blaise Pascal, *Pensées*, trans A. J. Krailsheimer (London: Penguin, 1966), 423:154. This is taken up elsewhere by Pascal in relation to impossible reasons for love: "The mind has its own [order] which uses principles and demonstrations. We do not *prove* that we ought to be loved by setting out in order the *causes* of love; that would be *absurd*" 298:122 (my emphases).

77 *On Loving God*, 49.

78 Ibid., 66.

79 Ibid., 49.

80 I am only surprised that one never finds this translation, which, despite its awkwardness, gives precisely the perspective of *On Loving God* and is based on the ambiguity of the Latin itself. (See Félix Gaffiot, Dictionnaire: *Latin-Français* (Paris: Hachette, 1934), article on "modus.") We can see a trace of it, or at least a reference, in Meister Eckhart's famous sermon on the vision of St. Paul on the road to Damascus, "Paul rose from the ground and with open eyes he saw nothing" (Acts 9:8): "We must take God as without mode, and essence without essence, for He has no modes. Therefore St. Bernard says, 'He who would know thee, God, must measure thee without measure.'" See *The Complete Mystical Works of Meister Eckhart*, trans. Maurice O'C Walshe (New York: Crossroad Publishing Company, 2009), sermon 19. See also my commentary in *God, the Flesh, and the Other*, trans. William Christian Hackett (Evanston, IL: Northwestern University Press, 2015): "Reduction and Conversion (Meister Eckhart)," 79–112. We can find the same suggestion, although not developed, and not linked with Meister Eckhart, in Guillaume de Stexhe's, "Entre le piège et l'abîme: l'ambiguïté du discours sur l'amour," in the collection of essays in honor of Daniel Coppieters de Gibson, *Qu'est-ce que Dieu?* (Brussels: Presses de l'Université Saint-Louis, 2019), 421: "The initial question gives us the space in which it is to be deployed, which is that of duty/necessity, of reason/cause and of *manner/measure*" (my emphasis).

81 *On Loving God*, 73.

82 Ibid.

83 *The Wedding Feast of the Lamb*, trans. George Hughes (New York: Fordham University Press, 2016), 73.

84 On the conflict of interpretations, see Pacifique Delfgauuw, "La nature et les degrés de l'amour selon saint Bernard," *Analecta Sacri Ordinis Cisterciensis* (ASOC) 1953, 234–52 and Jacques Blanpain, "Langage, mystique, expression du désir" in *Collectanea Cisterciensa*, 1974, no. 36 (II), 226–47. The discussion of the ambiguity is brought up to date, though not resolved, in Lode van Hecke, *Le Désir dans l'expérience religieuse, L'homme réunifié, Relecture de saint Bernard* (Paris: Éditions du Cerf, 1990), 140–2.

85 *On Loving God*, 74.

86 See Scheler, *The Nature of Sympathy*.

87 *On Loving God*, 74.

88 Ibid.
89 Husserl, *Cartesian Meditations*, §42, 90. As for the exemplary positioning of the "question of the other" in medieval philosophy, and in particular for Aquinas, who is often said, mistakenly, to be the most "objectifying," see my *God, the Flesh, and the Other*, "Angelic Alterity," 231–53.
90 *On Loving God*, 74–5.
91 Ibid., 75.
92 Ibid. (my emphasis).
93 See precisely in this context how the "Letter on Charity" addressed by Bernard and inserted in *On Loving God* (85–93) is not a simple addition or a reminder. It shows on the contrary how *eros* and the degrees of love are transformed by *agapê* or *caritas*, the Christian name of love in the Trinity. "Love [*caritas*] is the law then, and the law of the Lord, which in some manner holds and unites the Trinity [*quae Trinitatem in unitate*] in the bond of peace. But let no one think that I am taking this love as a quality [*qualitatem*] or an accident [*aliquod accidens*]. If I did, I should be saying—perish the thought—that there is something in God that is not God. But it is that divine substance that is in no way other than itself, as John says, 'God is love' [*Deus caritas est*] (1 Jn 4:8)." (*On Loving God*, 87). Jean-Luc Marion's view in *The Erotic Phenomenon* seems to me justified, but not decisive, in that it remains unilaterally "erotic" or simply "human." Marion's addition at the end of God as the "best lover," in a pure univocity of *eros* and *agapê*, suggesting that God loves in the same sense as us, is not sufficient as a way of *inserting* and *transforming* human love into divine love. In this way we can easily lose the specificity of *agapê*, not as a flight from, or a suppression of, *eros*, but as its assumption and deepest transformation. See my *The Wedding Feast of the Lamb*, "Desire and Differentiation," 154–66 (in particular 156–8), as well as my article "Dieu charité," *Communio*, no. XXX, 5–6 (September-December 2005): 75–87.
94 *On Loving God*, 74; *Life and Works of Saint Bernard, Abbot of Clairvaux*, vol. 4, sermon 50:7, 306.
95 *Life and Works of Saint Bernard, Abbot of Clairvaux*, vol. 4, sermon 50:7, 306.
96 Ibid., sermon 50:7, 306.
97 Ibid., sermon 50:7, 307: "Charity ... does not allow that you should refuse to any man, even to your most bitter enemy, some small measure of affection."
98 *On Loving God*, 75.
99 *Life and Works of Saint Bernard, Abbot of Clairvaux*, vol. 4, sermon 50:8, 307.
100 A directly phenomenological formulation of "love of the enemy" in Christianity as a paradoxical mode of a denial of reciprocity can be found in Jean-Luc Marion's *Being Given: Toward a Phenomenology of Givenness*, trans. Jeffrey L. Kosky (Stanford, CA: Stanford University Press, 2002): "Only the enemy makes the gift possible; he makes the gift evident by denying it reciprocity—in contrast to the friend, who involuntarily lowers the gift to the level of a loan without interest" (89). As for the debate on the "abstraction of the gift" and the necessary "recognition" of the *non-marketable* value of exchange (but without supposing an exchange or reciprocity as such), see chap. 3 "The Debt for the Gift": "recognition" (Ricoeur) and the "ceremonial gift" (Henaff), as opposed to the hypothesis of a "gift of the gift" (Marion) or a "definitive rejection of all reciprocity" (Derrida).
101 *On Loving God*, 76: "The second degree of love."
102 Ibid.
103 Ibid. (my emphasis).

104 Ibid., 77. (The second and third degree of love come together in the same section of *On Loving God* to show their profound unity and the way they are generated, and not simply as a juxtaposition.) [Trans.—the English translation by G. R. Evans does not follow the sections found in the original but divides them up.]
105 Ibid., 77.
106 Ibid. [Trans.—Text modified in line with Falque's translation.]
107 Ibid., 78.
108 Ibid.
109 Ibid.
110 Ibid.
111 See Meister Eckhart, "On Detachment" [*Von Abgeschiedenheit*]. French edition trans. Gwendoline Jarczik and Pierre-Jean Labarrière, *Du Détachment et autres textes* (Paris: Rivages poche, 1995), 49–52: "Detachment gets rid of all creatures … It is so close to nothing that between perfect detachment and nothingness there could be nothing else."
112 Étienne Gilson, *La Théologie mystique de saint Bernard* (Paris: Vrin, 1947), 151. Gilson adds, to show the difference from Meister Eckhart, "All the difficulty that one thinks one will find in Saint Bernard's works on this point can be reduced to a misinterpretation, because the soul which *comes apart*, which is *detached* from itself, from *renouncing what it is*, is established in its own particular *substance, such that divine love changes it*" (my emphases).
113 See my *The Metamorphosis of Finitude*, "The Resurrection Changes Everything," 62–80. The transformative and transforming sense of the Resurrection is underlined by Guillaume de Stexhe in his exegesis of the same text by St. Bernard in *Qu'est-ce que Dieu* (Brussels: Presses de l'Université Saint-Louis, 1985), "Entre le piège et l'abîme," §6, "'la gloire de la finitude,'" 445–9: "Eschatology does not speak of the abolition of the body but of the transfiguring Resurrection … It is solely in fully taking it on *in its finite condition* and thus as corporeity, that humankind can lay claim to the glory that is promised in the fourth degree of love. What is promised here is glory in the full integration of the body into the dynamic of the will stripped of any possessive fixation onto the self" (my emphasis).
114 *On Loving God*, 79.
115 Edith Stein, *On the Problem of Empathy*, trans. Waltraut Stein (Washington, DC: ICS Publications, 1989), 16. It is worth comparing this with Max Scheler's *The Nature of Sympathy* (1923) on the subject of (1) empathy, (2) affective participation, and (3) affective fusion. See also, on the phenomenological debate around the example of the "acrobat" and the distinction between "affective fusion" [*Einsfühlung*] and "empathy" [*Einfühlung*], connected to the *theological* mode of detachment in Meister Eckhart, my contribution "Edith Stein: L'empathie comme problème" in Jean-François Lavigne, *Edith Stein philosophe* (München-Göttinger: Ed. Ad Fontes, Studien zur Frühen Phänomenologie, 2017). The debate is also treated, brilliantly and at length, in Bénedicte Bouillot, *Le Noyau de l'âme selon Edith Stein* (Paris: Hermann, 2015), 63–9: "Une stricte separation des consciences: débat avec Lipps."
116 *On Loving God*, 80 [translation modified]. I translate "*substantia*" here by "human nature" and not by "substance" to avoid a reading of Bernard of Clairvaux that is absolutely not my object here, and that would be too substantializing and metaphysical. [Trans.—The Evans translation into English prefers "substance."]
117 I am returning here, with substantial modifications, to certain pages of *God, the Flesh, and the Other*, "Compassion": 212–18. Initially inserted in that book in a

section concerning Origen and the impassibility of the Father [*ipse Pater non est impassibilis*] these pages find here their proper context—that is to say in a discussion of Bernard and the monastic perspective (the book of experience) rather than Origen and the patristic debate over "patripassionism." My thanks to the Presses Universitaires de France for their permission to include the pages in this book with modifications.

118 *On Loving God*, 79.
119 Scheler, *The Nature of Sympathy*, 15.
120 *On Loving God*, 79–80. For the play between love or "affection" [*affici*] and becoming like God or "deification" [*deificari*], see the significant analysis of Jean Leclercq, to which I am indebted here, in *Maurice Blondel lecteur de Bernard de Clairvaux*, 83–93, and particularly 84–5. As for the theme of the "transfer of fluxes" in Husserl, as a central aspect of human intersubjectivity, but also as I see it of mystical empathy, see Edmund Husserl, *Zür Phänomenologie de Intersubjektivität*, in Husserliana 15 (1929–35), §43. This passage has been cited and commented upon by Depraz, *Transcendance et incarnation, Le statut de l'intersubjectivité comme altérité à soi chez Husserl*, §20, 251–9.
121 Origen of Alexandria, *Exegetical Works on Ezekiel*, trans. Mischa Hooker (Norwich: Chieftain Publishing, 2014), Homily 6:6, 195. For a commentary on this passage and exegesis of the thesis of the "passibility of the Father" see my *God, the Flesh, and the Other*, 208–12. François Varillon sees the possible passage from Origen to Bernard but simply suggests it without developing the idea. See *La Souffrance de Dieu* (Paris: Le Centurion, 1975): 46–7 (Origen), and 48 (Bernard).
122 It seems likely that Bernard had read Origen's Commentary on the Song of Songs, at least at the time of his encounter with William of Saint-Thierry in the sick bay at Clairvaux. But there is no proof that he would have had access to the Homilies on Ezekiel, which were not so easily available in the medieval world. See *Œuvres complètes de saint Bernard de Clairvaux* (Paris: Éditions du Cerf, 1992), vol. 1 (*Sources chrétiennes*, no. 380), J.-P. Bouhot "La Bibliothèque de Clairvaux," 141–53; and P. Verdeyen, "Une théologie de l'expérience," 564–72.
123 *Life and Works of Saint Bernard, Abbot of Clairvaux*, vol. 4, sermon 26:5, 159.
124 This is a charge that is often addressed, usually wrongly, at medieval philosophy as a whole. See, for example, Hans Jonas, "The Concept of God after Auschwitz; A Jewish Voice," *The Journal of Religion*, vol. 67, no. 1 (January 1987), 8: "For the sake of any viable theology, we cannot uphold the time-honored (medieval) doctrine of absolute, unlimited divine power." And see on this point my response in *The Guide to Gethsemane*, 50–2.
125 See Bernard Of Clairvaux, *De la Considération* (Paris: Éditions du Cerf, 1986), 133. (Translated as "He is not affected, he is love.")
126 Emmanuel Housset, *L'Intelligence de la pitié, Phénoménologie de la communauté* (Paris: Éditions du Cerf, 2003), 145–75. Housset's analysis is impressive, though it is all the more surprising that there is no mention of Bernard of Clairvaux, who would probably have been more suitable than Origen as the basis for the thesis. See also my *The Metamorphosis of Finitude*, where Bernard serves precisely as corrective to Origen on this topic: §17 "The Apperceptive Transposition of the Son," 67–74.
127 See Claude Romano, *Event and World*, trans. Shane Mackinley (New York: Fordham University Press, 2009), xi: "The human being is not interpreted here as *zôon logon echon*, nor as a Cartesian '*res cogitans*,' nor as *Dasein*, but instead as one to whom something happens, the one alone who is 'capable of events.'"

128 "Thus it is with the Holy Scripture [which starts with a kiss]; it has an attractive countenance [*iucundum eloquium*], which wins upon us at once [*facile afficit*] and carries us on to the reading of it [*allicit ad legendum*], in such wise that, however laborious it may be to investigate the hidden mystery it employs [*quod in ea latet*], that labour becomes pleasure." *Life and Works of Saint Bernard, Abbot of Clairvaux*, vol. 4, sermon 1:5, 9. [Trans.—the Eales translation omits the kiss].
129 Ibid., sermon 26:2, 156.
130 Ibid., sermon 26:3, 157.
131 See my *Guide to Gethsemane*, part 3: "The Body-to-Body of Suffering and Death."
132 *Life and Works of Saint Bernard, Abbot of Clairvaux*, vol. 4, sermon 26:5, 159.
133 Ibid. [Trans.—Text modified in line with Falque's translation.]
134 Ibid., sermon 26:14, 166.
135 Ibid., sermon 26:9, 163. [Trans.—Text modified in line with Falque's translation.]
136 [Trans.—See chap. 9 on "Openness (*apérité*) and Freedom." On the term "*aspérité*" see chap. 6, note 51.]
137 See Martin Heidegger, *On the Way to Language*, trans. P. D. Herz and Joan Stambaugh (New York: Harper and Row, 1982).
138 [Trans.—See Gabriel Marcel, *The Mystery of Being 1: Reflection and Mystery* (London: Harvill Press, 1950), 70: "Heidegger … has emphasized the importance of the notion of openness for any theory of truth—or the notion perhaps of being opened. His German word is '*Offenständigkeit*,' and the French translators have coined the word '*apérité*' as an equivalent."]

Chapter 9

1 *Life and Works of Saint Bernard, Abbot of Clairvaux*, vol. 4, *Cantica Canticorum: Eighty-Six Sermons on the Song of Solomon*, trans. Samuel J. Eales (London: John Hodges, 1893), sermon 26:3, 157.
2 [De Gratia et Libero Arbitrio] The Treatise of St. Bernard, Abbat of Clairvaux, Concerning Grace and Free Will, trans. Watkin W. Williams (London: SPCK, 1920).
3 See René Descartes, *The Philosophical Works of Descartes* (Cambridge: Cambridge University Press, 1911): *Meditations on First Philosophy*, trans. Elizabeth S. Haldane, meditation iv: 1–21.
4 Emmanuel Kant, *Critique of Pure Reason*, trans. Paul Guyer and Allen W. Wood (Cambridge: Cambridge University Press, 1998), A448/B476, 486; *Critique of Practical Reason*, trans. Werner S. Pluhar (Indianapolis, IN: Hackett, 2002), §8 Theorem IV, 49.
5 G. W. F. Hegel, *Elements of the Philosophy of Right*, trans. H. B. Nisbet (Cambridge: Cambridge University Press, 1991), §104, 131.
6 Thomas Aquinas, *Summa Theologiae*, trans. English Dominican Province (New Advent: Online edition, 2017. Retrieved January 7, 2020.) Prima pars, question 77, article 3, answer.
7 Marie-Joseph Nicolas, in Thomas Aquinas, *Somme théologique* (Paris: Éditions du Cerf, 1984), 77, note 1.
8 See my article, "Limite théologique et finitude phénoménologique chez saint Thomas d'Aquin," *Revue des sciences philosophiques et théologiques* vol. 92 (July–September 2008), 527–56.

9   *Summa Theologiae*. Prima pars, question 83, article 2 (Whether free-will is a power?), answer.
10 Ibid., Prima pars, question 83, article 2, reply to objection 2.
11 See Descartes, *Meditations on First Philosophy* iv: 1–19.
12 See, for example, Étienne Gilson, *La Liberté chez Descartes et la théologie* [1913] (Paris: Vrin Reprise, 1987), 239–43: "There is no doubt when he considers free will as the most obvious stamp left by God on his work, it is not to St. Thomas or to theologians of his school that he is affiliated … But it is principally to St. Bernard that it is customary to attribute such an affiliation." Indirect filiation of Descartes with St. Bernard has been established through the intermediary of Marin Mersenne in his *Quaestiones in Genesim* (1623), 1, 26, question 15, proposition 9: "The ninth position establishes the image of God in free will—on this subject see the divine Bernard, *Sermons on the Song of Songs* and chapter 1 of *Meditations on the Human Condition*." This is cited and commented upon by Jean-Luc Marion in "L'image de la liberté," in *Saint Bernard et la philosophie*, ed. Rémi Brague (Paris: PUF, 1993), 64.
13 *Concerning Grace and Free Will*, chap. 6, 28.
14 Respectively Marion, "L'image de la liberté," 52–3, and Étienne Gilson, *La Théologie mystique de saint Bernard* (Paris: Vrin, 1947), 64–5. See also the instructive debate on the subject between Jean-Luc Marion and Jean-Luc Vieillard-Baron in *Philosophie*, no. 42, 1994: "Réponse à J.-L. Vieillard-Baron à propos d'une hypothèse sur saint Bernard et l'image de Dieu."
15 *The Philosophical Writings of Descartes*, trans. John Cottingham et al. (Cambridge: Cambridge University Press, 1991), vol. 3, 245.
16 *Concerning Grace and Free Will*, chap. 1:5.
17 Ibid., chap. 6:28. [Trans.—modified in line with Falque's translation.]
18 Ibid., chap. 1: 4–5.
19 [Trans.—See chap. 6, note 51.]
20 Martin Heidegger, *Being and Time: A Revised Edition of the Stambaugh Translation*, trans. Joan Stambaugh (Albany: State University of New York Press, 2010), §44: 212 and *The Essence of Truth*, trans. Ted Sadler (London: Continuum, 2002), 29.
21 *Concerning Grace and Free Will*, chap. 2:10-11 and Heidegger, *The Essence of Truth*. A link between "consent" and the Heideggerian aim of unhiddenness (*apérité*) is confirmed (and thus at least in part justified) by Emmanuel Martineau, *La Provenance des espèces: Cinq meditations sur la liberation de la liberté* (Paris: PUF, 1982), 81 note 35: "There are in the West *three doctrines of freedom* and no more: that of *Phèdre*, that of Bernard and that of Schelling. It is not a question of gratuitous hyperbole or a personal choice: what we call a doctrine of freedom is thought capable of seeing *as such*, that is to say *outside any essential connection with a willed faculty*, even of 'free will,' an expression that in St. Bernard's work has no psychological function, nor even (primarily) any anthropological function" (my emphases).
22 See my *Crossing the Rubicon*, trans. Reuben Shank (New York: Fordham University Press, 2016), 112–13: "There Is No Choice."
23 Søren Kierkegaard, *Either/Or*, part 2:75, in *The Essential Kierkegaard*, ed. Howard V. Hong and Edna H. Hong (Princeton, NJ: Princeton University Press, 2000).
24 See my *Crossing the Rubicon*, part 2: chap. 3 "Always Believing" and chap. 4 "Kerygma and Decision": [§13] "Philosophy of the Decision," particularly "Philosophy of Religion and Philosophy of Religious Experience," 104–6.
25 *Concerning Grace and Free Will*, chap. 1:3 [Trans.—translation modified.]

26 [Trans.—The Pelagian heresy maintains that human nature is not affected by original sin, and thus we are still able to choose good or evil without divine assistance. Augustine insisted that perfection with grace was impossible because we are all born sinners. The heresy was condemned by the Council of Ephesus (431).]
27 St. Augustine, *The Retractions*, trans. Sister M. Inez Bogan (Washington, DC: Catholic University of America Press, 1968), chap. 92:268.
28 *Descartes' Meditations—Trilingual Edition*, trans. John Veitch (1996); Retrieved January 7, 2020, on https://corescholar.libraries.wright.edu/philosophy/8. Book iv:8 "Nor, moreover, can I complain that God has not given me freedom of choice, since, in truth, I am conscious of will so ample and extended as to be superior to all limits." The link with Bernard has been shown and demonstrated by Marion, "L'image de la liberté," 49–72, and see in particular "La postérité métaphysique de la doctrine de saint Bernard: Descartes," 64–7.
29 *Concerning Grace and Free Will*, preface, 1–2.
30 Ibid., chap. 1:3-4.
31 Ibid., chap. 6:32. Also cited in chap. 1:4 as "how to perform I find not." Rom. 7:18 is modified by Bernard. He suppresses "performing the good" [*perficere autem bonum*], talking simply about the will in free will and then later brings it back when talking about will for the good in the freedom of grace.
32 See Robert Javelet, "La reintroduction de la liberté dans les notions d'image et de ressemblance conçues comme dynamisme," *Miscellanea mediaevalia*, Berlin, 1971, 21–2 (a double misinterpretation as I see it): "Bernard is the first to link image and metaphysical freedom, to affirm the human personality and, however, avoid [suggesting] the equality of mankind with God … The unfailing freedom which makes man an equal with God is in fact a *possibility of saying 'yes 'or 'no'*; it is not at all 'essential' but at the same time it permits everything: animalization and divinization depending upon whether they open up to animality or grace" (my emphasis).
33 *Concerning Grace and Free Will*, chap. 1:5.
34 Ibid.
35 Ibid., chap. 1:4.
36 Emmanuel Levinas, *Otherwise than Being, or Beyond Essence*, trans. Alphonso Lingis (Dordrecht: Springer Science+Business Media, 2010), 149: "The Infinite is not in front of its witness, but as it were outside, or on the 'other side' of presence, already past, out of reach, a thought behind thoughts which is too lofty to push itself up front. 'Here I am, in the name of God,' without referring myself directly to his presence. 'Here I am,' just that."
37 *Concerning Grace and Free Will*, chap. 1:5.
38 Jean-Luc Marion, *Being Given: Toward a Phenomenology of Givenness*, trans. Jeffrey L. Kosky (Stanford, CA: Stanford University Press, 2002), 285.
39 See Henri de Lubac, *La Mystère du surnaturel* (Paris: Aubier, 1946), 394.
40 *Concerning Grace and Free Will*, chap. 6:28-29 [Trans.—Translation modified].
41 Jean-Luc Marion [*De Surcroît*], *In Excess: Studies of Saturated Phenomena*, trans. Robyn Horner and Vincent Bernard (New York: Fordham University Press, 2001).
42 See St. Augustine *Contra Julianum (Opus Imperfectus)*, 1:78.
43 *Concerning Grace and Free Will*, chap. 7:39.
44 Ibid., chap. 1:5.
45 [Trans.—*capax Dei*: capable of receiving God. See Augustine, *De Trinitate*, xiv, 8, 11: "The mind is the image of God, in that it is capable of Him and can be partaker of Him."

46 *Concerning Grace and Free Will*, chap. 1:5 (my emphasis).
47 The passage of a hermeneutic of culpable, or guilty, man. See *Finitude et culpabilité*, vol. 2 of *Philosophie de la volonté* (Paris: Éditions Montaigne, 1960), which is the preface to a hermeneutic of "capable man" in *Memory, History, Forgetting*, trans. Kathleen Blamey and David Pellauer (Chicago IL: University of Chicago Press, 2004). This progress is shown in Michaël Foessel, "De l'homme coupable à l'homme capable," *Esprit* no. 316 (July 2005), 99–103. See also Jean Greisch, *Paul Ricoeur, L'itinérance du sens* (Grenoble: J. Million, 2001), pt. 3, 285–435: "Une phénoménologie de l'homme capable," and the volume of essays *Paul Ricoeur, De l'homme faillible à l'homme capable*, ed. Gaëlle Fiasse (Paris: PUF, 2008).
48 Jean-Luc Marion, *Cartesian Questions: Method and Metaphysics* (Chicago: University of Chicago Press, 1999), 91.
49 *Concerning Grace and Free Will*, chap. 3:14; see also chap. 4.
50 Ibid., chap. 8:41.
51 Ibid., see chap. 14.
52 Marion, "L'image de la liberté," 51: "The univocal interpretation of the image (in St. Augustine) … leads to having to accept an image that is always equally achieved (which is false), under the pretext that it constitutes integrally the creature (which is true)." Without making it an issue here, I would point to the fierce debate on the subject opposing Jean-Luc Vieillard-Baron and Jean-Luc Marion concerning the doctrine of the image and *capax Dei* in mankind. See *Philosophie*, no. 42, June 1994. Jean-Luc Vieillard-Baron, "Nouvelles réflexions sur l'homme image de Dieu," 46–61, and Marion's reply, "Réponses à J.-L. Vieillard-Baron à propos d'une hypothèse sur saint Bernard et l'image de Dieu," 62–8.
53 St. Augustine, *De Trinitate: On the Trinity*, trans. Arthur West Hadden in *Nicene and Post-Nicene Fathers*, First series, vol. 3 (Buffalo, NY: Christian Literature Publishing, 1887), bk. 14: chap. 8:11.
54 See Étienne Gilson, *The Mystical Theology of Saint Bernard*, trans. A. H. C. Downes Sheed (Kalamazoo, MI: Cistercian Publications Inc., 1990), 46: "While Augustine seeks it [the image of God] for preference in intellectual cognition where the Divine illumination attests the continuous presence of the Creator to the creature, St. Bernard puts it rather in the will, and very especially in freedom." And Marion, "L'image de la liberté," 51: "What was missing in this tradition [inherited from St. Augustine] was the introduction in the theory of the image of a function that would guarantee the power both to remain indispensable and to tolerate variables, that is to say to respect different periods in the economy of salvation … It was Bernard who was to make these notable steps ahead."
55 *Concerning Grace and Free Will*, chap. 1:5.
56 Ibid.
57 Ibid.
58 Ibid., chap. 13:75.
59 See Thomas Aquinas, *Contra Gentiles: On the Truth of the Catholic Faith*, trans. Vernon J. Bourke (New York: Hanover House, 1955–7), vol. 3, chap. 67: "That God is the cause of operation for all things that operate," as well as chap. 77: "That the execution of divine providence is accomplished by means of secondary causes."
60 *Concerning Grace and Free Will*, chap. 13:75–6.
61 Ibid., chap. 2:8 and chap. 1:6. The formula is given twice by Bernard to distinguish between habit or disposition and assent.

62 *Summa Theologiae*, Prima pars, question 83, article 2, objection 2: "Whether free-will is a power?"
63 *Concerning Grace and Free Will*, chap. 7:39.
64 Martin Heidegger, *Being and Time: A Revised Edition of the Stambaugh Translation*, §28: 132–133: "The being which is essentially constituted by being-in-the-world *is* always its 'there.' According to the familiar meaning of the word, 'there' points to 'here' and 'over there.' The 'here' of an 'I-here' is always understood in terms of an 'over there' at hand in the sense of being toward it which de-distances, is directional, and takes care. The existential spatiality of Dasein which determines its 'place' for it in this way is itself based upon being-in-the-world. The over there is the determinateness of something encountered within the *world*. 'Here' and 'there' are possible only in a 'there,' that is, when there is a being which as the being of the 'there' has disclosed spatiality. This being [Seiende] bears in its ownmost being [Sein] the character of not being closed off [Unverschlossenheit]. The expression 'there' means this essential disclosedness [Erschlossenheit]. Through disclosedness this being (Dasein) is 'there' for itself together with the there-being [Da-sein] of the world … *Dasein is its disclosedness*" (emphases in original).
65 Ibid., §7: 27, 26. "The Phenomenological Method of Investigation": "The expression 'phenomenology' signifies primarily a *concept of method*. It does not characterize the what [*quid*] of the objects of philosophical research in terms of their content, but the *how* of such research" (emphases in original).
66 Ibid., §54. "The Problem of the Attestation of an Authentic Existential Possibility."
67 Marion, "L'image de la liberté," 71–2. This relies as I see it directly on an interpretation of free will as "[to decide] oneself through one's will" that is obviated by Bernard. One should note, however, that publication of this text dates from 1993 and that since then the author seems to have recognized the merits of "inauthenticity." See *Being Given*, 291, on how recognition of the "fundamental inauthenticity" of "originary" inappropriation allows access to the truth of the given.
68 *The Philosophical Writings of Descartes*, vol. 3; *The Correspondence*, trans. John Cottingham et al. (Cambridge: Cambridge University Press, 1991), 326: 85. Letter to Queen Christina, November 20, 1647.
69 Anselm, *Freedom of Choice: De Libertate Arbitrii*, in *Complete Philosophical and Theological Treatises of Anselm of Canterbury*, trans Jasper Hopkins and Herbert Richardson (Minneapolis MN: The Arthur J. Banning Press, 2000), chap. 3: 197. [Trans.—Text modified in line with Falque's translation].
70 The link between Bernard of Clairvaux and Anselm of Canterbury is developed at length, indeed overdetermined, in Michel Corbin, *La Grâce et la liberté chez saint Bernard de Clairvaux* (Paris: Éditions du Cerf, 2002), 290–4, "Anselme du Bec et Bernard de Clairvaux."
71 *Concerning Grace and Free Will*, chap. 1:6. [Trans.—The Williams translation of Bernard's text into English gives "self-determining" for *liber sui*. Falque uses the French translation "libre de soi" and "libre de soi-même" so that "free of the self" and "free of oneself" seem closer to Falque's reading of the text and the discussion that follows.]
72 Marion, "L'image de la liberté," 53–4 (my emphasis).
73 Michel Corbin, *La Grâce et la liberté chez saint Bernard de Clairvaux*, 67–8.
74 *De Adventu domini*, IV, 4 (PL 183, 48, d). See also the excellent article and commentary by Rémi Brague, "L'anthropologie de l'humilité" in *Saint Bernard et la philosophie*, 128–52 (and in particular 136–9, "humilité et vérité").
75 *Concerning Grace and Free Will*, chap. 6:31.

76 Ibid., chap. 6:31-32.
77 Ibid., chap. 6:31.
78 Ibid.
79 Ibid.
80 Anselm, *Freedom of Choice: De Libertate Arbitrii*, chap. 8:205.
81 *Concerning Grace and Free Will*, chap. 14:90.
82 Ibid., chap. 1:6.
83 *Summa Theologiae*, Prima pars, question 1, article 8, reply to objection 2: "God therefore does not destroy nature but perfects it, natural reason should minister to faith as the natural bent of will ministers to charity."
84 *Concerning Grace and Free Will*, chap. 7:38.
85 Ibid., chap. 9:49.
86 Ibid., chap. 7:38.
87 Ibid., chap. 3:15. I have changed the order of "necessity" and "sin" in order to maintain the coherence of the full quotation.
88 Ibid., chap. 6:28.
89 Ibid., chap. 10:57.
90 "The power of will consists only in this, that we are able to do or not to do the same thing (that is, to affirm or deny, to pursue or shun it), or rather in this alone, that in affirming or denying, pursuing or shunning, what is proposed to us by the understanding we so act that we are not conscious of being determined to a particular action by any external force" (bk. 4:8). *Descartes' Meditations—Trilingual Edition*, Meditation 4, trans. John Veitch. Retrieved October 16, 2019, on https://corescholar.libraries.wright.edu/philosophy/8
91 *Concerning Grace and Free Will*, chap. 3:14 (my emphasis).
92 Ibid., chap. 3:14–15.
93 Ibid., chap. 14:82. [Trans.—Text modified in line with Falque's translation].
94 Ibid., chap. 9: 49. [Trans.—Text modified in line with Falque's translation].
95 Ibid., chap. 3:16. [Trans.—Text modified in line with Falque's translation].
96 Ibid., chap. 7:39.
97 Ibid., chap. 7:38.
98 Ibid., chap. 4:38. [Trans.—Bernard is quoting Rom. 12:2].
99 *Descartes' Meditations—Trilingual Edition*, Meditation 4, bk. 4:8; bk. 4:12.
100 Ibid., bk. 4:8; *Concerning Grace and Free Will*, chap. 4:18.
101 *Concerning Grace and Free Will*, chap. 7:38.
102 *Descartes' Meditations—Trilingual Edition*, bk. 4:10.
103 *Concerning Grace and Free Will*, chap. 3:16. [Trans.—Text modified in line with Falque's translation].
104 Ibid., chap. 3:26-7. [Trans.—Text modified in line with Falque's translation].
105 Ibid., chap. 5:27; chap. 6:28.
106 Ibid., chap. 6:28.
107 Saint Augustine, *Confessions*, trans. Henry Chadwick (Oxford: Oxford University Press, 1991), VIII. viii–ix (20–1), 147.
108 *Concerning Grace and Free Will*, chap. 1:4. [Trans.—Text modified in line with Falque's translation].
109 Ibid., chap. 8:43.
110 *Life and Works of Saint Bernard, Abbot of Clairvaux*, vol. 4, *Cantica Canticorum: Eighty-Six Sermons on the Song of Solomon*, trans. Samuel J. Eales (London: John Hodges, 1893), sermon 43:4, 269.

111 *Concerning Grace and Free Will*, chap. 7:39–40.
112 Ibid., chap. 8:41. "For there neither belongeth, nor ever hath belonged, to freedom of choice, as such, to possess either power or wisdom, but simply willing."
113 Ibid., chap. 3:17.
114 See Thomas Aquinas, *Summa Theologiae*, Prima pars, question 77, article 3, answer.
115 *Concerning Grace and Free Will*, chap. 8:43.
116 Ibid., chap. 6:28.
117 Ibid., chap. 11: 58–9. [Trans.—Text modified in line with Falque's translation].
118 Ibid., chap. 11:59.
119 Ibid., chap. 11:59. [Trans.—Text modified in line with Falque's translation].
120 Ibid., chap. 14:87.
121 Ibid., chap. 14:79.
122 Ibid., chap. 10: 52–3. (Bernard is quoting Heb. 1:3).
123 Ibid., chap. 10:53.
124 Étienne Gilson, *La Théologie mystique de saint Bernard*, 70.
125 *Concerning Grace and Free Will*, chap. 10:53. [Trans.—Text modified in line with Falque's translation].
126 Ibid., chap. 10:56.
127 *Life and Works of Saint Bernard, Abbot of Clairvaux*, vol. 4, *Cantica Canticorum: Eighty-Six Sermons on the Song of Solomon*, sermon 26:5, 159. [Trans.—Text modified in line with Falque's translation].
128 *Concerning Grace and Free Will*, chap. 10:56.
129 St. Augustine, *On the Trinity*, trans. Arthur West Haddan, in *Nicene and Post-Nicene Fathers* (Buffalo, NY: Christian Literature Publishing, 1887), first series, vol. 3, 15:8:14. On New Advent site, ed. Kevin Knight. Retrieved October 23, 2019 (my emphases). https://www.newadvent.org/fathers/130115.htm
130 *Concerning Grace and Free Will*, chap. 10:55-56.
131 Ibid., chap. 13:73.
132 Ibid., chap. 1:3 [see §27].
133 Ibid., Bernard's commentary on 1 Cor. 4:7 in chap. 4:83.
134 Ibid., chap. 14:89.
135 Ibid., chap. 13:78.
136 Ibid., chap. 11:59. Quoting from *Song of Songs*, 1:3.
137 Ibid., chap. 2:59. In effect a return to and a reply to the question "What then is thin own work?"
138 Ibid., chap. 11:59.

Epilogue

1 [Trans.—"I AM WHO I AM" is from NRSV. "I AM WHO I SHALL BE" is an English version of the translation in the *Traduction œcuménique de la Bible* (Paris: Société biblique française et Éditions du Cerf, 2010): "JE SUIS QUI JE SERAI." According to the notes in this bible, it implies, "I am here, with you, as you shall see."] Pindar, *Olympian Odes: Pythian Odes*, trans. William H. Race (Cambridge, MA: Harvard University Press, 1997), 2:72 "Become such as you are, having learned what that is."
2 See Henri Maldiney on "transpassibility" [Trans.—The openness of our experience to radical change] in *Penser l'homme et la folie* (Paris: Grenoble, Jérôme Millon,

1991), 285. This is a formula that Heidegger does not just repeat in *Being and Time* §31: 145 ("Become what you are"), but that he modifies and thoroughly overturns. The formula is also taken up in Maldiney's *L'Art, l'éclair de l'être* (Paris: Éditions du Cerf, 2013), 175: "Such is the meaning of the invitation: *Become what you are*—and that you have to be in your own right, in making it your own possibility. What you *are*, you are only to *become* in existing" (emphases in original). See also the commentary on this point (but without specific reference to Maldiney) in Claude Romano, *L'Événement et le temps* (Paris: PUF, 1999), §15: "Le présent et la transformation," 246: "The formula that would most closely correspond is not 'Become who you are' (Pindar), but rather 'Be what you become.'"

3   Friedrich Nietzsche, *Beyond Good and Evil*, trans. R. J. Hollingdale (Harmondsworth: Penguin, 1973), §62: 69.

4   *Crossing the Rubicon*, trans. Reuben Shank (New York: Fordham University Press, 2016), chapter 1: "Is Hermeneutics Fundamental?"

5   *Parcours d'embûches: S'expliquer* (Paris: Éditions Franciscaines, 2016), §27 "Vivre Anselme."

6   *Saint Bonaventure and the Entrance of God into Theology*, trans. Brian Lapsa and Sarah Horton (St. Bonaventure, NY: Franciscan Institute Publications, 2018).

7   *God, the Flesh, and the Other*, trans. William Christian Hackett (Evanston, IL: Northwestern University Press, 2015).

8   It would be possible here to mark out a triple triptych of books that I have now completed: "patristic and medieval": *Saint Bonaventure and the Entrance of God into Theology, God, the Flesh, and the Other*, and *The Book of Experience*; "phenomenological and methodological": *Crossing the Rubicon, Le combat amoureux, Parcours d'embûches*; and of the order of "philosophy of religion" or perhaps "philosophy of religious experience": *The Guide to Gethsemane, Metamorphosis of Finitude*, and *The Wedding Feast of the Lamb*. These last three in French versions have been reprinted in one volume as the *Triduum philosophique*.

9   See *Parcours d'embûches*: §1 "La source franciscaine," §28 "Fidélité bonaventurienne et thomasienne," §5 "La racine ignacienne."

10 Charles de Bovelles, *Le Livre du Sage (Liber de Sapienta)* (Paris: Vrin, 2010), 201: "Do not degenerate, Oh man, either into stone or into plant, or into brute animal. *You are man: stand firm as man … Hold to it, be decided in your diet*, resting on what you are. Eat what is living. Domesticate what is animated. Be master of yourself."

11 A notable exception is Pierre Magnard's fine work, *La Couleur du matin profond, Dialogue avec Éric Fiat* (Paris: Les Dialogues des Petits Platons, 2013), 92–5: "Looking closely at it I have to agree rapidly that this legend of a man produced by spontaneous generation in response to these crises was the product of a *misunderstanding* of the Middle Ages … If there was an invention of man in the Renaissance, that could only have been made in the dynamic of that *Christology* whose secularization would not stifle the original inspiration … Looked at closely, humanism is *no longer the effect of a rupture*. It fits into a tradition that goes back to late antiquity, I would dare say to the mists of time. One would have to cite Cicero and his generous concept of *communis humanitas*, a shared humanity, first affirmation of a concrete universal. The effort at definition that springs from the *great Greek philosophers* would only serve to clarify things for the *Fathers of the Church*" (my emphases).

12 *Parcours d'embûches*, 166–7.

Index

Abelard, Peter 79, 144, 229
Aelred of Rievaulx x, 6–7, 11, 43, 114, 128, 130–41, 143, 149, 156, 179, 201, 203–4, 209, 236–8
Aeschylus 2–3, 207
Alain of Lille 76, 111
Ambrose of Milan 57
Anselm of Canterbury x, 3–4, 11, 14–15, 17–27, 29–66, 70, 75, 107, 111, 113–19, 122, 124–5, 128, 130, 138, 140, 145, 149–50, 156, 173, 179, 187, 190, 200–1, 203, 211, 213, 215–21, 235, 238, 252
Aquinas, Thomas 50, 66, 76, 79, 85–6, 111, 114–19, 122, 124–5, 175–8, 185–187, 190, 197, 218, 233, 245, 251
Arendt, Hannah 130
Aristotle 99, 118–19, 207
Augustine (Saint) 6, 11, 21–7, 29, 31–4, 36–7, 56–8, 76, 79, 83, 120–1, 134–5, 144, 148, 154, 179, 181, 183–5, 187, 196, 199, 211, 213, 215, 223, 234, 238–40, 242, 250–51
Avicenna (Ibn Sina) 134, 237

Balthasar, H. U. (von); 17, 46, 51, 81, 127, 219, 225, 234
Barbaras, Renaud 206
Baron, Roger 228
Barth, Karl 14, 17, 30, 35, 40–2, 214, 218
Beauchamp, Paul 234
Berengar of Tours 79, 224
Bergson, Henri 41, 100, 211, 216
Bernard of Clairvaux x, 3–4, 6–9, 11, 18, 43, 79, 99, 108, 111, 114, 128–32, 136, 143–73, 175–201, 203–4, 210, 236, 239–42, 244–52
Blanpain, Jacques 161, 244
Blondel, Maurice 239–40, 247
Boethius, A.N.S. 21–2, 24–7, 29, 36–7, 122, 243

Bonaventure (Saint) 7, 10, 50, 66, 74, 84, 87, 92–3, 114, 117–20, 124–8, 154, 204, 209–10, 213, 226–8, 232–5, 239
Bonnnefoy, Jean-François 233
Boquet, Damien 236, 237
Boso (Abbot of Bec) 53–4, 59, 62–3, 220
Bouchot, J.-P. 240
Bougerol, J.-G. 209–10, 235
Bouillard, Henri 14, 30, 211
Bouillot, Bénédicte 246
Boulnois, Olivier 21–2, 239
Bourdaloue, Jacques 51, 62
Bouyer, Louis 51
Bovelles, Charles (de) 204–5, 255
Brague, Rémi 144, 188, 210, 240, 252
Bruaire, Claude 61, 62
Buber, Martin 120, 234
Bultmann, Rudolf 30, 33, 214

Caravaggio 182
Casagrande, Carla 106, 108
Cezanne, Paul 88, 227
Chatillon, Jean 223, 243
Chauvet, Louise-Marie 224
Chrétien, Jean-Louis 109, 225, 240
Cicero 24–5, 29, 36–7, 100, 106, 255
Claudel, Paul 111
Colin, Pierre 241
Corbin, Michel 14, 17, 21–2, 188, 211, 219, 222, 252

Dahan, Gilbert 76
Damien, Pierre 79
Daniel, Walter 130, 137, 236
Declève, Henri 52
Decorte, Jos 75
Deleuze, Gilles 208
Delfgauuw, Pacifique 161, 244
Depraz, Natalie 206, 242, 247

Derrida, Jacques 42, 49, 55, 65, 82, 111, 220, 235, 237, 245
Descartes, René 21, 26, 34, 135, 175–7, 180–1, 184, 187, 192, 194–5, 208, 230, 237, 249–50
Dika, Tarek R. 206
Dilthey, Wilhelm 73, 208
Duns Scotus, John 111

Eadmer 17–19, 53, 212–13
Eckhart (Meister) 6, 74, 151, 154, 167–8, 209, 223, 244, 246
Eco, Umberto 20, 213
Escoubas, Éliane 136, 237

Fink, Eugen 5, 155
Flasch, Kurt 14, 39
Foessel, Michaël 251
Foucault, Michel 8–9, 38, 210
Francis (Saint) 150–1

Gabellieri, Emmanuel 65
Gadamer, Hans-Georg 1–2, 5–6, 71, 73, 92, 114, 153, 171, 207–9
Galileo Galilei 4
Gaunilo of Marmoutiers, 30, 37–9, 46, 218
Geoffrey of Auxerre 241
Gerard of Clairvaux (brother of Bernard) 144–5, 167, 169–72, 175
Gerson, Jean 205
Giard, Luce 224
Gilbert de la Porrée 144
Gilbert, Paul 42, 219
Gilduin (abbot) 78–9, 224
Gilson, Étienne 14, 17, 39, 41, 150, 168, 177, 184, 199, 211, 241, 243, 246, 249, 251
Goff, Jacques (le) 213
Gouhier, Henri 215
Gramont, Jérôme (de) 206
Gregory the Great (Saint), 21
Greisch, Jean 208, 239, 251
Guiges du Chastel 145
Guillevic, Eugène 10, 210

Hackett, William C. 206
Hecke, Lode (van) 235, 244
Hegel, G. W. F. 175–6, 178

Heidegger, Martin 3, 5, 7–10, 33, 52–3, 55, 59–60, 62, 91, 97, 114, 125, 130–3, 136, 171, 176, 178–9, 181, 186–7, 206–7, 210, 219–21, 235–9, 243, 248–9, 252, 255
Henaff, Marcel 49, 245
Henry, Michel 2, 6, 51, 134, 136, 157, 208–9, 237, 243
Hermann, Friedrich-Wilhelm (von) 7, 210
Housset, Emmanuel 170, 247
Hugh of Saint-Victor x, 3–4, 6, 11, 43, 66, 70–1, 73–111, 113–14, 120, 122, 124–5, 128, 130, 139, 147, 156, 201, 203–4, 223–231, 240
Husserl, Edmund 3, 5, 9, 43, 88, 97, 99, 114, 116, 130–3, 138, 148, 150–2, 155, 157, 162, 169, 171, 206–9, 212, 216–17, 227, 233, 237, 241–3, 245, 247

Ignatius of Loyola 146, 154
Illich, Ivan 75, 225
Irenaeus 183
Isaac of Stella 134
Isidore of Seville (Saint) 79

Javelet, Robert 250
Jean of Fécamp 238
Jerome (Saint) 10
Joachim of Fiore 126–7
John of Salisbury, 206
Jolivet, Jean 217, 229
Jonas, Hans 247
Jousse, Marcel 100, 230

Kant, Immanuel 35, 39, 86, 151, 175–6, 207, 216
Kierkegaard, Søren 179, 207
Klee, Paul 88
Klossowski, Pierre 242
Köpf, Ulrich 128, 235–6

Lacoste, Jean-Yves 242
Landgrebe, Ludwig 1
Lanfranc 25, 79
Lavigne, Jean-François 246
Leclercq, Jean 7, 210, 223–4, 229, 239–40, 247
Leclercq, Jean J. (Dom) 76

Lemoine, Michel 78
Leo the Great 21
Levinas, Emmanuel 2, 17, 51, 60, 103–4, 113, 116, 118, 140, 161, 181, 221, 231, 233–4, 250
Libera, Alain (de) 14
Lipps, Hans 5, 9
Lipps, Theodor 155, 167–8
Lombard, Peter 79
Lubac, Henri (de) 182
Luther, Martin 207

Magnard, Pierre 255
Maldiney, Henri 5–6, 171, 203, 207–9, 254, 255
Margerie, Bertrand (de) 234
Marion, Jean-Luc 2, 22, 41, 49, 51, 55, 64–5, 101, 116, 177, 182–4, 187–8, 207, 213–14, 218–21, 226–7, 232–3, 244–5, 249–52
Marsenne, Marin 249
Martineau, Emmanuel 249
Mauss, Marcel 49
Meessen, Yves 209, 223
Merleau-Ponty, Maurice 2, 88, 90, 92–3, 98–9, 105, 107, 113, 130, 138, 143–4, 156, 206, 229, 243
Mirandola, Giovanni Pico (della) 205
Mondrian, Piet 227
Mottu, Henry 235
Murdach, Henry 149

Nancy, Jean-Luc 126
Nicholas of Cusa 205
Nicolas, Marie-Joseph 175
Nietzsche, Friedrich 179, 192, 203
Nouzille, Philippe 6–7, 10, 136, 209–10, 236, 240, 242
Noye, Irénée 228

O'Loughlin, Thomas 211
Olivetti, Marco M. 51–2
Origen 56–8, 73, 111, 146, 148, 154, 169–70, 240, 247

Paliard, Jacques 48
Pascal, Blaise 29, 86–7, 89, 160, 179, 226–7, 244

Paschasius 79
Paul (Saint) 56, 59, 97, 136, 169, 180, 182, 185, 190–2, 198, 244
Péguy, Charles 100, 135, 230
Pernot, Laurent 230
Petkovsek, Robert 221
Petrus Comestor 21, 213
Pindar 203, 254–5
Pius X (Pope) 139, 149, 241
Plato 104
Plotinus 22, 24, 29, 36–7
Pöggeler, Otto 7, 210
Poirel, Dominique 85, 92, 99, 228–30
Poulet, Robert 217
Pseudo-Dionysius the Areopagite 21–2, 41–2, 50, 85, 117, 120, 213, 219

Radbertus 79
Rahner, Karl 35, 212, 216
Ratramnus 79
Regnon, Théodore (de) 117, 233
Richard of Saint-Victor 6, 11, 43, 65–6, 70–1, 111, 113–28, 130, 149, 156, 162, 175, 201, 203–4, 223, 232–5
Ricoeur, Paul 2, 30, 33, 49, 55, 62, 64, 71, 73, 90, 92, 113, 118, 148, 183, 189, 214, 222, 245
Robert of Molesme 4
Robert (Canon of Saint-Victor) 95
Romano, Claude 6, 9–10, 206–9, 247, 255
Roques, René 14, 219–20
Rule, Martin 212–13

Samain, B.-J. 210
Sartre, Jean-Paul 104, 121, 161, 181
Saussure, Ferdinand (de) 107
Scheler, Max 5, 130, 148–9, 155, 168, 241–3, 246
Schleiermacher, Friedrich 73, 149, 208
Schmitt, Jean-Claude 98–9, 103, 106
Schmitt, Yann 206
Scotus Eriugena 76
Seboüé, Bernard 63
Seneca 25, 29, 36–7
Sicard, Patrice 88, 228
Southern, R. W. 15, 211
Spinoza, Benedict (de) 43, 192, 216–17

Stein, Edith 5, 9, 99, 130, 155, 167–8, 246
Stercal, Claudio 240
Stexhe, Guillaume (de) 240, 244, 246
Stock, Brian 240

Tauler, Johannes 151

Urban II (Pope), 53–4, 220

Varella, Francisco 206
Varillon, François 169, 247
Vecchio, Silvana 106, 108

Verdeyen, Paul 240–1, 247
Vermersch, Pierre 206
Viallet, Ludovic 211
Vieillard-Baron, Jean-Luc 249, 251
Vignaux, Paul 14, 30, 34, 211, 215–16

Weizsäcker, Victor (von) 209
Wiedebach, Hartwig 209
William of Saint-Thierry 134, 143, 145–7, 150–1, 169, 180, 240–2, 247

Zombory-Nagy, Piroska 238

www.ingramcontent.com/pod-product-compliance
Lightning Source LLC
Chambersburg PA
CBHW071816300426
44116CB00009B/1335